Qualitative Research With Diverse and Underserved Communities

A volume in
Current Social and Cultural Issues: Challenges and Solutions
Jeton McClinton, Arthur E. Hernandez, and Alma L. Thornton, *Series Editors*

Current Social and Cultural Issues: Challenges and Solutions

Jeton McClinton, Arthur E. Hernandez,
and Alma L. Thornton, *Series Editors*

The purpose of this book series is to provide a description and explanation of various research and evaluation theories, methods, instruments, and techniques which can serve as a "practitioner guide" to action in the context of current and emerging social and cultural challenges. Although the books included in the series may be organized in various ways, each will include specific guides, book chapters, case study examples, and other resources intended to provide the reader/user with clear recommendations for practice. The books in this series will be distinct from other works in the fields of research and evaluation in that they will focus on "learning from action and action from learning" rather than merely exposit theoretical frameworks. In addition, this book series is designed from its inception as a guide to inquiry with individuals and groups which are underrepresented, marginalized and/or disadvantaged. With this purpose, the book series focuses on the meaningfulness of these approaches framed by a commitment to social justice and considers research and evaluation with the imperative of involving voiceless, marginalized, unrepresented, or devalued populations.

We anticipate the books in the series will be useful for teachers of research and evaluation, practitioners, dissertation students, and most importantly, as a ready reference (i.e., a field guide).

Qualitative Research With Diverse and Underserved Communities

edited by

Jeton McClinton
Jackson State University

Arthur E. Hernandez
University of the Incarnate Word

Alma L. Thornton
Jackson State University

INFORMATION AGE PUBLISHING, INC.
Charlotte, NC • www.infoagepub.com

Library of Congress Cataloging-in-Publication Data

A CIP record for this book is available from the Library of Congress
http://www.loc.gov

ISBN: 979-8-88730-387-1 (Paperback)
       979-8-88730-388-8 (Hardcover)
       979-8-88730-389-5 (E-Book)

Printed in the United States of America

CONTENTS

v

CASE STUDIES SECTION I

CASE STUDIES SECTION II

CASE STUDIES SECTION III

FOREWORD

This introductory text book on *Qualitative Research for Diverse and Underserved Communities* is designed to provide a description and explanation of various qualitative approaches and methods, with illustrations of how they can be utilized in the study of underrepresented, marginalized, and disadvantaged individuals and groups. This book fills an important gap in the need for knowledge and understanding of phenomena pertaining to the emergence and increasing prevalence of a wide variety of marginalized and underrepresented groups, using a continuum of methodologies from case study, grounded theory, narrative, ethnography, and phenomenology, to photovoice, sociolinguistics, Black feminism, Black storytelling, teacher as activist, mothercentric, and critical race theory. In addition to demonstrating how qualitative theories and methods can be used to study often neglected and marginalized groups, these articles provide an abundance of substantive knowledge about the social and structural factors (i.e., educational status, national origin, immigration status, and political alignment) that influence their development, behavior, achievements, and integration into the larger society. These methods are demonstrated from the professional and lived experiences of the authors or study participants.

The articles in this book are multidisciplinary in scope, representing scholars from various disciplines, including education, psychology, sociology, social work, health, speech, nursing, art, counseling, communication, and community action. These original research articles demonstrate how qualitative inquiry can be used to study a variety of individuals and groups, including single-parent families, gay and lesbian teachers, underrepresented

Qualitative Research With Diverse and Underserved Communities, pages xi–xii
Copyright © 2024 by Information Age Publishing
www.infoagepub.com
All rights of reproduction in any form reserved.

groups in STEM (science, technology, engineering, and mathematics), first generation Latino college students, gay immigrants, Black women, Black males, Chinese students, Muslim students, rural HIV residents, and students with disabilities. The qualitative designs and techniques employed in the study of these groups not only enhance our knowledge and understanding of diverse groups, but also provide a model for researchers who wish to advance their methodological and content area specialties. The authors illustrate the required training, skills, and expertise needed to engage in qualitative research on marginalized groups, which can present a daunting challenge, especially for the beginning researcher.

Finally, the articles in this book illustrate the basic and traditional value of qualitative research, which seeks to gain a more complete understanding and in-depth knowledge about a given phenomenon by collecting, analyzing, and interpreting data from subjects, based on their experiences, meaning, and context, especially in exploring questions pertaining to "what, where, how, and why." The authors intend for this book to be useful to students, college professors, social action researchers, and practitioners, who need information and illustrations of a wide range of qualitative approaches and methods for the study of marginalized and underrepresented groups and vulnerable populations.

—**Thomas J. Durant, Jr., PhD**
Emeritus Professor of Sociology & African American Studies
Louisiana State University
Former Professor of Education/Qualitative Research Methods
Executive Higher Education Leadership, College of Education
Jackson State University

INTRODUCTION

This book's purpose is to provide a description and explanation of various qualitative methods, mechanisms of analysis with case study examples. This book is intended to provide a primer, a ready reference or field guide that can accompany and support students, researchers, and evaluators conducting qualitative research with underrepresented and marginalized populations. The book should provide an introduction to theory, methods, and techniques which can serve as a guide for reflection and practice. Though there are many books which describe qualitative research, this book is designed from its inception as a guide to inquiry with individuals from and groups which are underrepresented, marginalized and/or disadvantaged. With this purpose, the book focuses on the meaningfulness of these approaches framed by a commitment to social justice and considers qualitative research with the imperative of actually considering—and even better—involving voiceless, marginalized, unrepresented, or devalued populations. Each chapter introduces, explains, and dissects qualitative inquiry, rationale, information, meaning, sharing and processes. Chapter 1 explains the rationale for qualitative research and the importance of inquiry when assessing issues among marginalized and minoritized groups. Chapter 2 addresses the appropriate nature and quality of research and methods. Chapter 3 discusses the nature of information for individuals from different groups and how information is recognized, defined, and collected. Chapter 4 debates meaning and the guidelines for meaning making while ensuring voice, relevance, and authenticity. Chapter 5 discusses sharing and the essential requirements for equitable use of knowledge gained

Qualitative Research With Diverse and Underserved Communities, pages xiii–xiv
Copyright © 2024 by Information Age Publishing
www.infoagepub.com
xiii

from inquiry. Chapter 6 discusses the approaches, tools, and techniques necessary to work ethically and meaningfully with individuals and communities from marginalized and minoritized backgrounds. The final chapter provides some case study examples not as examples but as important work for critical consideration and learning.

There are many books about qualitative research in literature, and these books have been available to researchers for decades. However, work in the area of social justice and the area of reaching out to voiceless, marginalized, unrepresented, or devalued populations is very limited. *Qualitative Research for Diverse and Underserved Communities* is specifically designed not only to teach fundamental and foundational notions and actions related to and intending to advance social justice through the process and product of qualitative research, but it attempts to frame the research inquiry around those qualitative questions: "How?"; "When?"; "What?"; and so on, the authors believe that this type of book will incite and expand national conversations about social justice, especially voids in the literature about social justice, gaps in public policy about social justice and generally the body of knowledge concerning equity, social justice and the role of qualitative research.

—**Jeton McClinton**
Arthur E. Hernandez
Alma L. Thornton

CHAPTER 1

RATIONALE

Importance of Qualitative Inquiry in Assessing Issues Among Marginalized and Minoritized Groups

Jeton McClinton
Jackson State University

WHAT?

The application of the qualitative methodology allows researchers to assess and understand the meaning individuals, communities, or groups ascribe to a human or social problem. Information about actual experiences and circumstances of marginalized and minority respondents negotiating problems can be collected using qualitative approaches (Eyisi, 2016). Because qualitative methodology promotes exploration of the ideas and actions in a social environment in context, applying such methodologies provides a greater likelihood of inclusive perspective and a more authentic appraisal of the complexity of the difficulties and challenges faced by minority and marginalized communities and their members. A researcher can assess a variety of occurrences affecting marginalized populations through their

Qualitative Research With Diverse and Underserved Communities, pages 1–10
Copyright © 2024 by Information Age Publishing
www.infoagepub.com
All rights of reproduction in any form reserved.

lived experience and minimize the potential for bias and misunderstanding which can result in the absence of that perspective. Appropriate qualitative approaches provide an avenue for accessing participants' ideas, logic, interactions, and conventions (Eyisi, 2016). Additionally, appropriate qualitative inquiry characteristics provides a vehicle for community development and action which serves the causes of social justice and equity. The significance of qualitative inquiry in analyzing problems among underserved and marginalized populations is thoroughly discussed in this chapter.

In all cases, qualitative researchers must engage in rigorous inquiry grounded in a known philosophical or theoretical framework. While it is regularly stated that qualitative research applied to social problems should be credible, trustworthy, consistent, and transferable, these requirements are all the more essential when working with individuals from minoritized or disadvantaged groups (O'Kane et al., 2019). However, unlike empirical research, qualitative research does not have a ready formula for achieving these ends. This means the responsibility for accuracy and authenticity lie solely with the researcher rather than the adequacy of some protocol or instrument. The rise in diversity, the expansion of inequities, and the development of social justice concerns in the United States have all contributed to an increased interest in the study of the situations and conditions of marginalized and underrepresented populations. Thus, qualitative research can advance social justice by undertaking studies that increase access, equity, harmony, and participation for vulnerable and diverse communities.

WHY?

The comprehensive investigation of social phenomena, including the experience, behavior, functionality, and interactions of intended participants, is supported by a qualitative technique. Questions on meaning, perspective, and experience are addressed from the participants' points of view rather than that of the researcher or some "theory." Qualitative research yields data that is richer and more elaborate than frequencies or averages. The questions under investigation include the experienced and lived attitudes, beliefs, notions of normative behavior, circumstances, and individual viewpoints. Since marginalized or minoritized groups are usually distinguished by others in terms of gender, race, sexuality, class, religion, physical characteristic, belief, or location, qualitative methodology can be an essential means of inquiry applied to problems of dominance, oppression, suppression, hegemony, and alienation.

Many researchers may opt to perform qualitative inquiry when exploring complicated situations that require a thorough understanding of the system of belief and action in context. For example, a narrative research design can be used to explore participants' accounts of the topic under investigation and how people view themselves. An issue, concept, or phenomenon may be explored through a phenomenological design. This approach seeks shared meaning in the participants' lived experiences. As a result, a researcher may be able to "extract" a generalizable lesson which goes beyond merely examining the system or individual and provide an understanding or explanation that is recognizable by the individuals experiencing the phenomena of study. Grounded theory approaches seek to develop a general model of (inter)action which describes or explains referent phenomena or to develop a description of the "mechanism of action." This methodology can be important for understanding complex phenomena and how those phenomena are experienced and interpreted by individuals from minority and underprivileged groups. Researchers conducting ethnographic studies focus on the attitudes, customs, and language of a group of people who share a common culture seeking to define or explain the influence of culture on experience, interpretation, and action. A case study qualitative research design makes it possible to evaluate problems in a practical setting (Yin, 2017). Therefore, it is clear that the qualitative methodology's nature and underlying principles support its significance for gathering information that can be used to develop a thorough understanding of the common difficulties and problems among underserved and marginalized groups. Qualitative methods of inquiry—in particular—can ensure that the research is founded in how people see their own realities and priorities rather than just the researcher's realities and objectives.

HOW?

Qualitative research enables the application of social justice interpretative frameworks to explore problems or subjects that result from the exclusion, marginalization, or disenfranchisement of people, communities, or cultures. This framework addresses issues and topics that serve to disadvantage and exclude people or cultures, such as hierarchy, hegemony, racism, sexism, unequal power relations, identity, or social injustices. The problems and research questions that are being investigated are intended to give the researcher an understanding of these issues or topics. Researchers can explore social, educational, and health-related issues affecting underserved and marginalized groups by using qualitative methodology to examine and analyze how events occur and what they mean to all stakeholders including essentially individuals from minoritized and marginalized groups.

For evaluating the experiences of Black, Indigenous, and racialized students in any context, qualitative research is a practical tool. For example, one-on-one and web-based telephone interviews for the data collection on the perception of African Americans and Hispanics in a medical school admission process, researchers might use a grounded theory approach to understand the system of action rather than merely identify the "deficiencies" of the referenced group and thereby identify the systemic causes and inappropriate mechanisms which result in disparate admissions rates. The resultant model or grounded theory can provide the researcher, students, faculty, administrators, and even policymakers better perspectives from which to make decisions concerning appropriate system changes rather than the usual reaction of "blaming the victim."

Suppose researchers explore the success of the qualitative methodology in pinpointing the problems that lead to disparities in mental health among marginalized and minoritized populations. And using an epidemiology research design makes it possible to analyze and comprehend the problems with treatment inequalities. Epidemiological research is used to plan and explore methods to prevent illness and as a guide to managing patients whose illness has already developed. Similarly, research methods such as in-depth interviews can support effectiveness in revealing how restrictive immigration laws, Latinx immigrants' social exclusion, concealment, and fear of deportation cause mistrust in their communities and frequently cause healthcare services to be delayed.

In the medical profession, considering breast cancer cases, conducting in-depth interviews with underserved breast cancer survivors may be able to assist the researchers in determining the characteristics that support the group's adherence to anti-hormonal medicine. In-depth interviews use open-ended questions, often beginning with "why" or "how," giving participants the freedom to use their own words, and are worded so that respondents expound on the topic, not just answer "Yes" or "No." Qualitative investigation can be used when analyzing how stress affects marginalized and underrepresented groups, including people of color, lesbians, gay men and women, and transgender persons. Findings in current research indicate that applying the qualitative research methodology facilitates the collection of data that can be applied to influence educational policies and practices, specifically those focused on promoting social justice, supporting equitable learning, decreasing disparities in the access to healthcare (De Kock et al., 2017; Hadinger, 2016; McConnell et al., 2018; Memon et al., 2016; Tilley, 2019; Valentin-Cortes et al., 2020; Wells et al., 2016).

Data Collection Tools

There are a variety of software tools that have aided qualitative research by streamlining the majority of qualitative methodological procedures, especially those incorporating multimedia digital data. This data can be assessed using computer-aided qualitative data analysis software (CAQDAS) such as MAXqda, Atlas.ti, HyperRESEARCH, and NVivo (Creswell & Creswell, 2018; O'Kane, 2019). Following is a brief overview of each CAQDAS, highlighting its fundamental use as well as the editor's perceptions of its advantages and disadvantages. MAXqda was developed by researchers for researchers and is helpful in the fields of business and education. Advantage: MAXqda is simple to use, supports a variety of languages, and employs artificial intelligence to assist users with audio transcription. Disadvantage: Users must save their work and then merge the versions making MAXqda difficult for individual users who want to work collaboratively (Wolff, 2021).

ATLAS.ti supports large amounts of graphics, video data, and textual information. Due to the additional features and cost, it is most useful for enterprises, academic institutions, and research groups. Advantage: ATLAS.ti has a user-friendly interface, which makes collaboration simpler than with other CAQDAS and it includes both sentiment analysis and autocoding. Disadvantage: ATLAS.ti may be pricey for students or individuals and the coding features are not considered intuitive (Wolff, 2021).

HyperResearch is a cross-platform software for those working in a collaborative environment. Advantage: Among all CAQDAS providers, HyperResearch offers the most versatile license options. It is also among the most reasonably priced CAQDAS products, and its student license and all other licenses are time unlimited. Disadvantage: Compared to the other CAQDAS, HyperResearch has fewer features, a less appealing aesthetic, and worse PDF handling, all of which can be regarded as minor negatives.

NiVio is best used by researchers in academic environments. Advantage: NVivo's user interface is simple to use, especially for those familiar with Microsoft Office. Additionally, it provides automatic transcribing and coding. NVivo's weaknesses include its inability to handle massive data sets and its difficulties with character-based languages. And data must be manually analyzed after it has been coded, which can be time-consuming.

The use of CAQDAS supports the transparency and trustworthiness of the qualitative data analysis process. CAQDAS provided basic building blocks that can be used for exploring data, clarifying codes, and studying patterns. These techniques help the researcher to understand the data and recognize sense-making of the output especially for inductive researchers (Wolff, 2021)

WHERE?

The activities involved in a qualitative inquiry include identifying the target facility or population, gaining approval, performing purposive sampling, and collecting, recording, storing, and analyzing the data. In narrative research, data are collected from one or more individuals who are willing to participate, who are accessible, and possess unique insight into the phenomenon of study. Among minoritized and marginalized groups, researchers can decide whether to conduct first or second-order narratives to collect data from the recommended maximum of 2–3 participants. The first-order narrative is a reflective story that draws a composite picture of the phenomenon emerging from the participants. The composite is not a simple re-telling, it is an interpretation by the researcher through her knowledge of the phenomenon under inquiry, through listening to and hearing the stories told by the participants, and through her reflexivity during the process. Second—order narrative is researchers conducting a qualitative inquiry based on the phenomenology design to collect data from individuals who have experienced the phenomenon of study. In grounded theory-based qualitative inquiries, the researchers include individuals who have participated in the action or process of study. Data for ethnographic research are occasionally collected from a single site that has a group with shared beliefs, values, and assumptions. Comparably, data for case studies are collected from one or more sites. In the design, data can be collected from different individuals, who are regarded as cases. By nature, the sample size for qualitative inquiries is usually small because of the saturation concept. Saturation is the point in data collection when no additional insight is found and data collected starts to become repetitive, and further data collection is redundant, suggesting that a sufficient sample size is attained. Although there is no generalized sample size, various qualitative researchers have provided recommendations. In grounded theory, ethnography, narrative research, phenomenological, and case study designs, the recommended sample sizes are 20–30, 30–50, 1–2, 5–25, and 4–5, respectively (Boddy, 2016; Creswell & Creswell, 2018; Creswell & Poth, 2016; Yin, 2017). Sampling techniques are used to produce detailed data consistent with the chosen methodological approach. Making sure that the sample size selected is neither too large nor too small is crucial. It is challenging to thoroughly understand the phenomenon under study if the researcher has a small number of participants. The researcher's analysis is likely flawed or, at the very least, deceptive if there are too many participants and that data is considered during coding.

Malterud et al. (2016) indicated that qualitative researchers could apply information power to guide the selection of an adequate sample size. The concept of information power is based on the aim of the study, quality of dialogue, analysis strategy, application of established theory, and sample specificity. Thus, applying purposeful sampling enables the researcher to select available participants who possess the experience and knowledge about the issues analyzed (Creswell & Poth, 2016). To designate a purposive sample, a researcher chooses participants based on the characteristics that the researcher desires. For instance, if a researcher wants to explore how students use campus mental health support systems, the researcher will purposefully select a subset of those students who are currently receiving mental health support, those who have stopped receiving it, and those who are still seeking to use it. Document reviews, interviews, and observations are among the methods used to acquire data regardless of qualitative design. These tools, and open-ended inquiries, field in-depth interviews are best employed in gathering data from study participants in their "natural environments." This means that qualitative researchers explore the environment as it is and do not alter their surroundings, whereas experimental and control groups are used to collect data for quantitative research. Qualitative methodology requires the careful consideration of the particular expression of the identity of individuals from diverse and underserved communities. A well-defined recruitment strategy must be devised if a participant population with various cultural backgrounds is to be included for research objectives. Understanding what a diverse population should look like and providing support that removes barriers are the first steps in doing this. Removing obstacles that do not include diverse representation begins with integrating technologies to create a culturally sensitive system that uses materials in many languages as appropriate, adapted to the target group's literacy level, linguistic needs, and cultural requirements. By using these kinds of resources, researchers can analyze participants' attitudes, beliefs, and perceptions and gather information that can be used to help ameliorate problems that affect underprivileged and minoritized populations.

WHEN?

The observational or interviewing techniques created by qualitative researchers are employed to gather data. In order to sample the proposed research protocols, data collection instruments, sample recruitment strategies, and other research techniques in advance of a larger study, pilot testing is carried out on a limited scale to establish the "validity" of the instruments. Before fully completing the intended study, the researcher can use the pilot study to identify and address any potential issues or flaws. Therefore, it is the responsibility of the researcher to provide data collecting instruments that are appropriate for getting authentic and accurate information from the target participants from varied and underprivileged communities.

For example, Reisner et al. (2018) used structured and semi-structured interview protocols to collect data about the participants' attitudes, beliefs, and perceptions on an issue of interest. Reisner suggested that the tools, which were administered via an online platform, provide unique advantages to researchers with interest in assessing rare and sensitive issues among geographically dispersed marginalized groups. In particular, qualitative research inquiry may ensure that the research is grounded in how people see their own realities and priorities rather than just the researcher's realities and objectives.

SUMMARY AND RECOMMENDATIONS

To examine and understand attitudes, beliefs, concepts, experiences, conditions, and personal viewpoints, qualitative inquiry analyzes picture and text data while keeping in mind that the researcher is the primary instrument. Complex reasoning is used in the process, and the participants' subjective viewpoints, interpretations, and meanings are the main points of emphasis in data collection. Establishing whether or not the particular approach to the issue is suitable for answering the research question with the particular population is the first step of any research investigation. A case study, phenomenology, ethnography, grounded theory, or narrative approach to research are all options available to the researcher (Yin, 2017).

The qualitative approach is also crucial since it provides a means to gather data that may be analyzed for implications for theory, subsequent research, actions, and treatments. Assessing social, health, and educational challenges of underserved and marginalized groups is facilitated by qualitative approaches to inquiry. Qualitative research-based studies examining hegemony, sexism, hierarchy, identities, unequal power relations, or societal injustice have been carried out and serve to inform both the topics of consideration and provide a model for inquiry to be considered by others with similar concerns. In qualitative research, the method of gathering data entails securing consent, sampling, and choosing the tools for data capture. Although there is no agreement on the ideal sample size, qualitative researchers looking at problems in the community of the marginalized and minoritized should choose people who can adequately provide information on the concept being studied. The first recommendation is that there is a need for more qualitative research that explores issues of concern among marginalized and minoritized groups and produces reliable results that can be incorporated into programs and policies. Second, it is important to analyze if new data gathering methods, such as focus groups and online interviews, are feasible and acceptable to underrepresented and marginalized groups. Third, applying CAQDAS in the approach will help qualitative researchers who analyze problems affecting marginalized and minoritized groups increase the openness and credibility of their study.

REFERENCES

Boddy, C. R. (2016). Sample size for qualitative research. *Qualitative Market Research: An International Journal, 19*(4), 426–432. https://doi.org/10.1108/qmr-06-2016-0053

Creswell, J. W., & Creswell, J. D. (2018). *Research design: Qualitative, quantitative, and mixed methods approaches* (5th ed.). SAGE Publishing.

Creswell, J. W., & Poth, C. N. (2016). *Qualitative inquiry and research design: Choosing among five approaches* (4th ed.). SAGE Publishing.

De Kock, C., Decorte, T., Vanderplasschen, W., Derluyn, I., & Sacco, M. (2017). Studying ethnicity, problem substance use, and treatment: From epidemiology to social change. *Drugs: Education, Prevention, and Policy, 24*(3), 230–239. https://doi.org/10.1080/09687637.2016.1239696

Eyisi, D. (2016). The usefulness of qualitative and quantitative approaches and methods in researching problem-solving ability in science education curriculum. *Journal of Education and Practice, 7*(15), 91–100. https://files.eric.ed.gov/fulltext/EJ1103224.pdf

Hadinger, M. A. (2016). Underrepresented minorities in medical school admissions: A qualitative study. *Teaching and Learning in Medicine, 29*(1), 31–41. https://doi.org/10.1080/10401334.2016.1220861

Malterud, K., Siersma, V. D., & Guassora, A. D. (2016). Sample size in qualitative interview studies: Guided by information power. *Qualitative Health Research, 26*(13), 1753–1760. https://doi.org/10.1177/1049732315617444

McConnell, E. A., Janulis, P., Phillips, G., II, Truong, R., & Birkett, M. (2018). Multiple minority stress and LGBT community resilience among sexual minority men. *Psychology of Sexual Orientation and Gender Diversity, 5*(1), 1–12. https://doi.org/10.1037/sgd0000265

Memon, A., Taylor, K., Mohebati, L. M., Sundin, J., Cooper, M., Scanlon, T., & de Visser, R. (2016). Perceived barriers to accessing mental health services among Black and minority ethnic (BME) communities: A qualitative study in Southeast England. *BMJ Open, 6*(11), 1–10. https://bmjopen.bmj.com/content/6/11/e012337

O'Kane, P., Smith, A., & Lerman, M. P. (2019). Building transparency and trustworthiness in inductive research through computer-aided qualitative data analysis software. *Organizational Research Methods, 24*(1). https://doi.org/10.1177/1094428119865016

Reisner, S. L., Randazzo, R. K., White Hughto, J. M., Peitzmeier, S., DuBois, L. Z., Pardee, D. J., & Potter, J. (2018). Sensitive health topics with underserved patient populations: Methodological considerations for online focus group discussions. *Qualitative Health Research, 28*(10), 1658–1673. https://doi.org/10.1177/1049732317705355

Tilley, S. (2019). The role of critical qualitative research in educational contexts: A Canadian perspective. *Educar em Revista, 35*(75), 155–180. https://doi.org/10.1590/0104-4060.66806

Valentin-Cortes, M., Benavides, Q., Bryce, R., Rabinowitz, E., Rion, R., Lopez, W. D., & Fleming, P. J. (2020). Application of the minority stress theory: Understanding the mental health of undocumented Latinx immigrants. *American Journal of Community Psychology, 2020*, 1–10. https://doi.org/10.1002/ajcp.12455

Wells, K. J., Pan, T. M., Vazquez-Otero, C., Ung, D., Ustjanauskas, A. E., Munoz, D., Laronga, C., Roetzheim, R. G., Goldenstein, M., Carrizosa, C., Nuhaily, S., Johnson, K., Norton, M., Sims, E., & Quinn, G. G. (2016). Barriers and facilitators to endocrine therapy adherence among underserved hormone-receptor-positive breast cancer survivors: A qualitative study. *Supportive Care in Cancer, 24*(10), 4123–4130. https://doi.org/10.1007/s00520-016-3229-8

Wolff, R. (2021, September 29). 8 great tools to perform qualitative data analysis in 2022. *Monkey Learn.* https://monkeylearn.com/blog/qualitative-data-analysis-software/

Yin, R. K. (2017). *Case study research design and methods.* SAGE Publications.

CHAPTER 2

INQUIRY

What is the Appropriate Nature and Quality of Researchers and Methods?

Jeton McClinton
Jackson State University

WHAT?

Qualitative inquiry is used in a variety of fields, disciplines, focusing on a range of issues as an approach to scientific investigation. For example, a naturalistic research method (NRM) known as qualitative inquiry aims to gain a thorough understanding of social phenomena in the context of the participants' everyday lives. NRM involves the researcher observing participants' actions in their everyday environments. The researcher then stays out of a naturalistic observation and does not influence anything. This approach might be compared to purposeful "people watching."

Case study, historical analysis, ethnography, grounded theory, and phenomenology are just a few of the different methodologies that qualitative investigation might use to supplement other analytical and statistical methods. Therefore, because it aids in understanding people's social

Qualitative Research With Diverse and Underserved Communities, pages 11–18
Copyright © 2024 by Information Age Publishing
www.infoagepub.com

environments, qualitative inquiry is an important component of research with both underrepresented and underserved populations.

Qualitative research is appropriate for gathering information that can be used to improve comprehension, provide descriptions, or generate theoretical, conceptual understanding of phenomena that affects a particular population which can inform problem definition and provide a basis for resolution. Applying the qualitative methodology to a minority or disenfranchised population may have the following potential benefits: understanding complex social processes, gathering values and beliefs that underlie issues among individuals in a diverse or underserved population and identifying crucial aspects of a phenomenon based on the participants' perspective. Focus groups, for instance, can be used to assess the obstacles that hinder members of Black and other underrepresented ethnic populations from receiving mental health care. Using this technique, researchers can identify the contextual factors that need to be altered to decrease care disparities and improve the delivery of culturally competent care.

The application of qualitative methodology is most appropriate given one or more of the following requirements. The first is when the foci of study are complex phenomena that are challenging or impossible to measure (quantitatively). Second, when collecting numerical or statistical data would not result in a comprehensive understanding of the problem; third, when the goal is to gain insight into casual concepts; fourth, when the objective is to have a basis of knowledge and understanding for the development of quantitative instruments or processes; and fifth, when applied to a specific population, such as individuals from underserved and marginalized groups (Creswell & Creswell, 2018). For example, a researcher ought to choose a qualitative method appropriate for investigating complex concepts, relationships, and dynamics related to healthcare delivery such as organizational change, patients' perception of quality care, and the role of clinical leaders in the implementation of evidence-based guidelines aimed at decreasing health disparities among diverse and underserved populations (Creswell & Poth, 2016). These concerns are likely best informed by qualitative approaches which provide opportunities to observe complexity and nuance which sometimes can be tested using quantitative methods.

Applying qualitative methodology is recommended when researching issues like criminal injustice, discrimination, racial profiling, and limited access to healthcare because complete understanding of these topics in context, requires knowledge about attitudes, experiences, beliefs, concepts, perceptions, and conditions among underserved and diverse populations. For example, Davis et al. (2019) conducted seven telephone interviews and 14 focus groups, which helped the researchers identify barriers hindering participation of African Americans in clinical trials. LaVaccare et al. (2018) demonstrated that a qualitative methodology was suitable for understanding issues among an underserved population such as women of color who identify as lesbians or bisexuals. Similarly, Davis et al. (2019), LaVaccare et al. (2018), Memon et al. (2016), and Erves et al. (2017) supported the applicability of qualitative research in providing in-depth understanding of issues affecting diverse and underserved populations.

WHY?

An open mind is one of the most crucial traits a qualitative researcher can develop. When speaking with a research participant, always probe further. As new, intriguing paths of investigation emerge, the researcher should follow them. Avoid allowing prior knowledge to prevent learning new things and approach the research as an emergent inquiry with each new insight informing the research process. A competent researcher must be patient and able to relate to people of many personalities, histories, and cultural backgrounds. This can be achieved by approaching each person as an individual whole rather than merely a "case" or "subject" listening in a way that lets them know they are being heard. The nature, characteristics, and qualities of the participants as well as the study topic should be considered when choosing the research methodology. The researcher should be aware of and include all relevant stakeholders in order to comprehend the subject under investigation fully and aware that there is minimal time for limited communication during the research process and return with findings in a short period. Try alternative note-taking techniques during interviews to help summarize information more quickly and easily. Consider what is most effective for the researcher: paper and pen or concept-making software that allows the researcher to annotate instantly. Keep in mind that the researcher may occasionally need help taking notes so they can focus more clearly and complete the interview more quickly. In this case, the researcher should be ready to have one person conduct the interview while the other takes notes, allowing both of them to concentrate on the participant as the researcher conducts the interview.

Disproportionalities in a variety of industries, including healthcare, education, and employment, could be caused by the underrepresentation of marginalized and diverse communities in research. For instance, in the healthcare sector, a dearth of participants from diversely sampled communities could be linked to the disproportionate burden of chronic diseases on minority populations. Another issue is the inequities caused by the underrepresentation of marginalized people. To ensure that the study's findings are transferable and credible the researchers must use the best methodology and include a broad population.

HOW?

Qualitative inquiry allows researchers to describe a range of complex issues or phenomena affecting the diverse and underserved populations. By its nature, qualitative methodology enables researchers to collect data that can be applied to understand consequences and precursors of a phenomenon. The text, visual, or verbal-based data are collected in natural settings, rather than experimental environments and use observations and open-ended discussions.

When a researcher wishes to count occurrences, statistically test hypotheses, and conduct random-control or quasi-experiments, which results in data collection using established processes looking for specific responses, a quantitative approach is appropriate (Creswell & Creswell, 2018; Creswell & Poth, 2016). Comparatively, qualitative research is frequently exploratory because it enables researchers to create new hypotheses using inductive rather than deductive methods. Conducting observations and formulating hypotheses are examples of inductive techniques. In contrast, deductive methods require testing existing hypotheses through focused observations. Anecdotal, non-scientific life experiences and persecutions are frequently the basis for qualitative techniques.

In qualitative research, credibility—especially with diverse and underrepresented populations—is promoted by ensuring that findings are adequately described and recognizable to individuals who shared and conveyed their experience. Researchers can then promote the credibility of qualitative studies through triangulation, and reflexivity that includes verbatim quotations. Qualitative researchers can ensure the transferability or applicability of their studies by including adequate samples who are representative in terms of ethnicity, race, culture, and socioeconomic backgrounds (Gagani, 2019; Hammarberg et al., 2016). Researchers also guarantee conformability by outlining instances of bias based on a person's gender, culture, or historical heritage. Essentially, conformability aids researchers in demonstrating that the conclusions are based on data and are not the product of the researchers' imagination (Korstjens & Moser, 2018). Once dependability, transferability, and credibility have been established, conformability happens, which gives the study's findings credibility. Transferability is achieved when the researcher gives in-depth explanations of the research participants' behaviors and experiences, and context, so that the reader may understand their behavior and experiences. Credibility is achieved when the research findings reflect the population's opinions. It is considered the initial standard so the researcher can establish the integrity of the research study's conclusions by directly relating the findings to the populations' opinions. Credibility emphasizes the two methods (triangulation and member checking). Member-checking is a strategy that allows participants to clarify their objectives, rectify mistakes, and supply extra information as needed. It establishes credibility and involves sharing the participants' facts, interpretations, and conclusions.

WHERE?

Researchers can employ in-depth interviews, focus groups, document reviews, and observations as effective data gathering techniques for ethnography, narrative, phenomenology, grounded theory, and case study research. When conducting an ethnographic study, researchers can keep a professional distance while using observation to better understand individuals and group behavior. Narrative data collection explores and conceptualizes the human experience in textual form from topical stories, personal narratives, or entire life stories such as biographies with the intent to collect data with personal knowledge of an event and the meaning that people give to their experiences. Phenomenological research explores the human experience through the descriptions provided by the people involved, these experiences are called lived experiences. Phenomenological research aims to explain the significance that experiences have for each individual. Studies using a "grounded theory" approach collect and explore evidence before developing a theory that is based on the findings. The study and development of concepts take place after data collection since the theory is "based" in actual data. Case studies are in-depth explorations of specific individuals or groups of individuals. Depending on the objectives of the study and the design selected by the researcher, a case study may be classified as either quantitative or qualitative research. For a case study to be classified as a qualitative study, just like other kinds of qualitative studies, the researcher must be more interested in what the participants' experiences mean to them personally than in extrapolating findings to other groups of individuals. Case studies are not used to test theories, but they can be used to develop theories.

Interviews allow the researchers to establish rapport with the participants and gain an in-depth understanding of the respondents' perceptions and experiences. The resulting data can enable researchers to direct subsequent discussions in a manner which may more fully describe experience, decision-making or action. Researchers who use in-depth interviews are required to be skilled in passive listening and use neutral, nonjudgmental, and culturally sensitive language. Quality researchers conduct effective interviews using appropriate verbal and nonverbal feedback based on the participants' response (Creswell & Creswell, 2018; Olson et al., 2015; Pelzang & Hutchinson, 2017).

Focus groups assist researchers in gathering the experiences of a cohort of people who share characteristics crucial to the problem, topic, or phenomenon under study (Creswell & Creswell, 2018). The method works well for gathering information from marginalized groups because they are likely to encourage participants to feel at ease, especially when the subject of interest is potentially private or "delicate." The researcher can observe, engage with, and gather detailed information from participants in their natural surroundings. The researcher can better appreciate and understand the culture and population under investigation thanks to this approach to data collection. Researchers evaluate written materials during the document review.

The literature related to ideal sample size for qualitative inquiry includes varied suggestions. However, many authors suggest between 20 and 30 people for interview methods and between 6 and 8 people for focus group approaches. While there is no definitive standard for sample size, qualitative researchers must include sufficient informants so as to reach saturation. Saturation, when used in a more general sense, refers to the point in data collecting when no new problems or insights are found and data start to repeat, indicating that an appropriate sample size has been achieved (Boddy, 2016; Creswell & Creswell, 2018; Hammarberg et al., 2016; Haven & Van Grootel, 2019).

WHEN?

Pilot studies are carried out to determine the cultural relevance and appropriateness of the instruments or techniques to support the researchers in recognizing and responding to cultural and linguistic nuances, even though the data collection tools created by qualitative researchers are not standardized (Creswell & Creswell, 2018; Pelzang & Hutchinson, 2017; Wardale et al., 2015). Let's examine an instance of how a research project might use a pilot study. It is crucial to have a representative sample of people from various communities to understand the causes and effects of persistent health disparities and offer local, state, and federal policymakers and healthcare professionals' evidence-based remedies. Still, diverse and underrepresented populations are largely underrepresented in contemporary biomedical and population research. A pilot study can be designed using bilingual, bicultural field interviewers and interpreters to establish trust with this group and elicit their opinions to help create recruitment methods and clear, culturally relevant terminology. In preparation for a study, the pilot study is used to examine applicability of the proposed approaches, feasibility, accessibility, reach, dose, receptiveness, and so forth, of the research process with the target audience. Additionally, the pilot study provides evidence of the reasonableness and credibility of inquiry methods and outcomes.

There are multiple technologies available to collect data from diverse, underserved and underrepresented research participants. According to Upadhyay and Lipkovich (2020), gathering data from a diverse population can be made more accessible by employing online tools like Zoom and video chat. Participants in their study reported feeling at ease when answering questions from researchers about delicate topics. subjects. Therefore, the authors believed that using these technologies might help increase the diversity of research samples that include people from traditionally underrepresented groups in research.

Limited inclusion of diverse and underserved populations in research has resulted in disproportionalities, lack of equity and injurious outcome disparities. A qualitative methodology is appropriate for gaining in-depth understanding of real-world problems focusing on the "why," "what," and "how" research questions. The intention of inquiry with marginalized and minoritized populations should be understanding the participants' perceptions, experiences, and beliefs in their "natural" setting including their "relationship" with existing systems to result in an authentic description of phenomena rather than one that fails to consider the dynamic interaction between social groups, social systems, and organizational systems. Researchers can apply qualitative methodologies to generate a more comprehensive understanding of issues affecting diverse and marginalized populations gaining insights into potential systems based as well as individual and group causal mechanisms. When identifying and describing problems related to inequities among underserved and varied communities, qualitative methodologies are most helpful. When conducting interviews, focus groups, and observations with diverse and marginalized communities, qualitative researchers pay attention without interjecting their opinions, recognize the possible bias from their experience, and speak in a way that is respectful and responsive of the cultures of their participants. To maximize credibility and transferability, qualitative researchers should regularly pilot test in advance of inquiry to assess the suitability of methods and to explore the influence of their own lived experience so as to recognize its influence in data analysis and interpretation. In the end, qualitative researchers seeking to explore experiences of individuals and groups from marginalized and minoritized groups carefully examine whether their proposed approaches are trustworthy, replicable, credible, and verifiable at a minimum.

REFERENCES

Boddy, C. R. (2016). Sample size for qualitative research. *Qualitative Market Research: An International Journal, 19*(4), 426–432. https://doi.org/10.1108/qmr-06-2016-0053

Creswell, J. W., & Creswell, J. D. (2018). *Research design: Qualitative, quantitative, and mixed methods approaches* (5th ed.). SAGE Publishing.

Creswell, J. W., & Poth, C. N. (2016). *Qualitative inquiry and research design: Choosing among five approaches* (4th ed.). SAGE Publishing.

Davis, T. C., Arnold, C. L., Mills, G., & Miele, L. (2019). A qualitative study exploring barriers and facilitators of enrolling underrepresented populations in clinical trials and biobanking. *Frontiers in Cell and Developmental Biology, 7*, 74–84. https://doi.org/10.3389/fcell.2019.00074

Erves, J. C., Mayo-Gamble, T. L., Malin-Fair, A., Boyer, A., Joosten, Y., Vaughn, Y. C., & Wilkins, C. H. (2017). Needs, priorities, and recommendations for engaging underrepresented populations in clinical research: A community perspective. *Journal of Community Health, 42*(3), 472–480. https://doi.org/10.1007/s10900-016-0279-2

Gagani, R. F. (2019). Credibility in qualitative and quantitative research in education: A humean approach. *American Journal of Humanities and Social Sciences Research, 3*(6), 134–139. https://www.ajhssr.com/wp-content/uploads/2019/06/R1936134139.pdf

Hammarberg, K., Kirkman, M., & de Lacey, S. (2016). Qualitative research methods: When to use them and how to judge them. *Human Reproduction, 31*(3), 498–501. https://doi.org/10.1093/humrep/dev334

Haven, L. T., & Van Grootel, D. L. (2019). Preregistering qualitative research. *Accountability in Research, 26*(3), 229–244. https://doi.org/10.1080/08989621.2019.1580147

Korstjens, I., & Moser, A. (2018). Series: Practical guidance to qualitative research. Part 4: Trustworthiness and publishing. *European Journal of General Practice, 24*(1), 120–124. https://doi.org/10.1080/13814788.2017.1375092

LaVaccare, S., Diamant, A. L., Friedman, J., Singh, K. T., Baker, J. A., Rodriguez, T. A., & Pregler, J. (2018). Healthcare experiences of underrepresented lesbian and bisexual women: A focus group qualitative study. *Health Equity, 2*(1), 131–138. https://doi.org/10.1089/heq.2017.0041

Memon, A., Taylor, K., Mohebati, L. M., Sundin, J., Cooper, M., Scanlon, T., & de Visser, R. (2016). Perceived barriers to accessing mental health services among Black and minority ethnic (BME) communities: A qualitative study in Southeast England. *Bio-medical Journal Open, 6*(11), 1–10. http://dx.doi.org/10.1136/bmjopen-2016-012337

Olson, K., Young, R. A., & Schultz, I. Z. (2015). *Handbook of qualitative health research for evidence-based practice.* Springer.

Pelzang, R., & Hutchinson, A. M. (2017). Establishing cultural integrity in qualitative research: Reflections from a cross-cultural study. *International Journal of Qualitative Methods, 17*(1), 1–10. https://doi.org/10.1177/1609406917749702

Upadhyay, U. D., & Lipkovich, H. (2020). Using online technologies to improve diversity and inclusion in cognitive interviews with young people. *BMC Medical Research Methodology, 20*, Article 159. https://doi.org/10.1186/s12874-020-01024-9

Wardale, D., Cameron, R., & Li, J. (2015). Considerations for multidisciplinary, culturally sensitive, mixed methods research. *Electronic Journal of Business Research Methods, 13*(1), 37–48. https://academic-publishing.org/index.php/ejbrm/article/view/1329/1292

CHAPTER 3

INFORMATION

What is the Nature of Information (for Individuals From Different Groups)? How is Information Recognized, Defined, and Collected?

Alma L. Thornton
Jackson State University

WHAT?

Members of historically underrepresented groups have frequently been subjected to abuse, stereotyping, and exclusion from social science. A repair of this past and a resolution to the moral requirement for socially equitable qualitative research have been demanded by academics and others. It is unwise to assume that qualitative research is inherently socially just or more appropriate for studying populations with different cultural backgrounds than other scientific approaches. The book's purpose is to carefully consider how researchers may gather qualitative data in a socially just manner, especially with populations that are culturally diverse.

Qualitative Research With Diverse and Underserved Communities, pages 19–28
Copyright © 2024 by Information Age Publishing
www.infoagepub.com
19

WHY?

Appropriate qualitative inquiry with underserved populations is helpful when little information exists on a topic and when the appropriate language, concepts, or questions to ask are unclear. Qualitative information collection within diverse groups is necessary to understand the critical ideas of members of these groups and provide guidance in asking the correct questions using the correct language. Qualitative approaches are suited for research targeting vulnerable and underserved populations whose voices have not been equitably included and represented in the larger body of literature historically. A reexamination of each step of the research process is needed in the conceptualization, data collection, data analysis, and data applications to ensure equity for and inclusion of these communities. A key consideration of qualitative methods is the grounded nature of the research approach. Qualitative methods rely largely on the lived experiences and explores how individuals construct and mediate reality (Clement et al., 2018).

Qualitative inquiry answers the question: "What is X and how do underserved communities perceive X in different situations, and why?" Exploring the subjectivity and complexity of phenomena, qualitative information can demonstrate how individual experiences and identities influence (and are influenced by) sociocultural, environmental, and contextual elements. It is believed that using this information can better help the understanding of marginalized communities by recognizing, conveying, and amplifying their voices and lived experiences.

It is legitimate to wonder as a researcher what information to collect. A qualitative research question is best based on a specific or explicit statement of the problem, issue or challenge that needs to be addressed. The question should not only specify who the participants should be, but it also directs the data gathering techniques required to get the most in-depth (i.e., useful and meaningful) answers. The best query needs to be focused on, for example, a single health condition and be both precise and direct. These data could be used to collect information on a wide range of subjects of interest in the healthcare, education, and other industries involving underrepresented populations.

Qualitative data can be collected using several strategies. It can be witnessed and filmed or video recorded and collected through observation, one-to-one interviews, and focus groups. Qualitative data is descriptive and open-ended—allowing respondents to express themselves fully (Creswell, 2018; Given, 2008; Rosenthal, 2018).

HOW?

There is a national call concerning what methods can be used to evaluate the extent to which systems advance racial equity and authentically represent the experience of underserved communities in the United States. There is a nationwide quest for inquiry tools that can be used to overcome traditional biases against and lack of representation of marginalized communities in the United States and advance the cause of racial justice through accuracy and authenticity. This call is groundbreaking because it acknowledges among other things that elements contributing to historically based inequity include a lack of all stakeholder engagement. Quantitative analysis even with detailed and validated theoretical frameworks cannot fully capture the nuanced experiences of underserved and underrepresented communities, but qualitative information may.

The collection and analysis of rigorous qualitative data is not just a technique to give life to quantitative evidence about policies or programs, although it often does that powerfully. The qualitative researcher can amass deep contextual insights about how people actually experience policies, programs, and power dynamics and how this experience explains the nature of the action and provides evidence regarding the basis for associated outcomes. Qualitative research can be helpful in comprehending how and why a given program or intervention may or may not work as intended (from the perspective of those on whom such is applied), the cultural and social influences that advantage some but not others and give voice and agency to those for whom those efforts were putatively mounted in the first place thus advancing equity for underserved and marginalized populations. Because people exist at the intersection of multiple identities, impacted by conditions and context (as perceived by those in a given experience, qualitative inquiry also enables policy researchers, administrators, social scientists and others to embrace, rather than "flatten," different perspectives regarding the same concept, experience, or activity.

There are four common methods used to collect information qualitatively. They are case study, ethnography, phenomenology, and grounded theory. Case study methods can be used to enable the participation of marginalized groups by exploring phenomenon within a real-life setting and is based on in-depth exploration of a single individual, group, or event to explore underlying relationships, judgments, decisions, expectations and assumptions and ideally provides an authentic exploratory and descriptive analysis. Case study with marginalized groups requires cultural responsiveness—an awareness and appreciation for the context of cultural identity within which all experience occurs. Ethnography involves direct observations of study participants in their real-life environment, sometimes over extended periods. Through observing social interactions within identified groups often using interviews and documentary data, ethnography can provide detailed and comprehensive accounts of different communities, organizations, and other groups. It documents and provides rich, comprehensive understanding of individual culture, worldview, actions, and habits situated within their personal spaces (Hughes, 1992). Ethnographic study is an essential contributor to understanding specific groups in context and location since both influence cultural identity formation, maintenance, and expression. Often, marginalized and underrepresented groups are categorized based on meaningless observable characteristics rather than the defining character of their cultural identity. Ethnography provides a vehicle for examining that identity that goes beyond the superficial and spurious. Grounded theory is an approach that is often based on face-to-face interviews, focus groups or other community observations to explore, describe, and explain particular phenomena. This method sometimes helps in explaining or framing a less-well-understood mechanism of action, problem or situation and intends to result in a useful and authentic theoretical grounding. Because grounded theory research is emergent, inductive, and comparative in nature, it is especially well-suited to elucidate the mechanisms by which elements related to racial and ethnic diversity affect various societal concerns (Delve, n.d.; Glaser & Strauss, 1967; Strauss & Corbin, 1990). Phenomenology shares features with grounded theory such as employing comparable methods to collect data and focusing on understanding how human beings experience their world. In some respects, it allows researchers to "insert" themselves in another person's shoes to understand the experiences of the participant. For example, the experiences of people of color in the health care systems or academic systems can be studied phenomenologically as it stresses the lived and experiencing dimensions of identified constructs with the goal of explicitly explaining the distinctive, stable elements (variables), the relationship between those elements and the rules that govern those arrangements in the context of where individuals interact socially. Phenomenological data are frequently limited to interviews and findings are reported as rich accountings of experience grounded in characteristics identified during data analysis (Clement et al., 2018; Corbin & Strauss, 2015; Denzin & Lincoln, 2011; McCall & Edwards, 2021).

WHEN?

Examples of qualitative information can include "variables" such as race and ethnicity. By highlighting the ambiguity and constructed nature of racial and ethnic categorizations, qualitative inquiry can help advance an anti-racist social system and worldview. For example, qualitative approaches to research usually demonstrate that notions of race and ethnicity are meaningless absent the consideration of relevant associated culture even while these ubiquitous but meaningless notions are the main factors that separate people. Regardless, race and ethnicity have historically been utilized as primary explanation and justification for grouping and blaming marginalized and minoritized people as a deleterious consequence to equitable access to social opportunity and social support and distribution of resources. In addition, qualitative inquiry can well demonstrate the pernicious impact of historical and ongoing social inequity since it provides for the consideration of lived experience as evidence and explanatory in the interaction between people and activity (e.g., "intervention") in a practically inescapable social system. Qualitative researchers should endeavor to collect complete and precise information on race and ethnicity to increase data richness, reduce the chance of inaccurate assumptions about the identity of participants, and improve the likelihood of authenticity.

Researchers are increasingly shifting to qualitative methods to understand underserved groups and how they interpret their experiences in recognition that neither individuals nor groups can be described in purely mechanistic terms. The three most used qualitative research tools for information collection are observations, focus groups discussions (FGD), and in-depth interviews (Marshall & Rossman, 1998; Rosenthal, 2018; Savin-Baden & Major, 2013; Taylor & Bogdan, 1984). Observations are used when researchers collect information by exploring behaviors or events in natural settings. For example, researchers may use observation to evaluate community needs and discern appropriate ways to frame intended projects during the planning phase. There are two types of observation: covert and overt. Covert observations are when the participant does not know they are being observed and the observer is hidden. An example is when the researcher, trying to understand seminars at community colleges, poses as a student to observe what is occurring. In overt observations, participants know they are being observed. For example, a researcher at a community college seminar may explain his study to the teacher and class and use a video camera to record the seminar. Typically, overt observations are usually favored because watching individuals without their knowledge or permission can raise ethical problems. Unlike inquiry involving covert observations, approval for the conduct of which obviously requires an independent assessment of risk and benefit, informed consent must be obtained for overt observation before any observational data is collected (Family Health International, n.d.). Observations are most useful when (a) the researcher attempts to understand a continuous process or situation, (b) the researcher is gathering information on individual actions or interactions between people, (c) the collection of data from people (e.g., interview) is not realistic.

Researchers should prepare for observation by ensuring the research questions or processes being observed are well structured and clearly defined (Lindlof & Taylor, 2002). In addition, it is imperative the researcher is aware and respectful of any cultural requirements of the community of interest in decisions related to methods and design.

The observer(s) must be well-trained in the data collection process, knowledgeable and respectful of the culture of the community, and focused on producing practical, valuable, and impartial shrewdness. Observers can be the researchers themselves or other trained individuals (such as students, interns, research assistants, or stakeholders) to act as observers (Given, 2008; Marshal & Rossman, 1998; Rosenthal, 2018; Taylor & Bogdan, 1984).

A few methods that may be used to collect data through observation include: (a) recording notes and checklists with preset questions and responses (which is considered one of the most traditional methods of collecting observation data); (b) developing observation guides which are lists of the interactions, processes, or behaviors to be observed, with space to record open-ended narrative data; and (c) writing field notes: open-ended narrative data that can be written (on paper or digitally) or dictated (on a audiorecorder). A lesser-used method for collecting observation data does not include preset questions but uses digital tools (such as a data collection app, digital recorder, laptops, video camera) to enable more in depth and considered processing of information and is often easier (Given, 2008; Marshall & Rossman, 1998; Rosenthal, 2018; Taylor & Bogdan, 1984).

There are many advantages to using observational methods including the observational method enables researchers to gather first-hand data from where the activity is happening, and researchers can get answers from groups that have limited time or readiness to respond to questions (Babbie, 2014, pp. 303–304). The limitations of the observation method include that it can be time-consuming and expensive, and observer bias can be an issue. The overt observation criterion can lead to the Hawthorne effect, meaning people tend to act more appropriately (i.e., social desirability) when they know they are being observed (Marshal & Rossman, 1998; Rosenthal, 2018).

Focus group discussions (FGDs) are another commonly used qualitative research method. It is generally recommended that participants be unknown to each other and share characteristics and experiences in common which are relevant to the topic of interest. It is equally important that focus groups be composed and conducted in such a way to ensure that members of minoritized and marginalized groups feel comfortable sharing their experiences and perspectives. This requires the consideration of social status, positionality, power differentials and other social influences which may compromise the authenticity of collected information. There is no set recommendation for focus group size. However, the qualitative researcher must carefully consider the focus of the inquiry, the likely nature of targeted participants, possible adverse repercussions/consequences of participation, with the requirements for the collection of "valid" data. Though collecting information from multiple groups can result in more in-depth and diverse information, providing for greater opportunity for insight, this recommendation must be considered against any possible adverse individual or group consequences. Focus groups should last between 60–90 minutes as less time may make it difficult to fully explore the discussion topic and more may be unduly arduous and fatiguing. Permission to participate is necessary, and researchers must obtain informed consent for all participants. Still, participation should be voluntary, although some researchers chose to offer incentives. However, the use of incentives is not without some controversy since it may be considered coercive or disrespectful as an insufficient token gesture rather than full compensation for time, effort, and information. It should be noted at the onset that the incentive is considered a form of trade and not compensation or coercion (Given, 2008; Marshall & Rossman, 1998; Rosenthal, 2018; Taylor & Bogdan, 1984).

Focus groups are most useful for

1. identifying program recommendations, weaknesses, and program strengths;
2. recognizing participants' views on program outcomes and impacts;
3. creating new ideas;
4. identifying and interpreting problems;
5. understanding quantitative findings;
6. pre-testing topics or ideas to focus the research questions; and
7. advancing equity in policy.

The researcher is not trying for group consensus. The goal is to explore participants' perceptions on the topic, resulting in exploratory rather than definitive findings. This approach is used to study the research questions rather than offer solutions to issues. A successful FGD requires an experienced moderator who will ensure participants are comfortable and involved in the discussion and that all participant *voices are heard.* Data are collected using audio or video digital recorders if available, alternatively a person can take notes. However, the ideal procedure is to obtain a recording in order to assure accuracy and authenticity of the collected information. It is essential to immediately transcribe the recordings, so that nuances are not lost over time (Given, 2008; Marshall & Rossman, 1998; Rosenthal, 2018; Taylor & Bogdan, 1984).

Regardless of recording, the researcher is encouraged to note the affect and nonverbal interactions to annotate transcriptions to provide detail for the processing of collected information. In all cases of method—it is essential the researcher is informed, respectful, and responsive to the cultural perspectives, assumptions, values, and so on, in order than any interpretation of information is authentic and meaningful from the perspective of the community rather than that of the researcher. There are several advantages of utilizing FGD, such as:

1. When participants address a topic, they may be more actively engaged, which drives more information gathering. The key to this in-

formation gathering is the moderator ability to ensure and encourage continuous participation in a culturally responsive manner.

2. Allows in-depth conversations about the topic informed by the conversation with interested and invested others.

3. Unlike a paper survey, FGDs will enable researchers to explain or describe the question or issue for better (more relevant) responses.

4. Permits researchers to guide policies and programs informed by how people experience a program or service in practice and its impact on their day-to-day lives which is more likely to be culturally responsive.

There are several challenges when utilizing FGDs, including:

1. Moderators cannot show bias since it may deflect/contaminate participants' conversation content and trajectory in unknowable ways. Moderators must also be engaged in guaranteeing that active participants do not overwhelm subdued participants during the discussion.

2. Since FGD data is qualitative, it might not be generalizable to a broader population. This is because qualitative information is often context-specific and depends on the nature of sampling, population, and so forth.

Another method of information collection is the in-depth interview (IDI), which is the most often used qualitative research method. They are semi-structured, which means the questions to be asked and issues to be addressed are focused on the purpose of the inquiry, this approach generally allows the process and content to be emergent—that is guided as much by the participant as by the researcher. Alternatively, some IDIs can be unstructured which means that only the general topic is introduced by the researcher and the particular research questions are not preplanned. Finally, some interviews are completely structured although it is a less commonly used approach. In-depth interviews traditionally last 60–90 minutes and are conducted face-to-face (either in person or virtually). As with all forms of inquiry IDI requires informed consent (Given, 2008; Marshall & Rossman, 1998; Rosenthal, 2018; Taylor & Bogdan, 1984). The description of the inquiry process, focus, and intentions communicated to potential participants must be in accordance with their cultural "worldview" and fully considerate of community values, and so forth.

Regardless of approach, the collection of accurate and authentic information from inquiry participants requires experienced, knowledgeable, compassionate, empathic, and culturally respectful and responsive researchers. The interviewers or focus group moderators should work from a inquiry guide (e.g., focus group moderator's guide, interviewer's guide, etc.). As with other narrative approaches, the interview should be recorded and transcribed immediately so that hidden information such as body language and expressions are not lost over time (Given, 2008; Marshall & Rossman, 1998; Rosenthal, 2018; Taylor & Bogdan, 1984).

Advantages of IDI include: (a) promoting face-to-face communications, (b) allowing the interviewer an opportunity to explain questions, (c) producing rich data and new insights, and (d) encouraging in-depth discussion about the topic being studied. Some challenges associated with IDI include: (a) the need to use qualified interviewers; (b) need to create exploratory, not conclusive, results; (c) findings cannot be generalized to the entire population; (d) need to obtain a large amount of data, which may make transcription and data analysis difficult or unfeasible; and (5) resource demands which may be expensive or cost prohibitive.

WHY?

Often underrepresented communities are skeptical about their ability to participate in qualitative research because of obstacles to their involvement, especially historical abuse and exploitation, lack of understanding about the inquiry process, researcher unrecognized perceived risk of or some social constraint which discourages participation, concern over power differentials or positionality, language or obvious cultural differences, and lack of interest in the focus of inquiry (it may be interesting or important to the researcher but not to the community). Beyond this, it is important to recognize the nature of information and perspectives related to the nature or reality may differ between researcher and informant/participant. Culture is a matter of collective or community identity with implications for individual identity and identity perspectives are informed by the philosophical foundations of that group. Cultural differences between community and research may cause misalignment between the intent and meaning of participants and interpretation and understanding of the researcher. Researchers with marginalized or underrepresented communities must consider carefully the impact of cultural differences on the nature, intent, process and meaning making, conclusions and implications of the work they do. Ideally, in every instance regardless of the cultural background of researcher or participant, inquiry planning and decision-making including regarding instrumentation should include and be informed by members of the community from which research participants will be drawn. Failure to do so, runs the risk of accurate but inauthentic information, meaning-making, and/or conclusions with deleterious consequences for individuals and their community.

REFERENCES

Babbie, E. (2014). *The basics of social research* (6th ed.). Wadsworth Cengage.

Clement, C., Edwards, S. L., Rapport, F., Russell, I. T., & Hutchings, H. A. (2018). Exploring qualitative methods reported in registered trials and their yields (EQUITY): Systematic review. *Trails, 19*, 589. https://doi.org/10.1186/s13063-018-2983-y

Corbin, J., & Strauss, A. (2015). *Basics of qualitative research.* Sage.

Creswell, J. (2018). *Qualitative inquiry and research design: Choosing among five approaches.* SAGE Publishing.

Delve. (n.d.). *Practical guide to grounded theory research.* https://delvetool.com/groundedtheory

Denzin, N. K., & Lincoln, Y. S. (2011). *The Sage handbook of qualitative research.* SAGE Publications.

Family Health International. (n.d.). Qualitative research methods: A data collector's field guide. http://www.techsociety.com/cal/soc190/fssba2009/ParticipantObservation.pdf

Given, L. M. (Ed.). (2008). *The Sage encyclopedia of qualitative research methods.* SAGE Publications.

Glaser, B., & Strauss, A. (1967). *The discovery of grounded theory: Strategies for qualitative research.* Sociology Press.

Hughes, C. C. (1992). "Ethnography": What's in a word–Process? Product? Promise? *Qualitative Health Research, 2*(4), 439–450. https://doi.org/10.1177/104973239200200405

Lindlof, T. R., & Taylor, B. C. (2002). *Qualitative communication research methods* (2nd ed.). SAGE Publications.

Marshall, C., & Rossman, G. B. (1998). *Designing qualitative research.* SAGE Publishing.

McCall, C., & Edwards, C. (2021). New perspectives for implementing grounded theory. *Studies in Engineering Education, 1*(2), 93–107. https://doi.org/10.21061/see.49

Rosenthal, G. (2018). *Interpretive social research: An introduction.* Universitätsverlag Göttingen. https://doi.org/10.17875/gup2018-1103

Savin-Baden, M., & Major, C. (2013). *Qualitative research: The essential guide to theory and practice.* Routledge.

Strauss, A., & Corbin, J. M. (1990). *Basics of qualitative research: Grounded theory procedures and techniques.* Sage Publications, Inc.

Taylor S., & Bogdan R. (1984). *Introduction to qualitative research methods: The search for meanings.* John Wiley.

CHAPTER 4

MEANING

What Are the Guidelines for Making-Meaning, Ensuring Voice, Relevance, and Authenticity?

Arthur E. Hernandez
University of the Incarnate Word

WHAT?

Meaning is a complicated topic to consider with philosophical and methodological bases and implications. While it has often been said that the research questions drive methodology, that simply cannot be the case. The choice of method must be determined with an eye to philosophical integrity (i.e., researcher internal consistency)—it is a researcher's epistemological, ontological, axiological, and so on, assumptions which set the stage and the parameters for all inquiry. This means that the starting step for any inquiry is to recognize and carefully consider the philosophical choices which have been made and ensure that the methods chosen are consistent with those choices.

Qualitative Research With Diverse and Underserved Communities, pages 29–38
Copyright © 2024 by Information Age Publishing
www.infoagepub.com
29

In general (always with disadvantaged, historically marginalized, or disenfranchised people), research and evaluation requires consideration of multiple ways of knowing and making meaning and the relationship between the philosophy of study participants/informants, that of the researcher, as well as those who will use/interpret that information. Misapplications and inauthentic judgments, decisions and adverse consequences can occur when the values of one group are incompatible or inconsistent with those of another (i.e., cultural differences). In its most basic sense, meaning is a matter of interpretation, judgment, and decision. It is the sense or appreciation of reality an individual makes from an observation, sensation, or other cognitive, kinesthetic and/or affective "input" in the context of previous experience. That is, meaning-making is always scaffolded by prior meaning-making and is something that is learned, practiced and self-reinforcing.

The influences on meaning-making are numerous and varied and include but are not limited to identity, culture, context, conditions, arousal, expectations, and philosophical assumptions among other things. Thus, regardless of the activity or object about which meaning is constructed, it is always possible for observers to make meaning or appreciate reality in different ways and to draw different conclusions which are "real" and "valid" from the perspective of their own particular point of view. This is not to suggest that meaning-making in qualitative research is somehow less "rigorous," accurate or valid. In fact, good qualitative research seeks to clarify the conditions and the basis on which meaning is constructed and provide a reasonable and credible rationale for judgment about its authenticity. While a discussion about all the ways that quantitative methods are no less "subjective" than qualitative methods is beyond the scope of this chapter, it is the case that the myriad of assumptions related to relevant variables, interrelationships and the rules (i.e., theory) governing those relationships, the quality and power of the selected metrics and indicators, and the generation of explanatory or mediating "hypothetical constructs" involves significant decision-making based on prior meaning-making which is subject to the same conditions and limitations as described for qualitative approaches. In any case, it is important to recognize the central role of decision-making based on and intended to result in meaning-making in all forms of inquiry as well as the influence of experience in recognizing information, decisions regarding appropriate analyses and the conclusions to which the results of those analyses lead.

Further complicating the understanding of the notion of meaning in qualitative research are the ideas of reciprocity and intersectionality. Reciprocity suggests that simple assumptions of "cause and effect" are very limited in their ability to describe something as multidimensional and dynamic as human behavior. Reciprocity, in essence, regards the nature of the relationships between those factors which influence behavior including the behavior itself as dynamic and mutually and probably differentially influential on each other varying as a result of a host of other variables at any given moment. This is not to say there are no trends in behavior some of which are quite persistent and durable but, beyond quite simple reflexive behavior, there is always the possibility of a different outcome than before (whether due to mechanistic or humanistic influences). In research, this means accepting the reality that any model of behavior is limited by *specification*, that is identification of relevant variables which influence the phenomena of interest, the relationships between those influences, the mechanisms which govern those relationships, and the conditions under which those relationships operate as hypothesized. In a sense this refers to the scope of the consideration and recognition of the limitation that much of what is supposed to govern human behavior is at best hypothetical, that is, not directly observable and thus a matter of inference (which is in itself meaning-making). In addition, the notion of reciprocity suggests that the influences on group behavior are likely to be even more complicated. While perhaps similar and possibly impacted by the same concerns as those that affect individual behavior, these factors are complicated by the relationships and interaction between individuals. These interactions and relationships are a matter of individual experience and meaning-making in the context of and conditioned by group affiliation and identification among other things.

Intersectionality is a matter of complex identity in context composed of multiple "senses of self" which combine to construct or define the "self" which interacts with the world at any given moment. While some aspects of self may predominate in a given situation and circumstance, all elements of self (including some that may appear inconsistent) are always present and always influence perspective and meaning-making. The notion of intersectionality is not new; however, for its wide usage it is not often well considered (if at all) in research and evaluation contexts. This is probably due to the ease of categorization and the subsequent facility with which categories can be examined. While undeniably of some usefulness, this approach to defining reality (i.e., making meaning) usually results in at best approximate descriptions of the tendencies of a group but hardly encompasses the full range of individuals who comprise that group and has the associated danger of stereotyping. This is in large measure because of the operation of intersectionality at the individual level and the range of values related to the associated characteristics of the grouping. For example, race is often considered a category of interest but the assignment of individuals depends on either the assessment of some observable characteristic or self-identification. In either case, this assignment is subject to a wide variety of possible influences resulting in wide ranges within categories and some unavoidable overlap between categories. This is all the more the case given that most categorizations are social constructions and reflect the perception of difference when in fact little or none exists beyond social preference or desirability. Though this is the case, it is also the case that these categories of identity and associated implications have become normalized and impact our understanding of others, often in inaccurate and unfortunate ways including discrimination, bias, and social and individual injustice.

So, given all the previously described considerations and perspectives, in the end, "What is "meaning"? Perhaps it can be described as an understanding that is generated or emerges from experience which is based and organized by meaning that has been generated or emerged from prior experience. "Prior experience" pertains to both personal and other (vicarious) experiences which have been shared. Of course, experience and the communication of experience is fundamentally value and language based, also derived from meaning constructed from prior experience. As a result, appreciation of meaning can be said to be continuous and developing.

Research and evaluation are structured approaches to examining phenomena, organizing meaning around the frame of theory or some other extant framework and making decisions based on experience. While this approach to meaning-making has the advantage of internal consistency (good theory should have no exceptions) and should be relationship and rule based, when applied to groups, it suffers from the dual challenges of artificiality and abstraction. Theories are ultimately limited by their inability to encompass all of the reality of a given phenomenon given its size, dynamics and differences including particular conditions and context, "unexplainable" exceptions, and assumptions related to universality. These limitations result in artificiality or inauthenticity since theory cannot address every possible variable nor account for the dynamics, the unreliability of human interpretation, decision, and action and the dynamic action of development of people, conditions, and circumstances.

Meaning-making in the social sciences is complicated and challenging and regardless of method of inquiry means that the outcome of any study is limited in its ability to provide a basis for meaning or interpretation in large part by the individual and collective differences between actors and observers. Fundamentally, this is because meaning is a matter of judgment and decision therefore, meaning-making is never complete but *always in process*, informed by different approaches, researchers, and inquiries over time.

WHY?

Meaning-making is the ultimate purpose or intent of any inquiry—to understand in order to leverage that understanding to advance, protect or advantage human well-being—the definition all of which is subject to the same mechanisms and founding philosophical starting points—as the inquiry process itself. Since meaning is the penultimate currency and purpose of inquiry, it is the basis on which its value is judged and the basis for the credibility of the evidence which serves to find it.

In the end, inquiry by any method is value bound and directed, the goal and result of which is meaning. Meaning becomes understanding through judgment, which is a part of the process of inquiry from the beginning. All inquiry is based on multiple decisions including "rules" for its conduct, assumptions, and presumptions because meaning-making is dependent on previous meaning-making and is why meaning-making is always ongoing. In the end, making meaning is ultimately valuable as defined by the researcher, the social/academic/professional community of which she or he or they is a part and the social groups about which or on which the inquiry was focused. All of this means that the values which ground, and which result from inquiry cannot be understood separate from the social context, constructions, or conditions within which the research is situated. The underlying value systems of science are subject to the same social/historical pressures and influences as any social system and research authenticity is determined by those systems ultimately as a matter of trust or faith in the capacity of the applied systems to result in something that is "true." All researchers/evaluators operate from within intersecting systems and the nature of their judgment and decision making regarding what is true depends on the influences and imperatives which predispose that researcher/evaluator to particular ways of knowing, interpretations, choices, and conclusions. It is always their value system which provides the parameters for meaning-making and offers the anchoring points for deduction or induction, recognizing, describing, and ultimately understanding causality and developing a framework which is generalizable or transferable beyond the "sample" from/on whom the original observations were made. The applicable and applied value system is all too often unquestioned and unrecognized but regardless, meaning-making is the reason for or the intention of all inquiry.

Relatedly, though the "validity" of inquiry is often determined by its ability to predict, given particular inputs and conditions, it should be clear that the nature of elements (variables) and presumed rules and relationships which characterize the phenomena of interest may be in fundamental error. This is true for all inquiries. The starting point for most is the conceptualization of phenomena (which itself is the product of prior meaning-making). Therefore, one important consideration in meaning-making always is the possibility that predictive power notwithstanding, the described model or mechanism of action (theory), either at the start or as a result of inquiry may be wrong. This is at least in part because all meaning-making involves presumption framed by and developed through experience. In other words, since meaning constructed from inquiry is always based on prior meaning-making, it may in fact be in error; that is, despite its "accuracy," it does not actually explain, represent, or describe the phenomena of interest.

Meaning-making in social science is about understanding ourselves and others and it is almost always purposeful, that is related to problem solving (i.e., application) rather than "pure science" or "validation" of theory. To be of maximum value, it requires structured, organized, and systematic observation (all which is guided by values, philosophical pre-assumptions, and world view, i.e., cultural perspectives and all of which make for diversity of thought and understanding) to "make sense" or meaning of what is observed. These same also fundamentally influence the manner and outcome of our efforts to "translate" observations into understanding which explains and provides a rationale for individual and social action (i.e., application). In the end, we make meaning to make sense of experience and *the meaning we make offers the perspectives and the means from which we make meaning.* This means, meaning derived from inquiry, is always used to question or support existing perspectives including world views about the characteristics and nature of human experience. Unfortunately, as experience indicates, meaning-making (understanding) can be used to support and reinforce repressive and injurious human conditions which adversely impact individual and collective human lives perhaps even more easily than the opposite. Since this is so, ethics require that the ultimate goal of meaning-making is that its conclusions and implications be used to equitably improve the state of life for all through institutionalizing and maintaining social systems (society, education, politics, etc.) which achieve that end. Knowingly doing otherwise is nothing less than the weaponization of inquiry through the deliberate, uncaring, or unknowing construction of meaning, which is destructive, injurious, and counter to purpose. Therefore, a minimum ethical requirement for all researchers, but in particular, those working with minoritized and disadvantaged groups, is that they seek authenticity—that is, that they constantly interrogate the basis for the assumptions, judgements, decisions and conclusions they make at every step of the inquiry to ensure that both the process and outcomes are to purpose—to advance well-being for all.

HOW?

Meaning-making is a matter of interpretation of and judgment about experience. This interpretation is usually influenced by how our experience has been interpreted and judged by others and how those judgements and interpretations have been communicated to and have affected us. This is especially the case of communication from our "significant others" including our family, teachers, and mentors and this interpretation and judgment serves as a foundation and framework for our cultural identifications and affiliations. Through inquiry from this developed point of view and sense of identity, we seek to structure our meaning-making in a way that is observable, recognizable, acceptable, and valuable to others in concert and consistency with social (including disciplinary and professional) norms and expectations.

Observation in the service of inquiry is always based on some structure which bounds, directs, and organizes it. Ideally that structure is known and understood so that it provides for internal consistency of the inquiry process (process fidelity) though sometimes processes are guided by implicit rather than explicit structure or norms. However, for most researchers and evaluators, successful inquiry requires a known structure which guides action (i.e., methodology) which is credible and provides a framework for meaning-making by virtue of its acceptability to others. Regardless, the selection of and the guiding structure itself must be ethical and informed by evidence which is derived from frameworks which themselves have been tested for ethics, validity, reliability, authenticity, genuineness, and so on. And the first requirement of "honest" inquiry is openness to the possibility that what is widely considered acceptable is in fact in error.

Observation in/of inquiry seeks to be "complete" in the sense that it encompasses everything that is relevant to the purpose (i.e., problem, hypothesis, or question) which precipitated the inquiry. Since this is often impossible for practical reasons, the conduct of research and evaluation involves decision-making about the focus and scope of what observations/information should be included and considered by and through the inquiry. This decision making related to all relevant influencers of action (e.g., mediators, moderators, social and cultural context, etc.) and a final design which is parsimonious but not artificially so, leads to the development of inquiry protocols or specification of methods. Ultimately, this decision making is a fundamental process of inquiry which guides the organization of observation at the same time resulting in and constrained by meaning-making. This in itself indicates that all inquiry is dependent on judgment and decision-making and it is the *quality of judgment* rather than merely the applied methods which determines the authenticity of information and conclusions. The penultimate criteria of quality in regard to inquiry is authenticity and accuracy. Accuracy is a matter of "correctness" while authenticity is a matter of relevance and applicability. Thus, it is essential the qualitative researcher recognize the constructed basis on and process by which meaning is ultimately derived and subject their working assumptions (e.g., theories) to examination as a matter of course in the conduct of any inquiry.

Qualitative inquiry involves observation which is knowingly guided by assumptions and presumptions and involves the translation of observation into structured perspectives concerning the phenomena of interest. These observations/perspectives should inform the questions of the inquiry (i.e., address its purpose) and provide the basis for meaning-making (evidence). This perspective i.e., useful observational structure is organized into frameworks which represent data which are manipulatable through mechanisms which are accepted by consensus (e.g., statistics, narrative analysis) as providing reasonable and credible means of aggregating and transforming data into evidence. Evidence, then is data organized as argument which directs/informs understanding and consequent action. Obviously, in no case does evidence constitute proof. However, as an argument it provides reason and rationale for assertions and contributes to credibility.

Inquiry with individuals from minoritized and disenfrancised groups requires preplanning, the development of relationship, and mutual trust and respect. This means that unlike typical application of qualitative research approaches, qualitative research with individuals from these groups instead seeks and considers historical, geographical, anthropological, and ethnographic perspectives of the community as well as that of the researcher. This consideration has not been well addressed in the literature which includes the preponderance of reference to cultural competence, respect, humility, responsiveness, and so on. While these notions are laudable in intent, they fall short of what is most desirable. The ultimate of preparation for "intercultural" inquiry requires at a minimum, the establishment of a deep knowledge and understanding of cultural epistemology and its relationship to the epistemology of the researchers. This understanding is not possible simply from an external study but requires "immersion" in the community of interest recognizing the inherent expertise of those living with a particular cultural identity regarding their own experience, and understanding that as with everything else, identity is not "monolithic," but for both individuals and groups exists as a constantly evolving range of values. This implies ongoing effort is necessary to ensure that values, indicators, analyses, and interpretations constantly pursue authenticity and suggests that the best qualitative research is conducted by those with experience not only in the topic or domain of interest but with the lived experience of those interests. This lived experience must be pursued and understood for qualitative inquiry to result in meaningful interpretations and ultimately, understanding.

Thus, it is not enough to examine perspectives, philosophy, language, history, and so on, of a community in advance of inquiry but, throughout its execution, checking constantly to ascertain methods and instrumentation are appropriate for the community in addition to the topic, theory, or research question. What is essential, is the recognition and understanding of the fact that any phenomenon of interest occurs in context, when conditions, experience, expectations, and interests play a part. Further that these things make sense at the individual level and aggregation of findings must be done thoughtfully and intentionally to ensure that what results as a "group finding" does not distort the reality of the individual experience.

However, community familiarity is not the same as authentic cultural identification which should be the goal of researchers working with individuals and groups from cultures other than their own. *Authentic cultural identification* is the positioning of the researcher in the cultural perspective of the individual or group of interest, with knowledge and authentic appreciation for the values and understanding of the world of those persons as well as expertise with the phenomenon of interest. This means, that in addition to a deep understanding and appreciation for the community, theoretical perspectives which explain or describe phenomena, and which are used to frame inquiry must be interrogated for cultural authenticity prior to their application to the research enterprise.

In qualitative research with groups who have been historically marginalized and subject to social injustice, meaning-making must include the information and be informed by the perspective of that historical injustice. This is critical to effectively understanding contextual and conditional psychosocial phenomena that influences individual and collective action.

WHEN?

Meaning-making is always the intended result and product of inquiry. Meaning is fundamental to understanding whether it is about the nature or operation of the focus of inquiry. In essence, it is the pursuit of meaning which is the impetus and motivation for research as the vehicle for understanding. This requires a thoughtful and deliberate attention to the processes involved and consideration of the alternative possibilities (e.g., counterfactuals) for any conclusion. In the end, since it is the purpose of research, assertions of meaning should always and ideally be subject to examination, verification, and criticism. This suggests that every aspect of inquiry involves judgment and decision making and thus constant self and activity reflection should be a requisite exercise for the conduct of research. This is an important idea since often researchers think about meaning-making only at the end of the process—making meaning of the "results" in light of the theory or topic and drawing conclusions which relate to some current or future questions. However, accuracy and authenticity require attention, judgment, and decision-making at every stage of the work and this admonition applies not only to judgments and decision-making about sample and method but requires ongoing critical self-reflection.

WHO?

Generally, ethical and authentic qualitative research with minoritized and disenfranchised individuals and groups requires the active presence of members of those groups in the planning and execution of that research. Those engaged in inquiry and those using the results/interpretations must accept and realize that any interpretation which fails to carefully consider the experience and authentic perspectives of those individuals from whom information is gathered is subject to bias, prejudice, and conflict of interest at a minimum. Researchers should also recognize that simply "coming from" the population of interest is insufficient by itself for "cultural competence" or "cultural responsiveness." It is experience rather than characteristics (e.g., race or ethnicity) which determines cultural identity and perspectives and at least differences in educational level, interest, experience, and so on, between researcher and "subject" renders the degree of authentic relationship subject to test.

Given the nature of the inquiry, it is the responsibility of the qualitative researcher to be responsible beyond protocol or process—in a sense "validity" is centered on the researcher since she/he/they are the "instrument" and "mechanism" of analysis. Obviously then, the qualitative researcher must be accountable for decisions made regarding all aspects of the inquiry since each decision impacts the nature of information, how it is processed and what meaning is constructed as a consequence.

WHERE?

These perspectives regarding the nature and conduct of meaning-making are important for both formal and informal inquiry. It is important that researchers understand the implications of interpretations and other meaning-making for all concerned (not simply for the community of interest/focus). This means that any meaning-making begins with what are questions of interest and/or import, the nature of the data to be collected to inform those questions and the methods by which that data will be collected and analyzed must be informed by authentic cultural knowledge and cultural identification or the risk for harm is high. This is the case regardless of the nature of the inquiry or the participant informants.

CHAPTER 5

SHARING

What Are the Essential Requirements for Equitable Use of Knowledge Gained From Inquiry?

Alma L. Thornton
Jackson State University

This chapter focuses on what is necessary to avoid exploitation and exacerbation of unearned and inequitable power and prestige differentials based on ethical practice.

WHAT?

Increasingly, attention has been given to equitable research practices. More awareness and consideration of cultural differences and understanding of varied and often distinct community voices, particularly voices in communities of color, which are less likely to be heard and represented are needed. Research steeped in traditional practices has often excluded, exploited, or misrepresented voices of vulnerable populations as data collectors and analyzers

Qualitative Research With Diverse and Underserved Communities, pages 39–54
Copyright © 2024 by Information Age Publishing
www.infoagepub.com

failed to provide opportunities for input on how data from their communities were collected, analyzed, communicated or used. Authentic qualitative research requires increased understanding of the intricacies of race, culture, social structures and equity in disparate research analyses, processes, and application of results. Issues related to equitable sharing of research have included (a) evaluation and scrutiny of existing research practices, (b) grounding government and philanthropic funding in practice of equity, (c) efforts to increase trust in research processes and practices among communities of color, and (d) more equitable inclusion of stakeholders in research practices.

"Equitable research" refers to the greater inclusion of all those involved in research endeavors as equally/mutually participating partners. This usually includes funders, researchers, participants, community members, and relevant and applicable community organizations and means that all parties should be included in problem definition, research design, data collection, analysis, interpretation and problem resolution decisions, and sustainability efforts. Finally, greater efforts should be made for equitable sharing in any benefits including knowledge gained resulting from the work. In addition to qualitative research, this approach has also been broadly described as applied or action research. Action research is an umbrella term that refers to several different applied research approaches where a key or essential element is the designing of programs or projects to meet the needs of the studied population as defined and directed by the applicable community.

WHY?

Why is equitable research needed and why is it valuable? Often a research topic is conceived focusing on theory, or "accountability" based on models and criteria which have been uninformed by and possibly not applicable to the community based on cultural or other differences. This is despite the intention sometimes, to engage in inquiry with the goal of advancing progress toward the resolution of social problems in that community. Research initiatives should be developed with a good understanding of participants' experience, assumptions, values, or philosophical foundations which requires the active involvement and inclusion of that community in research planning, execution, and data analyses as opposed to simply providing "data" or input relating to experience or perspectives. While participants may not have experience in conducting research, they are often more knowledgeable about how programs should be developed and implemented in their community as well as a better sense of what will work and what will not work. For example, research on poverty might ask the informants to describe their lived experiences with poverty and make recommendations from their perspectives on strategies to collect authentic information which can inform and guide efforts to remediate the problem. In this case, participants may feel greater consideration should be given to childcare needs or they may need assistance in addressing the educational challenges faced by their children when they, the parents, lack the skills to provide the help or they may need support for travel to attend meetings regarding the educational needs of their children at school or identify resources to address needs such as access to tutors. Parents as participants are often better able to define the dynamics of the problem as well as aid in designing and developing interventions. Consideration of the culture of research participants is important so as not to violate cultural norms. For example, a friend related a problem she encountered implementing a program in a developing country that illustrates an example of community involvement. She found that community residents preferred yellow corn to white corn. Although white corn was more disease resistant, there was no local market for the product—that is, it was not a culturally responsive solution to the local food shortage.

WHEN?

Moving Away From Traditional Research Practices

Typically, the researcher defines the primary focus and methods of study. The researcher generally directs data collection and analysis processes, evaluation/processing of findings and develops reports, and written summaries. One result of such practices has been the low participation of communities of color in research contributing to or because of community distrust and suspicion. Endo Inouye et al. (2005) recommend conceptualizing and engaging research with a shifting focus to multicultural investigations which includes identifying key questions, audiences, and determining appropriate budgets and approaches, conducting evaluations focusing on multi-cultural factors in guidance, review processes, selection of culturally competent evaluators, and increased attention to the funder's roles in fostering multicultural inquiry. However, while researchers may consider themselves and may be viewed by some members of the community as "culturally competent" with experience steeped in traditional languages and customs of the community, they likely have limited life experiences in the community of interest.

Research has not adequately addressed community concerns and in some instances, communities have been exploited and/or harmed and some vulnerable communities face an array of barriers to participation in research (Kaur et al., 2006; Scharff et al., 2010). In response, some researchers have utilized several models of community engagement-oriented research centered around promoting greater equity, engagement, and inclusion and largely focusing on increased community participation (Henderson et al.,

2017). Community-centered research participatory research models value and emphasize the importance of participation (Cornwall & Jewkes, 1995; Flaspohler et al., 2008). Action research, another equitable inclusion approach, places greater emphasis on inclusion in the process and beneficial outcomes for the community. Action research has a long history and is mostly known as an approach used in community development including internationally. It has been referred to as participatory action research among other things (Stringer & Ortiz Aragón, 2020). Exploring the significant wrongdoings, history of exclusion, and power imbalances in policy research and putting tools in place to incorporate the voices of communities most affected by these injustices are crucial steps toward attaining more racial equity. Researchers, governmental organizations, private businesses, and nonprofit organizations are encouraged by action research to involve the communities whose work will most impact in data-driven decision-making. In order to promote equality in the research process, it is important to recognize and resolve power dynamics, show that community voices are important and included, pay community members for their time and expertise, and give priority to their needs. By including participants in the research team and collaborating to solve some of their needs outside of research, these collaborations may empower traditionally underserved populations.

HOW?

Principles for Integrating Equity Into Research

Gaddy and Scott (2020) addressed the importance of equity, fairness and ethical considerations in conducting research throughout the various stages of the research process. In keeping with the three guiding principles in the Belmont Report, beneficence (maximizing benefits and doing no harm), respect for person (right of individual to make decisions in their own best interest), and justice (fair distribution of burden and benefits), equity is needed at each stage of the research life cycle including acquisition, conception, instrumentation, collection, analysis, and dissemination and disposition. Equity at the acquisition stage is needed for the underserved and vulnerable populations, who are often affected by research to benefit from its outcomes and have equal opportunities to contribute to it. Conception is forming ideas around what the data should reveal. The "what" and "who" can be attained through focus group discussions that include the community leaders, residents, local service agencies, and activists to learn what data the community thinks are relevant to improve their lives. During the instrumentation process, researchers informed by the community of interest should choose the best data gathering methods, take into account how information is shared in the community, and choose a methodology that effectively addresses the study issue while also removing any biases in measurement or approach. During the collection phase, the research team should be ethnically and culturally diverse and bring a range of viewpoints to the study's planning, execution, and conclusions. The researchers should think about how information is exchanged across the community and whose information is prioritized when choosing data collection methods. At the data analysis stage researchers should ask explicit questions about the communities concerns and what they think contribute to those issues and apply an interpretation of racial and ethnical equity from the community's perspective. This step is critical because researchers should understand that communities and populations are not simply sources for research "subjects," they should be involved and respected, therefore transparency and reciprocity is necessary. Researchers are not omniscient; the community perspective adds to and enriches the researcher's methods framing knowledge by providing contextual information that may affect how findings are interpreted. At the dissemination stage, language used by researchers to report findings must be appropriate for the audiences they have identified and must not victimize study participants. The method utilized to disseminate findings should also be appropriate for the community's needs and include face-to-face presentations at community gatherings, exhibits in community centers or forums, and media interviews. The dissemination process must go beyond the report of findings and include suggestions for the community that are ongoing for sustainability planning or to address the concerns that have been highlighted.

Andrews et al. (2019) have identified several guiding principles for integrating racial and ethnic equity in research. They recommend researchers inclusive principles as a way of creating greater equity. Although researchers seek to recognize and control their own perspectives in the collection and analysis of those of others, it is important to recognize that researchers inclusive principles bring values, background, and experience-based biases which influence decisions throughout the research process. Every effort should be made to recognize and control possible personal, ethnic, cultural, and experiences with privilege which have the potential to influence research. Secondly, researchers must closely examine outcome differences and not simply attribute research findings to racial and ethnic differences. Rather, researchers should closely scrutinize data to examine context and assess possible influence of (historical) antecedents belying racial and ethnic differences in outcomes. The Annie Casey Foundation (2006) provides a racial equity impact analytical tool for assessing policies, programs, and practices to promote equitable research. "What's Race Got to Do With It?"; "The Racial Equity Impact Analysis"; and "How to Talk About Race" are three resources included in the Annie E. Casey Foundation Race Matters Toolkit that can be used to begin racial equity work. It is designed to support decision-makers, advocates, and elected officials who want to achieve outcomes that provide opportunity for all children, families, and communities, regardless of race. This toolkit explains how to quickly address racial injustices, how to expose the causes of racial inequities, how to develop practices and policies that help eliminate racial gaps, and how to communicate effectively about race to a variety of audiences. Thirdly, it is important to understand how the research process impacts people and communities. Researchers should continuously consider their role in ensuring that the outcome of research benefits the community. For example, the American Public Health Association (2009) recommends benefits through improved community services within a predetermined time frame through interventions created and approved by the researchers. Furthermore, the community's capacity should be built through training, employment, and funding provided by the research in all areas of the research process. This results in an equitable perspective that underscores the pervasive impact research can have on vulnerable communities.

Research practices may result in outcomes which reinforce existing power paradigms and lead to or sustain existing abuse and exploitation. Transparency of research processes and activities is needed to ensure participants clearly understand the nature of the research and expected benefits. Transparency is a precursor to equitable and ethical research. Transparency, which is seen as a core ethical duty, is described as the responsibility to make the data, analysis, techniques, and interpretive decisions that underlie research conclusions available in a way that enables others to evaluate them. Readers will have a harder time appreciating, evaluating, debating, replicating, or extending a piece of study if research findings are inaccessible, analysis is unclear, or underlying decisions concerning the selection of data, theories, and methodologies are opaque. As such, researchers should focus greater attention and efforts to ensure that all stakeholders have clarity and understanding and are all included in decisions at the various stages in the research process. Fourthly, stakeholder communities should participate as partners in research undertakings and be given credit for their contributions. While credit for contributions may be limited, community members as stakeholders should be involved in the directions and applications of research outcomes. Further, many community members have experienced or know others who have experienced "being researched" and may offer an interpretative perspective different from that of the researcher. Accurate, authentic community insight and understanding requires collaboration and engagement with the community. Finally, Andrews et al. (2019) recommend that researchers should guard against explicit assumptions that may be normative but may not reflect conditions and lived experiences of the community being studied. Typically, research outcomes are interpreted as goalposts or normative standards. Research outcomes in some racial, ethnic, and vulnerable communities may vary from usual social expectations, be viewed as disparate, or not meet the expectations of these communities. Simply determining outcomes using Eurocentric, colonialistic standards fails to consider the historical and structural antecedents of inequities which may be influencing or even causing the observed actions, attitudes, and perspectives. Long-standing barriers to wealth, education, and decision-making may result in technical experts who may not recognize, much less value the lived experience and knowledge of community members who are perceived as different, which has resulted in so-called "data-informed decision-making" that has marginalized many people (Gaddy & Scott, 2020). This type of data-informed decision involves determining the political and social traits, preferences, prejudices, and asymmetries that those participating in the process of the data-informed decisions transferred to it and which may have an impact on the decision or its outcomes. Asking questions of the data collecting, management, and analysis process is one way to do this. Another is to determine whether the data correctly reflect the voices of underrepresented communities and a representative population (if relevant).

Gaddy and Scott (2020) have also proposed principles for advancing equitable data practices. They argue decisions made about what data to collect, what data to process, what outcomes are paramount, how outcomes are disseminated, and what programs will be developed and implemented are salient factors often reflecting biases in assumptions and interests of researchers. To advance equity in research, careful consideration must be given to factors which impact the validity and legitimacy of data-informed decisions. Consideration should also be given to possible harm resulting from each decision about vulnerable communities. This points to a need to expand and extend the equity lens to better manage and use data responsibly with data managers, stewards, and users. Equitable research begins with a more just, equitable, and less harmful data environment across the data cycle from conception to data informed decision-making and outcomes. The data cycle involves how data are collected, analyzed, interpreted, and disseminated from an equity perspective. It highlights the unequal access to data that marginalized people have, as well as the damage that might sometimes result from data abuse. Gaddy and Scott (2020) recommend the inclusion of the following equity principles:

1. Inclusion of community interests in design considerations
2. Awareness of how sensitive topics can affect people and communities
3. Minimization of the amount of personally identifiable information collected
4. Conciseness of re-identification risks
5. Avoidance of undue burden on people and communities
6. Incorporation of informed consent whenever possible, even if not formally required

7. Transparency about the limits of the data
8. Incorporation of communities' interpretation of the data
9. Consideration of how publication may reinforce inequities or close disparities
10. Data sharing to reduce the burden of duplicate data collection
11. Return data and research results to community members in a form they can use
12. Empower individuals to order the destruction of their data
13. Transparency about plans for the data after the conclusion of the project
14. Empower individuals to order the destruction of their data

Participatory research models embrace equitable involvement of researchers, community members, and other stakeholders and require mutual respect of the knowledge and skills of each partner across every stage of the research life cycle (Collin et al., 2018). Based on a model of international development, Fransman and Newman (2019) advocate for greater stakeholder inclusion in establishing research agendas as well as approaches and schemes allocating funding. The model named rethinking research collaborative (RRC) is an international network of networks made up of academics, civil society organizations, transnational movements, international NGOs, and research support organizations. These groups are dedicated to cooperating in order to investigate the politics of evidence and take part in the mobilization of knowledge for international development. To increase the output of pertinent research for social justice and global development, RRC seeks to promote more inclusive, responsive, and transformative collaboration. Its four main goals are to mobilize a community of practitioners, encourage critical engagement, build research capacity, and inform and transform policy and practice.

Fransman and Newman also consider development goals and outcomes. They argue stakeholders possess profound knowledge and understanding of realities on the ground, types of impacts needed to make real and meaningful change, and the complexities and nuances of everyday barriers to implementation. Fransman and Newman (2019) argue that equitable research should go beyond translating research findings into practice and policy but also provide an understanding of how complex processes of development unfold. They have proposed the following codifying practices and policy reflecting eight principles for fair and equitable partnerships:

Principle 1: Put Poverty First

Research impact pathways should be situated within existing practice-based development work/impact systems. Poverty is a major concern in development efforts around the world. Researchers must understand all interventions must have at their heart the elimination, eradication, or reduction of poverty and improving wellbeing. The bottom line is that research must at its core, grapple with a practice-based theory of change. Designers of research must therefore have a deep understanding and grasp of the needs of the communities served, processes and interventions currently provided within that community, and the nature and pace of relevant and social change to fully understand how their research fits into the schema of work in the field.

Principle 2: Critically Engage With Contexts

Consideration should be given to the multiple facets of research impact, equitable inclusion, and understanding and interpretation of impacts, and the meanings assigned to those impacts. Influences include where research is located, what is prioritized, the response to evidence, how the evidence is framed, and finally, our understanding and interpretation of the issue.

Principle 3: Redress Evidence Hierarchies

It is important to acknowledge different evidence and research questions based on preferences, expectations, and needs of the researchers, funders and other stakeholders and be open to new assumptions at different stages of the research process. Researchers should be leery of hierarchies of evidence marginalizing knowledge and confining roles to data collectors. A hierarchy of evidence is a heuristic utilized to rate the comparative strength of results or findings obtained from scientific research. Stegenga (2014) defined a hierarchy of evidence as a rank-ordering of methods according to the possibility for that method to suffer from systematic bias.

Principle 4: Adapt and Respond

When considering complexities of research and rapidly changing social and structural conditions, researchers must be able to adapt practices as while research processes are often based on linearity, the reality of social dynamics are seldom linear. Complex and rapidly changing developmental contexts require flexibility allowing for needed modifications in program definition, understanding, delivery and outcomes.

Principle 5: Respect Diversity

Equitable research requires knowing, valuing and respecting the vast range of the knowledge, perspective, skill, experience, aspirations, and expectations of all partners (including research informants/participants).

Principle 6: Commit to Transparency

Transparency across all phases of the research is an important element of trust, commitment, and relationship building among partners. Maximization of impact is facilitated when all processes inclusive of budgets and funds distribution are open, clear, and transparent avoiding any stakeholders exercising unfair privilege.

Principle 7: Invest in the Relationship

Strong and sustained relationships influence research impact. Relationship building involves developing shared vision and agendas, devoting time to understanding each other and developing trust. Building relationships can be time consuming and exhausting but a strong research team must develop common understanding and full involvement to conceptualize, design, and implement research with equitable inclusion of all partners.

Principle 8: Keep Learning

In research partnerships, we often work with individuals with whom we might not usually collaborate and with researchers who bring new skills, perspectives, understanding and knowledge. In environments valuing diversity, although not always comfortable, opportunities for learning are created by investing time for individual reflections on varying research experiences and interpretations of reach outcomes and impact.

WHERE?

Community Based Participatory Research— A Model for Equity and Inclusion

Increasingly researchers have looked to community-based participatory research (CBPR) as an approach fostering equitable community engagement

(Israel et al., 2003). In the model, partners, particularly non-academic collaborators, share expertise, responsibilities, and ownership in creating knowledge to increase understanding and improvement in the well-being of community members (Israel et al., 1998). Unlike traditional community-based research, the community-based participatory research model recognizes and values the role and contributions of participants and promotes active engagement and influence of community members in all phases of the research process (Shultz et al., 1998). Historical roots of CBPR can be found in the development of participatory action research, traced to the work of Kurt Lewin (1946), and has been applied in many disciplines including the social sciences, education, health care, and business. Lewin coined the term "action research" referring to critical research to address problems by involving the community that affects and described the comparative research process leading to social action (Collins et al., 2018).

CBPR emerged from social justice and action research traditions which have focused on strengths and perspectives of community partners. The goal of CBPR approaches is to develop tangible and beneficial outcomes for the community and require real collaboration and partnership between the researcher and the community. Working in partnership, community members, organizational representatives, and researchers equitably design studies, collect and interpret data, and disseminate findings. Equitable partnerships require sharing of power, resources, results, credits, and knowledge and mutual respect for each partner strengths and skills. The aim of CBPR is to better understand the study phenomenon and integrate knowledge gained into policy or social change beneficial to the community. Viswanathan et al. (2004) in a review of 60 CBPR projects noted the importance of community involvement in all phases of the research. They argued that to promote equitable partnerships, the community should be involved in setting the priority and direction of the research, defining the problem, selection of study methods and study design, conducting the research, interpretation of research findings, determining how the research will be integrated into the community, and developing sustainability and capacity building efforts.

According to Israel et al. (2001) advantages of community-based participatory research include increased relevance and usefulness of data for all research partners, brings together skill, knowledge, and expertise of diverse partners, improves validity and reliability of data by incorporating local knowledge of people involved, enhances trust of the community members who have historically been subjects of such research, and provides access to resources to communities involved. Israel et al. (2003) has developed key design elements in CBPR which provide guiding principles which are summarized below though not intended to be exhaustive or comprehensive.

Community is the unit of identity. The CBPR approach views community structures such family, friendship networks, and geographical neighborhoods as socially constructed components of collective and individual identity. Through collective engagement, CBPR seeks to strengthen community identity and identify community resources that may benefit from external support.

CBPR builds on strengths and resources with the community. Community-based participatory approaches seek to identify, support, and expand existing community skills and assets, trusting and cooperative relationships, and community structures such as churches and community-based organizations.

CBPR facilitates collaborative, equitable partnership in all research phases and involves an empowering and power-sharing process that attends to social inequities. All partners share control and agree in all phases of the research cycle including defining nature and extent of the problem, data collection procedures, definitions of outcomes, and applications of results. Particular emphasis is placed on avoiding or redressing power and resource inequities in marginalized and vulnerable communities through explicit attention given to information, power, and resource sharing.

CBPR promotes co-learning and capacity building among all partners. Reciprocal sharing of skills, knowledge, and capacity is facilitated. In the CBPR model, researchers and community stakeholders have resources and skills that can be shared such as management and engagement styles.

CBPR integrates and achieves balance between research and action for the mutual benefit of all partners. Community-based participatory research seeks to expand the body of knowledge regarding the phenomenon under investigation while developing workable and meaningful outcomes for the community.

CBPR emphasizes (public health) problems of local relevance and ecological perspectives that attend to the multiple determinants of health and disease. CBPR addresses the multiple dimensions of social problems emphasizing physical, mental, and social well-being. The approach values the individual in the broader context family and social networks and the individual as situated in the larger community. An ecological approach, CBPR examines the social, economic, cultural, and physical environmental factors as influencers of research outcome.

CBPR involves systems development through a cyclical and iterative process. The CBPR model is an approach where the entire partnership (the system) develops competences that are institutionalized and maintained through all phases of the research process including problem definition, research design, data collection and analysis, data interpretation, action steps development, policy implications, results dissemination, actions steps, and sustainability efforts.

CBPR disseminates findings and knowledge gained to all partners and involves all partners in the dissemination process. Findings are disseminated to all members of the partnership and are written in a fashion that is understood and respectful, and co-owned by all partners involved. Ownership may extend to dissemination efforts including co-authorship of publications and co-presentations of results.

CBPR requires a long-term process and commitment to sustainability. Because, trust is essential to sustainability of outcomes and requires investment of time and effort, commitments must be on-going and extend beyond a single project and may take decades to realize.

CBPR addresses issues of race, ethnicity, racism, and social class and embraces "cultural humility." Community-based participatory research generally involves racial, ethnic, and vulnerable communities. To acquire what Tervalon and Murray-García (1998) calls "cultural humility," requires self-examination and reflection on one's own motives and drives, past experiences with racism and elitism, grappling with the dynamics of power and privilege, and forging real partnerships embracing trust and understanding. Although cultural humility has been widely discussed in the literature, not always favorably, it is a path of self-reflection and lifelong learning intended to acknowledge a person, a group, or a community's lived experiences while taking a closer look at the care and services provided to various populations. The emphasis is on respecting the words or narratives that describe that person's, group's, or community's wants, wishes, or cultural desires and on incorporating this knowledge to grow loyal relationships and achieve the best results.

GROUNDING RESEARCH IN EQUITABLE PRACTICE

Traditionally, research narratives have been primarily framed from a largely Eurocentric worldview encompassing persisting ideologies that have rationalized and, in some instances, unconsciously influenced inequity. According to various definitions, Eurocentrism is an attitude, a conceptual framework, or a group of empirical beliefs that portrays Europe as the main force behind an architect of world history, the carrier of universal principles and logic, the apex, and consequently a model for progress and development. As a result, the reality that Africa is the officially recognized cradle of humankind was overshadowed by the Eurocentrism thesis of human history, which prioritizes the Greek and classical Roman world as the cradle of human civilization. Some of the negative results of eurocentrism are the degradation of natural resources, capitalism, urbanization, and the introduction of alien illnesses to livestock and people. Ignoring or undervaluing what other cultures have accomplished inside their own societies or seeing the history of non-European nations solely in terms of Europe are examples of its civilizing influence. The question to ask is "How do we overcome or manage Eurocentrism?" Diversity and inclusion of diverse groups in research may result in questioning long held assumptions undergirding practices and normalizing social processes. Greater inclusion of more diverse individual and group voices for shaping opinions and narratives and implementing solutions to societal problems as defined and priorities by the communities impacted is needed. Stories should also be told from the viewpoints of the underrepresented, underserved, and sometimes disenfranchised with consideration given to multiple realities from different communities having varying identities in our complex society. A perspective of inclusion and equity is needed for greater understanding of the lived experiences of individuals from multiple viewpoints. Using inclusion criteria for validity means that researchers can confirm that participants are representative of the target community while recruiting participants. Authenticity and inclusion are two sides of the same coin and ensure that everyone feels free to share their voices and trusts that their ideas will be equally considered by all involved as valuable and worthy before decisions are made.

Equitable research practices require greater focus on culture and the community, stressing the importance of community empowerment and social equity. It is important that culture is not discounted in the research process. As researchers, it is important to closely examine results and generalized findings relative to the culture and contextual application of results. Diversity, or the recognition of the full range associated with a given social characteristic, equity or fairness, and inclusion, the antithesis of exclusion, must be organized in an operational framework that guides researchers to consider both the process and the positive and negative consequences for individuals from diverse and limited resource communities. Equity considerations in research are important because they bring crucial and often very different individual and group defining life experiences into consideration for meaning making that is fair, inclusive, and leads to productive and beneficial outcomes for individuals with diverse voices and perspectives. Researchers must identify and develop effective working strategies, and methods where everyone has equitable opportunity. It is imperative that research is designed and implemented that addresses critical drivers of social and structural inequalities and complexities associated with structural conditions being weighed and measured by the given inquiry initiative. Culturally responsive and equitable research is essential for a more diverse and just society. Social science researchers more and more engage individuals from various religious, ethnic, racial, language, and gender groups requiring a commitment to inclusion and responsiveness to different cultural groups in their work. Cultural competence is critical and important to conducting equitable and addressing often neglected variables in project design and evaluation. In conclusion, equitable research considers the perspective of all stakeholders including participants, staff, and community program supporters and entails the need to communicate programmatic successes, strengths, weaknesses, and applications.

REFERENCES

American Public Health Association. (2009). *Support for community-based participatory research in public health.* https://apha.org/policies-and-advocacy/public-health-policy-statements/policy-database/2014/07/23/14/58/support-for-community-based-participatory-research-in-public-health

Andrews, K., Parekh, J., & Peckoo, S. (2019). *How to embed a racial and ethic equity perspective in research: Practical guidance for the research process.* Child Trends.

Annie E. Casey Foundation. (2006). *3 tools for getting started with the Race Matters toolkit.* https://www.aecf.org/resources/3-tools-for-getting-started-with-the-race-matters-toolkit

Collins, S. E., Clifasefi, S. L., Stanton, J., The LEAP Advisory Board, Straits, K. J. E., Gil-Kashiwabara, E., Rodriguez Espinosa, P., Nicasio, A. V., Andrasik, M. P., Hawes, S. M., Miller, K. A., Nelson, L. A., Orfaly, V. E., Duran, B. M., & Wallerstein, N. (2018). Community-based participatory research (CBPR): Towards equitable involvement of community in psychology research. *American Psychologist, 73*(7), 884–898. https://doi.org/10.1037/amp0000167

Cornwall, A., & Jewkes, R. (1995). What is participatory research? *Social Science & Medicine, 41*(12), 1667–1676. https://doi.org/10.1016/0277-9536(95)00127-S.

Endo Inouye, T., Cao Yu, H., & Adefuin, J. (2005). *Commissioning multicultural evaluation: A foundation resource guide.* Social Policy Research Associates. https://www.spra.com/resource/commissioning-multicultural-evaluation-a-foundation-resource-guide/

Flaspohler, P., Duffy, J., Wandersman, A., Stillman, L., & Maras, M. A. (2008). Unpacking prevention capacity: An intersection of research-to-practice models and community-centered models. *American Journal of Community Psychology, 41*, 182–196.

Fransman, J. , & Newman, K. (2019). Rethinking research partnerships: Evidence and the politics of participation in research partnerships for international development. *Journal of International Development, 31*(7), 523–544. https://onlinelibrary.wiley.com/doi/full/10.1002/jid.3417

Gaddy, M., & Scott, K. (2020). *Principles for advancing equitable data practice* [Report]. Urban Institute. https://www.urban.org/sites/default/files/publication/102346/principles-for-advancing-equitable-data-practice_0.pdf

Henderson, L., Shigeto A., Ponzetti, J. J., Jr., Edwards, A. B., Stanley, J., & Story, C. (2017, October). A Cultural-variant approach to community-based participatory research: New ideas for family professionals. *Family Relations, 66*, 629–643. https://doi.org/10.1111/fare.12269

Israel, B. A., Schulz, A. J., Parker, E. A., & Becker, A. B. (1998). Review of community-based research: Assessing partnership approaches to improve public health. *Annual Review of Public Health, 19*, 173–202. doi: 10.1146/annurev.publhealth.19.1.173. PMID: 9611617.

Israel, B. A., Schulz, A. J., Parker, E. A., & Becker, A. B. (2001). Community-based participatory research: Policy recommendations for promoting a partnership approach in health research. *Education Health, 14*(2), 182–197. https://doi .org/10.1080/13576280110051055

Israel, B. A., Schulz, A., Parker, E. A., Becker, A. B., Allen, A., & Guzman, R. (2003). Critical issues in developing and following community-based participatory research principles. In M. Minkler & N. Wallerstein (Eds.), *Community-based participatory research for health: From process to outcomes* (pp. 53–76). Jossey-Bass. https://www.scholars.northwestern.edu/en/publications/critical-issues -in-developing-and-following-community-based-parti-2

Kaur, J. S., Dignan, M., Burhasstipanov, L., Baukol, P., & Claus, C. (2006). The "Spirit of Eagles" legacy. *Cancer* (Suppl), *107*(8), 1987–1994.

Lewin, K. (1946). Action research and minority problems. *Journal of Social Issues, 2*, 34–46. http://dx.doi.org/10.1111/j.1540-4560.1946.tb02295.x

Newman, K., Bharadwaj, S., & Fransman, J. (2019). Rethinking research impact through principles for fair and equitable partnerships. *IDS Bulletin 50*. 10.19088/1968-2019.104.

Scharff, D. P., Matthews, K. J., Jackson, P., Hoffsuemmer, J., Martin, E., & Edwards, D. (2010). More than Tuskegee: Understanding mistrust about research participation. *Journal of Health Care for the Poor and Underserved, 21*(3), 879–897. https://doi.org/10.1353/hpu.0.0323

Schulz, A. J., Israel, B. A., Selig, S. M., Bayer, I. S., & Griffin, C. B. (1998). Development and implementation of principles for community-based research in public health. In R. H. MacNair (Ed.), *Research strategies for community practice* (pp. 83–110). Haworth Press.

Stegenga, J. (2014). Down with the hierarchies. *Topoi, 33*, 313–322.

Stringer, E. T., & Ortiz Aragón, A. (2020). *Action research.* SAGE Publications.

Tervalon, M., & Murray-García, J. (1998). Cultural humility versus cultural competence: A critical distinction in defining physician training outcomes in multicultural education. *Journal of Health Care for the Poor and Underserved, 9*, 117–125.

Viswanathan, M., Ammerman, A., Eng, E., Garlehner, G., Lohr, K. N., Griffith, D., Rhodes S., Samuel-Hodge, C., Maty, S., Lux, L., Webb, L., Sutton, S. F., Swinson, T., Jackman, A., & Whitener, L. (2004). *Community-based participatory research: Assessing the evidence.* Agency for Healthcare Research and Quality.

CHAPTER 6

PROCESS

What Are the Approaches, Tools, and Techniques Including Modification of Existing Practice Necessary to Work Ethically and Meaningfully With Individuals From Marginalized and Minoritized Groups?

Arthur E. Hernandez
University of the Incarnate Word

WHAT?

The methods of practice of qualitative inquiry are informed by philosophical assumptions which are rarely considered outside the classroom and even more rarely reported in the literature. It is these assumptions which form the basis and criteria for determining relevance, relationships and the rules that govern in any given phenomenon. These assumptions related to epistemology, ontology, axiology, and so on, must be identified

Qualitative Research With Diverse and Underserved Communities, pages 55–64
Copyright © 2024 by Information Age Publishing
www.infoagepub.com

and examined in relation to the assumptions of the individuals and groups which are to be participants in any study in all cases but even more so in instances of research related to individuals and communities which are different from the researcher. This suggests, at a minimum, philosophical congruence is essential in consideration of and decision-making regarding the appropriate approaches, tools and techniques including modification of existing practice necessary to work ethically and meaningfully with individuals from marginalized and minoritized groups. This consideration cannot be conducted absent the input and information from those about whom these judgments are to be made and require authentic cultural identification as a starting point. Authentic cultural identification implies appreciation and respect rather than simply knowledge—it requires an understanding that is grounded in the cultural experience and identity of the research participant which is only possible from genuine mutual relationships. While the particular approaches to qualitative inquiry may not necessarily require modification, when working with minoritized or marginalized individuals or groups the nature of the prompts, questions, priorities, information, and so on, which are the contents of and the mechanisms for qualitative research are certainly subject to serious consideration beyond the goal of addressing the intent of the inquiry (i.e., the "research questions"). Researchers should constantly ask whether their own point of view, cultural identity, approaches, instrumentation, and methods of analysis, are appropriate (i.e., authentic) and ethical. This suggests that unlike other approaches to inquiry, qualitative research with these individuals and groups is more likely to result in authentic meaning when their design is emergent rather than a priori protocol driven, and qualitative research questions and methods are informed by the community of interest rather than solely determined by the researcher's interest. For qualitative inquiry methods to be authentic, they must be fully understood in practice by the community as well as the researcher. Inquiry participants must know and understand how information gathered will be used to result in meaningful descriptions and explanations of the phenomena which is their experience and should at least indirectly (i.e., cultural competence-cultural humility-cultural responsiveness) inform those explanations to ensure accuracy and authenticity. Some examples of these types of approaches include community-based and participatory research and (participatory) action research. In any case, ultimately, the progression of research-based knowledge discovery or creation moves from observation to data, to evidence.

"Observation" is noting the phenomena of interest, guided by the purpose of inquiry. We observe the world around us and our experience of that phenomena. However, in qualitative research we are challenged to observe phenomena as experienced by others. This is accomplished through the application of methods which are intended to "harvest" the perceptions and judgments of others in a credible and potentially "transferable" manner. Observation becomes "data" when it is the basis for addressing (research) questions and is acceptable to others by logic, consensus or agreement. (This is one of the bases of contention between qualitative and quantitative researchers.) These data are useful when subjected to analysis which seeks to organize information in a manner that is interpretable, and results in meaningful judgments concerning the nature, characteristics, or functioning of phenomena. Data becomes "evidence" as a result of interpretation and is used to make an argument (e.g., relationship, differences, nature of action, defining characteristics, etc.) about the phenomena of interest. Ultimately, the goal of research is to describe or explain—evidence provides a basis for credibility and authority of assertions related to what is understood related to the referent experience or phenomenon.

The conduct and/or review of qualitative inquiry (making meaning) with or about individuals from marginalized or disenfranchised groups should always precede the collection and analysis of information by other means. This requirement acknowledges that theory related to the phenomena of interest by itself is insufficient for understanding that phenomena authentically, that is "lived experience" and making decisions regarding what "variables" are important and how and why they are related since social-psychological theory represents a conceptual generalization of "human experience" and neglects inherent diversity. This is in part due to the nature of the conditions and context (historical and transgenerational social injustice, inequity, bias, etc.) within which those individuals find themselves, and the impact for that context on perception, judgment and most especially, the nature and demonstration of values. Developing a respectful/authentic understanding of the cultural context and cultural identity of those from or with whom research is conducted is essential to the development of authentic information. At a minimum, this should be recognized as an ethical imperative and as such it is always necessary to pursue authenticity.

WHY?

Careful consideration and application of authentic approaches is important not only for the sake of ethical conduct of inquiry but for the sake of ensuring justice and equity. However, in addition, it is important for the result of authentic rather than merely accurate information and interpretation which forms the basis of meaning-making, decision-making, and understanding. "Accuracy" describes the degree to which a description of phenomena is congruent with what happens (action), while "authenticity" involves a genuine and honest description of experience (willful behavior). It is often the case that those from whom information is collected and about whom inquiry is focused are subject to decisions which affect their experience and wellbeing without the opportunity to provide any input beyond what has been determined by others to be important, meaningful, essential, relevant, and valuable. This is emblematic for individuals and communities who are and have been marginalized and minoritized. The application of any information to decision-making about or for others and the integrity of inquiry from which that information was derived depends on the authenticity as well as the accuracy which requires at a minimum the input of the participants/informants. It is essential that the qualitative researcher examine his/her/their process and perspective to ensure congruence between the research activity and the understanding (i.e., worldview) of those who are the focus of the inquiry. This congruence forms the minimum requirement for authenticity and thus the minimum standard for the conduct of inquiry. Anything else is nonsense, regardless of how others perceive it.

Ethical and authentic research requires attention to the consequences of the work. Inquiry which supports and sustains social injustice, inequities, subjugation of individuals and groups and results in practices or beliefs which are injurious or damaging, is by definition unethical and inauthentic. For example, the reductionist practice in research and evaluation of categorization of cultural identity such as gender, race, or ethnicity to superficial observable characteristics (e.g., skin color or language) for purposes of "diversity," "inclusion," or differentiation of social groups seems obviously to value ease of practice at the cost of authenticity.

Problem-solving which is informed by social science inquiry typically deals with problems of people in groups often localized or influenced by specific geographical location. While this may not be the only reason for engaging in social science inquiry, it is arguably most important from the perspective of the participants/subjects who inform that inquiry. In the past, driven by western epistemological frameworks, research was intended to inform or validate extant theory as a way of describing and explaining referent phenomena for the purpose of leveraging that theory to determine or validate practices and processes which affect those populations. However, this indirect effect was more often presumed than actual, of differing degrees of effect for those constituting the group and there was little attention to whether or not impact for improvement actually occurred.

Finally, the application of traditional research paradigms, including qualitative research has usually if not primarily been for the advancement of personal and professional agendas especially for researchers with university affiliation (i.e., career trajectory). Focusing on the nature and impact of the work with regard to specific or particular populations is an important aspect of moving away from an exploitative research process and provide "value" or "benefit" to the participant/subject or that person's community. This is arguably a fundamental basis for making judgments concerning the authenticity, much less the ethics of the work and something that should be an explicit consideration of all researchers and especially qualitative researchers focusing on phenomena in populations which are minoritized, marginalized, and disenfranchised. This is the case even for inquiry which doesn't aspire to achieving advocacy. While it is entirely legitimate for inquiry to be purposed for facilitating, supporting, or even precipitating social, political, or policy change, in order to argue for legitimacy and credibility, inquiry should be crafted in a way that demonstrates that resulting information and evidence is authentic and accurate. This may require that researchers relate their methods to extant or "new" methods acceptable (to the intended audiences and stakeholders including the community represented by the "sample") and provide a rationale and argument for the "legitimacy" of the methods, esults, and constructed meaning.

HOW?

As with all research, qualitative research is informed by or results in theory— a model or description of experience in aggregate. Briefly, at a minimum, "theory" is an explanation or description of phenomena which identifies defining characteristics, the relationships between those characteristics and the rules which govern those relationships. In qualitative research, theory provides the parameters, serves to identify relevant constituents or "variables," dynamics which describe, explain, govern, and organize action into conceptual terms and frameworks. This theory may be formally and collectively or informal and individually constructed and may be recognized by others or implicit to the researcher. Thus, to be authentic, decisions researchers make concerning what, where, and how to attend to any phenomena of interest should begin a problem of understanding (ideally identified by the community) which results in questions that guide inquiry and informs, improves or remediates the problem. The focus and act of observation should be recognized as deliberate (a decision on the part of the researcher) which is facilitated and informed by theory and prior inquiry but not dictated by it. All too often social "science" ignores social/environmental/historical context and conditions in which phenomena occur since many practitioners seek to describe a universal mechanism of action as a matter of research epistemology. This is particularly problematic in the case of inquiry which focuses on human identity and action since all human experience is grounded in context and conditions at least some of which are transitory, situational, and subject to individual and cultural interpretation. In the case of inquiry with historically marginalized or minoritized groups this includes the influence and impact of historically unjust systems (e.g., societies) and associated presumed power and privilege perspectives and values which generally go unrecognized (except by the "victims"). Decisions concerning the object of observation must be informed by these considerations and tempered by regard for both intended and unintended consequences.

Failure to critically examine the perspective of the researcher and reach cultural identification is likely to result in misunderstanding and irrelevant meaning-making. "Collected" observations, data and evidence can consist of a wide variety of demonstrations or indicators of perceptions, perspectives, and presumed relationships which are organized in a fashion that lends to understanding through information structure/organization. Researchers who fail to be appropriately and critically self-reflective tend to move to meaning based on a priori expectation and experience which direct the selection of the questions and methods which guide and focus the inquiry. Frequently, it is the nature of the questions as much as the methods which provide a clear indication of the researcher's perspective and provide an indication of that a priori expectation. This is demonstrated by the popular phrase "the questions drive (determine) the methodology" which is often applied to decisions regarding qualitative or quantitative approaches. However, this simplistic orientation presumes a great deal. At a minimum, it fails to recognize the typically "researcher centered" nature of inquiry and absolves the researcher of the ethical responsibility for decisions and definitions related to all aspects of the conduct of the inquiry.

The ethical and responsible (qualitative) researcher examines those assumptions which delimit, drive and direct inquiry decision-making and determines their value, applicability, impact, and consequences recognizing that their orientations and beliefs influence determinations of relevance, mechanisms of action (including model specification), instrumentation and more. This self-reflection and self-awareness is essential to informed and meaningful meaning-making and begins by influencing the questions being asked which guide both the focus of observation and the development of data (which comes from the specification of the questions!).

Converting observations to data involves the "transformation" of information into manageable "chunks" usually through aggregation of some kind (e.g., measures of central tendency, codes, categories, etc.) which is amenable to usual and "scholarly" means of analysis (e.g., narrative analysis, ANOVA, etc.) which is generally accepted as applicable by other researchers. While this acceptability should ultimately be determined by the likelihood that it will result in "honest answers" (authenticity) it is also influenced by pressure within the discipline which generally has to do with consensus resulting from familiarity, history, practice, and so on. For example, in quantitative research though many questions might be better informed by Bayesian analysis, most reported research still relies on the "statistics of distribution" or in qualitative research the emphasis on thematic analysis rather than "gap analysis" (see Action Research). Regardless of method, this transformation is guided by the questions to which the data will be applied and the philosophical and personal perspectives and values of the researcher.

Data analysis is the presumptive way in which researchers make meaning, but analysis is merely a way for organizing observations so that they are meaningful for constructing arguments. In science, arguments are advanced through and by evidence. Evidence is the organization and marshaling of data to provide a rationale or basis for assertions of fact (or truth). It is in the examination of evidence that one can ascertain the perspective, beliefs and assumptions of the researcher and it is only in those cases where perspectives, beliefs and assumptions are shared by both the research and the "consumer" (of research) is meaning-to be conveyed. While meaning-making by the researcher is an essential outcome of inquiry, it is ultimately without value if that meaning is not recognized and accepted by others. This means presumptions that guide inquiry significantly influence meaning-making and the resulting "understanding," and is one reason that some researchers fail to recognize the interpretation of others based on "methodology" (e.g., the "quant" vs. "qual" argument).

The quality of "data" depends on many factors, all of which are the result of judgments and decisions on the part of the researcher. The determination of relevance and thus important for observation is one of the first steps in research. Often this determination if not based on extant theory is influenced by previous inquiry. In this case, the scope, depth, and direction of the observation is decided by what has been previously demonstrated and associated arguments of fact. The referenced model or theory serves to direct observation to those variables or elements of importance and the relationships between those elements. In other cases, it is a combination of understandings (various theories or models) which guide observation. In these instances, a general framework of elements recognized as important and influential are identified and the theory pertaining to each is applied. Still in other cases there is no model of reference. The goal of the inquiry then is to begin to identify those elements which are relevant to the phenomenon of interest and begin to describe the nature and actions of the relationships between those elements. It is easy to see how researcher perspective, experience, worldview, and so on, can influence every aspect and element and associated decision-making.

Since most of the factors or elements implicated in the social science examination of human activity are hypothetical or operationally defined (e.g., motivation, race, society, intelligence, history, heritage, etc.), it is essential to understand the assumptions and bases for those constructs. In some cases, these constructs arise from reification, and others merely as a result of the inability to directly observe the phenomenon of interest.

Clearly in every case, this conceptualization is a matter of judgment and decision-making and influences and is influenced by the manner in which these constructs reflect experience. This influence comes most readily as a result of instrumentation which requires assumptions among which are the "validity" or authenticity of selected indicators. Despite being "scientific," one egregious example of this can be seen in the notion of "intelligence" which over its history has been examined by "intelligence tests" in a spectacular example of circular definition with disastrous social consequences. Regardless, decisions regarding the nature and quality of an indicator (the interpretation of some observation as being uniquely or significantly related to some construct) can impact on meaning-making in profound ways. Researchers and consumers of research should pay special attention to the ways in which observations are collected or gathered (instrumentation) and the manner in which results are constructed and judgments and conclusions are determined/constructed when judging their credibility.

Beyond mechanisms for capturing or harvesting data, the means and mechanisms must be organized to construct evidence—the basis for argument which advances a particular perspective concerning the nature and operation of the phenomena of interest. Although empiricists might argue that "evidence" is merely information which is descriptive, explanatory, or predictive, it should be recognized as a lever which advances a particular perspective which only makes sense from the "right worldview." That is, a worldview which provides the basis for understanding, argument, and of "making sense" of what is "learned" in the inquiry.

WHERE?

Authentic practice is genuine to the community from which or about which information is pursued. Typical social *scientific* endeavors seek to describe the mechanisms which are responsible for observable behavior. However, unlike other science, many aspects of those hypothetical mechanisms (i.e., theory) in social science are not directly observable. In addition, much traditional social science ignores the mediation and actualization of mechanisms for action by individuals and groups and seeks instead to develop universal descriptions and explanations (one size fits all models) of behavior that is unaffected by a particular population or group's experience. The history of research in social/human sciences where study samples were restricted (e.g., White undergraduate students in psychology) has amply demonstrated the inaccuracy and unauthenticity of results as applied to members of groups which were not represented. Examples range from medicine and psychology to sociology and public policy. Thus, while it is important in all research including qualitative research, it is absolutely essential that this effort be a part of any research which seeks to provide information about and which will be applied to populations which are disenfranchised, marginalized, and minoritized.

WHEN?

Process decisions are typically made a priori to the research/inquiry whether it is qualitative or quantitative. However, in practice it can happen that a priori process decisions must be revisited due to either conditions or to unanticipated factors which arise, or about which researchers become aware as a result of or which result from process learning. This suggests that process is actually a matter of constant attention to the action of inquiry most especially with minoritized and marginalized communities. This is due to a variety of considerations. One reason for process decision-making during inquiry and procedural change may be the cultural realization which results from immersion in the community, through the knowledge which arises from the mechanisms of observation, data development and/or the construction of evidence. Another reason for process adaptation includes qualitative research which may be designed from an action research or community based and participatory research framework where process, instrumentation, priorities, and even research questions may intentionally be designed to be "emergent."

Process decision-making is a matter of perception and judgment—underlying epistemology, values, ontology, and so on, establish the parameters and provide the guidelines or rules for understanding. Thus, it is clear that research is not a matter of application of method or design. In a very real way, research is personal—both for the researcher and for the community of the informants. Clearly, "seeing" something which is outside of expectation is so often so very hard to do. This is one reason that cultural competence, humility, and responsiveness are so essential when working with minoritized communities. However, cultural identification is something that is always developmental in nature with different starting points, the degree to which otherness is challenging to cultural knowledge/certainty and the transitory and developmental nature of culture itself. Cultural competence is not a state—it is an ongoing honest effort on the part of the researcher to share the perspectives/experiences of the research participants/"subjects." Process decision-making is something about which the researcher should always reflect and something that should be subject to change as the researcher discovers ways in which planned process may result in inauthentic results, conclusions, and impact.

WHO?

Obviously individual researchers are responsible for the conduct of their inquiry. However, much process decision-making is bounded by what is acceptable to the respective discipline. While these boundaries for inquiry are important for consistency and internal integrity of research within the discipline, they often result in "blinders" beyond which researchers seldom see. This is not necessarily surprising since it is impossible for anyone to act beyond their experience and the training of researchers is almost always within the framework of a particular discipline. While there has been some formal effort to become more interdisciplinary in health services delivery for example, even here this interdisciplinarity does not usually expand the known and accepted frameworks for and boundaries of inquiry. Researchers (and disciplines) who engage in inquiry with minoritized and marginalized communities must be active learners, willing to explore and expand their epistemological frameworks and their methods of meaning-making. This often means moving beyond Western knowledge frameworks. For example, while Freire's liberatory pedagogy has influenced research methods, researchers influenced by these ideas often neglect significant epistemological and liberatory perspectives of the communities with which they work (e.g., indigenous liberatory epistemology). More superficially, this can be expanded beyond solely qualitative or quantitative methods, recognizing the access to knowledge creation or discovery provided by each which is beyond the other. This inquiry (self) consciousness is essential for the pursuit of authentic knowledge/information which is consistent not only with some theoretical perspective but with the lived experience of those about whom and on whom theory is applied. Thus, it is not enough for researchers to adapt and grow but they must also be committed to action which expands notions of acceptable/credible meaning-making and mechanisms for drawing conclusions within their disciplines. Knowledge about reality must be approached from all perspectives if it is to be close to actual reality.

INTRODUCTION TO CASE STUDIES

The case studies in Chapter 7 demonstrate efforts to engage in qualitative research projects with individuals from communities which have been marginalized, minoritized, or disenfranchised. Though the approaches demonstrated are not consistent and some frankly fail to reach the standards described by the previous chapters, all demonstrate different aspects of what could be considered the ideal. This is by no means a pejorative criticism of the projects. In many cases, projects are reported as they are due to the constraints of publication or the presumption of basic expectations for the conduct of inquiry including meaning making. In other cases, this is due to the nature of the parameters imposed by discipline and background. However, all have been selected as strong examples of work which are fruitful for consideration and reflection. We encourage all readers to learn from what is included but also to interrogate each of the studies reported for it is from practice, experience, and reflection that the best learning occurs. Every reader will identify something they would do differently or questions they would ask of the authors or even things that they might argue were inappropriate. It is important to consider all of this and especially the rationale for the critique. These case studies can provide a strong basis for individual and community reflection and as with all work in (social) science, serve as a basis for learning and improvement.

Qualitative Research With Diverse and Underserved Communities, pages 65–66
Copyright © 2024 by Information Age Publishing
www.infoagepub.com
All rights of reproduction in any form reserved.

As you read each of the case studies, you are encouraged to think about what is intended, the methods described, the observations and conversion to data, and the final arguments which are made. What meaning is described and advanced? How does that relate to the worldview of all participants (e.g., researchers, data analysts, reports, stakeholders, etc.)? How do the results impact and/or inform the precipitating question or problem, that is what are some likely consequences (whether intended or not)? To what extent the researchers are engaged with the community of interest, showing through process and product community? This book is intended to provide a basis for reflection, insight, and reflexivity rather than be simply a "how to" or recipe book, the former a matter of human and professional development, the latter a matter of artificiality and standardization which would necessarily reduce or even replace the requisite attention to the important elements and requirements for authentic and ethical inquiry.

—**Jeton McClinton**
Arthur E. Hernandez
Alma L. Thornton

CASE STUDIES SECTION I

INTRODUCTION TO CASE STUDY 1

This exciting and powerful research inquiry seeks to answer the questions of who, how, and why. It is significant how the author established the conditions for this exploratory study so that other researchers and readers can understand the environmental constraints and context that influenced participants' behaviors and outcomes. This case study's participants were 51 Kansas City, Missouri residents who had experienced school desegregation. Also, a unique and distinguishing feature of the study is the population of choice, participants who had gone through school desegregation. The participants were exemplary, considering they portrayed a population influenced by two significant legislations: *Brown v. Board of Education* in 1954 and *Jenkins v. Missouri* in 1995.

At that time, the participants were students, teachers, or educational administrators at the school or school district levels, parents, and community activists. This is an ideal illustration of snowball sampling and how it can be used by recommendations from individuals to collect the required sample sizes for a research project. These researchers used snowball sampling because these types of samples are chosen based on characteristics that are not easily identified in the general population.

This population is frequently neglected, considering we read books on the subject but not the participants' actual lived experiences. Also, noteworthy is how the authors applied unique methods to include the inquiry's arts-based and experiential nature. Another novel method was the author's creation of a website with artifacts, resources, photos, videos of oral histories and documentaries, and a community yearbook. The inquiry asked

Qualitative Research With Diverse and Underserved Communities, pages 69–79
Copyright © 2024 by Information Age Publishing
www.infoagepub.com

what it would take for schools and communities to collaborate on initiatives to deliver a racially integrated, equitable, and outstanding education for all students.

CASE STUDY 1

BEARING WITNESS TO MOBILIZE CHANGE

Narratives of Experience of School Desegregation

Candace Schlein
University of Missouri–Kansas City

Loyce Caruthers
University of Missouri–Kansas City

Jennifer Friend
Rockhurst University

CONTEXT FOR THE INQUIRY

Brown v. Board of Education's historical U.S. Supreme Court ruling rendered the segregation of Black children and White children in public schools unconstitutional. Although this ruling occurred in 1954, the Kansas City Missouri School District (KCMSD) managed to avoid adhering to this ruling through shifting attendance boundaries and a lenient transfer policy,

Qualitative Research With Diverse and Underserved Communities, pages 71–79
Copyright © 2024 by Information Age Publishing
www.infoagepub.com
All rights of reproduction in any form reserved.

in association with changes in neighborhoods caused by blockbusting and White flight. This was supported by housing and financial lending practices that effectively limited the areas where Black families could buy homes, and therefore, where Black children could attend school (Gotham, 2002). Consequently, most schools remained racially segregated through these attendance boundaries.

CONDITIONS WITHIN WHICH THE INQUIRY IS SITUATED

The Kansas City Missouri School Board eventually implemented *Desegregation Plan 6-C* nearly 20 years after *Brown v. Board of Education*. The legal system was again brought forward for guiding schooling in Kansas City when the *Jenkins v. Missouri* case (1995) led to an educational overhaul that would entice school integration through a $2 billion investment aimed at improving school facilities and resources and creating several magnet schools (Thomas & Hoxworth, 1991). The magnet schools brought to Kansas City enriched programs that were centered around themes, such as Central Computers Unlimited, Language Magnet Schools, Classical Greek Magnet High School (Ciotti, 1998).

During this period of time, cities across the United States added bussing programs so that Black students in urban areas would attend suburban schools with a mostly White student population (Siegel-Hawley, 2016). Suburban school districts surrounding Kansas City did not voluntarily participate in school desegregation, and they were not held liable in the *Jenkins v. Missouri* case (1995). Instead of bussing Black students from city schools to the suburbs, White students from surrounding districts were provided with bus or taxi rides to attend the magnet schools in Kansas City. Eventually, the funding for improved facilities and magnet schools dried up, and the end result is a sustained lack of equitable and integrated education (Gotham, 2002; Mawdsley, 2004; Moran, 2005).

INQUIRY FOCUS

Our overarching inquiry focus was to puzzle over the following line of questioning: "What would it take for schools and communities to collaborate around efforts to provide a racially integrated, equitable and excellent education for all students?" Our investigative efforts were further tightened for deliberation over these research questions:

1. Drawing on their experiences, what do educators and students: (a) want to share about their school integration experiences through

images and narratives posted on an interactive, public website (b) have to say about what is needed to change outcomes for students in today's urban public schools?

2. In what ways can historical materials be made accessible to elucidate the period of school integration in Kansas City?

3. How can online resources and educator workshops provide opportunities to focus on local regimes of truth with individuals constructing new knowledge forms related to equal educational opportunities?

CASE

The participants for our study were drawn from the pool of residents of Kansas City, Missouri who had experienced school desegregation. Importantly, we strove to include participants who were involved in the initial period of school integration following *Brown v. Board of Education* (1954) as well as those who had experienced the later period of school desegregation following *Jenkins v. Missouri* (1995). The case examined within this inquiry comprised a total of 51 participants; representing 18 males and 33 females who were either students (10), teachers (10), or educational administrators (15) at the school or school district levels, as well as parents (2) and community activists (14). The majority of the participants, $N = 31$ of 51, had multiple roles as students, teachers, parents and community members. While our numbers depict two participant interviews in the role of parents, 10 of the 51 participants were parents following *Brown* and *Jenkins v. Missouri*. Our focus was on the voices of African Americans, but we also wanted to hear diverse voices. A second round of interviews included six White and two Latinx participants.

Incorporating the experiences of educators alongside students, administrators, parents, and community stakeholders enabled us to attend to some of the storied tensions of teaching and learning from multiple viewpoints. It also enabled us to uncover how district, school, and classroom shifts resulted in changes to actual teaching and learning. Lastly, this set of participants was uniquely positioned to shed light on how the communities and families were impacted by educational policies that arose during efforts to desegregate schools in Kansas City and some of the enduring consequences of these efforts.

METHODOLOGY

This inquiry consisted of several stages. Our participants were recruited for inquiry participation utilizing snowball sampling. We each reached out to current or former students, teachers, school administrators, parents, and other community members who had experienced school desegregation efforts in Kansas City. We also asked participants for recommendations for additional potential participants. Over the course of 2 years, we met with 51 participants for informal video-recorded interviews. These digital videos focused on the historical and "resonating" (Conle, 1996) experiences of school desegregation. Our participants included students, educators, parents, and community members who have lived, worked, and/or were educated in the Kansas City, Missouri area.

Another central component of this inquiry was the collection of artifacts. We invited our participants to bring to their interviews any documents or other objects that they wanted to share from their experiences with school desegregation. During our interviews, we asked our participants to describe the artifacts that they had brought with them and to highlight their perceived relevance for understanding school desegregation efforts. The artifacts that we gained from our participants included pictures of students, teachers, and schools; school yearbooks; school and/or school district meeting minutes; and related newspaper items. We scanned all artifacts into digital files during the course of the scheduled interviews.

Artifact collection for this study included compiling scans of documents and photographs related to desegregation in local schools. We visited the Black Archives of Mid-America Kansas City and the Kansas City Public Library on several occasions during the 2-year data collection phase of the investigation. Some members of the research team had previously completed a documentary project on Eugene Eubanks, chair of the district's desegregation monitoring committee, and the litigation lawyer for *Jenkins v. Missouri* (1995), Arthur Benson. The documentary and the experiences of working on it were also accounted for in this study.

We then created a website Kansas City Speaks: Stories of School Desegregation (https://kcdeseg.com) to voice the experiences of school desegregation. The website includes video interviews, documentary films, and historical artifacts. The website was shaped to provide content and to engage in social justice oriented educational and societal transformation.

We developed several lesson plans that make use of the website content surrounding the themes of students, teachers, and community. The goal of the lesson plans are for teachers and students to engage in discussion about school desegregation as a means of building awareness and as a platform for change. The lesson plans are available on the website free of charge.

This study is a generative investigation that is structured to continually engage with educators, students, parents, and other community members. We established a community yearbook on the website where site visitors can share their own stories and upload pictures and other artifacts. This content can then serve to both continue the dialogue and provide ongoing data sources displaying possible new dialogic turns.

Methodological Rationale

This study was structured with a methodological base of general qualitative methods (Creswell, 2012). However, this study was influenced by different methodological strands to account for the arts-based and experiential nature of this inquiry. In particular, we desired to loosen the boundaries of formal qualitative research in order to capture some of the fluctuations of story and experience among our participants. We especially recognized that the focus of the investigation intertwined historical and contemporary layers of curricular engagement via desegregation movements. For this reason, we looked to St. Pierre (2015) to transition beyond traditional qualitative inquiry toward engaging in post qualitative methods.

Adopting a post qualitative perspective in our study enabled us to explore new understandings of experience that were understood as discrete and/or related phenomena with historical, social, and cultural meanings. The qualitative tradition of narrative inquiry (Clandinin, 2007) further pushed us to envision story, experience, and the storying of experiences of school desegregation as incorporating elements of the past, the present, and the future that shift and merge across these temporal landscapes.

Soja's (1996) framework of space was also seminal for our work, as it allowed us to break through the walls of the traditional qualitative research paradigm through the interactive medium of a website. In this framework, the "firstspace" is seen as material space, such as schools in Kansas City. "Secondspace" can be understood as the thoughts of students, teachers, and community members in Kansas City. We applied "thirdspace" in this inquiry as the online environment of the Kansas City Speaks website. This thirdspace allows for the local and broader public to both consume and contribute to the content on the website.

In this way, our study involves public voicing. While we recognize the power of lending voice and a platform to bear witness to past and ongoing experiences of school desegregation, we further recognize the need to mobilize change through our work. Critical race theory (Ladson-Billings & Tate, 1995) provided a useful lens for framing our work and analyzing our data in ways that attend to the historical and contemporary racial tensions in schools and society, and thereby, to challenge knowledge (Hill Collins, 2003) and dominant discourses through counter-stories (Solorzano & Yosso, 2005, p. 72).

Data Analysis

The major source of data for this study was the video recorded and audio-recorded interviews, which were placed on our research website. In this way, our data collection and analysis processes were meshed with issues of public voicing. We transcribed and coded interviews using Ethnograph 6 software (Seidel, 1984) and posted the interview videos to the website along with scanned files of any artifacts that participants may have brought. We took note of the content categories for each of these collected artifacts.

Major themes were disseminated through public presentations and journal article and book chapter publication. The common narrative themes of our study were: In reviewing our collected interview data, we uncovered five common narrative themes and 14 related sub-themes. The theme of "desegregation plan" incorporated the sub-themes of "integrate schools," "traditional schools," and "provisions of plan." The theme of "community's reactions to desegregation" included the following sub-themes: "impact of community," "mixed feelings," "parent involvement," and "charter schools." The theme of "lessons from a contested field" comprised the sub-themes of "focus on academic outcomes," "reclaim children," and "preparation and recruitment." The theme of "views about integration" highlighted the sub-themes of "benefits" and "mixed achievement." The final theme of "dangerous memories of institutional racism" outlined the sub-themes of "differential treatment" and "racial attitudes."

To represent the themed findings from this research through arts-based methods, we developed two documentary films. These films included edited portions of full interview videos that were organized by theme. Making the documentary films involved further meaning-making during the post-production process in which we edited videos and paired the pictures and words of various participants together with title cards to showcase our findings. Friend and Militello (2015) examined video production methods in education research and discerned that "video as a research instrument has the potential to transform research from something we do to subjects to something we do with participants—co-generation of knowledge through inclusion of authentic voices that can be shared with a wide audience" (p. 91).

Our lesson plans stand as another outgrowth of our data analysis. Once we identified the themes from among our data, we attended to shaping lesson plans that were reflective of these themes. They were thus fashioned to represent the current discussion and move the conversation forward on race and equity in schooling and society.

ANTICIPATED AND UNANTICIPATED CONSEQUENCES

When we began this inquiry, we recognized that this was a study that would prove to be meaningful to local community members. We did not anticipate the extent to which this study would garner excitement among people in Kansas City. Our participants included a current U.S. representative and a former Missouri senator. After we concluded our data collection, a few potential participants asked us to be included in the study. While we had to deny them participation due to time limitations to conduct video-recorded interviews, we are excited to see that there is an ongoing pool of possible participants for future phases of this research.

This study began as a research project that was focused on public voicing, but the need for public outreach soon became apparent to us. We have led two research conferences in the region stemming from this investigation. Each of these conferences included local educators, educational researchers, and community members. We had documentary viewings, we hosted question and answer sessions, and we organized panel sessions with some of our local and state leaders to address the audience regarding their experiences and their hopes for the future of local schooling. This outreach has continued following completion of this initial research project, as team members have established contact with other researchers in places such as New Orleans and St. Louis examining facets of racial segregation and desegregation.

INQUIRY EVOLUTION

In the section above, we underscored some of the ways that the study surprised us in terms of the breadth of interest and the depth of the available participant pool. We also displayed how the original research plan of data collection, website development, and data analysis took new shapes in acknowledging the need to enhance the voicing of participants' experiences. We attended to this need in organizing two full-day conferences that examined the intersection of research and narratives of experience on school desegregation.

During the first set of interviews, we concentrated only on the experiences of African American participants. However, as our participants shared their stories with us, we realized that we were only getting one racial perspective on issues such as the rise and fall of magnet schools, bussing programs, community school and community disruption, and housing practices in relation to schooling. We therefore intentionally evolved the inquiry to include a wider set of participants from different racial backgrounds.

CONCLUSION: LESSONS ABOUT QUALITATIVE RESEARCH

Often when researchers prepare to enter the field to collect data they focus on academic considerations. Although we immersed ourselves in data collection out of academic interest, we also did so within our own fervent passions for transformative education. There was an immediate need to position ourselves as researchers within the study and carefully consider the lines between our biases and our interest in the study. Talking about these issues among the research team revealed our biases so that we could account for them during data analysis. We thus recommend that qualitative researchers document their struggles of moving between subjectivity and objectivity in order to lend clarity to the context of interpretive findings.

Additionally, as we listened to stories of the reality of school desegregation that included students of color being taught on separate floors of the school and different lunch times for students based on race, we shifted from invested researchers to witnesses of injustice and inequality. This experience highlights for us the potential impact of engaging in research with community members and the position of power that researchers may hold over participants and knowledge claims. We understood the power of representing the telling of their stories. For us, bearing witness to these experiential narratives demanded that we honor our participants through voicing to mobilize change. We invite all qualitative researchers to account for context and power issues as major factors of data collection and analyses, as well as for the dissemination of outcomes from such investigations.

REFERENCES

Brown v. Board of Education, 347 U.S. 483 (1954). https://supreme.justia.com/cases/federal/us/347/483/

Ciotti, P. (1998). *Money and school performance: Lessons from the Kansas City Desegregation Experiment* (Vol. 298). Cato Institute.

Clandinin, D. J. (Ed.). (2007). *Handbook of narrative inquiry: Mapping a methodology.* SAGE Publications.

Conle, C. (1996). Resonance in preservice teacher inquiry. *American Educational Research Journal, 33*(2), 297–325.

Creswell, J. W. (2012). *Educational research: Planning, conducting, and evaluating quantitative and qualitative research* (4th ed.). Pearson Education.

Gotham, K. F. (2002). Missed opportunities, enduring legacies: School segregation and desegregation in Kansas City, Missouri. *American Studies, 43*(2), 5–42. https://journals.ku.edu/amsj/article/view/3050

Hill Collins, P. (2003). Toward an Afrocentric feminist epistemology. In N. K. Denzin & E. J. Lincoln (Eds.), *Turning points in qualitative research: Tying knots in a handkerchief* (pp. 47–72). AltaMira Press.

Jenkins v. Missouri, 515 U.S. 70 (1995). https://supreme.justia.com/cases/federal/us/515/70/

Ladson-Billings, G., & Tate, W. F. (1995). Toward a critical race theory of education. *Teachers College Record, 97*(1), 47–68. https://doi.org/10.1177/016146819509700104

Mawdsley, R. D. (2004). A legal history of Brown and a look to the future. *Education and Urban Society, 36*(3), 245–254. https://doi.org/10.1177/0013124504264095

Moran, P. W. (2005). *Race, law, and desegregation of public schools.* LFB Scholarly Publishing.

Seidel, J. V. (1984) *Qualitative data analysis* (Ethnograph 6.0) [computer software]. Qualis Research.

Siegel-Hawley, G. (2016). *When the fences come down: Twenty-first-century lessons from metropolitan school desegregation.* The University of North Carolina Press.

Soja, E. W. (1996). *Thirdspace: Journeys to Los Angeles and other real-and-imagined places.* Blackwell.

Solorzano, D., & Yosso, T. (2002). Critical race methodology: Counter-storytelling as an analytical framework for education research. *Qualitative Inquiry, 8,* 23–44. https://doi.org/10.1177/107780040200800103

St. Pierre, E. A. (2015). Practices for the "new" in the new empiricisms, the new materialisms, and post qualitative inquiry. In N. K. Denzin & M. D. Giardina (Eds.), *Qualitative inquiry and the politics of research* (pp. 75–95). Left Coast Press.

Thomas, J. C., & Hoxworth, D. H. (1991). The limits of judicial desegregation remedies after *Missouri v. Jenkins. Publius: The Journal of Federalism, 21*(3), 93–108. https://doi.org/10.1093/oxfordjournals.pubjof.a037960

INTRODUCTION TO CASE STUDY 2

It is exemplary how these authors employed a culturally responsive research approach to recognize culture as central to the research process and employ both the researchers and the researched cultural perspectives as a method for research design, data collection, and data interpretation. Also, this case study is an example of how purposeful sampling can be used to include populations not traditionally represented in STEM research. The sample represented a diverse demographic, geographic, and cultural context in five PREP locations. This is a case that also demonstrates the benefit of establishing relationships with a history of trust, which allowed the researchers to collaborate with site directors to find students who matched their research populations criteria needed to understand and provide a voice to students who are usually underrepresented in STEM fields. Also included in this case study are the terms gender minorities to represent the trans population and URM, which is another example of underrepresented minorities.

Qualitative Research With Diverse and Underserved Communities, pages 81–92
Copyright © 2024 by Information Age Publishing
www.infoagepub.com
All rights of reproduction in any form reserved.

CASE STUDY 2

SOCIAL AND LEARNING EXPERIENCES OF UNDERREPRESENTED STUDENTS IN STEM SUMMER PROGRAMS

A Culturally Responsive Case Study

Guan Saw
Claremont Graduate University

Kahi Hedrick-Romano
Claremont Graduate University

Ryan Culbertson
University of Texas at San Antonio

Pesha Mabrie
University of Texas at San Antonio

Vicki Lynton
Northwest Vista College

Qualitative Research With Diverse and Underserved Communities, pages 83–92
Copyright © 2024 by Information Age Publishing
www.infoagepub.com
83

In the United States, statistics consistently show that women, racial/ethnic minorities (particularly Blacks, Hispanics/Latinx, and Native Americans), low-income youth, and rural and small-town students have a lower level of career interest and are severely underrepresented in science, engineering, technology, and mathematics (STEM) fields (National Science Foundation [NSF], 2019; Saw & Agger, 2021; Saw et al., 2018). To address the STEM diversity issue, numerous out-of-school time (OST) STEM programs have been developed and offered to support the STEM educational and career pathways of underrepresented students (e.g., Afterschool Alliance, 2014; Saw et al., 2019). While the existing, yet limited, studies on the effectiveness of OST STEM programs are promising, research evidence regarding *under what circumstances* an OST STEM program promotes STEM outcomes of underrepresented students is scarce (National Research Council [NRC], 2015). This article describes a culturally responsive case study (CRCS) that fills this critical research gap by addressing two key research questions:

1. How do underrepresented students describe their social and learning experiences in OST STEM programs?
2. How do various program components and processes of OST STEM programs influence STEM learning, motivation, and participation of underrepresented students?

CULTURALLY RESPONSIVE CASE STUDY

Culturally responsive case study (CRCS) is an emerging case study approach involving individuals from underserved and marginalized communities (e.g., Santamaría, 2014; Yamamoto et al., 2017). It draws on theoretical perspectives from indigenous epistemologies, social advocacy theories, and critical race theory (Hood et al., 2015; Hopson, 2009). A case study approach is considered culturally responsive if it considers the culture and context of the case that is being examined, as well as the needs and cultural factors of those who are being involved in the case (Frierson et al., 2002; Hood et al., 2015). CRCS seeks to understand the lived experiences and strengths of participants or studied communities. As such, it is well-suited for the purpose of this study, which aims to explore the OST STEM learning experiences and outcomes of students who have been underserved and minoritized in STEM education.

The Case: The Prefreshman Engineering Program (PREP)

This case study focuses on the prefreshman engineering program (PREP), an OST STEM program, which was founded at the University of

Texas at San Antonio (UTSA) in 1979 and was originally established to help high school seniors from underrepresented backgrounds prepare for college math classes. With financial support from funders like the National Aeronautics and Space Administration (NASA), NSF, and Texas Legislature, PREP expanded to include 35 sites located across the Southwestern United States. PREP, a multi-year program taking place over seven weeks each summer, began shifting its focus from math to include all STEM subjects during the 1980s. Participants can enroll in the program as early as the sixth grade and can continue until their junior year of high school. PREP has continually maintained a mission of recruiting underrepresented students—particularly women, Blacks/Hispanics/Native Americans (or underrepresented and racially/ethnically minoritized people [URM]), and low-socioeconomic status (SES) youth. In recent years prior to the COVID-19 pandemic, PREP served about 5,000 students across sites every summer. However, during the COVID-19 pandemic (in the summer of 2020 and 2021), the enrollment number dropped across PREP sites. Each PREP site is located on a college/university campus and is managed by a site director, with general oversight of the entire program done by an administrative team located at UTSA.

ENTERING THE COMMUNITY AND BUILDING A DIVERSE RESEARCH TEAM

In early Spring 2019, PREP staff from UTSA and an external researcher (two of the coauthors; one White man and one Asian man) launched a mixed methods research project, which included the CRCS described in this article, that aims to examine the impact of PREP on student outcomes. In an early phase of the project, late Spring 2019, the research team visited more than 20 PREP sites across several states to learn about their history, cultural context, and communities, while building research–practice partnerships and discussing what research questions needed to be answered and prioritized. An outcome of the visits was the revision of the original research objective, to understand PREP's impact (*explanatory investigation*), to now include research questions that explore the social and learning experiences of PREP participants (*descriptive investigation*). A focus on recruiting underrepresented students for the research project was decided to address equity, diversity, and inclusion issues in STEM. In early Spring 2020, the research team was expanded and diversified to include two Latinas and one Black woman (three of the coauthors). One of them is a PREP alumna and a parent of two PREP participants. Together, the research team is a demographically and culturally diverse group of researchers, practitioners, and stakeholders.

STUDY DESIGN

The PREP-CRCS uses an embedded, single-case study design with culturally responsive approaches to explore underrepresented students' experiences within an OST STEM program and to examine how the program influences their STEM outcomes. Using a single-case study design is appropriate to understand how students and stakeholders from various demographic and cultural backgrounds perceive and describe contextual factors of an OST STEM program and how the program shapes students' STEM learning, motivation, and participation (Stake, 1995; Yin, 2017). A culturally responsive case study approach is particularly useful because the study aims to understand the shared experiences of students who have been underserved and minoritized in STEM education but participate in the same OST STEM program (Yin, 2017). Employing an embedded design, we can draw from multiple sources of data valued by various stakeholders—including students, parents, instructors, and program staff—across sites within the program (Yin, 2017).

SAMPLING STRATEGIES

Five PREP sites were purposefully selected for the first stage of the PREP-CRCS study. Sites were selected based on established relationships with site directors, and together represent diverse demographic, geographical, and cultural contexts of PREP across the Southwestern United States. By selecting sites with established trust between the research team and program staff, it was believed that open and forthcoming conversations among participants, practitioners, and researchers would occur. Participants were also purposefully selected. In order to understand and give voice to students who are traditionally underrepresented in STEM including women, URMs, and low-SES youth, researchers worked with site directors to recruit students who fit these characteristics. The final student sample consisted of 32 students, which included 41% girls, 79% URMs, and 25% low-SES youth (whose parents have not earned a 4-year degree). Furthermore, 16 additional stakeholders, including four parents, four instructors, four near-peer mentors (or program assistants), and four site directors, were also interviewed to supplement student data.

DATA COLLECTION

The research team traveled to each of the five selected PREP sites in early Spring 2020 to conduct in-person, semi-structured interviews and focus groups. Data collection was approved by UTSA's institutional review board and conducted with participants' and parents' informed consent. Interview questions were designed to understand experiences from each participant's perspective. We anticipated interviewing a large number of Hispanic/Latinx participants and therefore considered some participants might prefer an interview conducted in Spanish. When the interview questions were translated into Spanish, each question was vetted with a native Spanish speaker to ensure each was culturally appropriate and easily understood. In addition to interview and focus group data, various documents and artifacts were collected from across PREP sites, including curriculum materials, training documents, program reports, and video recordings of PREP activities.

DATA ANALYSIS

Two of the coauthors, who conducted the interviews and were familiar with the sites' context, conducted a thematic analysis of the focus group and interview transcript data. A deductive approach was taken to coding the data and an initial codebook was created based on a literature review of student experiences at OSTs and their influence on learning and motivation and from familiarization with the transcript data (Elo & Kyngäs, 2008). After several rounds of refining the codebook, two independent cycles of coding were undertaken using MAXQDA to reach inter-rater reliability of 0.86., after which the remaining data was coded and collapsed into key themes of students' social and learning experiences present in PREP. Particular attention was given to the perspectives and experiences of underrepresented students (i.e., girls, URMs, and low-SES youth). Further, to achieve an accurate interpretation of the data and gain feedback from program stakeholders, our research team presented preliminary findings to PREP site directors from across the country, who are familiar with the culture and context of PREP.

BRIEF SUMMARY OF FINDINGS

Comprehensive results of the PREP-CRCS are reported elsewhere (Romano et al., 2021). This section provides a summary of findings.

Enhanced STEM Human and Social Capital of Underrepresented Students

Findings indicated that underrepresented students—especially girls, URMs, and low-SES youth—described particularly positive social and learning experiences within PREP, which were not mutually exclusive. Collaboration with other students on group projects allowed them to work on "challenging yet fun" projects in STEM and to "work together to accomplish goals." Participants discussed how collaboration was helpful because many of the STEM topics were new to them, and by working together they could learn from each other. Underrepresented students also valued being a part of a supportive community with shared interests in STEM. By participating in PREP, participants expanded their social networks to include a broader array of individuals with whom they shared similar STEM interests. Many underrepresented students emphasized that they enjoyed learning with people to whom they could relate and shared that they valued the new friendships created with other individuals who also enjoy and help them in learning STEM subjects.

Equity and Inclusion: Access to Advanced Learning and Mentorship in STEM

Several program components and processes of PREP were found to influence STEM learning, motivation, and participation of underrepresented students. Analysis revealed that students in PREP have early access to advanced STEM learning which both directly ties to their schools' curricula as well as exposes them to real-world STEM knowledge they may not receive in their school setting. Mentorship was found to be an influential component of PREP. Underrepresented students described feeling supported and encouraged by peers, instructors, and program staff to persist in the program and in STEM education. Such findings corroborate those documented through online post-program survey in the summer of 2019 (Saw et al., 2020). Students felt that PREP instructors and staff were invested in their learning and pushed them to excel in STEM. PREP near peer mentors, who were college students, also served as "role models in STEM" and as easily approachable adults who could help with content understanding and provide advice on learning and college transitions in STEM fields.

CHALLENGES AND CHANGES

Identifying (Understanding) Marginalized Minority Populations

To design a case study that is responsive to cultural context, one important preparation step is to understand the characteristics of the populations involved in the study. In an early phase of the PREP-CRCS, an online survey was administered to the participants across all PREP sites in Summer 2019 to identify underrepresented students in STEM, including those who are women, gender minorities (e.g., transgender, gender non-confirming), URMs, low-SES youth, and undocumented students. However, given the political climates in the Southwestern United States, where transgender and immigration issues are controversial among local community members, some related demographic items were excluded from the questionnaire for several PREP sites. Omitting these items limited the ability to identify and thus understand the experiences of gender minorities and undocumented students who have been underserved and marginalized in STEM education. As a result, focus was placed on girls, URMs, and low-SES youth—the three "popular" underrepresented groups in STEM—in the first phase of our PREP-CRCS.

Recruiting Hard-to-Reach Low-SES Participants

Effective recruitment of participants with relevant backgrounds is essential to the overall success of a case study. While the gender and racial/ethnic composition of the students interviewed in this CRCS reflect PREP's overall population, recruiting students from low-SES families was a major challenge (though it is not unique in research studies; Mendelson et al., 2021). Most of the students interviewed (62.5%) had at least one parent who earned a 4-year college degree or above (considered as middle and upper SES), whereas only a quarter of the students interviewed had parents who had never earned a 4-year degree (considered as low-SES; 12.5% reported being unsure about their parental education level). In the PREP-CRCS, recruiting participants was done by the individual site directors. It was observed that those who used email for recruitment received more responses from high-SES participants, whereas those who reached out to participants directly were able to target and successfully recruit low-SES students. Furthermore, during the COVID-19 pandemic, the enrollment number of low-SES students in online PREP program across sites disproportionately decreased. This difference in participation reflects the difficulty of accessing OST STEM programs for students from low-SES households, which imposes more challenges for researchers to reach and engage socioeconomically disadvantaged students in the time of crisis.

LESSONS LEARNED AND RECOMMENDATIONS

In this final section, lessons learned from the PREP-CRCS are discussed and recommendations are offered to researchers who conduct case studies involving diverse and underserved communities.

From, By, and For Diverse Communities

Studying a culturally diverse community, like PREP, requires a culturally diverse research team. In building a CRCS research team, the principal investigator (the first author) carefully considered and recruited trained researchers from diverse backgrounds. The research team, which includes PREP alumna and program staff, was culturally diverse and representative of the PREP community in terms of gender, race/ethnicity, SES, immigration generation, languages, and regions of upbringing. Such diverse lived and cultural experiences of the research team members propelled close work with PREP stakeholders in facilitating the design and implementation of PREP-CRCS and to connect with interview participants by sharing experiences during formal and informal interactions. During the PREP-CRCS interviews and focus groups, participants were willing, open, and, at times, excited to share and discuss their experiences and perspectives of the program, which yielded invaluable data for answering the research questions and for informing the improvement of program, particularly in addressing the needs of underrepresented students in STEM. From our CRCS experience, we recommend researchers invest time and resources in forming mutually trusting and respectful relationships with participants and communities, which will lay a strong foundation for designing and conducting CRCS research.

Critically Examining Researchers' Own Cultural Positionalities/Biases

Working in a socially and culturally diverse team/community provides constant opportunities for discussions and debates with individuals from different backgrounds which challenge researchers to be cognizant of their own positionalities and biases. During the PREP-CRCS experience, each research team member appreciated the formal and informal conversations had during work meetings and travels that prompted each to critically examine their own social and cultural positions and biases, especially in relation to the issues associated with underrepresented students in STEM. For example, how participants from diverse and underserved groups perceive and define "learning" or "STEM diversity" may be different from that of researchers. It is important for researchers to refrain from imposing their own definitions on participants, which violates the fundamental principle of culturally responsive approach. From our CRCS experience, we recommend researchers continuously and critically reflect on their own social and cultural positionalities with respect to participants and communities, and the influence of their own values and biases in the CRCS process.

Inclusion of Multiple Stakeholder Perspectives Throughout the CRCS

One key success factor of our PREP-CRCS is engaging stakeholders from different status and cultural positions in every study phase, including research questions development/prioritization, study design, instrument development, data collection and analysis, and results interpretation. During the PREP-CRCS experience, the constant input of cultural and contextual knowledge from multiple stakeholder perspectives helps to promptly adjust study strategies in response to the needs of participants and communities, avoiding major clashes or conflicts that could impede the study progress and long-term relationship building. From our CRCS experience, we recommend researchers working with diverse and underserved communities engage stakeholders with different status and cultural positions over the course of a CRCS to ensure the study design, implementation, and interpretation are responsive and responsible to the culture and context. This recommendation is even more pertinent in times of crisis and constant change, such as the COVID-19 pandemic.

ACKNOWLEDGMENTS

We thank all PREP community members who made this study possible. This article is based on work supported by the National Science Foundation (grants: DRL-2113395, SMA-2221994, SMA-2221995, SMA-2221996).

REFERENCES

Afterschool Alliance. (2014). *America after3pm: Afterschool programs in demand.* https://www.wallacefoundation.org/knowledge-center/documents/America-After-3PM-Afterschool-Programs-in-Demand.pdf

Elo, S., & Kyngäs, H. (2008). The qualitative content analysis process. *Journal of advanced nursing, 62*(1), 107–115. https://doi.org/10.1111/j.1365-2648.2007.04569.x

Frierson, H. T., Hood, S., & Hughes, G. B. (2002). Strategies that address culturally responsive evaluation. In J. F. Westat (Ed.), *The 2002 user friendly handbook for project evaluation* (pp. 63–73). National Science Foundation.

Hood, S., Hopson, R., & Kirkhart, K. (2015). Culturally responsive evaluation: Theory, practice, and future. In K. Newcomer, H. Hatry, & J. Wholey (Eds.), *Handbook of practical program evaluation* (4th ed.; pp. 281–317). Wiley.

Hopson, R. K. (2009). Reclaiming knowledge at the margins culturally responsive evaluation in the current evaluation moment. In K. Ryan & B. Cousins (Eds.), *International handbook of educational evaluation* (pp. 429–446). SAGE Publications.

Mendelson, T., Sheridan, S. C., & Clary, L. K. (2021). Research with youth of color in low-income communities: Strategies for recruiting and retaining participants. *Research in Social and Administrative Pharmacy, 17*(6), 1110–1118.

National Research Council. (2015). *Identifying and supporting productive STEM programs in out-of-school settings.* National Academies Press.

National Science Foundation. (2019). *Women, minorities, and persons with disabilities in science and engineering: 2019* (Special Report NSF 19-304). National Center for Science and Engineering Statistics.

Romano, K., Saw, G. K., & Culbertson, R. (2021). *Enhancing adolescents' human and social capital in STEM: Evidence from the prefreshman engineering program (PREP).* University of Texas at San Antonio.

Santamaría, L. J. (2014). Critical change for the greater good: Multicultural dimensions of educational leadership toward social justice and educational equity. *Education Administration Quarterly, 50*(3), 347–391. https://doi.org/ 10.1177/0013161X13505287

Saw, G. K., & Agger, C. A. (2021). STEM pathways of rural and small-town students: Opportunities to learn, aspirations, preparation, and college enrollment. *Educational Researcher, 50*(9), 595–606. https://doi.org/10.3102/0013 189X211027528

Saw, G. K., Chang, C.-N., & Chan, H.-Y. (2018). Cross-sectional and longitudinal disparities in STEM career aspirations at the intersection of gender, race/ ethnicity, and socioeconomic status. *Educational Researcher, 47*(8), 525–532. https://doi.org/10.3102/0013189X18787818

Saw, G. K., Romano, K., & Culbertson, R. (2020). *Increased STEM inclusion and career interest among racial/ethnic minorities and low-income students in the prefreshman engineering program (PREP).* University of Texas at San Antonio.

Saw, G. K., Swagerty, B., Brewington, S., Chang, C.-N., & Culbertson, R. (2019). Out-of-school time STEM program: Students' attitudes toward and career interests in mathematics and science. *International Journal of Evaluation and Research in Education, 8*(2), 356–362. http://doi.org/10.11591/ijere.v8i2.18702

Stake, R. E. (1995). *The art of case study research.* SAGE Publications.

Yamamoto, K. K., Black, R. S., & Yuen, J. A. W. (2017). Lessons learned from a culturally responsive case study approach. *International Journal of Learning and Development, 7*(3), 210–228. https://doi.org/10.5296/ijld.v7i3.11716

Yin, R. K. (2017). *Case study research and applications: Design and methods* (6th ed.). SAGE Publications.

INTRODUCTION TO CASE STUDY 3

This case study explores the widely debated issue of police reform through the prism of George Floyd's preventable death at the hands of a Minneapolis police officer, which is exemplary for academics interested in community policing and police reform. The methods for recruiting individuals, gathering data, analyzing that data, and interpreting the results are valuable to researchers who are considering similar research that challenges the status quo. The population of interest includes representation of women and racial and ethnic minorities. This study pushes for appeals to realize the significance of reestablishing trust within the communities they serve and undertaking the mission of policies with accountability, respect, dignity, and policing that restores legitimacy. In a field where white men dominate, the researchers believed that the problem was the scarce representation of women in the executive branches, which included a lack of opportunities for advancement, acrimony from male officers, and a dearth of female mentors. It is important to consider nontraditional approaches to data collection when attempting to reach groups that are traditionally difficult to connect. To secure the population of interest, the researchers attended and publicly announced their intent at specific law enforcement conferences, outreach on a social media platform named LinkedIn, which is a professional engagement network, sent private messages to potential participants, and made contact with male chiefs of police and others who had familiarity with their research as part of their recruitment process. Another note is the uniqueness of this research is that the authors' combined grounded theory to explore the impact of the systemic design and situational analysis to understand the topic's dense complexity.

Qualitative Research With Diverse and Underserved Communities, pages 93–109

CASE STUDY 3

WOMEN AT THE TOP IN POLICING

Centering Their Voices Through Grounded Theory and Situational Analysis Methodologies

Nicola Smith-Kea
Antioch University

Elizabeth L. Holloway
Antioch University

As we experience the current civil unrest sweeping the United States after the avoidable death of George Floyd under the knee of a Minneapolis officer; there is a sense of urgency, and a call for major reform in policing. We now hear the constant refrain that "the time is ripe for change in policing," with significant attention being paid not only on what police do, but also on who police are. Advocates and researchers alike are now challenging the status quo, looking more closely at what they consider in recruitment, what

Qualitative Research With Diverse and Underserved Communities, pages 95–109
Copyright © 2024 by Information Age Publishing
www.infoagepub.com
All rights of reproduction in any form reserved.

they value in promotion, and what is essential for fair and effective policing. At a time when there is severe underrepresentation of women and racial and ethnic minorities, there is a mandate for increased diversity. Policing leaders are being asked to lead with dignity and respect, restore legitimacy and accountability, with appeals to recognize the importance of rebuilding trust within the communities they serve. This can only be achieved by changing their way of operation, by changing the way they look and lead, and by encouraging more diversity throughout the rank and file and leadership. This study was designed to probe deeply into the professional lives of women who had made it to top ranks of policing to understand their rise and the systems of power that marked their journeys.

Women police are an underrepresented and marginalized group, particularly at the executive level. In this study, we sought to pivot the dominant narrative and put this diverse group of women at the center, highlighting their agency and acknowledging their experience of a system that has never welcomed them. We will discuss our research approach to the overarching research question: What is the experience of women who have reached top executive leadership positions in policing in the United States?

THE PROBLEM: LOW FEMALE REPRESENTATION IN POLICING

For more than 25 years, female representation across the nation's approximately 18,000 law enforcement agencies has remained stuck around 12.5% (Federal Bureau of Investigation, 2018); with women merely 3% of top executives (Reaves, 2015). There is considerable research on the challenges and barriers women face in this white, male-dominated profession, including, lack of opportunity for promotional advancement; resistance and hostility from male officers and supervisors; and a paucity of women mentors. These circumstances lead to few women being promoted into positions of authority (Gau et al., 2013; Guajardo, 2016; Holdaway & Parker, 1998; Irving, 2009; Morash & Haarr, 2011; Yu, 2015). However, research has shown that women officers are less likely to be named in lawsuits or citizen complaints, are less likely to use force or to be accused of excessive force (Lonsway, 2008), and are more successful in defusing violent or aggressive behavior, overall (Rabe-Hemp & Schuck, 2007). Although having more women in the profession can make a positive difference, efforts to increase women in policing must ensure not only an expansion in numbers but a sufficient pipeline with equitable opportunities to impact leadership at the top (Smith-Kea, 2020).

METHODOLOGIES OF CHOICE

To understand the women's journeys of achievement we felt it essential to embrace their experience at the interactional (micro), organizational (meso), and socio-cultural (macro) levels. With the aim of understanding the full contextual experience, we applied a methodological approach that integrated the findings of grounded theory ([GT]; Charmaz, 2014; Glaser & Strauss, 1967) and situational analysis ([SA]; Clarke, 2006).

We wanted to understand the individual experience within the context of the policing system; this avoided problematizing women for the lack of representation and maximized the opportunity to understand the systemic issues that situate their experiences, that is, the complex interaction of political, social, economic, cultural, and institutional forces of policing (Burke, 2011; Maguire, 2003).

Grounded theory can be especially advantageous when exploring marginalized perspectives on familiar settings that have largely been defined by the dominant group (Holloway & Schwartz, 2018). However, because policing is deeply embedded in intersecting systems in our society and GT does not fully explore the perceived dynamic nature and influence of these systems on everyday social encounters, we chose to add Clarke's (2006) SA to understand the dense complexity of context (Clarke et al., 2018). Situational analysis embraces a critical social justice edge, having deep feminist and antiracist roots (Clarke, 2006, 2008, 2015). It intentionally looks at both human as well as nonhuman and discursive elements. Data collection includes different types of discourse materials, such as policy and procedure documents, images, artifacts, and so forth. Situational analysis of organizational and societal experience begins with cartographic representations of major elements that emerge from the different discourses in the environment as well as the distribution and withholding of power (Clarke et al., 2018); a process that is particularly relevant to "understanding the intersection of macro institutional structures and the marginalization and exclusion of individuals and groups" (Holloway & Schwartz, 2018, p. 43).

DATA COLLECTION PROCESS

We sought a purposeful sample of women policing executives, aimed at getting insight about the phenomenon of interest and not empirical generalization from a sample to a population (Patton, 2002). With no locatable comprehensive list of women police executives, the first author used her network of connections to invite participants that would meet our inclusion criteria:

- Female;
- over the age of 20 years old;
- must be or have been in an executive leadership position in a local police department, a municipal police department, or a university police department; and
- must be or have been a deputy chief, assistant chief, chief of police, deputy commissioner, or commissioner of police.

Recruitment included: (a) attending major law enforcement conferences and making public announcements during relevant sessions, (b) outreach on LinkedIn (the professional engagement network) and through private messages sent to potential participants, and (c) making connections through male chiefs of police and others who had familiarity with our research. This resulted in a list of 40 potential participants, which was reduced by using a maximal variation technique (Creswell & Clark, 2011), that resulted in a diverse set of 21 participants across race, ethnicity, sexual orientation, age, educational attainment, and geographic location. For the SA, our sample included both men and women of diverse demographic characteristics, that would speak to the cultural, organizational, and structural forces that were identified by our women executive participants as instrumental in their career attainment. This diverse sample allowed for the triangulation of individual perspectives and systemic attributes embedded in policing.

With the list of study participants finalized, the first author began in-person interviews. For SA data gathering, on-site interviews allowed us to see imagery within the department; and more specifically to see the physical space in which they worked, the details of that space, the way they expressed their own journey through images, the relationship with staff and response from staff, and most importantly their expression and movement during the conversation. The nonverbal response was equally important in understanding their journey. What made them pause, smile, laugh, or cry? How did they relate to the first author, as a black female who was not within or a part of the profession? One participant, for instance, spoke with pride about being asked to sing the national anthem at a major event which included President Bill Clinton. As she spoke, she looked at the image that was positioned in a space you immediately saw when you entered her office. The placement showed the importance placed on that significant recognition of her career attainment.

Unfortunately, we had to change to virtual meetings halfway through interviewing, because it became increasingly costly to travel to the numerous locations across the United States, only to be told minutes before the scheduled interview, that the chief was no longer available because she had to tend to an unexpected matter. We quickly pivoted to videoconferencing and attempted to draw out as much depth and richness as was possible given the virtual medium.

DATA ANALYSIS PROCESS

Data was reviewed and organized for analysis using all elements of the GT approach including, a coding team, memoing, constant comparison, and dimensional analysis and theorizing (see Figure 3.1); and complemented by the SA mapping process (see original map Figure 3.3). Given the diverse and large volumes of data collected, NVivo, a qualitative data analysis computer software package by QSR International, was used for data organization.

Coding

We engaged in a process of *constant comparison*, to help generate categories during focused coding, by taking one piece of datum and examining it against another in order to determine if the two are conceptually the same or different (Corbin & Strauss, 2015). This allowed us to engage in *initial*

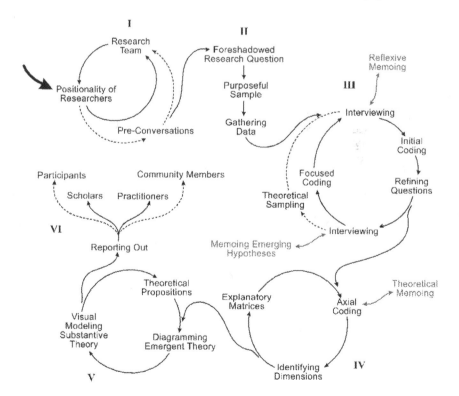

Figure3.1 Phases of grounded theory research process (Holloway & Schwartz, 2018, p. 675). *Note:* Used with permission.

and *focused coding* as depicted in area III of Figure 3.1. The order in which the initial set of interviews were coded was also important to ensure we had diverse representation across the conceptual categories that were being formed. This was critical, so that the narrative of the dominant culture did not monopolize the conceptual understanding during initial coding. This process was enriched using a coding team with different cultural and discipline perspectives to enhance trustworthiness, an important criterion for rigor in qualitative research. The team met to review individual's coding process, to compare and discuss codes used, to review initial code book and emerging themes, and to clarify any major inconsistencies that surfaced.

The next step involved the identification of primary conceptual dimensions and placing those dimensions within the structure of explanatory matrices (see area IV of Figure 3.1). This is a central organizing feature within GT that on the micro-level, social processes of everyday life, the conditions under which they transpired, and the perceived consequences of these occurrences (Kools et al., 1996). Although in GT larger contextual variables are identified as relatively static factors (Clarke, 2006), in which human interactions take place, SA uncovers a more dynamic and multidimensional context, thus mapping meso and macro level factors that appeared to be critical influences.

Memo-Writing

Analytic memo-writing, an exercise of documenting thoughts, ideas, issues, and experiences with the data and defining categories, was done throughout the analytic process. Note in Figure 3.1 that memos serve different purposes at various stages of the analysis (see Figure 3.1 reflexive, emerging hypotheses, and theoretical in areas III & IV). Memos were critical in identifying those elements that would be investigated in the SA mapping process.

Explanatory Matrices

Arriving at the core dimension, which is a unifying concept that relate to all the primary dimensions (Kools et al., 1996), was time consuming and difficult as we explored numerous iterations of potential models. We had to ensure that the concept selected was sufficiently broad yet remained at the heart of the social processes that flowed through these women's lives, ultimately, we chose the core dimension of *wanting change*. In Figure 3.2 we represent it as a band that influences all primary dimensions—*being visible*,

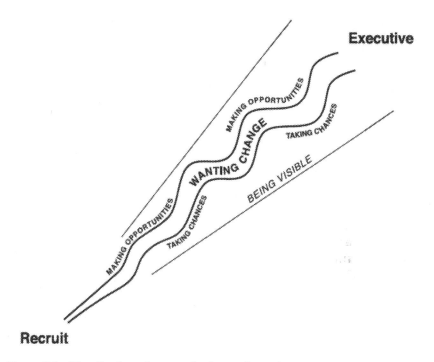

Figure 3.2 Visualization of core and primary dimensions.

making opportunities, and taking chances—as the women move from recruit to executive.

The explanatory matrix, considered the cornerstone of the GT dimensional analysis, flowed from the core dimension and included three primary dimensions. This conceptual structure moved us beyond the primary conceptual modeling and led to understanding the conditions of occurrence and the consequences of these processes, as well as describing in rich detail their properties (see Table 3.1).

The Situational Analysis Process

Situational analysis was used to construct the "situation." Situations emerged from the in-depth interviews and were those the participants considered significant to their experience. Other situations were selected from the analysis of discourses collected through ethnographic observations made during visits to departments and museums, as well as imagery, documents, websites, social media postings, written news articles, and other relevant sources.

TABLE 3.1   Explanatory Matrix for Understanding the Journey of Women Reaching the Top

Dimensions	Properties		
	Conditions	Processes	Consequences
Wanting Change (Core Dimension)	• Need for change in the profession • Strained police-community relations • Palpable atmosphere of discrimination and harassment • Legitimate power	• Being self-aware • Learning to lead • Having a higher purpose • Doing it for the right reason	• Moving up the ranks • Recruited or assigned to higher position • Women brought in to clean up stuff • Different type of leadership • Greater commitment to service • Self-actualization
Being Visible	• Diversity of experiences • Exposure and engagement opportunities	• Being heard • Intentionally showing up • Being at the table and having a voice • Saving a seat for a sister	• Discriminated against and harassed • Pigeonholed • Supported • Shoulder tapped to advance career
Making Opportunities	• Other avenues for career development • Special assignments	• Being flexible • Collaborating • Being supportive	• Well-rounded career • Visibility • Negative impact on family
Taking Chances	• Progressive leadership • Changing environment	• Being strategic • Being courageous • Having grit and determination	• Recognition • Gender role perceptions

At this stage, we began to develop messy maps (Clarke, 2006) of the discourse materials and ethnographic representations that we had catalogued. The messy map was the beginning of conceptualizing the larger terrain of policing and the space that women executives held within it (see Figure 3.3). We reconceptualized numerous times as we considered new information that emerged, and in some situations, various elements initially considered germane lost their significance as the research progressed. Ultimately, through this conceptual refinement process we created an ordered map which allowed us to examine the fullness of their situation more critically and systematically.

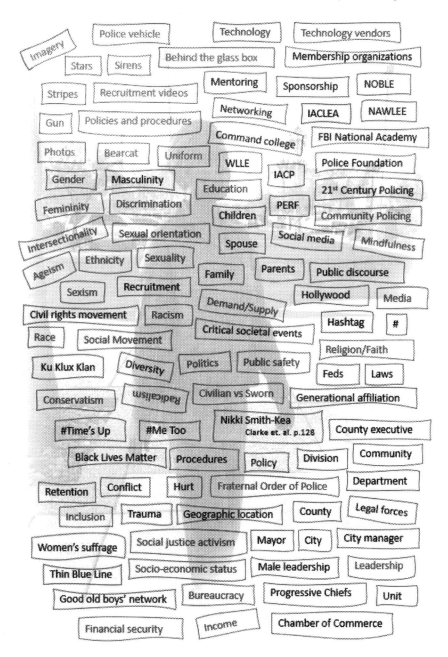

Figure 3.3 Abstract situational map: Messy map showing contextual factors.

Next, we tackled the development of social worlds/arenas maps, as depicted in Figure 3.4. This map illuminated the power dynamics constructed from the participants' interviews and multiplicity of data sources. It was critical in recognizing the relationships among the policing, political, economic, and sociocultural arenas. Each of these broader forces is made up of smaller arenas that overlap and intersect. The relationships are reflected by placement and size of the circles and lays out all of the major groups,

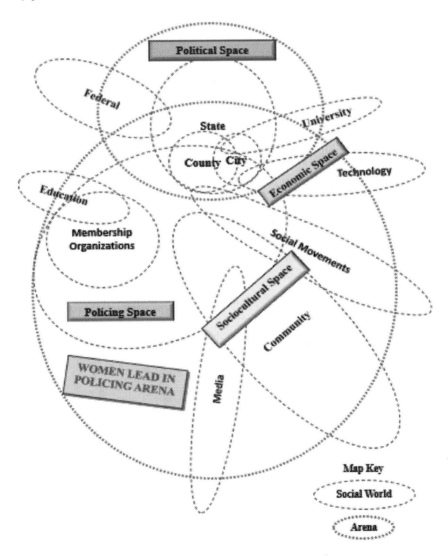

Figure 3.4 Social worlds/arena(s) map of women leading in policing arena.

organizations, institutions, and other collective actors that emerged as key forces in the *Women Lead in Policing Arena*. It was from this mapping that a heuristic model of the women's journey emerged.

THE THEORETICAL MODEL: A WEB OF INTERSECTIONS

Visual representation of conceptual discoveries is not uncommon in GT (Holloway & Schwartz, 2018). Our challenge was to visualize a model that both merged and transformed the findings from both analytical tools—GT and SA—and showed the layers of conditions at the micro, meso, and macro levels within the policing situation as a whole. In Figure 3.5 both the analysis from the participants' lived experiences, the core dimension, and primary dimensions—*wanting change, being visible, making opportunities*, and *taking chances*—which all played a critical role in the women's achievements, and the SA that unearthed four interrelated domains of influence—*policing, political, economic,* and *sociocultural spaces*—deepened understanding of

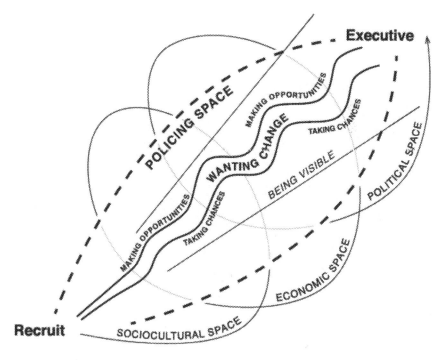

Figure 3.5 Web of Intersections: Visual Representation of both Grounded Theory and Situational Analysis Findings

the discourses that are prevalent in the lives of women police at the top of their profession.

The *Web of Intersections* is the larger construct that describes these women's passages and speaks to the challenges of understanding a world that has never embraced them. The model suggests a dynamic labyrinth with challenges both from inside and outside of the department. The model represents their "lived" intersectionality (Hankivsky, 2014; Shields, 2008) and it promotes an understanding of these women navigating an unashamedly "male" space layered by a ubiquitous White culture.

THEORETICAL PROPOSITIONS

A distinctive feature of GT is the opportunity to create "middle-range" theory (Glaser & Strauss, 1967) or theoretical propositions that provide a roadmap for future research and practice. The purpose is to drive research and practice from "the ground up," that is, to influence understanding of others by the experiences of those groups that have lived, and in our case thrived in the situation of policing. Three theoretical propositions present an explanation that these women are not simply being acted upon, but rather, they are acting as agentic and intentional participants in their journey.

Proposition 1

Women make the decision to advance to top executive positions because they want change inside and outside of the profession, with their journey and positioning not just being happenstance, but calculated and intentional, showing a great deal of agency.

Proposition 2

Women are self-aware and intentionally practice self-leadership, all while recognizing and learning the importance of deliberately making themselves visible as they make the choice to move towards top executive positions.

Proposition 3

No matter the form, support is important for advancement to executive position for women, with different supports playing a different role at different times in their journey.

CONCLUSION

Throughout this journey, one of the complexities we faced was the need to constantly move between and among larger contexts and human experiences that forced us to operate in a space of foreground and background, making meaning of the situation. We would recommend that any researcher who is interested in understanding the different levels across which their participants operate should consider utilizing GT in combination with SA. This combination made vivid and more concrete, the life trajectory and the situational elements that shaped the journey of these women.

As qualitative researchers, we should:

1. Ensure we select an appropriate methodology to aptly articulate the complexity of our participants' experiences, providing a more comprehensive understanding of their navigation and thinking throughout their journey.
2. Strive for a co-creation of theory which will only arise from the stories of real people, living real experiences, recounting as best they can. This is coupled with the researchers' understanding and articulated as best to represent the participants' journey as situated in a wider reality that also has significant impact on this journey.
3. Recognize that type of analysis which relates to culture, context, and time, constructs or reconstructs both the participants' and the researcher's way of thinking.
4. Understand that the results of analysis represent the researcher's interpretive understanding, rather than the researcher's explanation, of how the participants create their understanding and meaning of reality (see Hallberg, 2006).

This article is intended to help the reader understand the iterative processes involved in using this combination of methodologies that piloted this exploration and led to an articulation of the micro, meso, and macro forces that explain the many ways these women survived and thrived. The SA was particularly important to capture the changing situations in policing through the various iterations of the mapping process, clarifying the context and the power dynamics that existed. There is room for more of these distinct yet compatible methods working together to bring situational understanding as well as the lived experience of the underrepresented and marginalized to the center.

AUTHOR NOTE

This chapter is based on the first author's dissertation—*Saving a Seat for a Sister: A Grounded Theory Approach Exploring the Journey of Women Reaching Top Policing Executive Positions*, https://aura.antioch.edu/etds/609—and supervised by the second author. Correspondence concerning this chapter should be addressed to Nicola Smith-Kea, nsmithkea@antioch.edu

REFERENCES

Burke, W. (2011). A perspective on the field of organization development and change: The Zeigarnik effect. *Journal of Applied Behavioral Science, 47*(2), 143–167. https://doi.org/10.1177/0021886310388161

Charmaz, K. (2014). *Constructing grounded theory* (2nd ed.). SAGE Publications.

Clarke, A. E. (2006). Feminisms, grounded theory, and situational analysis. In S. Hesse-Biber (Ed.), *Handbook of feminist research: Theory and praxis* (pp. 345–370). SAGE Publications.

Clarke, A. E. (2008). Sex/gender and race/ethnicity in the legacy of Anselm Strauss. In N. K. Denzin, J. Salvo, & M. Washington (Eds.), *Studies in symbolic interactionism* (pp. 161–176). Emerald. https://doi.org/10.1016/S0163-2396(08)32012-2

Clarke, A. E. (2015). Feminisms, grounded theory, and situational analysis revisited. In A. E. Clarke, C. Friese, & R. Washburn (Eds.), *Situational analysis in practice: Mapping research with grounded theory* (pp. 119–154). Routledge.

Clarke, A. E., Friese, C., & Washburn, R. S. (2018). *Situational analysis: Grounded theory after the interpretative turn* (2nd ed.). SAGE Publications.

Corbin, J., & Strauss, A. (2015). *Basics of qualitative research: Techniques and procedures for developing grounded theory* (4th ed.). SAGE Publications.

Creswell, J., & Clark, V. (2011). *Designing and conducting mixed methods research.* SAGE Publications.

Federal Bureau of Investigation. (2018). 2017 *Crime in the United States.* https://ucr.fbi.gov/crime-in-the-u.s/2017/crime-in-the-u.s.-2017/tables/table-74

Gau, J. M., Terrill, W., & Paoline, E. A., III. (2013). Looking up: Explaining police promotional aspirations. *Criminal Justice & Behavior, 40*(3), 247–269. https://doi.org/10.1177/0093854812458426

Glaser, B., & Strauss, A. (1967). *The discovery of grounded theory: Strategies for qualitative research.* Aldine de Gruyter.

Guajardo, S. (2016). Women in policing: A longitudinal assessment of female officers in supervisory positions in the New York City Police Department. *Women & Criminal Justice, 26*(1), 20–36. https://doi.org/10.1080/08974454.2014.997418

Hallberg, L. R.-M. (2006). The "core category" of grounded theory: Making constant comparisons. *International Journal of Qualitative Studies on Health & Wellbeing, 1*(3), 141–148. https://doi.org/10.1080/17482620600858399

Hankivsky, E. (2014, April). *Intersectionality 101.* The Institute for Intersectionality Research and Policy, Simon Fraser University. https://resources.equity

initiative.org/bitstream/handle/ei/433/2014%20Hankivsky%20Intersection
allity%20101.pdf?sequence=1

Holdaway, S., & Parker, S. (1998). Policing women police: Uniform, patrol, promotion and representation in the CID. *British Journal of Criminology, 38*(1),
40–60. https://doi.org/10.1093/oxfordjournals.bjc.a014227

Holloway, E. L., & Schwartz, H. (2018). Drawing from the margins: Grounded theory research design and EDI Studies. In L. A. E. Booysen, R. Bendl, & J. K.
Pringle (Eds.), *Handbook of research methods in diversity management, equality and
inclusion at work* (pp. 497–528). Edward Elgar.

Irving, R. (2009). Career trajectories of women in policing in Australia. *Trends
& Issues in Crime & Criminal Justice,* (370), 1–6. https://www.aic.gov.au/
publications/tandi/tandi370

Kools, S., McCarthy, M., Durham, R., & Robrecht, L. (1996). Dimensional analysis:
Broadening the conception of grounded theory. *Qualitative Health Research,
6*(3), 312–330. https://doi.org/10.1177/104973239600600302

Lonsway, K. (2008). Are we there yet? The progress of women in one large law enforcement agency. *Women & Criminal Justice, 18*(1/2), 1–48. https://doi.org/
10.1300/j012v18n01_01

Maguire, E. (2003). *Organizational structure in American police agencies: Context, complexity and control.* State University of New York Press.

Morash, M., & Haarr, R. (2011). Doing, redoing, and undoing gender: Variation in
gender identities of women working as police officers. *Feminist Criminology,
7*(1), 3–23. https://doi.org/10.1177/1557085111413253

Patton, M. (2002). *Qualitative research & evaluation methods.* SAGE Publications.

Rabe-Hemp, C. E., & Schuck, A. M. (2007). Violence against police officers: Are female
officers at greater risk? *Police Quarterly, 10*(4), 411–428. https://doi.org/10
.1177/1098611107304326

Reaves, B. (2015, May). *Local police departments, 2013: Personnel, policies and practices.*
U.S. Department of Justice, Bureau of Justice Statistics. https://www.bjs.gov/
content/pub/pdf/lpd13ppp.pdf

Shields, S. A. (2008). Gender: An intersectionality perspective. *Sex Roles, 59*(5/6),
301–311. https://doi.org/10.1007/s11199-008-9501-8

Smith-Kea, N. (2020, September 2). *Why the gender gap in policing is a public safety
crisis.* The Crime Report. https://thecrimereport.org/2020/09/02/why-the
-gender-gap-in-policing-is-a-public-safety-crisis/

Yu, H. (2015). An examination of women in federal law enforcement: An exploratory analysis of the challenges they face in the work environment. *Feminist
Criminology, 10*(3), 259–278. https://doi.org/10.1177/1557085114545824

INTRODUCTION TO CASE STUDY 4

The authors used a unique data collection method, the photo voice technique, which is often used with the intent of a social change to respond to the research questions in this case study. Data was collected from the "resident experts" in three parts: photographs, in-depth group discussion, and collaborative analysis of 20 Black/African American middle school students guided by faculty mentors and pre-licensure nursing students as they conducted a community assessment of heart health. The authors found that social and environmental factors were significant causes of heart disease and the dangers that go along with it. To comprehend the links between the social environment and heart health, the authors determined that addressing social determinants of health was crucial. The capacity of this study highlights healthy practices and educates populations in harm's way. This unique population included middle school students who were members of an organization that promotes social change and provides opportunities for youth from under sourced communities. And the application of participatory action research enhanced their collaborations to understand the issue of one of many health factors, such as heart disease while paving the way to take action to bring about social change. The researchers' method of data analysis is exemplary, using the acronym SHOWED, which stands for See, Happening, cOmmunity, Why, Educate, and Do. This type of analysis can be earmarked for various community participatory action research projects that recognize and include individuals whose shared experiences contribute to the understanding and appreciating health and environmental issues.

Qualitative Research With Diverse and Underserved Communities, pages 111–121
Copyright © 2024 by Information Age Publishing
www.infoagepub.com
111

CASE STUDY 4

THE SOCIAL DETERMINANTS OF A HEART HEALTHY COMMUNITY

A Participatory Action Research Project

Adriana Glenn
George Washington University

Sandra Davis
George Washington University

Karen Dawn
George Washington University

CONTEXT

Social determinants of health (SDH) are the conditions in which people are born, grow, live, work and age. The relationship between social conditions, environmental factors, and health has been known for centuries. However, until recently, serious attention had not been given to the importance of

Qualitative Research With Diverse and Underserved Communities, pages 113–121
Copyright © 2024 by Information Age Publishing
www.infoagepub.com
All rights of reproduction in any form reserved.

social determinants in shaping health, healthcare, and health outcomes. The increasing focus on health disparities has triggered renewed interest in SDH. Over the past 20 years, it has become evident targeting individual behaviors does not significantly increase overall health and medical care. Additionally, focusing on an individual's behaviors does not adequately reduce health disparities. Social and environmental factors such as education, housing, neighborhoods, family, income and race all matter in the context of health, healthcare, and health outcomes.

In the United States, heart disease is the leading cause of death, affecting over 18 million adults (Centers for Disease Control [CDC], n.d.). Social and environmental factors affect heart disease and its risk factors. Underserved and underrepresented groups, especially Blacks/African Americans suffer a disproportion and burden of heart disease (Heron, 2019). One of the nation's cities with a large Black/African American population is Washington, District of Columbia (DC). Washington DC is one of the poorest cities in the United States and has one of the highest avoidable death rates from heart disease of all major U.S. cities (American Heart Association [AHA], n.d.). An adjacent Washington, DC area, Prince George's (PG) County, Maryland is another area with a sizeable Black/African American population suffering from poor outcomes.

The health outcomes in the situated communities of PG County, Maryland, and Washington, DC are ranked lower than the United States as a whole. Some of the notable examples of poor health outcomes in PG County include: rates of diabetes, access to health care providers, obesity/overweight and stroke. Health data for PG County shows diabetes rates at 13.9% compared to Maryland (11.1%) and the United States (10.9%); the numbers of PG County residents who can afford a healthcare visit is 15.2%, compared to Maryland (11.9%); adults who are overweight or obese are 71.3% compared to Maryland (66.2%) and the United States (65.8%; Community Health Dashboards, 2018) and the age-adjusted death rate due to stroke is 44/100,000 compared to Maryland 40/100,000 and US 37.3/100.000 (CDC, n.d.). In Washington, DC, similar disparities can be seen in wards where the study participants reside. Washington, DC has the 7th highest death rate from cardiovascular disease in the country (AHA, n.d.). Washington, DC's food insecurity prevalence includes 36,000 households (11.4% of residents), and in low-income households, 13% are food insecure (DC Health, n.d.). These communities also suffer from lower health literacy scores, with over 50% challenged with interpreting health information (National Health Literacy Mapping, n.d.).

CONDITIONS

The Washington, DC area is home to many under-resourced communities and these communities have a high percentage of Black/African American residents, lower income, and other social determinants impacting health. This project focused on enlisting middle school students in two of the communities where the risk for heart disease, and obesity is five percentage points higher compared to surrounding jurisdictions (AHA, n.d.; DC Health, n.d.). The overall purpose of this study was to engage middle school students in an interdisciplinary collaborative project to identify and address the facilitators and barriers to heart healthy communities in the Washington, DC area. Using a participatory action approach, the following goals were critical to the development of the participatory action approach:

Goal 1: Discuss heart disease, heart prevention & recognition, identification of risk factors for heart disease and creation of awareness of the disproportionate burden of heart disease on Blacks/African Americans and under-resourced communities on a local, national, and international level.

Goal 2: Describe SDH and their impact on health and the risk factors for heart disease.

Goal 3: Conduct a community assessment using Photovoice.

Goal 4: Using emerged themes from the Photovoice activity, students would explore the connection between health and the environment.

Goals 5: Development of a policy brief framing SDH issues and culminating in a presentation to Washington, DC policy makers, health care providers and community leaders.

Goal 6: Facilitate the presentation of students' photographs and policy briefs to legislators, public health officials, health care providers, and community members through presentation at schools, churches, and health fairs, a day on Capitol Hill and a public gallery exhibit.

RATIONALE

The selection and inclusion of middle school students from under-resourced communities was vital to the project as we sought to educate and empower a population that is often overlooked. Middle school youth are young, impressionable, and enthusiastic yet, mature enough to follow directions and think deeply when provided with education and guidance. It is clear from the research on SDH it is important to create awareness as early as possible to affect change and reduce health disparities (Huang et al., 2013).

METHODOLOGY

Participatory action research, specifically photovoice, was used to answer the research questions in this study. Photovoice is an approach integrating photography with critical discussion to examine issues from the perspective of "resident experts," the people who live, work, go to school, play, and pray in the community being examined (Haque & Eng, 2011). This methodology was chosen by the researchers as the most effective way to engage the middle school students in learning about heart health while simultaneously participating in a research process. We wanted to educate the middle school students about heart disease and SDH but, more importantly, we wanted to teach the students how to develop their voices and initiate action needed for change via knowledge, assessment, data collection, analysis, critical dialogue, and evaluation.

The research was conducted over a period of 6 months from May–December 2018 and was approved by the university's institutional review board. Middle school students met with pre-licensure baccalaureate nursing students weekly on Saturdays over the course of 6 months.

Student Researchers

This participatory action research study engaged 20 middle school students who resided in the metro Washington, DC area. The middle school students were participants of an organization that promotes social change by providing opportunities to youth from under-resourced backgrounds. The organization provides weekly Saturday learning and social opportunities for middle school students, aged 11–14 years. The middle school students in this study were all Black/African American with slightly more males than females. The middle school students were guided in the project by eight undergraduate (UG) nursing students from an accelerated baccalaureate nursing program in the DC area and their nursing faculty.

Preparation of the Nursing Students

There were several aspects of the study where preparation was critical to the development of working on a project including middle school students as well as nursing students. Three nursing faculty began preparing in July and August at a clinical site associated with the organization (herein referred to as *community partner*). Under the guidance of the nursing faculty, the nursing students assigned to the summer community partner clinical site completed health education projects on heart disease and SDH in preparation for the fall project.

In the fall, faculty began preparing the nursing students assigned to the community partner's Saturday site for community clinical. The project began with a "train the trainer" model whereas three nursing faculty trained, guided, and mentored the nursing students to work with the middle school students on SDH and the photovoice method. The faculty trained the nursing students on the photovoice methodology, instructional strategies for the middle school students in the areas of heart disease in the context of SDH, and faculty reviewed the ethics of photography. Subsequently, the nursing students were able to confidently provide education to the middle school students on recognizing heart disease and the identification of risk and preventative factors which included the SDH, photography and ethics of photography. The faculty were ultimately responsible for the delivery and clarification of content to the middle school students via the nursing students as well as making sure the nursing students met their community clinical course objectives.

Participatory Action Research—Photovoice Project

The study was conducted in two parts. Part one was comprised of education and review of heart disease, SDH, photography and critical dialogue about the photographs they obtained. The nursing faculty and nursing students distributed a digital camera and camera case to each of the participating middle school students for use in documenting their observations of heart healthy facilitators and barriers in their communities. Participating students were those students who provided their assent in conjunction with their parent's consent.

Using the ethics of photography, the middle school students were instructed to go into their communities and photograph what they perceived as facilitators and barriers to a heart healthy community. The middle school students were reminded while they were to have fun taking pictures, they needed to maintain the heart focus as well as being mindful of staying safe and respectful in the quest for their photos. While working in small groups of 2–3 middle school students per 1–2 nursing students, the photographs were then downloaded onto computers and reviewed. The middle school students were able to "tell their stories" about SDH within their own lived spaces. The nursing students were able to facilitate reflections and collective analysis from the middle school students about their photographs. The subsequent dialogue facilitated the development of themes. The themes centered on nature/environment, exercise, rebuilding, and safety. The themes were solidified by late October. In addition to the theme development, the middle school students titled each of their photographs, provided description(s) and decided which photographs would be shared in a public exhibit.

Part two involved a focus shift to the middle school students taking their experiences and expressing them in writing letters to local legislators and policy makers for attention and action. The project culminated with the themed pictures and letters displayed in December 2018 in the photovoice exhibit as a result of the education and guidance. The exhibit was viewed by students, parents, families, local community leaders and nursing faculty. The photographs were also displayed as part of an exhibit at the Smithsonian National Museum of African American History and Culture from May through August of 2019.

The analysis of our project was twofold. First, there was the need to work with the middle school and nursing students to develop the thematic content displayed in the exhibit. Second, it was critical to evaluate the learning regarding the SDH. Thematic content development for the exhibit was captured with several tools. These tools included: (a) reflection documentation sheet, (b) SHOWED (See, Happening, cOmmunity, Why, Educate, Do) worksheet, and (c) themes worksheet. A pre-post survey was used to capture and reflect learning about the SDH. Prior to the study, about half of the middle school students were not able to list any concerns in their community related to health. After their participation in the study, 95% of the students were able to identify community concerns such as environmental factors, how individual actions can bring about changes and support healthy living, and how policy can be used to create healthier environments for residents.

Participatory action research requires a level of trust that may be hard to obtain if one does not have a working relationship with a community partner that will facilitate acceptance and participation in the project. In this case, our research team had a long-standing relationship with the community partner and this subsequently aided the recruitment and retention of the desired sample population and proposed interventions. The main challenges in this study related to the need to be flexible and planning ample time when working with youth and nonprofit community partners. Specific challenges related to the aforementioned areas include: some students lost or forgot their cameras, staffing changes were common, there were weather issues requiring timeline and content delivery changes, and faculty were working with two student groups (UG nursing and middle school students) requiring different levels of support to meet educational objectives.

This research was conceptualized as a community engaged participatory action photovoice project. Photography was the medium for generating knowledge, insights, critical dialogue, and solutions. It was the conduit for understanding health disparities in heart disease from a broader lens that included connections to policy, economics, and the social environment. Moreover, this action-oriented approach focused on engaging students to recognize their agency and capacity for change through voice and action.

As the project ensued, the power of the stories associated with the photographs became increasingly salient. The richness of the individual lived experiences underscored the true value of the narratives. It became evident that as a research methodology, narrative inquiry was just as important as photovoice. Narrative inquiry was deemed by the researchers as necessary. It was essential that a written narrative accompany each photograph. The narratives ensured the photographs did not "speak for themselves," but rather were photo-narratives that gave voice to the individual. The research is best described as a narrative-photovoice project.

The students created both written and verbal narratives in addition to taking photographs. Their lived experiences, captured through photography, provided the data for oral and written stories. This process, both reflexive and reflective, generated rich and powerful narratives shared by the students in class, at the photovoice exhibit, and via their letters to political leaders. An original goal was to include educational instruction on how to write a policy brief, which was to be shared with a community or political leader. However, as middle school students told their stories, it became clear the focus needed to be on allowing the students to express themselves through written word and not learning a new writing technique. While collective themes emerged, it was the written or verbal storytelling of the individual's experiences and the analysis and interpretation of those experiences that evoked powerful emotions and reactions.

The photovoice project offered several opportunities to the two student populations involved. First, the project allowed middle school students from an under-resourced community, to learn about the impacts of social determinants of health on heart disease and how they could identify and mitigate their risk. Second, the middle school students were able to engage in research facilitating their knowledge and empowerment in today's data driven decision-making world. It is important that youth, especially from low resource areas, learn and become skilled in techniques and tools expanding their access to initiate change as well as stimulate scientific inquiry. Youth have remarkable insights and candor. In addition, youth have the capacity to engage in research and use the research experience in advocacy efforts for their own communities which is one of the main ways to bring about positive societal changes.

The use of photovoice with the undergraduate nursing students expanded their critical thinking, participation and understanding of qualitative research. The nursing students found research fun and relevant. Additionally, we discovered nursing students can be effective educators and partners in research when working with younger populations.

Qualitative research techniques are valuable and appropriate methods of scientific inquiry regarding human conditions. Nurses, educators, and other social scientists benefit from the consideration and use of qualitative methods where the participants and researchers are mutually engaged. Qualitative inquiry involves organization, planning and lots of interpretation. It is essential to establish what one wants to learn and the information that will need to be obtained; failure to establish the aforementioned puts one at risk for ineffective research questions and inappropriate methodology. The selection of a particular qualitative approach is based upon one's goals which subsequently aids in the identification of the processes needed to yield the best data and thus, results.

The use of photovoice for our project is the perfect example of how our team identified the need to teach different educational levels of students the importance of the social determinants of heart health. Additionally, there was a need for faculty to ensure the nursing students met their clinical course objectives. The use of photovoice satisfied the need to provide instruction to various levels of students while simultaneously creating engagement and intellectual curiosity regarding the research process.

The introduction of qualitative research to youth and undergraduate students builds confidence and understanding of the research process contributing to future generation's embrace of evidence-based practice and data driven decision making. Ultimately, we were able to facilitate learning about a significant community problem and create awareness in the community and beyond. The skills for understanding the human experience can be introduced as early as the middle school years. This study involved the recognition and inclusion of individuals whose shared experiences contributed to the understanding and appreciation of the many issues affecting heart health in today's society.

REFERENCES

American Heart Association. (n.d.). *DC state fact sheet: Leading causes of death in D.C. in 2017.* https://www.heart.org/-/media/Files/About-Us/Policy-Research/Fact-Sheets/Morbidity-and-Mortality-by-State/Quality-Systems-of-Care-Washington-DC.pdf

Centers for Disease Control. (n.d.). *Heart disease facts.* https://www.cdc.gov/heart disease/facts.htm

Community Health Dashboards. (2018). *Prince George's County health department: Indicators.* http://www.pgchealthzone.org/index.php?module=indicators

DC Health. (n.d.). *Health equity summary report: District of Columbia 2018—Social and structural determinants of health.* https://dchealth.dc.gov/sites/default/files/

dc/sites/doh/publication/attachments/HER%20Summary%20Report%20 FINAL%20with%20letter%20and%20table_02_08_2019.pdf

Haque, N., & Eng, B. (2011). Tackling inequity through a photovoice project on the social determinants of health: Translating photovoice evidence to community action. *Global Health Promotion, 18*(1), 16–19. https://doi.org/10 .1177/1757975910393165

Heron, M. (2019). Deaths: Leading causes for 2017. *National Vital Statistics Report, 68*(6). https://www.cdc.gov/nchs/data/nvsr/nvsr68/nvsr68_06-508.pdf

Huang, K., Cheng, S., & Theise, R. (2013). School contexts as social determinants of child health: Current practices and implications for future public health practice. *Public Health Reports, 6*(3), 128, 21–28. https://doi .org/10.1177/00333549131286S304

National Health Literacy Mapping to Inform Health Care Policy. (n.d.). *Health literacy data map.* University of North Carolina at Chapel Hill. http://health literacymap.unc.edu/#

INTRODUCTION TO CASE STUDY 5

Narrative research is the process of gathering and exploring the stories people tell about their experiences in order to provide interpretation. This study about the cross-cultural features of coming-out experiences displays a narrative approach using the participants' experiences. The author properly contextualized these coming-out stories with in-depth accounts instead of serving as resources for developing sexuality typologies. Narrative research also sheds light on how narrators negotiate sexual practices concerning the self, the interviewer, and sociocultural norms. This study emphasizes how these immigrants' sexualities are repositioned through narration inside the U.S. context for legitimacy by utilizing sociolinguistic interviews as the technique and narrative positioning as the analytical tool. Some theoretical and methodological reflection strategies are described in the section on qualitative research for marginalized groups and can easily be replicated for similar research populations.

The author gave attention to two timely issues, exploring the language of coming-out narratives and how it might produce valuable insights on (homo)sexuality. The selected theory asserts that narrative positioning emphasizes communicating and positioning self and desire. To demonstrate how sociolinguistic interviews and the analytical strategy of narrative positioning are utilized, this chapter focuses on an interview with an Indian immigrant who self-identifies as gay. In contrast to the overall framework of the coming-out narrative genre or the predominant identity-based theorization, this method elaborates the cross-cultural features of coming out for sexual minorities with immigration status.

Qualitative Research With Diverse and Underserved Communities, pages 123–133
Copyright © 2024 by Information Age Publishing
www.infoagepub.com

CASE STUDY 5

NARRATIVE POSITIONING IN SOCIOLINGUISTIC INTERVIEWS WITH "GAY" IMMIGRANTS' COMING-OUT EXPERIENCES

Ping-Hsuan Wang
Georgetown University

ABSTRACT

Analyzing the discourse of coming-out narratives can yield fruitful results for understanding (homo)sexuality when two considerations are taken heed of. Methodologically, interview data should be analyzed in depth. Theoretically, narrative positioning should highlight the expression and negotiation of self and desire. This chapter sketches the need for advancing research in this direction and presents an excerpt from an interview with a "gay" Indian immigrant in the United States to illustrate the implementation of the method of sociolinguistic interviews and the analytical tool of narrative positioning. This approach fleshes out the cross-cultural aspects of coming out for sexual

Qualitative Research With Diverse and Underserved Communities, pages 125–133
Copyright © 2024 by Information Age Publishing
www.infoagepub.com

minorities of immigrant status against the mainstream framework of the coming-out narrative genre or the dominant identity-based theorization.

Coming-out narrative has become an established genre that comes with a set of expectations (e.g., DiDomenico, 2015), building on the moral imperative of "honesty versus secrecy" (Rasmussen, 2004). However, while same-sex desire can be found around the world, disclosing one's sexual identification or sharing one's coming-out experiences is far from universal. In fact, Adan Sanchez (2017) critiques that, for people of color (POC) in the United States, mainstream coming-out narratives "imply a White subjectivity," with the influence of POC culture and heritage lost. Over decades of research into coming out, this is often a missed intersection: qualitative studies in the field of language and sexuality, whether based on naturally occurring conversations or interview data, have drawn primarily on English-speaking, White participants' accounts. Murray (2014) further notes that coming out can pose greater difficulties in the non-heterosexual diasporas where vocabularies or discourses "invoke different limitations."

For example, the population of Indian immigrants in the United States has doubled in the past 2 decades (mostly men for the purpose of education and employment) and, for same-sex desiring Indian immigrant men, the concept of coming out is new to them (Wang, 2017). Yet few qualitative studies have looked into how sexual minorities of this demographic adjust themselves to coming out after migration. While scholars have continued to call for more studies that discuss the cross-cultural aspects to sexuality (e.g., Cameron & Kulick 2003; Davis et al., 2014; Levon, 2015), addressing this issue requires more than including non-English data or non-White participants (del-Teso-Craviotto, 2008). Against this background, this chapter highlights the importance of using sociolinguistic interviews to examine how sexuality, as observed in coming-out narratives, is complicated by (transnational) migration. Furthermore, narrative positioning is adopted to capture how desire is translated into identity through Western theorization of sexuality.

RESEARCH UNDERPINNINGS: SOCIOLINGUISTIC INTERVIEWS AND NARRATIVE POSITIONING

Across disciplines, interviewing is arguably the most common and "the favorite methodological tool of the qualitative researcher" (Denzin & Lincoln, 2000, p. 353). Early adoption of this approach in sociolinguistics (e.g., Labov & Waletzky, 1967), however, is criticized for "decontextualizing" narratives (Patterson, 2008). Therefore, two considerations are instrumental in advancing research in a new direction that resituates interviews as a context for narratives (De Fina & Perrino, 2011) and narratives as a context for coming out (Wang, 2021). First, methodologically, coming-out narratives should be analyzed in depth to illuminate the contingent nature of sexuality in the turn-by-turn interaction. Traditionally, interviews are used to glean data for developing coming-out models (for an overview, see Sandler, 2022). Interview excerpts serve only as exemplars of certain thematic patterns. Under these circumstances, the interview's function as the locus for the expression and negotiation of desire in coming-out narratives is lost.

In short, although it cannot be denied that, in sociolinguistics, "much of the data in the field comes from interviews" (Fuller, 2000, p. 388), interviews are not just a means to an end. Rather, interview data can be a fertile ground for investigating social interaction without being reduced to patterns and statistics. After all, interviews can be used for investigating "cultural discourses of race, class, gender, sexuality, and other politicized identities" (Lindlof & Taylor, 2011, p. 181). More of late, researchers have begun to recognize the narrative approach to studying accounts of coming out in interviews (e.g., Faulkner & Hecht, 2011; Sala & De La Mata Benítez, 2017). A close examination of coming-out narratives offers insights into how sexual minorities with a history of migration define and negotiate (homo)sexuality.

Second, theoretically, literature on coming out has thrived largely in the West, especially the United States, where coming out is imbricated with local identity politics in order to increase the visibility of sexual minorities post-Stonewall (Armstrong, 2002). In this regard, when Sedgwick (1990) describes the closet as "the defining structure of gay oppression" (p. 71), she refers not only to the obvious fact that sexual minorities hold a marginal position in society; she is contending that coming out builds upon binarism that includes inevitable secrecy (see also Butler, 1993). The conceal/reveal conception of identity has long persisted in the research of language and sexuality. When the idea of sexual identity such as "gay" as a Western construct (Chan, 1995; see also Currier, 2012; Decena, 2008) is left unquestioned and applied indiscriminately, research risks stifling possibilities of a cross-cultural exploration among underrepresented populations. Sometimes the identity model can dilute sexual minorities' experience of (homo)sexuality when ascription is (mis)taken for identification.

To complement the extant research, a qualitative approach can make salient the nuances (Wang, 2020). To illustrate this point, this chapter adopts narrative positioning. Instead of "searching who s/he (really) is," narrators are believed to be "engaging in the activity of narrating" for situated purposes (Bamberg, 2006, p. 144). Davies and Harré (1990) propose the interactional notion of positioning in the examination of selves in discourse. This analytical lens encompasses three central elements: a "story line" that organizes the discourse for proper interpretation, "positions" that can be assumed, challenged, or otherwise negotiated, and "speech acts" that are realized in participants' mutual linguistic actions. In this case, the utterance "I'm gay" constitutes the speech act of identification for same-sex desiring Indian immigrant men to assume a "gay" position in the story line of coming out in the United States.

Adding to such theorization, Bamberg (1997) postulates three levels of narrative positioning: Level 1 deals with character positioning in the story world; Level 2 involves interactive positioning between the storyteller and the story recipient; Level 3 pertains to positioning the self "with regard to dominant discourses or master narratives" (Bamberg & Georgakopoulou, 2008, p. 391). This framework has since found a broad application in many fields (e.g., Bernhard, 2015; Lawson, 2017). In doing so, both coming out as a social practice and the telling of these narratives are fully contextualized in sociolinguistic interviews.

AN ILLUSTRATIVE EXAMPLE

Below I present an excerpt from a sociolinguistic interview with Reyansh, a same-sex desiring Indian immigrant man living in the United States. The research design was explained to him before consent was obtained. A crucial part of this process is to invite informants to share their understanding of coming out without imposing the researchers' presumptions. This is reminiscent of the interpretive approach to sexuality, which involves steps that "engage an individual in open interaction in a way where meaning could be located in active use" (Manning, 2013, p. 2509). Participants were asked to define what it means to come out and, subsequently, encouraged to recount personal experiences to substantiate. The interviews were audio-recorded and then transcribed for analysis (see Appendix for transcription conventions).

When Reyansh is asked to define coming out, the homo/hetero binary is leveraged to ratify his same-sex attraction, through which this desire is translated into the Western concept of gayness.

Excerpt 1

1. Reyansh: So for me, coming out was primarily me realizing that I am gay.
2.   Ping: Mhm.
3. Reyansh: And- and everything after that was
4.   More just another step of coming out
5.   To me, coming out was when I realized I was gay.
6.   Ping: Mhm.
7. Reyansh: And that I wasn't bisexual, wasn't just something,

8.		"Oh, I can be with women at some- just have some fun right now,"
9.		"And be with men later on."
10.	Ping:	Yeah.
11.	Reyansh:	Hehehe you know. So me realizing that, "no I am gay."
12.		"I cannot possibly marry a woman."
13.		"I'm only attracted to men."
14.		And not just physically but also emotionally.
15.		That even if I somehow (.) marry a woman,
16.		And am able to have sex with her,
17.		Just for the purpose of procreation.
18.	Ping:	Mhm.
19.	Reyansh:	Even then, I would never be straight.
20.		I would always be attracted to,
21.		Me realizing that is basically that main coming out.
22.	Ping:	Mhm.
23.	Reyansh:	After that, everything else was just adding on top of it?
24.		But for me coming out was me realizing that I was gay.

As a researcher, I provide just enough responses to show my attention while avoiding interrupting Reyansh's account. This helps to foreground his repetition of "me realizing I'm gay," which marks the opening and closing of an episode (Tannen, 2007). Viewing repetition as a strategy of involvement indicates my presence as the interviewer and the interactional context of the interview. For one, such repetition explains his understanding of coming out in response to my question; for another, it provides justification for his decision to come out (Wang, 2021), establishing coming out as a solution to the contradicting feelings he had. Reyansh thereby linguistically creates a sense of continuity by connecting himself as "the narrator" in the interview and the self as "the protagonist" in the repeated phrases. Likewise, Reyansh presents his inner thoughts as dialogue, which is evidenced by the change in tense (Lines 8 and 9). The constructed dialogue again connects his sense of self, simultaneously being aware of his same-sex desire and the social expectation of him marrying a woman. According to Tannen (2007), constructed dialogue is another performative strategy for creating involvement. Attending to these discursive details underscores the dynamics of storytelling in interviews: the researcher is present during data collection and narrative analysis needs to account for the role of the recipient/interviewer.

As mentioned above, the application of narrative positioning emphasizes the emergence of a sense of self from multiple relationships. However, supplementing to previous understanding (Wang, 2017), this "self" is not to be equated with "identity" as the latter is an intricate process of discursive approximation of one's presentation of self to one or more socially recognized categories (Wang, forthcoming). While identity categories are useful, qualitative researchers should be cautious when dealing with them so that these categories are not inadvertently imposed onto participants of minority communities. For instance, relating himself to other story characters, Reyansh expresses his "un-desire" toward women (Line 8) or marriage with them (Lines 15 and 16). Level 1 positioning builds on the hetero/ homo binary to create a same-sex desiring self. When such a position is mapped onto the story line in the U.S. context, a "gay" identity emerges and produces the force of coming out as a speech act.

Extending to level 2 positioning, Reyansh's definition answers my question, again stressing the storyteller-recipient relationship in a sociolinguistic interview. Positioning theory thus accentuates the interactional context of the interview, in which Reyansh is positioned as a conscious interviewee who interprets my questions and responds accordingly (De Fina, 2009) and positions me both as an interviewer who expects answers or even rationales for coming out and as a witness of his desire for other men in order to co-construct a "gay" identity (Wang, 2021). The interviewer's role can sometimes be overlooked, but it is indispensable for analyzing sexuality and subjectivity in coming-out narratives, which also holds true for other narrative genres and other disciplines that work with narratives.

Finally, by attending to Level 3 positioning in his narrative, the analysis reflects the salience of heterosexual assumptions about marriage. Reyansh casts himself against the prevailing phenomenon that in India, many same-sex desiring men still end up marrying women despite the decriminalization of homosexuality (Sharma, 2014; Zane, 2018). Because of the role that marriage plays in Indian society and the possibility of entering a heterosexual marriage, Reyansh's resistance becomes a touchstone of his homosexual desire. Using narrative positioning for analysis, the expressions of desire, for men and for women respectively, are shown to be translated into Western identity categories (e.g., "straight," Line 19). As a point of reference, contesting the Indian social tradition *illegitimates* his presumed "straight" identity and simultaneously *authorizes* his "gay" identity (see Bucholtz & Hall, 2005). As such, narrative positioning fleshes out the cultural nuances in Reyansh's definition of coming out and his experience as an Indian immigrant in the United States. Paradigmatically speaking, instead of a direct, one-step equation of his homosexuality to a "gay" identity, this analytical lens teases apart how desire is (re)molded into identity in Western theorization.

CONCLUSION

This chapter points out how a discourse-informed qualitative approach can contribute to the exploration of the cross-cultural aspects of coming-out experiences. To do so, it is necessary to treat interviews as real communicative events. As such, coming-out narratives can be properly contextualized and closely analyzed, not merely as materials for creating sexuality typologies. Also, narrative positioning illuminates narrators' negotiation of sexual practices in relation to the self, the interviewer, and the sociocultural norms. Taking full advantage of sociolinguistic interviews as the method and narrative positioning as the analytical tool draws attention to the process in which these immigrants' sexualities are resituated through narration within the U.S. context for legitimacy. This chapter outlines some ways of methodological and theoretical reflection in qualitative research for underserved communities. Diversity thereby comes from reevaluating the U.S.-based model of coming out and its associated Western identity categories. In this way, the elicited accounts provide a substantive look that moves beyond traditional identity-based theorization so that their experiences are presented as variations rather than deviations from the norm of coming out.

APPENDIX: TRANSCRIPTION CONVENTIONS

(.)   Noticeable pause
.   Falling intonation followed by a noticeable pause
?   Rising intonation followed by a noticeable pause
,   Continuing intonation
-       Self interruption

REFERENCES

Armstrong, E. A. (2002). *Forging gay identities: Organizing sexuality in San Francisco, 1950–1994.* University of Chicago Press.

Bamberg, M. (1997). Positioning between structure and performance. *Journal of Narrative and Life History, 7*(1–4), 335–342. https://doi.org/10.1075/jnlh.7.42pos

Bamberg, M. (2006). Stories: Big or small: Why do we care?. *Narrative Inquiry, 16*(1), 139–147.

Bamberg, M., & Georgakopoulou, A. (2008). Small stories as a new perspective in narrative and identity analysis. *Text & Talk, 28*(3), 377–396. https://doi.org/10.1515/TEXT.2008.018

Bernhard, S. (2015). Forms of identities and levels of positioning: A practice theoretical approach to narrative interviewing. *Narrative Inquiry, 25*(2), 340–360. https://doi.org/10.1075/ni.25.2.08ber

Bucholtz, M., & Hall, K. (2005). Identity and interaction: a sociocultural linguistic approach. *Discourse Studies, 7*(4–5), 585–614. https://doi.org/10.1177/1461445605054407

Butler, J. (1993). *Bodies that matter: On the discursive limits of sex.* Taylor & Francis.

Cameron, D., & Kulick, D. (2003). *Language and sexuality.* Cambridge University Press.

Chan, C. S. (1995). Issues of sexual identity in an ethnic minority: The case of Chinese American lesbians, gay men, and bisexual people. In A. R. D'Augelli & C. J. Patterson (Eds.), *Lesbian, gay, and bisexual identities over the lifespan: Psychological perspectives* (pp. 87–101). Oxford University Press.

Currier, A. (2012). *Out in Africa LGBT organizing in Namibia and South Africa.* University of Minnesota Press.

Davies, B., & Harré, R. (1990). Positioning: The discursive production of selves. *Journal for the Theory of Social Behavior, 20*(1), 43–63. https://doi.org/10.1111/j.1468-5914.1990.tb00174.x

Davis, J. L., Zimman, L., & Raclaw, J. (2014). Opposites attract: Retheorizing binaries in language, gender, and sexuality. In L. Zimman, J. Davis, & J. Raclaw (Eds.), *Queer excursions: Retheorizing binaries in language, gender, and sexuality* (pp. 1–12). Oxford University Press.

De Fina, A. (2009). Narratives in interview—The case of accounts: For an interactional approach to narrative genres. *Narrative Inquiry, 19*(2), 233–258. https://doi.org/10.1075/ni.19.2.03def

De Fina, A., & Perrino, S. (2011). Introduction: Interviews vs. "natural" contexts: A false dilemma. *Language in Society, 40*(1), 1–11. https://www.jstor.org/stable/23011781

Decena, C. U. (2008). Profiles, compulsory disclosure and ethical sexual citizenship in the contemporary USA. *Sexualities, 11*(4), 397–413. https://doi.org/10.1177/1363460708091741

del-Teso-Craviotto, M. (2008). Book review. In S. Kyratzis & H. Sauntson (Eds.), *Language, sexualities & desires: Cross-cultural perspectives.* Palgrave Macmillan.

Denzin, N., & Lincoln, Y. (2000). *Handbook of qualitative research* (2nd ed.). SAGE Publications.

DiDomenico, S. M. (2015). "Putting a face on a community": Genre, identity, and institutional regulation in the telling (and retelling) of oral coming-out narratives. *Language in Society, 44*(5), 607–628. https://www.jstor.org/stable/43904163

Faulkner, S., & Hecht, M. L. (2011). The negotiation of closetable identities: A narrative analysis of lesbian, gay, bisexual, transgendered queer Jewish identity. *Journal of Social and Personal Relationships, 28*(6), 829–847. https://doi.org/10.1177/0265407510391338

Fuller, J. (2000). Changing perspectives on data: Interviews as situated speech. *American Speech, 75*(4), 388–390. https://muse.jhu.edu/pub/4/article/2770/pdf

Labov, W., & Waletzky, J. (1967). Narrative analysis: Oral versions of personal experience. In J. Helm (Ed.), *Essays on the verbal and visual arts* (pp. 12–44). University of Washington Press.

Levon, E. (2015). Integrating intersectionality in language, gender, and sexuality research. *Language and Linguistics Compass, 9*(7), 295–308. https://doi.org/10.1111/lnc3.12147

Lawson, M. (2017). Narrative positioning and 'integration' in lifestyle migration: British migrants in Ariège, France. *Language and Intercultural Communication, 17*(1), 58–75. https://doi.org/10.1080/14708477.2016.1165242

Manning, J. (2013). Interpretive theorizing in the seductive world of sexuality and interpersonal communication: Getting guerilla with studies of sexting and purity rings. *International Journal of Communication, 7,* 2507–2520. https://ijoc.org/index.php/ijoc/article/view/2250/1023

Murray, D. (2014). Queering borders: Language, sexuality and migration. *Journal of Language and Sexuality, 3*(1), 1–5. https://doi.org/10.1075/jls.3.1

Patterson, W. (2008). Narratives of events: Labovian narrative analysis and its limitations. In M. Andrews, C. Squire, & M. Tamboukou (Eds.), *Doing narrative research* (pp. 23–40). SAGE Publications.

Rasmussen, M. L. (2004). The problem of coming out. *Theory Into Practice, 43*(2), 144–150. https://doi.org/10.1207/s15430421tip4302_8

Sala, A., & De La Mata Benítez, M. (2017). The narrative construction of Lesbian identity: A study using Bruner's self-indicators. *Culture & Psychology, 23*(1), 108–127. https://doi.org/10.1177/1354067X16650831

Sanchez, A. (2017, July 7). The Whiteness of 'coming out': culture and identity in the disclosure narrative. *Archer Magazine.* http://archermagazine.com.au/2017/07/culture-coming-out

Sandler, E. T. (2022). An overview of coming out research: Introducing a three-lens typology. *Sociology Compass, 16*(2), e12958.

Sedgwick, E. K. (1990). *Epistemology of the closet.* University of California Press.

Sharma, B. (2014, August 22). *Indian gay men's wives "trapped" in marriage.* Al Jazeera. https://www.aljazeera.com/indepth/features/2014/08/indian-gay-men-wives-trapped-marriage-20148226128111437.html

Tannen, D. (2007). *Talking voices: Repetition, dialogue, and imagery in conversational discourse* (2nd ed.). Cambridge University Press.

Wang, P.-H. (2017). Out of the country, out of the closet: Coming-out stories in cross-cultural contexts. *Southern Journal of Linguistics, 41*(2), 173–198. https://www.researchgate.net/publication/328017640_Out_of_the_country_out_of_the_closet_Coming_out_stories_in_cross-cultural_contexts

Wang, P.-H. (2020). Negotiating racialized sexuality through online stancetaking in text-based communication. In D. N. Farris, D. R. Compton, & A. R. Herrera (Eds.), *Gender, sexuality, and race in the digital age* (pp. 187–203). Springer.

Wang, P.-H. (2021). "When I came to the US": Constructing migration in gay Indian immigrants' coming-out narratives. *Narrative Inquiry, 31*(2), 338–357. https://doi.org/10.1075/ni.19088.wan

Wang, P.-H. (forthcoming). Querying peripheral identities with penumbral positionings in 'gay' immigrants' 'coming-back-in' narratives. In Y. Matsumoto & J.-O. Östman (Eds.), *Identity perspectives from peripheries.* John Benjamins.

Zane, Z. (2018, October 25). *A third of gay men report being married to a woman in India.* Out. https://www.out.com/news-opinion/2018/10/25/third-gay-men-report-being-married-woman-india

CASE STUDIES SECTION II

INTRODUCTION TO CASE STUDY 6

This report of a research project illustrates inquiry precipitated by a demonstrable inequity with a goal of understanding the lived experience of those subject to that inequity for the purpose of redressing that injustice. It is important to recognize that research is purpose driven whether it is for the discovery of knowledge, description of a phenomenon or to test a hypothesis or theory. These purposes are in themselves insufficient for researchers concerned with social justice for groups which are judged to be "less than" in and by "society." Recognizing this important basis for inquiry is essential for authenticity and to avoid the collection of information solely as an exploitative exercise (which is often the basis for inquiry especially on the part of university or college affiliated researchers for whom the conduct and publication of research is real currency in the advancement of career).

This study report also demonstrates the strong press of "protocol" in the conduct of research. Even though the researcher was aware of the need and prepared to adapt his inquiry as a result of the feedback and participation of his informants, he felt constrained and concerned about doing so. This can occur for many reasons including methodological bias, concern for notions of "validity" and "generalizability" or simple expedience. For whatever the reason, the qualitative research process, outcomes, interpretations, and implications must be carefully considered in terms of possible cost to obtaining authentic "rich, thick" information.

Finally, the present case amply illustrates concerns associated with participant-observer research. While the researcher in this study attempted to address the possibility of bias by recusing himself from teaching and by

Qualitative Research With Diverse and Underserved Communities, pages 137–148
Copyright © 2024 by Information Age Publishing
www.infoagepub.com

endeavoring to be cognizant of his own perspectives and beliefs, he was nevertheless surprised by at least some of what was reported by his research participants. This suggests that despite efforts at bracketing and disassociation from the community of focus, he was nonetheless susceptible to the press of his own experience which is quite reasonable. Since it is likely, it is something about which qualitative researchers should be concerned and endeavor to identify and manage.

CASE STUDY 6

EXPLORING THE LIVED EXPERIENCES OF LATINO FIRST-GENERATION STUDENTS IN A COMMUNITY COLLEGE BACCALAUREATE PROGRAM

Carmen Jones
California State University, Northridge

CONTEXT FOR THE INQUIRY

Governor Brown signed California State Senate Bill (SB) 850 (2014) authorizing 15 community colleges in California to confer baccalaureate degrees in 2014. One of the programs authorized was dental hygiene at Southern Pacific Community College (SPCC). I chose to study that program due to the college being designated as a Hispanic serving institution (HSI) and 50% of students enrolled in the program being Latino first-generation college students (FGCS) and because Latinos are disproportionately underrepresented in the field of dental hygiene, the disparity of dental professionals of

Qualitative Research With Diverse and Underserved Communities, pages 139–148
Copyright © 2024 by Information Age Publishing
www.infoagepub.com
139

color and the impact for this disparity on minority populations, as well the low degree completion rates reported for communities of color.

In 2018, 46% of first-time students enrolled in California community colleges were reported to be Latino/Hispanic (California Community Colleges, n.d.). And, although Latino FGCS reported an intent to transfer to a university, the percentage who actually obtained a bachelor's degree was quite low (Cahalan et al., 2019). The lack of Latinos pursuing higher degrees creates a disparity in healthcare, not only for professionals, but also patients of color.

According to the 2018 National Healthcare Quality and Disparities Report, Latino patients received lower quality healthcare than White, non-Hispanic patients (U.S. Department of Health and Human Services, 2019). Moreover, California is reported to be one of the worst states in the differences in quality of care for Black, Latino, and Asian patients when compared to White Patients (U.S. Department of Health and Human Services, 2019). Dentistry is included in the healthcare disparity. According to Daugherty and Kearney (2017), nationally, 85% of dental hygienists were Caucasian and 97.2% female. According to the American Dental Educators Association (2019), Latinos made up 6% of dental hygienist students enrolled in programs nationally in 2001–2002 and since then that percentage has increased to 14% in 2016–2017. Although there is an upward trend in diversification, the change is lagging. Diversification of the healthcare workforce can increase cultural competence practices, which can in turn increase patient satisfaction and compliance.

According to the legislation, there is currently a gap of 1.1 million baccalaureate degrees needed in order for California to remain economically competitive (California State Senate Bill 850, 2014). Yet, students who graduated with an associate's degree in dental hygiene were limited to employment in clinical practice. And, although working in a dental office/private practice provided a livable wage, alternative options require a bachelor's degree. Hence, the baccalaureate degree would create the potential of employment opportunities beyond private practice and for better wages.

Although California was the twenty-third state to authorize the conferring of baccalaureate degrees in community colleges, research has only provided a perspective on community college baccalaureate degree (CCBD) programs from the institutional lens related to policies and procedures, best practices, and lessons learned from program implementation perspective (Essink, 2013; Hofland, 2011; McKee, 2001; Person et al., 2017; Yeager, 2017). Thus, discourse was lacking on the academic and social experiences of students, particularly Latino FGCS in a CCBD program.

FOCUS FOR THE INQUIRY

To better understand the lived experiences of Latino FGCS pursuing a CCBD, the following questions guided the research:

> **RQ1:** *What factors influenced first-generation Latino college students to pursue a community college bachelor's degree? What do the students perceive as the benefits of such a program?*

> **RQ2:** *What are the academic and social experiences of first-generation Latino students in a community college bachelor's degree program?*

> **RQ3:** *What are some of the barriers/challenges that Latino first-generation college students face in their pursuit of a community college bachelor's degree? How have students navigated those barriers/challenges?*

SAMPLING/POPULATION

A mixed sampling strategy was used to select participants for the study. More specifically, a criterion (Patton, 2015) and snowball sampling (Durdella, 2019) were used to identify participants as my data sources. Criterion sampling was used since I had predetermined that I would study students that (a) self-identified as Latino, Chicano/a, or Latinx; (b) FGCS; (c) junior and/or senior level dental hygiene students; and (d) enrolled in the CCBD program at Southern Pacific Community College (SPCC) during the Fall 2019 through Spring 2020 semesters. The snowball sampling allowed for participants to identify and/or recruit additional participants to be interviewed (Durdella, 2019).

My objective was to recruit 8–12 participants. The recruitment process included posting flyers in the program's designated classrooms and laboratory spaces, as well as the individual student mailboxes of those who met the criterion. In addition, an informal invitation was sent via email to potential participants. The recruitment invitation and email included the criterion to participate, the researcher's contact information, and the compensation amount for participating.

INQUIRY AMIDST COVID-19 CONDITIONS

The interviews were scheduled to take place in mid-February through March 2020. However, the COVID-19 pandemic occurred during the month of March and the college decided to proceed with strictly remote learning, eliminating access to the campus for students and faculty. Prior to the campus closure, 10 of the 12 interviews were completed on campus.

The space selected to host the interviews was deliberate. The interviews were all scheduled to take place in the on-campus library. By separating the participants from the building where the program was housed allowed them to speak freely about their experiences. The library conference room was on the third floor and tucked away in a corner where interruptions or distractions were improbable; a measure taken to protect the privacy of the participants and to maintain confidentiality throughout the process. However, one interview was conducted in the Academic Affairs Vice President's Conference Room on campus due to a participant needing to reschedule the interview during a time when the library was closed. The vice president's conference room was on the first floor in a different building but was nonetheless private. The transition from being on-campus to suddenly only remote access created disruption and uncertainty amongst students, which resulted in communication barriers between me and the two remaining participants I had intended to interview. As a result, the interviews were concluded after 10 in-person interviews.

METHODOLOGY

Since I wanted to understand the academic and social experiences of Latino FGCS enrolled in the dental hygiene baccalaureate program, a narrative case study was used as the methodology. I chose a narrative case study design since the participants for the study were part of a bounded system, all of them were enrolled in the dental hygiene program at SPCC, and this was a particular contemporary phenomenon to California and the college (Merriam, 2009). This methodology allowed me to provide a rich, thick description of the phenomenon under investigation. According to Patton (2015), a narrative design enables the researcher to interpret stories and life history narratives to reveal cultural and social patterns through the lens of individual experiences. Nevertheless, being that a case study design was used, the results may not be generalizable to the larger population.

PROCESS/PROTOCOL FOR THE INQUIRY

A protocol guide was created in advance of the interviews to ensure consent forms were signed, surveys completed, the process of the interview was conveyed, and the audio recording process was explained. Also included was the right of the participants to end the interview at any time. Lastly, a post interview guide was developed that included compensation for participation in the study, and the explanation of validity/member checking the transcriptions. The guides served as a critical step-by-step reminder during the process of the interviews.

To understand the experiences of Latino FGCS, the researcher utilized two fundamental instruments, a background/demographic survey, as well as a semi-structured interview guide. The sessions were scheduled for 60 minutes, which included a 10-minute demographic survey and a 50-minute interview. Although 10 minutes was allocated for the completion of the short 8-question demographic survey, participants took no more than 3 minutes to complete it. And, although participants were sent the survey to review prior to the interview session, only two students brought a completed survey to the session. The semi-structured interviews lasted 35–45 minutes, at most. Most participants appeared comfortable sharing their stories.

CASE STUDY NARRATIVE

The case study narrative design was selected for this study as it allowed for the opportunity to engage students in discourse about their academic and social experiences in a community college baccalaureate program. Former research on Latino FGCS was mostly conducted through a deficit lens and lacked a focus on the students' voice/stories. Thus, to highlight the cultural capital of the participants, a critical race theory and community cultural wealth framework were used.

The setting for the study was deliberate; also, being an administrator and a faculty member at the college provided me access to the students via the connection with the program director, as she was the gatekeeper. To reduce perceived bias, I chose to recuse myself from teaching for two semesters.

The data recording protocol included two audio recording devices for interviews and note taking during the sessions to capture body language and expressions. McMillan and Schumacher (2001) consider nonverbal communication to be very important in qualitative studies, asserting that the recording of facial expressions, gestures, and movements can be triangulated with verbal data.

THEMATIC AND NARRATIVE PROCESS/ANALYSIS

A thematic and narrative analysis was utilized to code the transcriptions. The process began with having the audio files professionally transcribed and then uploading them to the ATLAS.Ti computer software. The software allowed me to create codes, sub codes, and major categories. I also used a manual process for narrative analysis using Microsoft Excel. The manual process allowed for immediate visualization/identification of commonalities, as well as the inequalities in the narratives expressed by the participants.

analysis involved segmenting, categorizing (or coding) and linking the codes to identify emerging themes with shared characteristics. I initially started with 43 codes but was able to combine and reduce them to 12 code families. I ultimately condensed the codes further to three major themes, with three subcategories for each theme. The final three major themes identified were community influence in higher education, access to higher education, and barriers and challenges.

INTERPRETATION

Once the thematic analysis was completed, I was able to interpret the data. With my method being narrative case study centered on critical race theory, after systematizing the data, I used a theory-driven process to interpret the data. I compared the findings from my analysis with existing literature on Latino FGCS using a critical race theory (CRT) lens (Ortiz, 2010; Patton, 2016) and a community cultural wealth (CCW) framework (Yosso, 2005). For example, the cultural wealth exhibited by the participant's proved to be valuable. I was able to align the findings from the responses of the participants to the six tenets of CCW to highlight the culturally rich capital in the responses from participants.

In an attempt to ensure accuracy in the transcriptions, as well as the appropriateness of representation of the participants' quotes, I used two forms of validity testing. The first was a member checking protocol requesting feedback on their transcribed data. I gave participants a deadline to return any edits, of which all 10 participants responded in a timely manner. Only two participants requested to clarify their responses. All other participants approved and accepted the transcriptions as presented. During the analysis process, member checking of quotes was conducted to ensure accuracy in the descriptions and interpretations of the quotes. Once again, the quotes were sent to each individual participant but only seven participants accepted my interpretation of their quotes, one of the seven participants requested minor edits to the quotes, which I obliged. Three participants did not respond to the email. Lastly, peer debriefing occurred with a tenured community college faculty who is a FGCS, person of color, in a doctoral program. Those processes helped to enrich my evidence as well as identify potential errors in the interpretation (Thomas, 1993, p. 39).

ANTICIPATED AND UNANTICIPATED EVENTS

I experienced challenges during the recruitment process which started with my assumption that once I posted the recruitment flyers, participants would come. Two weeks after posting flyers and placing them in the student's program mailboxes, I didn't receive any responses. Although I spoke to the program director about my study, I failed to ask for support in reaching out to the students on my behalf. After reaching out to the program director for support by sending an email to the students encouraging them to participate in the study, I began to receive correspondence from participants. I realized how important it was to include the gatekeeper in the process early on.

CHANGES IN INQUIRY FOCUS

Although I was able to get rich thick data from the questions I asked during the interview, the responses could have been even richer had I taken a step back after the first interview to reassess the interview questions. For example, I started the inquiry with a question on educational support from family, I realized afterward that I should have started with asking questions that would have allowed the participants to tell me about themselves first and then I could branch out to family, community, and institution topics. And, although I intentionally used a semi-structured interview protocol to have flexibility with the questions being asked, I kept to the script even though I knew I had the flexibility to modify the questions. At times I felt I had to pry responses from the participants and was uncertain how to proceed or whether or not I should continue to "nudge." For instance, one participant appeared skeptical and guarded and gave short answers, which in turn made me uncomfortable. Nonetheless, most participants seemed comfortable sharing their narratives and provided ample context and details about their experiences.

BRIEF SUMMARY OF FINDINGS

Latino FGCS bring a wealth of capital to the program, college, and community. The majority of participants came to the dental hygiene program with work experience as dental assistants. Although families encouraged them to attend college, most of the participants were influenced by their co-workers to pursue dental hygiene and college. Challenges they faced were navigating the institutional system, but they were able to figure it out independently, without the support of a counselor. They simply went on-line, identified the classes, and enrolled.

While in the dental hygiene program, the participants identified a racial disparity in the field of dental hygiene for both patients and practitioners. Participants reported a connection and a sense of comfort with their Spanish speaking patients. However, they also felt a sense of obligation to interpret for non-bilingual faculty and peers. They reported feeling anxious when they could not assist them. As a result, upon achieving their degree and obtaining licensure, most participants reported they plan to work in, and give back, to their communities.

Although my assumption was that the participants came to SPCC for the bachelor's degree, the participants stated they came for the dental hygiene program, and not necessarily the higher degree. However, they were proud to achieve the degree. Further, as a result of the baccalaureate degree, 100% of the participants intend to pursue a master's degree and, as a result of faculty role modeling and mentorship, some participants reported motivation to teach in the dental hygiene program.

WHAT WAS LEARNED ABOUT QUALITATIVE RESEARCH?

Qualitative research is an intense process so connecting with the participants is important. Participants are vulnerable and possibly defensive to open up to a stranger (the researcher) and share personal experiences. Moreover, although as a researcher the expectation is to disengage presumptions on the subject matter, it was challenging accepting the contrary. For example, from an emic perspective as a past graduate from the associate's degree program, past faculty, and current administrator supervising the program, I assumed the bachelor's degree was important to the participants. I had to contend with information that contradicted my expectation. Lastly, I learned that it is important for participants to feel at ease by explaining to them that you are not there to judge, challenge or dismiss their experiences, but that your principal role is that of a researcher/learner and merely to share their very valuable stories. Thus, I would recommend, using the term *conversation* opposed to interviews on recruitment flyers and when contacting potential participants. Interview has an interrogative connotation, while conversation, on the other hand, is explanatory.

REFERENCES

American Dental Educators Association. (2019, May 2). *Data, analysis and research: Applicants, enrollees and graduates.* https://www.adea.org/data/students/

Cahalan, M., Perna, L. W., Yamashita, M., Wright-Kim, J., & Jiang, N. (2019). *2019 indicators of higher education equity in the United States: Historical trend report.* The Pell Institute for the Study of Opportunity in Higher Education, Council for Opportunity in Education (COE), and Alliance for Higher Education and Democracy of the University of Pennsylvania (PennAHEAD).

California Community Colleges. (n.d.). *Baccalaureate degree program.* https://www .cccco.edu/About-Us/Chancellors-Office/Divisions/Educational-Services -and-Support/What-we-do/Curriculum-and-Instruction-Unit/Curriculum/ Baccalaureate-Degree-Program

California State Senate Bill 850. (2014). Baccalaureate degree pilot program *Cal. Education Code §78040 et seq. 2014.*

Daugherty, H. N., & Kearney, R. C. (2017, October). Measuring the impact of cultural competence training for dental hygiene students. *Journal of Dental Hygiene, 91*(5), 48–54. https://jdh.adha.org/content/91/5/48.short

Durdella, N. (2019). *Qualitative dissertation methodology: A guide for research design and methods.* SAGE Publishing.

Essink, S. E. (2013). *The community college baccalaureate: A mixed methods study of implementation and best practices* [Unpublished doctoral dissertation]. University of Nebraska. http://digitalcommons.unl.edu/cehsedaddiss/152

Hofland, B. (2011). *A case study of the community college baccalaureate: What happened in ten years?* [Unpublished doctoral dissertation]. University of Nebraska. http://digitalcommons.unl.edu/cehsedaddiss/75

McKee, J. (2001). *Factors and issues surrounding development of one community college baccalaureate degree program* [Unpublished master's thesis]. Oregon State University.

McMillan, J. H., & Schumacher, S. (2001). *Research in education: A conceptual introduction* (5th ed.). Addison Wesley Longman.

Merriam, S. B. (2009). *Qualitative research guide to design and implementation: Revised and expanded from qualitative research and case study applications in education.* Jossey-Bass.

Ortiz, L. (2010). Critical race theory: A transformational model for teaching diversity. *Journal of Social Work Education, 46*(2) 175–193. https://doi.org/10.5175/ jswe.2010.200900070

Patton, L. D. (2016). Disrupting postsecondary prose: Toward a critical race theory of higher education. *Urban Education, 51*(3), 315–342. https://doi.org/10.1177/ 0042085915602542

Patton, M. Q. (2015). *Qualitative research and evaluation methods: Integrating theory and practice* (4th ed.). SAGE Publishing.

Person, D., Blake, M. B., & Villagomez-Buus, A. (2017). *A research study of the California community college baccalaureate degree pilot program.* Center for Research and on Educational Access and Leadership. C-Real.

Thomas, J. (1993). *Doing critical ethnography.* SAGE Publishing.

Yeager, S. C. (2017). *The California community college baccalaureate degree pilot program: A case study of baccalaureate degree implementation* (ProQuest number:10442323) [Unpublished doctoral dissertation]. Drexel University.

Yosso, T. (2005). Whose culture has capital? A critical race theory discussion of community cultural wealth. *Race Ethnicity and Education, 8*(1), 69–91.

U.S. Department of Health and Human Services. (2019). *2018 national health-care quality and disparities report* (AHRQ Pub. No. 19-0070-EF). Agency for Healthcare Research and Quality. https://www.ahrq.gov/research/findings/nhqrdr/nhqdr18/index.html

INTRODUCTION TO CASE STUDY 7

This case study presentation is extraordinarily important for qualitative researchers who are interested in working with marginalized, disenfranchised, or disadvantaged groups. It clearly and well presents the importance of ongoing reflection and the constant process of monitoring self and the process of inquiry for the purpose of authenticity but also for the purpose of always being respectful and honoring the lived experiences and contributions shared by research participants. All too often the notion of cultural responsiveness or cultural respect are treated as "check boxes" rather than essential elements of ethical inquiry with some researchers seeking to identify characteristics or actions which are indicative of the same rather than understanding the fundamental requirements of relationship and mutuality as necessary but in themselves, insufficient bases for cultural responsiveness. Reflection is a crucial tool for self-discovery and self-awareness in the context of the inquiry and in relationship with those with whom the researcher is engaged.

Another important notion presented here is the idea that research guides, frameworks, and methods are not sacrosanct essentials to "good" research. It is important for researchers to explore the nature and intentions of those recommendations and to adopt and adapt as informed by the process and the people with whom the inquiry is being conducted. This includes the nature of analysis and recognizing and reporting multiple ways of knowing valuing and respecting respondent epistemologies and the historical foundations for cultural identity and cultural expression. Conformity to research mores which have arisen from one cultural perspective

Qualitative Research With Diverse and Underserved Communities, pages 149–160
Copyright © 2024 by Information Age Publishing
www.infoagepub.com
149

regarding knowledge and knowing can be crippling to the culturally re-sponsive researcher who seeks authenticity rather than merely accuracy. Including "participants" as co-researchers (see Action Research) enables the process of inquiry to be guided by, and essential knowledge prioritized and decided by those about whom that knowledge pertains and from whom it originates. This process involves inquiry which is an emergent process rather than one which is directed by an a priori determined protocol.

Finally, this submission concludes with recommendations for research-ers and research which are well founded and should be well received. Qual-itative research is subjective in nature and it provides an avenue for explo-ration, discovery, and meaning-making which is real, people rather than problem focused and serves to discover the nature and dynamics of lived experience rather than merely test a theory.

CASE STUDY 7

IN PICTURES AND WORDS

Centering Black Women's Experiences With Their Bodies With Narrative Photovoice Methodology

Y. Falami Devoe
Antioch University

Elizabeth L. Holloway
Antioch University

Philomena Essed
Antioch University

For six weeks, they gathered. They gathered,
exchanging stories and tears . . . memories and smiles.
Exchanging life stories from past to present . . .
reflecting on the future.
Sitting around the virtual "kitchen table," ten women,
ten "sisters" not by blood . . .
but shared experiences
came together to
share and unpack

Qualitative Research With Diverse and Underserved Communities, pages 151–160
Copyright © 2024 by Information Age Publishing
www.infoagepub.com
All rights of reproduction in any form reserved.

                    the lived experiences
                      of their bodies . . .
                         never before
                           had any
                             had
                      a conversation
                         like this.

At a time when horrific amounts of grief, anxiety, fear, loss, uncertainty are held captive within the bodies of communities of color, this essay is about healing and liberation. This research, particularly this methodology, is a culturally relevant and dignified way to honor Black women's experiences with their own words and images. African American women are under attack. Rooted centuries ago, when they were made captive to be enslaved, their bodies have been treated as different, less human, and of inconsequential worth (Morgan, 2011). African American women and their bodies have been used and seen as objects, subjects for scientific and medical experiments, and sites of assault and rape (Hill Collins, 1990; Washington, 2006). This study focuses on the impact of abuse and dehumanization on body perception and experience. The overarching question for this study was, "How do African American women experience their bodies?" Y. Falami Devoe with Philomena Essed and Elizabeth Holloway[1] explored this question through an intersectional approach, focusing mainly on the simultaneity of gender, race, sexual orientation and class through the frame of womanism. The quest for lifting and embracing the voice of the African American woman has been at the heart of womanism, which emerged from muted and marginalized voices and experiences within the feminist movement (Das, 2014; Phillips, 2006; Walker, 1985). From a social change perspective, the thrust of Womanism is liberation and self-determination (Phillips, 2006).

I chose to use a decolonizing methodology and I sought to counter residuals from slavery and colonization that continue to impact how researchers approach studying African American people. African Americans have been ignored frequently in mainstream research, or, if the focus of research at all, is typically being done "on" them and not "with" them (Guishard, 2018). The methodology chosen intended to amplify their voices and honor their meaning-making.

Utilizing a participatory action research method provided study participants the platform to be involved in the process, which was liberatory. Narrative photovoice was used as the central approach for data collection and interpretation. photovoice has proven to be an empowering tool and a counter storytelling praxis. Moletsane et al. (2007) asserted that photovoice sits within the larger scope of visual methodologies for social change, helping people process their lived experiences while framing their ideas for change. Narrative photovoice allowed me and the participants/co-researchers/sisters[2] to hear and see how gender, race, sexual orientation impact how women experience their bodies. I embarked on this research journey with my sisters by my side and the anticipation of the vulnerability and power that might ensue from choosing this topic and a methodology that invited deep reflective practice amongst us. Consistent with a liberatory approach, I used poetry to interpret the themes that emerged from the women's stories. This research has been inspired, in particular, by the example of Audre Lorde, one of the most inspiring early Black feminist poets who also wrote extensively on the experience of her body (Lorde, 2011).

POSITIONALITY AND ETHICAL CONSIDERATIONS

Touching upon sensitive issues around the lived, gendered, racialized body experiences of African American women drove the methodological choice and reflected the intentionality of acknowledging the marginalized voice in a culturally appropriate way. As a holistic practitioner/healer, who creates supportive, healing spaces for women of color, it was paramount that I carefully considered the choices I made when creating group sessions that would include delicate conversations about their bodies. These conversations could trigger powerful emotions and stories of denigration and abuse. Further, to protect the women's identities, careful consideration was given to the types of photographs shared in the group. In my initial contact with the participants, I explained that the photographs they would take would be images that did not identify them. They would not bring pictures that showed their face or other identifying images. This condition was critical in obtaining institutional review board (IRB) consent. Further, my experience with facilitating conversations of health and body awareness in women's groups allayed the ethical concerns of engaging in research that could lead to undesirable emotional disturbance. In keeping with my intent to create a safe space for sharing and to hold clear boundaries between my responsibilities as a researcher rather than as a holistic healer, I provided a mental health resource list that they could enlist if follow-up counseling were warranted.

THE SISTERS AS CO-RESEARCHERS

I invited women who considered themselves Black or African American, between the ages of 30 to 55, and who had a minimum of a bachelor's degree. This particular demographic was selected because there are limited research studies within this age and racial demographic. Since this was a methodology that required taking images, participants were expected to have photographic capability on their cellular device and access to the internet as group sessions and interviews were conducted via Zoom videoconferencing.

I identified two women whom I already knew from a historically Black sorority, and using a snowball sampling strategy, I invited them to contact women who might be interested in the topic. I found this approach appropriate considering the sensitive, private nature of the study and the importance that those who identified with women of African ancestry would be suited to reach out to potential participants (Biernacki & Waldorf, 1981).

I contacted the referrals and asked for an initial conversation to make sure they understood the process. During our conversation, I shared information about why I chose to research Black women's lived experiences of their bodies. I was careful to explain that the study would be done "with" them instead of "on" them. Action researchers conduct research "with" participants instead of "on." As an action researcher, I chose to enter into a partnership with my "co-researchers," and I intentionally called them my "sisters." Deeply connected to my culture, I knew calling them my sisters brought a closeness not only with them but honored us as a collective, linked to identifiers of our ancestry. As our time together progressed, the sisters began to refer to each other as "Sis" in conversation with each other.

THE RESEARCH PROCESS

During the 6-week study, the sisters shared their stories, photos, and experiences with their bodies. Figure 7.1 illustrates the research process's flow, beginning and ending with individual interviews with each woman. In the service of brevity, I will describe Sessions 0, 1, 3, and 4 in detail because of their critical experiential role in the group process. The agenda for each session is outlined in Figure 7.1. Sessions 0 and 1 set the stage for the project; I explained photovoice, offered an opportunity for suggestions from the group, and laid the foundation for member connection and trust. Session 2 continued the community building as the details of the photography project were discussed and a lesson in photo composition was included. Session 3 was the SHOWED method, a protocol for sharing in photovoice and described in more detail below. Session 4 and 5 was the apotheosis of the project as the sisters' shared their images with the group.

Session 0: Individual Interview

I discussed the overall theme, ethics, and potential risks of taking photographs in a non-secure environment (Session 0, Figure 7.1). Most

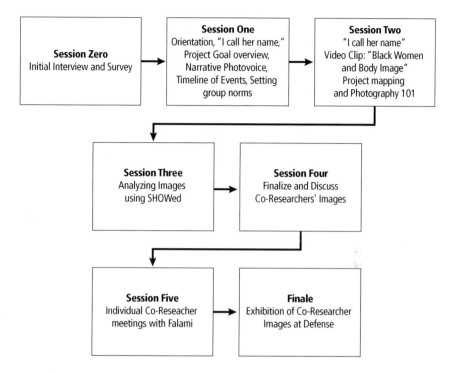

Figure 7.1   Overview of the participatory action research sessions for photovoice process.

importantly, I was able to connect with participants and respond to any concerns or trepidation that they might have about their involvement in the research process. In each interview, I was struck by the commitment and ardor that these women brought to the topic and their belief in its relevance to their growth and the next generation of African women. I realized how impactful these interviews were on me and began a reflective journal to document my feelings, thoughts, and sisters' experiences throughout the research process. This reflective journal became a home for the poems that I wrote throughout the research work (see Box 7.1).

Session 1

As a contemplative praxis, when the women entered the zoom room, they heard the sounds of Whitney Houston, singing, "I'm Every Woman," to energize the space and have the women connect to the song that touts the ferocity of women.

BOX 7.1 REFLECTIVE JOURNAL: ENTRY 1

Journal Entry (written after Session 0)

I am no words. I am emotional. I am humbled. I am grateful. The interviews today solidified the importance of my research. We don't know our body stories per sé or if we do, we don't think about them in the context of every day. We are mothers with daughters. We are our mother's daughters. We have a responsibility to instill in them importance of being who they are not a size, shape or color. I am excited about beginning this process, sharing my story, sharing our story.

Honoring my spiritual tradition (Evans-Winter, 2018; Maparyan, 2011), I began this session modeling what would become a practice for each session. As a practitioner of an African traditional religion, it was important to impart the significance of recognizing and honoring women who were influential in my life; that are now ancestors; connection to ancestors is integral as a practitioner. The session began honoring my mother and other influential women in my life with the traditional Yoruba tribute chant, "I Call Her Name." This practice continued and was shared for all our mothers and othermothers at the opening of every subsequent session.

To come to know each other, the women were asked to introduce themselves with "I am" statements, why they were participating in the study, and say one fun statement about themselves. In this session, the women viewed a video clip of Congresswoman Ayanna Pressley addressing her hair loss due to alopecia (The Root, 2020). I chose this video deliberately as an example of how Black women, who are in the public arena, navigate societal expectations regarding their appearance. I then went to the slides outlining the project goals, the introduction of narrative photovoice, and timeline of events with the participants. Also, participants were asked to reflect and share their feelings throughout the research process. Their input would be valuable in navigating the conversation. Because of the sensitivity of the subject, we constructed collectively group norms for providing feedback.

The 2 weeks in between meetings. Anticipating the third session, I made an entry to my researcher's journal (see Box 7.2).

Session 3 and 4

I began both sessions with "I call her name." The sisters shared their five selected photographs and discussed using the SHOWED method (Wang & Burris, 1997). To prepare them for the SHOWED session, they all received

---

BOX 7.2 REFLECTIVE JOURNAL: ENTRY 2

Journal Entry (written hours before the third session)

So today is the third session, it has been two weeks since I saw them In those two weeks, I have been all over the place with my emotions wondering if everybody was uploading pictures, did they get what they were supposed to do, what were they struggling with. During the two weeks, to keep them engaged, I posted video clips on the FB group. A video clip from the TV sitcom "Blacklish," were the character, Diane, is grappling with what to do with her hair. I asked questions about their experiences. On average, there was 95% participation on the posts!

It is a balancing act being a researcher and photographer. As I review the photos, at times I fight back the photographer instinct. I think how the picture could have been taken differently, but I also think about the possibilities.

---

an information sheet describing the acronym. This acronym represents the method that invites participants to answer these questions (note the bold first letter of the steps, which constitute the acronym, SHOWED).

- What do you See here? (Describe what the eyes see)
- What is really happening Here? (What is the unseen story behind the picture? What does the heart see?)
- How does this relate to Our lives?
- Why does this problem, concern or strength exist? What can we do about it? How might the photo EDucate?

The sisters analyzed the images, providing feedback, and sharing what resonated. I challenged them to discuss themes or issues that emerged. Session 3 was a challenging session. It was visibly noticeable in their facial expressions. Before concluding the session, a few of the sisters shared. "This was emotional, I had to take breaks (from the camera), yet I was empowered by the stories, listening to the stories made me think about how I always conform to others." One sister said she felt "safe and sacred with the sisters."

FINDINGS AND CONCLUSIONS

The findings were analyzed using narrative thematic analysis (Clandinin, 2007) and photovoice to uncover the meaning embedded in the stories told while sharing the photos. The thematic analysis resulted in the themes listed below:

1. hiding one's self from attention, shame, hurt, judgment, and abuse;
2. conforming or not conforming to Eurocentric standards of beauty;
3. colorism;
4. coming out and loving one's self; and
5. surviving cancer.

Evans-Winters (2019) spoke of the conjuring of creative expression. The findings seemed best imparted through poetry, for poems captured the stark, raw expression that emerged from engaging the photovoice methodology.

The sisters' voices, their words, and their stories became rooted in my everyday life as I struggled to discover the right words and form to honor their felt experience. The sisters had revealed through their photos and expressions the hurt and pain their bodies endured as the target of racist, sexist, hegemonic ideologies. Yet, they boldly shared their stories of resilience, resistance, and freedom. There was a strong theme within their accounts of liberation through body love and acceptance as an ongoing process that waxed and waned but was never predictable.

An example of translating from photo story to theme to poetry is presented in Table 7.1. Sister Eleven spoke of her journey to love her natural hair and not conform to the white European image of beauty. In Box 3, her words and the photo she brought to share are presented.

TABLE 7.1 Poetic Interpretation of Themes

Theme 2	Image	Poem
"Conform to Eurocentric Standards of Beauty		We were taught to hate our hair Conform to a more European standard of beauty And not even that was a standard of beauty just what was accepted. I have rejected that my entire Adult life conforming to that standard I appreciate the thickness the fullness The rejection of the conformity. ~Sister Eleven

CONCLUDING REMARKS

As a qualitative researcher, I have learned three important lessons that are also recommendations for others who plan to conduct qualitative research.

1. Trust the process. As I moved through unchartered territories, at times, doubt set in, questioning if I was doing everything "according to the book." After many self-talks, I began to trust the process.
2. Trust your processing. Reflection is essential to the process. It is key to connecting to and with the stories and experiences of your co-researchers.
3. Trust your co-researchers' processing. At the beginning of the process, would the information be triggering? How would they process? Would they grasp how to process their experiences and transfer them via their photographs, and would they provide information for me to tell their stories? I had to trust their way of processing. Trusting your co-researchers is critical in action research, particularly with narrative photovoice. With this type of research, not only do you rely on their stories to answer your research question, but also the images to compliment, provide context and more in-depth insight.

The use of poetry and the vulnerability of choosing this form to share the women's experiences was humbling and fortifying. In the words of Audre Lorde (1984), "Poetry is not a luxury" (p. 36) it is an illuminating force as a means of survival; a "revelatory distillation of experience" (p. 36). This "distillation," this project expressed the intensity, pain and triumph of ten African American women embodied experience.

AUTHOR NOTE

This chapter is based on the first author's dissertation—*In Pictures and Words: A Womanist Answer to Addressing the Lived Experience of African American Women and Their Bodies—A Gumbo of Liberation and Healing*, https://aura.antioch.edu/etds/611/—and supervised by the third author. Correspondence concerning this paper should be addressed to Y. Falami Devoe, https://www.linkedin.com/in/yfalami/

NOTES

1. The chapter will use "I" as representing Falami who implemented the dissertation research study under the supervision of the 2nd and 3rd authors.
2. These words will be used interchangeably through interviews and group sharing.

REFERENCES

Biernacki, P., & Waldorf, D. (1981). Snowball sampling: Problems and techniques of chain referral sampling. *Sociological Methods & Research, 10*(2), 141–163. https://doi.org/10.1177/004912418101000205

Clandinin, D. J. (2007). *Handbook of narrative inquiry: Mapping a methodology.* SAGE Publishing.

Das, S. (2014). Gender politics: A womanist reading of the short stories of Alice Walker. *International Journal of Humanities & Social Science Studies, 1*(3), 123–128. https://oaji.net/articles/2014/1115-1417594158.pdf

Evans-Winters, V. E. (2019). *Black feminism in qualitative inquiry: A mosaic for writing our daughter's body.* Routledge.

Guishard, M. A. (2018). Now's not the time! Qualitative data repositories on tricky ground: Comment on Dubois et al. (2018). *Qualitative Psychology, 5*(3), 402–408. https://doi.org/10.1037/qup0000085

Hill Collins, P. (1990). *Black feminist thought.* Atlantic Books.

Lorde, A. (1984). *Sister outsider.* Crossing.

Lorde, G. A. (2011). *Zami: A new spelling of my name: A biomythography.* Crossing Press.

Maparyan, L. (2012). *The womanist idea.* Routledge.

Moletsane, R., de Lange, N., Mitchell, C., Stuart, J., Buthelezi, T., & Taylor, M. (2007). Photo-voice as a tool for analysis and activism in response to HIV and AIDS in a rural KwaZulu-Natal school. *Journal of Child & Adolescent Mental Health, 19*(1), 19–28.

Morgan, J. L. (2011). *Laboring women: Reproduction and gender in New World slavery.* University of Pennsylvania Press.

Phillips, L. (2006). Introduction—Womanism: On its own. In L. Phillips (Ed.), *The womanist reader* (pp. xix–lv). Routledge.

The Root. (2020, January 16). *Exclusive: Rep. Ayanna Pressley reveals beautiful bald head and talks alopecia for the first time* [Video]. YouTube. https://www.youtube.com/watch?v=dAR5yuD7s-s

Walker, A. (1985). *In search of our mothers' gardens: Womanist prose.* Harcourt.

Wang, C., & Burris, M. A. (1997). PhotoVoice: Concept, methodology, and use for participatory needs assessment. *Health Education & Behavior, 24*(3), 369–387.

Washington, H. (2006). *Medical apartheid: The dark history of medical experimentation on Black Americans from colonial times to the present.* Anchor Books.

INTRODUCTION TO CASE STUDY 8

Critical race ethnography is an important methodological perspective when working with minoritized or disadvantaged, disenfranchised participant-collaborators. This approach seeks the political purpose of recognizing, acknowledging, and addressing social injustice and inequality for change. This type of research provides an avenue for socially discounted individuals and groups to have their voice heard and communicated in a respectful and caring manner to the advantage of those who are sharing that voice. This requires researchers to be self-aware and actively monitoring research decisions, and objective, recognizing the effort is impossible with the inclusion of their own perspectives, experiences, and objectives. Among other things, this means the culturally responsive researcher seeks honest self-reflection and reflexivity to discover the implicit political motivations and goals inherent in the research effort.

Another important element in this case study is the notion of valuing the time and the contributions of the participants in the research process. Culturally responsive and respectful researchers are well aware that simply engaging people for purposes of inquiry (gathering information for presentation, publication, advance of career, etc.) is exploitation at a minimum. However, researchers with individuals from minoritized populations must also be sensitive to the possibility that incentives can be coercive rather than inducements or indications of appreciation for what is offered in the research process. This requires the researcher to be well versed in the social and material conditions of those with whom they are engaged. The ethical researcher recognizes the challenge of identifying an appropriate

Qualitative Research With Diverse and Underserved Communities, pages 161–171
Copyright © 2024 by Information Age Publishing
www.infoagepub.com
161

recognition of value without offering something that is literally "too good to pass up."

Finally, this presentation demonstrates that awareness of the relationship between culture and language is essential and unavoidable. Cultural responsiveness and respect demand that language considerations be central to the development of research plans and their operationalization. This recognition thus requires that all aspects of the inquiry including recruitment, consent, questionnaires, and focus group and interview guides are carefully designed and that recordings are faithfully and authentically transcribed (or otherwise managed) and that translation cannot be merely literal but must also strive to be culturally faithful and authentic to the stories provided by the individuals who are co-researchers, co-creators of meaning.

CASE STUDY 8

MOTHERCENTRIC METHODOLOGY

Using Critical Race Ethnography for Mothering Students of Color in Post-Secondary Education

Cindy N. Phu
Pasadena City College

CONTEXT/BACKGROUND

In the United States, approximately 30% (4.8 million) of community college students are student-parents with young children (Guzman-Lopez, 2019). Student-parents need support beyond academics, including childcare, diapers, baby clothes, and mental health counseling (Guzman-Lopez, 2019). Pallas (2015) explains that among the 4.8 million college student parents nationwide, 71% are student-mothers, 43% are single mothers, and 11% are single fathers. Mothers of color have been historically invisibilized in research, academia, and policies (Anaya, 2011; Caballero et al., 2019; Gumbs et al., 2016). Because women of color are disproportionately likely

Qualitative Research With Diverse and Underserved Communities, pages 163–171
Copyright © 2024 by Information Age Publishing
www.infoagepub.com

163

to be student parents, the purpose of this qualitative study is to understand the unique experiences of mothering students of color (MSC) in community college as they face obstacles such as discrimination, sexism, and racism, as well as to explore how to support their college access and retention.

As such, my methodology is informed by a desire to capture the rich experiences of MSC and to center their perspectives in higher education discourse on parenting. I use critical race ethnography, which is informed by racialized experiences and substantiated through ethnographic research, and centers racial analysis in the process of data collection and analysis (Duncan, 2005; Ramos, 2013). This case study is an examination of my dissertation research titled, "Othering Mothers: Mothering Students of Color in Community College."

RESEARCH QUESTIONS

With more women-identified students entering higher education, I highlighted the multiple identities of mothering students of color (MSC) in higher education, including but not limited to, women-identified students who are mothers, single mothers, and first-generation mothering students. To do so, I used critical race ethnography to better understand the lived experiences of MSC who have a child(ren) during their time attending community college. The following were my research questions:

RQ1: *What are the experiences of MSC in community colleges?*

RQ2: *What barriers do MSC in community colleges encounter when attempting to pursue their education? How do they navigate such barriers?*

RQ3: *What do the narratives of MSC reveal about the climate and treatment of mothering students at community college?*

MOTHERING STUDENTS OF COLOR
IN COMMUNITY COLLEGE

I conducted my dissertation research at a local community college in the Southwestern region of the United States, which has over 30,000 students, 90 academic areas of study, and one childcare center connected to the main campus. The student population is approximately 50% Latinx, 25% Asian, 5% Black/African American, 15% White, and 5% Other. Due to its diverse student demographic, this community college was an ideal setting to recruit participants who self-identified as MSC.

I used a mix of criterion-, opportunistic-, and network-sampling strategies to recruit and select participants. For the criterion-sampling strategy for this research study, the criteria for inclusion were MSC who have been enrolled for at least one semester at a community college and with a child(ren). As part of the mixed-sampling strategy, I included a network of potential participants suggested by the gatekeepers. After the sample selection process, I had 13 semi-structured, face-to-face individual interviews.

RESEARCH CONDITIONS

This research interviews took place January–February 2020 right before the pandemic quarantine orders were implemented. I conducted 14 interviews with MSC at the community college, but one participant withdrawal. Therefore, my research is informed by 13 participants. During the pandemic when community colleges transitioned to remote learning, I still had half of my participants who needed to review their transcriptions.

METHODOLOGY

I used critical race ethnography to understand the experiences of MSC. First, ethnography is a study that "focuses on the culture and social regularities of every life" (Merriam & Tisdell, 2016, p. 229), which allows for rich descriptions [of what]. The ethnographic approach allowed me to situate myself as a mother of color researcher to examine the current discourse on MSC *with* MSC, as a mechanism to uncover inequity in community colleges. To engage with the critical part of my study, I placed my research within my own epistemological, theoretical, and methodological position to be in a place of reflexivity.

Critical race ethnography helped me examine the narratives, experiences, and observations of MSC who are pursuing higher education. I contend that their racialized mothering identities warrant further investigation. Critical race ethnography allows for the examination of ontological categories that could inform the way race functions within stratifying influences in community colleges and higher education. The ontological categories known as states of existence include objectivity, subjectivity, and uncertainty (Carspecken, 1996). According to Carspecken (1996), ontological objectivity claims that "objective-realm entities exist... to say that they are accessible to multiple observers" (p. 64) who will agree with the existence claim if they share specific features of language and culture.

With the understanding of ontological awareness, the approach with face-to-face transformative interviews with MSC allowed for self-disclosure, self-reporting, and helped me to "address layered subjectivity by facilitating the rise into awareness of subjective states routinely repressed or misinterpreted by an interviewee in most social settings" (Carspecken, 1996, p. 75). Furthermore, with the flexibility of interviews and observations, I had the ability to revise my own understanding and alter the interview protocol during or after the interview. Transformative interviewing allows for the development of trust, mutuality, and establishment of an environment of empathy and care (Kezar, 2003). Carspecken argues that participants may sometimes alter their own attitudes and feelings by the end of the interview, which represents evidence of change in self-awareness and produces rich data that an instrument can never attain.

As part of critical race theory (CRT), counterstories served to build and advance discourse surrounding MSC. In order to recognize the invisible voices that have not been adequately documented, I conducted interviews to empower these individuals to share their stories. The interviews helped accomplish the goals of CRT to reveal counterstories. Additionally, CRT offers researchers the ability to connect with qualitative data about the everyday experiences of people to reflect the larger social systems (Delgado & Stefancic, 2001). By using CRT on a micro-level, researchers can have a better understanding of how statements, claims, discussion, and/or discourse can reveal social trends connected to issues of race, racism, and racial progress (Winkle-Wagner et al., 2019)

It is imperative to note that the discourse—or lack of discourse—pertaining to MSC can be equally problematic. Critical race ethnography allows the researcher to focus on the questions of what and how we know based on critical analysis. This is essential when examining how MSC experiences forms of oppression and inequality based on their racialized mothering identities at institutions of higher education. CRT privileges the narratives of marginalized voices who have encountered inequalities in society and depend predominantly on stories as a methodology to showcase their experiences. The value of storytelling is consistent with the research tradition of critical race ethnography.

PROTOCOL

The first instrument was an interview protocol used for semi-structured interviews. Interview protocols can be designed with several themed questions intending to uncover the topic of the research study through covert categories (Carspecken, 1996). The interview protocol can help the researcher (a) keep the basic concept in their mind, (b) not forget any key questions or follow-up questions, and (c) anticipate the multiple directions the conversation can lead (Carspecken, 1996). However, as with the benefits of the semi-structured interview protocol, it is only beneficial as long as the researcher is able to be adaptable and reactive to their participants.

My protocol included a written questionnaire and interview guide, as well as questions that sought the following information: demographic background, experience and behavior questions about the obstacles and challenges as a MSC in higher education, and opinion- and values-based questions about institutional receptivity to MSC with special attention to participant perceptions of resources they believe would help support their academic journey. These questions were emailed to the participants once interview dates and times were scheduled.

During the semi-structured interviews, I took field notes reflective of observations. I also had memos before, during, and after each interview to help contextualize the experiences with observations that cannot or were not captured through the audio-recorder. The memos included noting if they had a child present, breastfed in the interview, and any discourse observations. These memos provide another way to memorialize the interview experience but were not directly coded in the data analysis.

The primary data source was interviews with MSC and secondary sources included discourse, events, and policies. For primary data sources, I transcribed audio-recordings of the interviews, as well as corresponding participant observation field notes and memos. I then reviewed documents and artifacts as secondary sources. I collected campus demographic data and artifacts, which included the campus website, social-media, and campus maps.

THEMATIC ANALYSIS

In ethnographic data analysis, include description, interpretation, and analysis to understand "what is going on here" (description), "what does it all mean" (interpretation), and "the identification of essential features and the systematic description of interrelationships among them" (analysis) according to Merriam and Tisdell (2016, pp. 229–230). After compiling the thematic data analysis, I interpreted the themes and patterns in relation to the existing empirical and conceptual literature on student-mothers in higher education to fill the gap of knowledge in regard to the experiences of MSC in higher education, specifically community colleges.

As critical race ethnography is my framework to explore the inequalities in social structures and uncover racialized patterns, I used the experiences of MSC in higher education to help me present the data through the lens of critical race theory, intersectionality, and double-consciousness (Crenshaw, 2008; Delgado & Stefancic, 2001; Du Bois, 1994). First, interviewing allowed me to gather data for the purposes of research through storytelling and the narratives of that experience to understand the MSC's experiences through higher education. This process helped me share a collaborative document that mutually construct stories out of the lives of both the researcher and the participants. I displayed direct quotes, summaries, and observations connected to the theme and stories.

Second, critical race ethnography is composed of multiple parts for interpretation. It will help create the notion of reframing and transforming the accessibility of higher education to mothering students through a process of critical critique, which is the critical ethnography component. The critical race ethnography will allow for me to analyze in greater detail, specifically looking at the narratives, artifacts, and discourse related to the context of the story.

UNANTICIPATED EVENTS

There were several unanticipated events. First, during the scheduling stage, there were numerous late, no-show, or lack of child-care participants. This was primarily a reflection of their busy schedules balancing motherhood, academics, work, and the added burden of this additional research interview. Second, I did not expect children to be present or have a mother breastfeeding her newborn during the interview. Third, I did not anticipate a participant withdrawal during transcription review as her interview went way beyond the time constraints of the interview. I ended up with 13 participants and had to turn some away and was not able to reconnect with the remaining two participants once the pandemic hit. Finally, one of the participants did parts of her interview in her native language, which was Mandarin. It was important to allow the participant to speak in the language she was comfortable with even though it made it harder for the researcher since there was a delay in accessing the information through the translation services.

CHANGES

In my research, there are several changes to my inquiry plan. First, I changed the office environment space to include toys, crayons, playdough, children's books, and wooden puzzles given that children might be present during the interview. Second, it was important to be even more flexible with scheduling, spacing out interviews, and providing time for debrief. Debrief after the interview was important as the experience for most was the first time many of them revealed their stories, so having a meta-communication afterwards made the interview more transformative in affirming and validating their reported obstacles.

Finally, financial incentives that reflect the needs of the demographic is essential to demonstrating in a concrete manner that their time was valuable. I knew they were working mothers going to school, and the research showed that a majority weresingle parents. I gave a $25 gift card for the initial interview and another $25 for the transcription review. When community colleges moved to remote learning during the pandemic, I emailed the remaining participants an electronic gift card. When I designed the study, I never would have imagined that the gift cards would have been used for medication for their children.

SUMMARY OF FINDINGS

MSC counterstories demonstrate how MSC (a) center their children as their superpower, (b) overcome barriers through learned navigational strategies acquired from intergenerational and/or contemporary traumas, and (c) find mothering mentors who serve as allies and increase their sense of belonging in community college. The implications of the findings are that although community colleges generally were characterized by participants as hostile, holding a deficit notion of children as a burden to MSC, participants persisted and identified institutional possibilities for a mother-receptive climate. I used MSC counterstories to develop recommendations for positive parenting practice, pedagogy, and policy towards the development of a mothering-receptive campus culture in community colleges.

LESSONS LEARNED

Critical race ethnography provided access to interviews, environment inquiry, and review of documents, data, and observations. The research process reflected the MSC experiences trying to go to their own classes while managing their life as a mother. When scheduling, it is imperative to set up email reminders for participants and provide multiple options and opportunities to reschedule. Also, to be open to "non-continuous" interviews over days or shorter duration interviews. It was important to send out the survey before the interview to allow participants time to reflect on the questions before the interview.

RECOMMENDATIONS

There are several recommendations for future qualitative research. First, most participants are sharing their stories for the first time so it should not be expected to be linear—it is up to the researcher to "uncover" the missing pieces. Second, centering scheduling around the needs of the participants will allow for more access, equity, and empathy. Third, remember that the participants are co-writers of your research project so allow organic conversations to emerge before, during, and after the interview. Also, give agency to the participants in the interview question by providing a question to allow them to reimagine their experience. I asked the participants for recommendations for how we can better their experience at the community college. Finally, taking Ginwright's (2018) healing-centered engagement (HCE) approach when listening to the participant's traumas so that they are not viewed from a deficit-notion.

In creating a mothercentric space in COVID-19 times, be patient, as pandemic parenting is hard while navigating student responsibilities in remote learning for both parent and child. When interviewing over the phone or with video, expect family and children to be in the Zoom space. It is also imperative to allow participants to have their video turned off to protect their privacy beyond what they are comfort with revealing during the interview. To use a mothercentric methodology, we must be intentional in creating safe spaces for our participants whose stories we explore and share.

REFERENCES

Anaya, R. (2011). Graduate student mothers of color: The intersectionality between graduate student, motherhood and women of color in higher education. *Intersections*, *9*, 13–31.

Caballero, C., Martinez-Vu, Y., Perez-Torrez, J., Tellez, M., & Vega, C. (Eds.). (2019). *The Chicana motherwork anthology*. The University of Arizona Press.

Carspecken, P. F. (1996). *Critical ethnography in education research*. Routledge.

Crenshaw, K. (2008). *A primer on intersectionality*. African American Policy Forum.

Delgado, R., & Stefancic, J. (2001). *Critical race theory: An introduction*. New York University Press.

Du Bois, W. E. B. (1994). *The souls of Black folk*. Outlet Book.

Duncan, G. A. (2005). Critical race ethnography in education: Narrative, inequalities and the problems of epistemology. *Race Ethnicity and Education*, *8*(1), 93–114. https://doi.org/10.1080/1361332052000341015

Ginwright, S. (2018). *The future of healing: Shifting from trauma informed care to healing centered engagement*. Medium.com. https://medium.com/@ginwright/the-future-of-healing-shifting-from-trauma-informed-care-to-healing-centered-engagement-634f557ce69c

Gumbs, A. P., Martens, C., & Williams, M. (Eds.). (2016). *Revolutionary mothering: Love on the frontlines*. PM Press.

Guzman-Lopez, A. (2019, March 29). *Nearly 1 in 3 community college students is a parent: Here's how to keep them in class*. LAist. https://laist.com/news/many-students-cant-balance-being-a-parent-and-going-to-college-this-is-how-one-center-helps

Kezar, A. (2003). Transformational elite interviews: Principles and problems. *Qualitative Inquiry, 9*(3), 395–415. https://doi.org/10.1177/1077800403009003005

Merriam, S. B., & Tisdell, E. J. (2016). *Qualitative research: A guide to design and implementation* (4th ed.). John Wiley & Sons.

Pallas, P. (2015). *Attending college as a student-parent: Balancing life with higher education for single moms, working dads and everyone in between.* Retrieved from https://www.affordablecollegesonline.org/student-parents-guide

Ramos, T. (2013). Critical race ethnography of higher education: Racial risk and counter-storytelling. *Learning and Teaching, 6*(3), 64–78. https://doi.org/10.3167/latiss.2013.060306

Winkle-Wagner, R., Thandi Sulé, V., & Maramba, D. C. (2019). Analyzing policy critically: Using critical race theory to analyze college admissions policy discourse. In R. Winkle-Wagner, J. Lee-Johnson, & A. N. Gaskew (Eds.), *Critical theory and qualitative data analysis in education* (pp. 193–203). Routledge.

INTRODUCTION TO CASE STUDY 9

This case study is illustrative and important for several reasons pertaining to the purpose of this book. First, the notion of rigor. The basis for the prejudice regarding the rigor of qualitative research seems to be the methodological differences with "empirical" research rather than an examination of the underlying philosophy and the nature of the effort. Well done qualitative inquiry is no less rigorous than any other approach to inquiry. Clear requirements and expectations regarding methods and subsequent credibility of findings and conclusions are well described in the literature and philosophical and logical guidelines require much better and more careful attention in practice. Qualitative research with individuals from minoritized or disadvantaged backgrounds especially requires rigorous attention to cultural as well as individual (personal) considerations.

The idea of generalizability as a standard for inquiry or research is likely another "carry over" from quantitative/empirical research practice. Culturally responsive and responsible qualitative practice requires authenticity of process as well as outcome—*authenticity rather than "generalizability" is the gold standard* and is based on and judged in terms of the lived experience of research participants with findings and interpretations ranging in applicability based at least in part on the "distance" from the "original story." While this does not mean to imply that qualitative research findings cannot be descriptive of or "transferrable" to others, it does mean that any effort to design a study which does so must even more so than usual have a strict and rigorous focus on the implications of culture and place.

Finally, this study also illustrates the notion of purposive sampling. Regardless of definition, a key element is "expert" knowledge of the domain, significant cultural experience and investment and careful consideration of decision making by the researcher to ensure that outcomes are reflective of and responsive to that knowledge and experience. Purposive sampling which is performed solely as a matter of researcher interest and fails to consider the context, conditions, experience and culture of the respondents is untenable and probably unethical.

CASE STUDY 9

EXPLORING ASSISTIVE TECHNOLOGY INFLUENCES ON KENTUCKY AGRABILITY PROGRAM RECIPIENTS' WORK LIFE

Nesma Osman
Mississippi State University

Donna J. Peterson
Mississippi State University

STATEMENT OF THE PROBLEM

Farming is one of the riskiest occupations in all industries (Allen et al., 1995; Mathew et al., 2011). Agriculture-related injuries ranked the second-highest origin of disability for farmers after chronic health conditions, such as arthritis and spinal cord injury (Meyer & Fetsch, 2006). Among the six types of disabilities recognized by the American Community Survey (hearing, visual, cognitive, ambulatory, self-care, and independent living),

Qualitative Research With Diverse and Underserved Communities, pages 175–188
Copyright © 2024 by Information Age Publishing
www.infoagepub.com
175

ambulatory disability was the most common health problem among all ages at 6.8% (Erickson et al., 2012). Roughly 2.13 million farms and ranches are responsible for producing a significant portion of the food and fiber consumed in the United States (Field & Jones, 2006). However, many of the individuals who operate these farms and ranches have various disabilities. The percentage of those farmers and ranchers with temporary or permanent disabilities in the United States has reached 19% of the agricultural population (Deboy et al., 2008).

Continuing farm occupations is one of the most significant challenges that face agricultural workers with disabilities. Disability has a considerable influence among the many things that could threaten farmers with disabilities losing their way of life (Molyneaux-Smith et al., 2003). Hancock (1998) found that providing modifications to farm equipment and using appropriate assistive technology (AT) helped farmers with disabilities overcome work barriers and gave them the confidence to return to farming. Assistive technology is defined as "a broad range of machines, services, strategies, or skills intended to assist disabled people in accomplishing activities independently" (Grisso et al., 2014, p. 1). Since most farmers with disabilities are owners or operators of their farms (Jackman et al., 2016), they need appropriate modified farm equipment and AT that fit their limitations and help them work independently (Field & Jones, 2006).

Many researchers have focused their studies on how agricultural workers with disabilities return to work through different AT. However, few studies compare farmers with disabilities' work-life before and after using AT or how AT influences their work motivation. More research is needed to explore how AT contributes to motivating agricultural workers with disabilities to continue farming. Also, there is a need to examine how AT improves agricultural workers with disabilities' work life.

The job characteristics model (JCM), designed by Hackman and Oldham in 1976, provided the framework for this study. The JCM consists of three major components: task features, psychological states of workers, and individuals' attributes toward dealing with challenges and difficulties at work. The model shows the relationship between job characteristics and employee performance and reaction to the profession through five dimensions: skill variety, task identity, task significance, autonomy, and feedback. These dimensions cause three primary psychological states in workers: experienced meaningfulness of the work, responsibility for work, and knowledge of the ultimate results of the activity. The three psychological states generate meaningful results in enhancing job performance, decreasing turnover, and boosting internal work motivation.

PURPOSE OF THE STUDY

Using the JCM (Hackman & Oldham, 1976), the purpose of this study was to document the experiences of agricultural workers with disabilities who were using assistive technology through the Kentucky AgrAbility program. Comparisons were made between work life before and after use of AT. We explored how using AT contributed to helping agricultural workers with disabilities in the following areas: capability of conducting tasks with different skills, capability of completing tasks from beginning to end, capability of performing tasks independently, and capability of doing tasks with a passion for benefiting themselves and others. These aspects contribute to an understanding of the psychological states of agricultural workers with disabilities. Work outcomes (i.e., internal motivation to work, work performance, satisfaction with work, and frequency of turnover) were explored to determine the influence of using AT on motivating agricultural workers with disabilities to continue farming. Personal characteristics that affected work motivation were also examined.

RESEARCH QUESTION(S)

The research questions of the study were:

1. How did agricultural workers with disabilities perform their work before using AT?
2. What influenced agricultural workers with disabilities' work motivation before using AT?
3. How do agricultural workers with disabilities perform their work using AT?
4. How does using AT influence work motivation among agricultural workers with disabilities?
5. How do personal characteristics (i.e., age, role on-farm) relate to work motivation?

DESIGN OF THE STUDY

This research study adopted a qualitative approach to get a better understanding and more in-depth information about the phenomenon under investigation (Bradley et al., 2007). The data derived from participants' experiences were "powerful and sometimes more compelling than quantitative data" (Anderson, 2010, p. 2). However, generalizing qualitative study findings to other settings, maintaining rigor, and consuming much time to collect and analyze data were the disadvantages of using a qualitative approach.

RESEARCH CONTEXT AND DESCRIPTION OF PARTICIPANTS

After conducting several communications with AgrAbility programs in four different states, we selected the Kentucky AgrAbility program as the study site. The two reasons for choosing the Kentucky AgrAbility program were (a) the project director helped provide sufficient information about the project and describe the general activities for which the project was responsible, and (b) the director assisted with recruiting participants who met the specific study inclusion criteria. Also, the Kentucky AgrAbility program had served agricultural workers with different disabilities for more than 18 years with several supports such as providing assistive technology, training, or education, which allowed them to overcome barriers while working ("Kentucky AgrAbility Project," n.d., p. 1).

We used a purposive sampling method to ensure participants met specific criteria. The first criterion was that participants had a disability—whether from birth or acquired due to work conditions. The rationale for selecting the first criterion was that farmers t had a disability that challenged their ability to do their job to examine how AT influenced their work life and their work motivation. Second, different types of disabilities were included to explore how individuals with various disabilities were affected by using AT. The third criterion was that individuals included mush have been using ATs for at least 1 year. The criterion was selected to ensure that agricultural workers with disabilities had fully interacted with AT to have enough experience to provide meaningful feedback.

The Kentucky AgrAbility program director provided a list of 15 names who met these criteria and who indicated possible interest in participating in the study. Five males and two females completed both the questionnaire and interview process. Participants in the study included—two who owned horse farms, two dairy farms, one a sheep farm, one a lawn service company, and one primarily gardened and mowed on his farm.

DATA COLLECTION TOOLS

A questionnaire and telephone interview were used for data collection. The questionnaire was divided into two parts. The first part included the demographic questions (e.g., age, gender, type of disability, the length of disability, and occupation). The second part had basic questions which covered the agricultural workers with disabilities' work life before and after using AT. The advantages of using the questionnaire were (a) collecting the participants' initial data to facilitate the telephone interview procedures and (b) double-checking what the participants said. On the other hand, sending the questionnaire to participants via mail before conducting the telephone interview instead of via email lengthened the data collection process. The Kentucky AgrAbility program director reviewed the survey to check the questionnaire's quality,

Interview questions were constructed based on the JCM (Hackman & Oldham, 1976) to explore the AT's influences on agricultural workers with disabilities' work motivation and work life. The questions covered the five dimensions of the JCM (skill variety, task identity, task significance, autonomy, and feedback) while using AT. The advantages of using telephone interviews were (a) reaching participants more easily at any time, (b) getting more in-depth information on how disabled agricultural workers performed their work before using AT and how using AT influenced their work motivation, and (c) allowing for revisions to questions since "interviews are not restricted to specific questions and can be guided/redirected by the researcher in real-time" (Anderson, 2010, p. 2). However, using a telephone for conducting the interview prevented observing participants' real reactions and may contribute to bias in understanding their actual meanings. We analyzed the data based on thematic analysis, which can be applied across different theoretical frameworks (Braun & Clarke, 2006).

The questionnaire and the interview questions were reviewed by three faculty members familiar with the study to check the questionnaire's quality and clearness and interview questions. The study was reviewed and approved by the Mississippi State University Institutional Review Board. It was granted exempt from review status and subsequently inactivated from further requirements.

DATA COLLECTION PROCEDURES

We collected the data from December 2016 to February 2017. The Kentucky AgrAbility program director contacted potential participants first to see if they were willing to participate in the study. The director used a script developed by the researcher for recruiting participants. After the individuals agreed to participate, the director provided a list of fifteen potential participants' names, addresses, and phone numbers to the researcher. Then, the researcher contacted the potential participants to inform them that they would receive (via mail) a questionnaire to fill out within a week that would take approximately 25 minutes to complete. Due to the difficulties of reaching potential participants by phone, the researcher mailed the questionnaire and a formal letter explaining the study and what was involved in participation.

After 2 weeks, when five participants out of 15 returned the completed questionnaire, a faculty member called those individuals to schedule an appointment to interview over the telephone and shared a list of the topics that would be covered in the phone interview. However, one of those five individuals mentioned that he would not be able to participate in the telephone interview due to its length. Also, because some participants did not return the questionnaire, the Kentucky AgrAbility program director re-contacted those individuals to see if they were still interested in participating. The faculty member contacted those who agreed and scheduled an appointment to complete the questionnaire and interview simultaneously over the phone. Ultimately, eight questionnaires were completed, but only seven individuals participated in the interview (complete data existed for seven).

Each interview was conducted by two interviewers (the researcher and one faculty member). One interview was conducted with a participant's mother due to his disability and difficulty in communicating. Before beginning the telephone interview, we informed the participants that all information would be confidential, their names would not appear in the study, and they were free to skip any questions. The interview lasted from 22 minutes to 45 minutes.

The interviews were audio-recorded for transcription purposes with permission from the participants. Transcriptions were used for analyses (pseudonyms only were used to identify participants in the transcriptions). We asked participants semi-structured questions; some of the questions were structured in advance, and others emerged during the interview to get more in-depth explanations about the topic. The interview took place in one faculty member's office at the researcher's institution. The total time participants spent on all phases of the study (questionnaire and interview) was approximately 1 hour. We offered participants a $15 gift card as an acknowledgment of sharing their stories and their contribution to the study.

DATA ANALYSIS PROCEDURES

Qualitative data were analyzed based on thematic analysis, a method that is used "for identifying, analyzing, and reporting patterns (themes) within data" (Braun & Clarke, 2006, p. 6). The idea behind using thematic analysis is to summarize large amounts of data and provide more description of the data set, which leads to developing unanticipated insights (Braun & Clarke, 2006). The analysis procedures began with transcribing the whole audio-recorded interview verbatim, and then the transcripts were read and re-read again to get a general understanding of the data (Braun & Clarke, 2006).

The second step was coding; in this analysis phase, a systematic process is used to highlight the interesting and important data from the interview across the data set and then group data related to each other (Braun & Clarke, 2006). For the coding process in this study, a preliminary coding list was developed based on the JCM; however, other codes emerged during analysis. Some responses fit more than one code, but only one emerging code was identified in all transcripts. The coding process was conducted by the researcher and checked by one faculty member. The two individuals reviewed coded transcripts for agreement in assigned codes with differences resolved through discussion and consensus.

After coding, the analysis focused on developing themes primarily identified by using theoretical or deductive analysis, in which the identification of the theme was related to the questions that were asked of participants (Braun & Clarke, 2006). The themes constructed from the interview were compared with those derived from the literature review and the JCM.

Themes were reviewed and checked on two levels: the coded extracts and the entire data set (Braun & Clarke, 2006). This step's significance was to ensure that each theme had sufficient data supporting it and to determine whether themes needed to be broken into subthemes. Finally, a thematic map of the analysis—a process in which all themes and subthemes were organized in a way that ensured the meaning of each theme, refined overlap between themes, and ensured that themes fit within the theoretical framework—was developed for generating an organized story about the data (Braun & Clarke, 2006). The demographic data from the questionnaires were only used to describe each participant. However, the rest of the questionnaire items were used to double-check the participants' responses and facilitate the telephone interview process.

TRUSTWORTHINESS

In a qualitative study, "the researcher is always part of the study and reflects upon the phenomenon under study while proceeding in the process of generating understanding" (Stenbacka, 2001, p. 553). Also, qualitative researchers depend on the views of people who conduct research, participate in a study, or read and review findings from the study, more than on psychometrics of specific instruments (Creswell & Miller, 2000). Therefore, trustworthiness, which consists of (a) credibility, (b) transferability, (c) dependability, and (d) confirmability, contributes to assuring the accuracy and the quality of the data and their interpretation (Lincoln & Guba, 1985).

First, credibility is a criterion to ensure that researcher's interpretations and findings are valid based on participants' responses with the (Lincoln & Guba, 1985). In this study, three techniques were used to ensure credibility. The first was using triangulation across different methods (i.e., an interview and a questionnaire) for relying on more than one piece of evidence to ensure the credibility of the data (Creswell & Miller, 2000). As an illustration, the interview method was the primary method for collecting in-depth data from participants. However, some of the questionnaire questions were used to double-check the participants' responses and facilitate the interview process.

Peer debriefing, which is "the review of the data and research process by someone familiar with the research being explored" (Creswell & Miller, 2000, p. 129), was the second technique used to establish credibility. The researcher involved one faculty member in reviewing each step in the analysis process, including reviewing coding, themes, and the thematic map to maintain objectivity and accuracy. A minor change was suggested by the faculty member on the coding process, and the researcher made the modification. The last technique is the thick description, which helps to establish credibility through describing the participants, the setting, and the themes in rich detail to give the reader a chance to "read a narrative account and are transported into a setting or situation" (Creswell & Miller, 2000, p. 129). We accomplished that by providing details about participants, full descriptions of each theme, and quotes from participants that illustrate the themes.

Transferability, which is equivalent to generalization in quantitative studies, was achieved through presenting a detailed description of the methodology (i.e., study design, sampling, data collection tools, data collection procedures, and data analysis procedures) and the results (i.e., participants' details, findings, and discussion) to give a clear picture on how this study was conducted (Lincoln & Guba, 1985).

The third criterion of trustworthiness is dependability, which helps to ensure that a researcher can "produce the same research result over and over again" (Stenbacka, 2001, p. 552). Since the qualitative study's nature is different from the quantitative research, dependability could be reached by providing sufficient information about the whole research process to help other researchers understand the entire process (Lincoln & Guba, 1985). Dependability was achieved by using the same technique as illustrated above in transferability.

The last criterion is the confirmability. It refers to how the data and interpretations are associated with participants' thoughts and responses, rather than being generated from the researcher's subjectivity (Lincoln & Guba, 1985). This criterion was reached by providing detailed descriptions of each theme with essential quotations representing what participants said to compare it with the researcher's and readers' interpretations.

RESULTS

Participant Descriptions

Overall, seven participants (two females and five males) completed both the questionnaire and the interview. The detailed descriptions for each participant are provided below.

Participant 1 was 74 years old, widowed, and retired. She has had a paraplegic disability for 35 years. She now lives in an assisted living facility in Kentucky. She had worked in an agriculture career all her life until she retired. She had a horse farm; her duties were to take care of the horses, mow the farm, and tend to a garden. She had worked in agriculture for 30 years since her disability and performed her farm work for 10 years without using ATs. She had used the leaders, reachers, a ramp to get on her golf cart, and a board to get on the tractor for 20 years. She had used hand controls to assist with driving her car for 30 years.

Participant 2 was 65 years old, single, and employed full-time as an Extension specialist and part-time farmer. She had been diagnosed with nearly 100 mini strokes leading to vertigo and balance issues requiring a walker for 4 years, bronchiectasis lung disease for 7 years, and general lung problems with bouts of pneumonia for 55 years. She had worked in an agriculture career before her disability for 45 years. She has a horse farm; her duties are feeding, training, and showing horses, hay handling, transporting horses in the trailer, foaling mares, and breeding stallions. Four years before the interview, she began having severe health problems but continued her work for 1 year without using ATs. She used a golf cart, shorter-length fences, redesigned waterlines, and a grain storage unit (that reduced the distance when transporting grain to the horses) for 3 years.

Participant 3 was 71 years old, married, and full-time employed. He had a diabetes sore on his leg that required part of his leg to be removed. He had worked in agriculture before his disability for 50 years and had spent 6 years performing his job since his disability. He has a sheep farm; his duties are feeding sheep and mowing. He had been using an artificial leg for 6 years.

Participant 4 was 32 years old, single, and employed full time during the summer. He has had CMT (Charcot-Marie-Tooth), which is a neuromuscular disease, for 18 years. He is an owner of Claire Lawn Services, and his work involves cutting yards. He had worked in lawn services for 14 years since his disability and performed his job without using the ATs for 8 years. He had been using a modified lawnmower for 6 years. (Participant 4's mother completed the interview for him.)

Participant 5 was 58 years old, married, and employed full time. He had a leg amputation 4 years before the interview. He had worked in an agriculture career before his disability for 45 years. He has a dairy farm; his duties are feeding calves and cows and opening gates. He had worked in his agriculture career for 4 years since his disability. He had been using hand controls on his tractor, a tractor with a lift, and a wheelchair for 4 years.

Participant 6 was 62 years old, married, and employed full time. He has quadriplegia but has some use of his hands. He had worked in an agriculture career before his disability for 15 years. He has a dairy farm; his duties are to do some custom hay bale rolling for people, cut hay, and feed moved bails to cattle. He had worked in an agriculture career for about 30 years since his disability. He used hand controls on his tractor, a golf cart with hand controls, and a gator with hand controls for 21 years.

Participant 7 was 66 years old, divorced, and employed part-time. He has had paraplegia for 10 years. He had worked in an excavating career for 30 years; his farming duties were gardening and mowing. He used hand controls on his tractor for 8 years and a modified lawnmower for 9 years.

OVERVIEW OF THEMES

We identified five main themes from analyzing the interview transcripts: work life before using AT, motivational factors for work before using AT, work life after using AT, motivational factors for work after using AT, and personal characteristics related to work motivation. We presented a summary of each theme and illustrative quotes below.

Work Life Before Using AT

Agricultural workers with disabilities' work life before using AT was slow, hard, took a long time, and could not be done without others' help. One participant described, "I couldn't mow until I got a farm tractor fixed up with hand controls. I had to get somebody else to mow it until I got my farm tractor fixed up, so I could do it myself."

Motivational Factors for Work Before Using AT

The primary reasons that kept participants motivated to work before using AT the desire to live and work on a farm, receive support from the community, and still complete at least part of one's farm tasks without having AT. For most, due to their ownership of a farm, their love of working on a farm, and their strong faith that disability would not keep them from continuing their job, they never thought about quitting farming: "I love the farm. I've always lived on a farm, and I wanted to stay on a farm."

Work Life After Using AT

Participants who received different AT (e.g., external devices such as hand controls on a tractor or having an artificial leg) had a chance to maneuver more easily on the farm and accomplish their farm tasks. Most participants indicated that AT did not require any specialized training or skills to use AT. Moreover, using AT did not influence agricultural workers with disabilities' work quality but did affect the speed at which a farm task was completed. One participant said,

> It's much easier now [farm work], much less effort. Time had gone down from what 5 years ago would take about 30 to 40 minutes, then took me an hour to an hour and a half about twice a day to feed horses. And now, I can do it in 15 to 20 minutes.

However, while using AT helped agricultural workers with disabilities to work independently, some still needed assistance to access and operate AT.

Motivational Factors for Work After Using AT

Using AT made participants feel more independent and increasing their self-worth. They could complete their work more quickly and maintain what they loved to do. AT also contributed to increasing agricultural workers with disabilities' passion for benefiting themselves and others. As one participant described,

> Imagine a picture of something that you were able to do daily that gave you a driving force of accomplishment within yourself, and now that ability was taken away. Assistive technology enables me to have that passion still and not give up on what I was trying to accomplish.

Personal Characteristics Related to Work Motivation

Personal characteristics of age, type of disability, and role on the farm were related to work motivation. For example, the more severe the type of disability and related health conditions and the aging process itself, the more negatively affected work motivation. As one participant explained,

> All of us don't have the physical capabilities at 30 as we do at 60, so it is a natural occurrence. But those prosthetic legs have been to me because without them, over half the things that I do I would not be able to do. it still enables someone to have a quality of life that you would not even begin to have if you didn't have them.

However, being the owner of the farm or agricultural business positively influenced motivation to continue agrarian work.

LIMITATIONS

Several limitations of this study need to be considered. The first limitation is generalizing results. Because the study had a small number of participants, generalizing results will be difficult. However, this small number of participants and a qualitative approach helped get more in-depth information about their stories, which could convey how the study could be replicated in other agricultural settings. Due to the difficulty in reaching agricultural workers with disabilities in different states, there could be a limitation based on geographic differences in farm settings.

Additionally, due to differences in specific characteristics such as age or gender, generalizing the results within a disability type or across different types is questionable. Conducting a telephone interview prevented observing participants' real reactions, which may contribute to bias in understanding the actual meaning behind their stories (compared to a face-to-face interview). However using additional data collection methods for triangulation purposes was an effort to reduce potential bias.

Another limitation of this study was the difficulty for some participants to understand the questionnaire, which led to conducting both the interview and completing the questionnaire simultaneously and lengthened the interview time. It could be improved by double-checking with the participants by conducting another telephone interview to get their feedback and comments on interpreting the findings (Rodger et al., 2001). It is also possible that because only seven of the fifteen individuals on the list of potential participants completed the interview, they could differ in their motivation to work than those who did not complete the interview.

The final limitation is struggling to engage the participants in the conversation and asking follow-up questions, especially for further clarification. Because the researcher is not a native English speaker, this sometimes led to difficulties in understanding whether the participants gave a full answer to the target question. It could also be improved with the previous technique where the researcher re-asks questions in a different way to get sufficient answers.

FUTURE RESEARCH

The qualitative approach will not contribute to generalizing the results. Thus, future studies could include additional participants with different disabilities to understand better the effect of using AT on their agricultural work life. Different demographic characteristics would also benefit from the future study. For example, including participants who work on others' farms (rather than being a farm owner) needs further investigation to explore if their motivation to continue working would change or stay the same as reported by farm owners in the current study. It would also be essential to assess how agricultural workers with disabilities' income levels relate to AT's use. There could be differences in motivation among those workers who have the financial ability to purchase AT on their own rather than needing assistance from a support program, or the AT that are used could differ based on an individual's financial situation. Also, recruiting participants with similar personal characteristics, such as age, gender, and role on-farm, need to be studied to explore the influence of ATs on workers with disabilities' work motivation within the same types of disabilities or farm settings.

REFERENCES

Allen, P. B., Field, W. E., & Frick, M. J. (1995). Assessment of work-related injury risk for farmers and ranchers with physical disabilities. *Journal of Agricultural Safety and Health, 1*(2), 71–81. https://doi.org/10.13031/2013.19455

Anderson, C. (2010). Presenting and evaluating qualitative research: Strengths and limitations of qualitative research. *American Journal of Pharmaceutical Education, 74*(8), 1–7. https://doi.org/10.5688/aj7408141

Bradley, E. H., Curry, L. A., & Devers, K. J. (2007). Qualitative data analysis for health services research: Developing taxonomy, themes, and theory. *Health Services Research, 42*(4), 1758–1772. https://doi.org/10.1111/j.1475-6773.2006.00684.x

Braun, V., & Clarke, V. (2006). Using thematic analysis in psychology. *Qualitative Research in Psychology, 3*(2), 77–101. https://doi.org/10.1191/1478088706qp063oa

Creswell, J. W., & Miller, D. L. (2000). Determining validity in qualitative inquiry. *Theory Into Practice, 39*(3), 124–131. https://doi.org/10.1207/s15430421tip3903_2

Deboy, G. R., Jones, P. J., Field, W. E., Metcalf, J. M., & Tormoehlen, R. L. (2008). Estimating the prevalence of disability within the U.S. farm and ranch population. *Journal of Agromedicine, 13*(3), 175–190. https://doi.org/10.1080/10599240802371763

Erickson, W., Lee, C., & von Schrader, S. (2012). *2010 disability status report: United States.* Cornell University, Employment and Disability Institute.

Field, W. E., & Jones, P. (2006). Disability in agriculture. In J. E. Lessenger (Ed.), *Agricultural medicine* (pp. 70–80). Springer New York.

Grisso, R., Perumpral, J., Ohanehi, D., & Ballin, K. B. (2014). *Assistive technologies in agriculture* (Publication 442-084). Virginia Tech.

Hackman, J. R., & Oldham, G. R. (1976). Motivation through the design of work: Test of a theory. *Organizational Behavior and Human Performance, 16*(2), 250–279. https://doi.org/10.1016/0030-5073(76)90016-7

Hancock, J. (1998). Kentucky AgrAbility: Helping disabled farmers return to the land. *Journal of Agromedicine, 5*(1), 35–43. https://doi.org/10.1300/J096 v05n01_05

Jackman, D. M., Fetsch, R. J., & Collins, C. L. (2016). Quality of life and independent living and working levels of farmers and ranchers with disabilities. *Disability and Health Journal, 9*(2), 226–233. https://doi.org/10.1016/j .dhjo.2015.09.002

Kentucky AgrAbility Project–University of Kentucky. (n.d.). Retrieved from https:// content.iospress.com/articles/journal-of-vocational-rehabilitation/jvr00107

Lincoln, Y. S., & Guba, E. G. (1985). *Naturalistic inquiry.* SAGE Publication.

Mathew, S. N., Field, W. E., & French, B. F. (2011). Secondary injury potential of assistive technologies used by farmers with disabilities: Findings from case studies. *Journal of Agromedicine, 16*(3), 210–225. https://doi.org/10.1080/105992 4X.2011.581542

Meyer, R. H., & Fetsch, R. J. (2006). National AgrAbility project impact on farmers and ranchers with disabilities. *Journal of Agricultural Safety and Health, 12*(4), 275–291. https://doi.org/10.13031/2013.22009

Molyneaux-Smith, L., Townsend, E., & Guernsey, J. R. (2003). Occupation disrupted: Impacts, challenges, and coping strategies for farmers with disabilities. *Journal of Occupational Science, 10*(1), 14–20. https://doi.org/10.1080/14427 591.2003.9686506

Rodger, S. A., de Jonge, D. M., & Driscoll, M. (2001). Factors that prevent or assist the integration of assistive technology into the workplace for people with spinal cord injuries: Perspectives of the users and their employers and coworkers. *Journal of Vocational Rehabilitation, 16*(1), 53–66.

Stenbacka, C. (2001). Qualitative research requires quality concepts of its own. *Management Decision, 39*(7), 551–555. http://dx.doi.org/10.1108/EUM00000 00005801

INTRODUCTION TO CASE STUDY 10

This report of inquiry is illustrative of the importance of relationship based on in-depth knowledge and understanding and trust developed both as a matter of engagement and as a matter of research procedure in the pursuit of authentic stories which provide a basis for judgment and understanding of others' lived experience. One way this is demonstrated is through the use of hermeneutic phenomenological interviewing. Hermeneutic phenomenology expects the researcher to recognize and accept the historical context of the individuals experiencing the phenomena of interest and the influence of the social context on the interpretive description of the individual's experience. This is a key consideration for any inquiry focusing on the experience of individuals from minoritized or disadvantaged groups since it bases judgments about meaning on the likely developmental basis for current perspectives—that is, it recognizes that experience is the key mechanism for socialization and the development of identity. Another way this is reflected in the current study, is the development and refinement of questions which were the basis for the interview guide. All too often, qualitative researchers artificially constrain their inquiry with requirements for quantitative methods which are not applicable. This includes inquiry which is regulated rather than guided by the initial protocol for research action. Qualitative researchers have the responsibility to be active "instruments"— that is, devices for eliciting information which is relevant and authentic or in other words, "valid" and "reliable."

Finally, researchers must be sensitive to and respectful of the perspectives of those who provide information about the focus of their inquiry. This is a

Qualitative Research With Diverse and Underserved Communities, pages 189–201
Copyright © 2024 by Information Age Publishing
www.infoagepub.com
189

far cry from the perspective of considering inquiry participants as "subjects" of research and instead acknowledges and celebrates that they are co-creators or meaning makers in the conduct, process, and outcomes of the study. Regardless of intentions or design, qualitative research *seeks to engage participants rather than merely utilizing them.* The value proposition for qualitative researchers should be not simply the pursuit of information but, instead meaning making which is authentic and useful—that is going beyond observation to evidence. Good qualitative researchers recognize that their objective and purpose is the study of the experience of phenomena (i.e., phenomena situated in context and identity) rather than solely the phenomena itself. This is always so but, essentially important in the study of that experience from the perspective of those who have been and continue to be discounted by the larger society or simply ignored as irrelevant or unworthy.

CASE STUDY 10

INTERPRETIVE INQUIRY INTO MUSLIM STUDENTS' ELEMENTARY SCHOOL EXPERIENCES IN CANADA

Afshan Amjad
Norquest College

Julia Ellis
University of Alberta

Anna Kirova
University of Alberta

SOCIETAL CONTEXT: RACISM, ISLAMOPHOBIA, AND HARASSMENT FOR MUSLIM STUDENTS

While Canada enjoys an international reputation as a culturally diverse state that is largely welcoming to newcomers, the fact is that Canada has not escaped the often contentious debates surrounding the social integration of Muslim communities seen elsewhere, especially since the

Qualitative Research With Diverse and Underserved Communities, pages 191–201
Copyright © 2024 by Information Age Publishing
www.infoagepub.com

world-altering events of the 11th of September 2001. Since then, concerns regarding the integration of Muslims in Canada have flared up around the use of religious law in family-based disputes in Ontario in 2005, over homegrown violent extremism both by Islamists (e.g., the "Toronto 18" arrests in 2006) and White supremacists (e.g., the mass shooting at a mosque in Quebec in 2017), over controversies and the legal battle surrounding the wearing of the niqab during the oath of citizenship, and over the admission of Syrian refugees during the 2015 federal election campaign (McCoy et al., 2016, p. 10). This indicates that perhaps not all immigrants feel equally welcomed in Canadian society. As Jeffrey Reitz (2009) has acknowledged, some of these debates have mirrored what has been seen in other Western states: "The questions in Canada as elsewhere have focused on religion, whether certain religious minorities have values, beliefs or practices that are difficult to integrate into Canadian society because they clash with Canadian ideas about gender equality or secularism in public institutions" (p. 9).

Given that the most current national statistics (the 2011 National Household Survey) indicate that in 2011 Muslims living in Canada comprised 3.2% of the national population, and therefore represented the second largest religious group (after Christianity) and are one of the fastest growing and younger segments of the Canadian population, the issue of integration of Muslim children in Canadian schools is of utmost importance. While adjusting to school is not an easy experience for most newcomer children, Muslim children in Canadian schools also face racism, Islamophobia, and harassment. In Zine's (2008) study, she examines the politics of piety, veiling, and gender segregation with special attention to the construction of gendered identities. She found that in school, boys reported being called terrorists and girls who wore hijab had stones thrown at them during their walks to and from school. Due to the multiple religious and cultural interpretations in society, schools have a significant responsibility (Merry, 2006). Prejudice among school age children against Arab Muslims has been identified by recent studies in North America (Brown et al., 2017). Syrian refugee children in a study conducted in Western Canada, recounted incidents of ethnic-religious discrimination when they were beaten up and told to go back to their "own" country when they attempted to pray outside of the school building (Guo et al., 2019, p. 86). Discriminatory attitudes on the part of students are often supported by teachers' lack of response to racist bullying or their penalizing of the victims (Zine, 2000). As a result, Muslim children develop feelings of disaffection and marginality because of the lack of social acceptance.

FOCUS OF INQUIRY: LEARNING MUSLIM STUDENTS' PERSPECTIVES

Most studies of the school experiences of Muslim students have included high school, college, and university students leaving a gap in the literature regarding the experiences of Muslim students in elementary schools (Amjad, 2016). Children have their own understandings of the world around them, which are not easy for an adult to understand (Green & Hill, 2005). Ellis (2006) calls children "social actors" who create their own culture through exploring the physical and social resources available to them (p. 111). Green and Hill (2005) state that in most societies, children "are valued for their potential and what they grow up to be but are devalued in terms of their present perspectives and experiences" (p. 3). The purpose of the study reported here was to explore how Muslim students had experienced and made sense of their everyday lives at elementary schools in a major city in Western Canada.

SAMPLE AND POPULATION OF INTEREST

There were seven participants in the study: 3 male and 4 females ranging in age from 11 to 18. All participants moved to Canada after the age of 8 and completed all or some part of their elementary grades in schools in the province in which the study took place. It was important to include both male and female students as participants given that female Muslim students have the visible hijab as part of their dress code whereas male Muslims do not have visual religious symbols in their dress prior to adulthood. Students 11 and older were intentionally sought as participants to reduce the risk of including students who might be in the midst of traumatic experiences in elementary school years. Ethics approval was granted by the ethics board at the university where the first author was a doctoral student.

CONDITIONS WITHIN WHICH THE INQUIRY WAS SITUATED

The study was undertaken as dissertation research by the first author (Amjad, 2016). Participants were recruited through the personal connections of the researcher within the East Asian community in the city in which the research took place. Yin (2017) has argued that all dissertation studies that involve case study research should be considered pilot studies for working out case study protocols for the problem of interest and that the researcher should work with sites or people who are friendly and will be patient as procedures are figured out along the way.

INTERPRETIVE INQUIRY: QUALITATIVE CASE STUDIES WITH AN INTERPRETIVE EMPHASIS

In this interpretive inquiry the first author developed qualitative case studies with an interpretive emphasis (Merriam, 1998). Guba and Lincoln (1994) explained that situating one's inquiry in the constructivist/interpretivist paradigm entails a commitment to narrative and hermeneutical methods. A key idea from hermeneutics that guided the researcher's work in interpretive inquiry was the importance of approaching the entity in a way that enables it to show itself (Packer & Addison, 1989; Smith, 1991, 2002, 2010). More specifically, to undertake the delicate work of inviting Muslim students to recall and share their school experiences, the researcher used a hermeneutic interview protocol that evolved over many years of being used and further developed in the context of a research graduate course instructed by the second author, Ellis. Mishler (1990) and Patterson and Williams (2002) have noted the failure in discussions of the interpretivist perspective to address the details of how to collect and analyze data. A mechanical cook-book approach would be inappropriate. The alternative they recommended is that researchers provide exemplars or case studies to illustrate possible methodological approaches. In the next section we describe the general format of the hermeneutic interview protocol with some of its rationale, and provide the specific protocol used in this study.

THE HERMENEUTIC INTERVIEW PROTOCOL

The hermeneutic interview protocol begins with a request for the participant to complete two or more pre-interview activities (PIAs) in the form of visual representations about experience (Ellis, 2006; Ellis et al., 2013; Tine & Ellis, 2022)—one about the person in general and one about the participant's experience with the research topic. The PIAs are brought to the interview or else completed upon arrival at the interview. Completing them provides an opportunity for participants to recall and reflect on experience and to choose what is comfortable to share with the interviewer. To start the interview, the participant presents the PIAs and talks about what is included in each. The use of the PIAs is consistent with the literature on conducting research with vulnerable children (Kirova & Emme, 2007).

Following the talk about the PIAs the interviewer can use the prepared groups of questions. The first group includes six or more "getting to know you" questions that help the researcher to learn what is important or interesting to the participant in life more generally. The remaining groups of open-ended questions are organized according to topics that move from either the general to the specific—or from the past to the present. Having these different foci for the groups of questions can help with identification of connecting themes and with discerning the meaning of the experiences of interest (Ellis et al., 2013).

Figures 10.1 and 10.2 show the specific protocol used in this study.

Please use the colored markers and pens and pages provided and complete one or more of the activities below, and bring it with you to our interview.

1. Draw a schedule for your day, week or year and use colors to indicate how time is spent.
2. Draw a diagram and use colours to show where your support or support systems come.
3. Draw a picture or make a diagram of a place that is important to you. Use key words to indicate the parts or what happens in each of the parts.
4. Think of an important event that changed things in your life. Make two drawings showing what things were like for you before and after this event.

And also please complete one or more of the activities below, and bring it with you to our interview.

5. Make a timeline showing important things that happened that changed what school was like for you during your elementary school years.
6. Make two drawings: one showing what you thought life would be like for you in when you were in your elementary school and another showing what it turned out to be like. You can use speech bubbles or thought bubbles.
7. Draw two pictures showing what being a student was like for you before and after you finished your years in elementary school in this city.
8. Make two drawings: one showing "a good day" being an elementary grade student and one showing "a not so good day" being an elementary grade student.
9. Make two drawings: one showing what you have liked about life in elementary school here and another showing what you have not liked so much.

Figure 10.1   Pre-interview activities.

INTERVIEW QUESTIONS

"Getting to know you" questions

1. If you had to go to school only three days a week, what are some of the things you'd like to do with the extra time?
2. Have you ever done anything that other people were surprised you could do?
3. What is the most difficult thing you have ever had to do or, is there something you've done that was really hard to do but you really wanted to do it?

Figure 10.2   Interview questions. *(continued)*

4. Have you ever done anything really different from what most people of your age have done?
5. Some people really believe in the power of wishing. Do you think you do?...Has it ever worked?
6. Do you ever get other people to go along with your ideas or what you want to do? What about in activities with friends or routines at home?
7. Sometimes we like to day-dream about things we'd like to do, or things we'd like to try, or things we'd like to become. Can you remember anything you've ever day dreamed about?
8. What's the best thing about being your age? .... [after answer] What's the hardest thing about being your age?
9. What would you like to be really good at doing?
10. Some people believe that willpower can take them a long way. Do you think that you've ever used willpower?

Questions about the participant's experience in schools in Canada generally

11. I'm going to ask you some different kind of questions now, questions about how you see things. For example who do you think makes the biggest difference to what happens in the classroom, the principal, the teacher, or the students?
12. What did you like about your school experience in Canada?
13. What is the best part of going to school in Canada? .... [after answer] What would you say is the most difficult part?
14. If you could choose to spend two weeks in either secondary school or elementary school what will be your choice and why?
15. What are some of the things you hope for in your future school years?

Questions about participant's experience in elementary school student in Canada

16. Before you came to Canada, what were you good at in school or most interested in at school?
17. What was it like to you when you first attended the elementary school in Edmonton? Were you happy or excited or scared?
18. When you first started going to school here, what surprised you most? Did anything surprise you about the teachers, the other students, or about the activities in school?
19. When you started going to school here, what was easier than you thought it would be? ...... [after answer] What was more difficult than you thought it would be?

Questions about participant's current experience in school in Canada

20. Right now, what is the best part of going to school every day?
21. What are some of the things you don't like so much about being at school?
22. Since you have been in Canada, how have things changed for you in school?
23. What is it like to be Muslim in your school? Does it make any difference to your school day? Does it make it easier or more difficult in any way?
24. If a student who is Muslim was going to start attending your school, what advice would you give to this student?

Questions to conclude the interview

25. What do you look forward to doing this summer?
26. Are there any questions you would like to ask me?

Figure 10.2 (continued)   Interview questions.

ANALYSIS

Data analysis entailed crafting individual narrative portraits (Ellis, 2006, 2009), identifying common topics across all seven portraits, and then searching for themes or key ideas in the stories about each of the topics. This process was informed by Polkinghorne's (1995) ideas about "narrative analysis" followed by "analysis of narratives."

SUPPORTING PARTICIPANTS AS CO-PRODUCERS AND CO-INTERPRETERS OF THE DATA

The researcher, Amjad, was already known to the participants as a family friend and a member of the larger South Asian Muslim community and therefore did not need to work extra hard to establish trust; it was already there. She was, however, extremely careful about collecting information from her participants that pertained to their families and she had the participants review the data several times. They were encouraged to delete and/or add information as they saw appropriate during their review of the data. In this way Amjad supported the participants in the role of co-producers and co-interpreters of the data (Patton, 2002).

FINDINGS

The study results provide important insights into the lives of Muslim immigrant children who are trying to adapt to their host country while maintaining their family and community religious beliefs and practices. The findings presented clear signs of the presence of Islamophobia in Canadian schools. Four main themes emerged from the data: relationships with peers; teachers' attitudes; neighboring community behavior; and the role of the media. The study participants felt that they were marginalized in their schools in various ways, either through biased curricula, discriminatory school cultures, or negative and unfair attitudes on the part of their peers, teachers, and school administrators.

WHAT WAS LEARNED ABOUT INTERVIEW-BASED QUALITATIVE RESEARCH

Many aspects of the research process made important contributions to the researcher's relationship with participants in the interview context and the quality of sharing that took place in these interviews. For one, it was very helpful to have more than one interview with each of the participants. Amjad (2016) shared the following observation of one of the participants:

Even though Shama is a very confident young woman, in her first interview, she was a little shy and hesitant to share her experiences openly. That is why her initial responses were brief and given very carefully. In her second interview, she suddenly opened up and shared her inner feelings about her school experiences. (p. 116)

For another, the PIAs contributed in important ways. As shown in Figure 10.3, sometimes a participant chose to produce and organize a large number of ideas on a PIA and that visual provided a map to support the

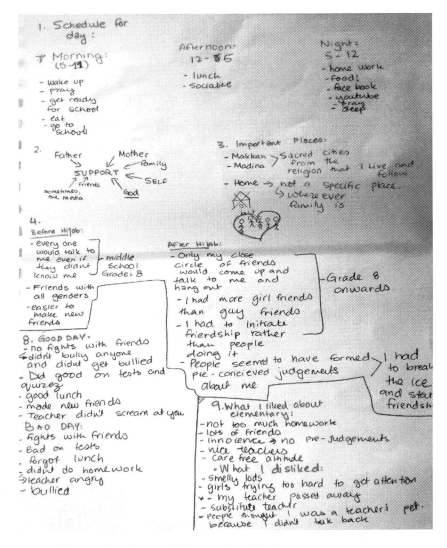

Figure 10.3 Pre-interview activities completed by Shama.

participant in talking about all the ideas in a focused, coherent way. Some participants used the space of the PIA to include an image that held a story. Figures 10.4 and 10.5 show an example of such a PIA and Amjad's writing about the story that was shared for the image.

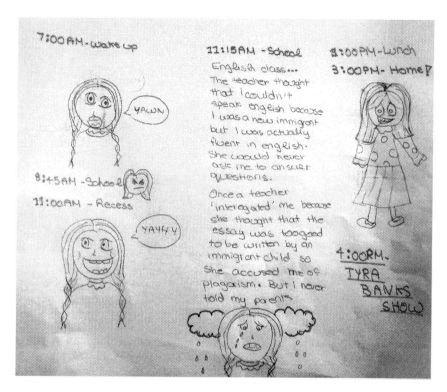

Figure 10.4   Pre-interview activities completed by Amina.

Amina said that although most of her teachers were good, her grade 3 teacher was not. Amina thinks the teacher did not like her. Even in class, the teacher made comments about Amina in front of her classmates. The teacher was suspicious of her about everything. Once Amina did an assignment on which she spent a lot of time in the hope that she could become the teacher's favourite child. Instead of praising her efforts, the teacher called her into her office to investigate whether anyone had helped her or where she had copied the assignment from. She said she stopped taking part in the class activities after that event because she was very disappointed. The teacher called Amina's mother and complained that Amina was not fully participating in class activities, which made her mother very upset. She still regrets not telling her mother about these things, but at the time she was new, and in her culture, respecting adults is considered an important quality for a child. (pp. 130–131)

Figure 10.5   The story about the image in Amina's PIA.

Thirdly, the "getting to know you" questions provided opportunities for students to share stories about accomplishments and aspirations that make them happy and proud. Celebrating those happy stories together further warmed the relationship between the researcher and participants. Altogether, the PIAs provided spaces for participants to choose experiences they would be comfortable to share and/or to have a visual organizer for speaking at length, and the "getting to know you questions" (Ellis, 2006) helped the researcher to have a more holistic view and appreciation of the participant.

REFERENCES

Amjad, A. (2016). *Multicultural education and immigrant children: The case of Muslim children in Canadian schools* [Doctoral dissertation, University of Alberta]. University of Alberta Educational Research Archives. https://era.library.ualberta.ca/items/a35034f9-48f9-4d03-a291-a515645e0acf

Brown, C. S., Ali, H., Stone, E. A., & Jewell, J. A. (2017). U.S. children's stereotypes and prejudicial attitudes toward Arab Muslims. *Analyses of Social Issues and Public Policy, 17*(1), 60–83. https://doi.org/10.1111/asap.12129

Ellis, J. (2006). Researching children's experience hermeneutically and holistically. *Alberta Journal of Educational Research, 52*(2), 111–126. https://doi.org/10.11575/ajer.v52i3.55151

Ellis, J. (2009). Interpreting results. In A. J. Mills, G. Durepos, & E. Wiebe (Eds.), *Encyclopedia of case study research* (pp. 484–486). SAGE Publications.

Ellis, J., Hetherington, R., Lovell, M., McConaghy, J., & Viczko, M. (2013). Draw me a picture, tell me a story: Evoking memory and supporting analysis through pre-interview drawing activities. *Alberta Journal of Educational Research, 58*(4), 488–508. https://doi.org/10.11575/ajer.v58i4.55541

Green, S., & Hill, M. (2005). Researching children's experiences: Methods and methodological issues. In S. Green & D. Hogan (Eds.), *Researching children's experiences: Approaches and methods.* SAGE Publishing.

Guba, E. G., & Lincoln, Y. S. (1994). Competing paradigms in qualitative research. In N. K. Denzin & Y. S. Lincoln (Eds.), *Handbook of qualitative research* (pp. 105–117). SAGE Publishing.

Guo, Y., Maintra, S., & Guo, S. (2019). "I belong to nowhere": Syrian refugee children's perspectives on school integration. *Journal of Contemporary Issues in Educatio,. 14*(1), 89–105. https://doi.org/10.20355/jcie29362

Kirova, A., & Emme, M. (2007). Critical issues in conducting research with immigrant children. *Diaspora, Indigenous, and Minority Education: An International Journal, 1*(2), 83–107. https://eric.ed.gov/?id=EJ814656

Merry, M. S. (2006). Islamic philosophy of education and western Islamic schools. In F. Salili & R. Hoosain (Eds.), *Religion in multicultural education* (pp. 41–70). Information Age.

McCoy, J., Kirova, A., & Knight, W. A. (2016). Gauging social integration among Canadian Muslims: A sense of belonging in an age of anxiety. *Canadian Ethnic Studies, 48*(2), 21–52. https://doi.org/10.1353/ces.2016.0012

Merriam, S. B. (1998). *Qualitative research and case study applications in education.* Jossey-Bass.

Mishler, E. G. (1990). Validation in inquiry guided research: The role of exemplars in narrative studies. *Harvard Educational Review, 60,* 415–442. https://doi .org/10.17763/haer.60.4.n4405243p6635752

Packer, M. J., & Addison, R. B. (1989). Evaluating an interpretive account. In M. J. Packer & R. B. Addison (Eds.), *Entering the circle: Hermeneutic investigation in psychology* (pp. 275–292). SUNY.

Patterson, M. E., & Williams, D. R. (2002). *Collecting and analyzing qualitative data: Hermeneutic principles, methods, and case examples.* Sagamore.

Patton, M. (2002). *Qualitative research and evaluation methods* (3rd ed.). SAGE Publications.

Polkinghorne, D. E. (1995). Narrative configuration in qualitative analysis. In J. A. Hatch & R. Wisniewski (Eds.) *Life history and narrative* (pp. 5–23). Falmer Press.

Reitz, J. (2009). Assessing multiculturalism as behavioural theory. In J. Reitz, R. Breton, K. Dion, & K. Dion (Eds.), *Multiculturalism and social cohesion: Potentials and challenges of diversity* (pp. 1–47). Springer.

Smith, D. G. (1991). Hermeneutic inquiry: The hermeneutic imagination and the pedagogic text. In E. C. Short (Ed.), *Forms of curriculum inquiry* (pp. 187–210). SUNY Press.

Smith, D. G. (2002). Hermeneutic scholar. In M. P. Woolfe & C. R. Pryor (Eds.), *The mission of the scholar: research and practice—A tribute to Nelson Haggerson* (pp. 183–200). Peter Lang.

Smith, D. G. (2010). Hermeneutic inquiry. In C. Kridel (Ed.), *Encyclopedia of curriculum studies* (Vol. 1, pp. 432–435). SAGE Publishing.

Yin, R. K. (2017). *Case study research: Design and methods* (6th ed.). SAGE Publications.

Zine, J. (2000). Redefining resistance: Toward an Islamic subculture in schools. *Race, Ethnicity, and Education, 31*(2), 293–316.

Zine, J. (2008). *Canadian Islamic schools: Unravelling the politics of faith, gender, knowledge, and identity.* University of Toronto Press.

INTRODUCTION TO CASE STUDY 11

This submission illustrates the importance of situating any inquiry in a philosophical/theoretical perspective in order to provide structure and meaning as a basis for interpretation and drawing conclusions. In this work, the researchers began with a CRT lens, fully intending to discover *confirmation* of the resulting expectations. While traditional "empirical" researchers might decry this a priori intentionality as an example of the introduction of bias, it is little different from the manner in which they operate. Simply, all inquiry whether formal or informal is based on a particular notion regarding the nature of the phenomena and expectations as to how it "should work." These expectations generally serve as guides regarding what merits attention and how the observations should be interpreted. Further, this starting point predisposes researchers to make meaning in a manner which is consistent with the a priori framework and expectations.

While this might seem to contradict the stated intention of the researchers to provide participants with an opportunity to share their own "voice"—it doesn't necessarily do so. In this case, participants were provided opportunities to reflect on their observations and conclusions, to make adjustments and "corrections" to the text of their comments as well as to provide feedback. These multiple opportunities were intended to ensure "authenticity" through efforts directed at examining consistency ("reliability") and accuracy. In addition, this project demonstrates an effort to pursue beneficence—to improve the welfare and wellness of the participants.

Qualitative Research With Diverse and Underserved Communities, pages 203–214
Copyright © 2024 by Information Age Publishing
www.infoagepub.com
All rights of reproduction in any form reserved.

CASE STUDY 11

CAN YOU HEAR ME NOW?

Voices of First-Generation College Students About Their Experiences to Remain and Graduate From High School as Explained by Critical Race Theory

Gloria Dansby-Giles
Jackson State University

Jacqueline Dansby
St. Mary's University

ABSTRACT

Behind every early warning indicator of a student at risk for leaving school without a diploma is a real human being with a story (MacIver, 2011). By listening to the voices of students, educators and policymakers can better understand factors that contribute to the success of students to remain in school and graduate. This study is significant in that much of the research that has been associated with educational reform has focused on quantitative data. In addition, many of the theoretical approaches used to examine factors that

Qualitative Research With Diverse and Underserved Communities, pages 205–214
Copyright © 2024 by Information Age Publishing
www.infoagepub.com
All rights of reproduction in any form reserved.

may impact the dropout rate of high school students have failed to take into consideration sociological and cultural factors of society.

This qualitative study included critical race theory (CRT) as a theoretical and methodological framework to examine race and inequity in exploring the experiences of first-generation college students' decision to remain and graduate from high school. The results indicated that potential first-generation college students may have to work to supplement the family income while dealing with personal problems and that school services were not made available to them. Other findings were feelings of uncertainty and fear and the lack of a responsible, caring adult as a role model. Since the participants in this study had the courage to lift their voices, the researchers hoped to broadcast their concerns to stakeholders, school administrators and others to inform them of practices that make a difference in promoting high school graduation for students from marginalized groups.

Behind every early warning indicator of a student at risk for leaving school without a diploma is a real human being with a story (MacIver, 2011). By listening to the voices of students, educators and policymakers can better understand factors that contribute to the presence of indicators identified largely through an analysis of quantitative data. This study is significant in that much of the research that has been associated with educational reform has focused on quantitative data. In addition, many of the theoretical approaches used to examine factors that may impact the dropout rate of high school students have failed to take into consideration sociological and cultural factors of society. Thus, the CRT was used to as a theoretical and methodological framework to explore appearance and significance of race and inequity in American society and the educational system. In addition, this theory examined the intersection of identities within race, class, gender, and sexuality.

To increase the understanding of factors that may influence high school graduation rates among potential first generation college students, this study investigated the perceptions of students impacted by educational reform so that their voices may become part of the conversation among stakeholders, provide broader understanding of underlying experiences that may shape existing behavioral patterns, and stimulate ideas about increasingly effective interventions to spur the next wave of reform. In addition, the voices of students are amplified as their experiences will be examined within the context of CRT.

PURPOSE OF THE STUDY

The purpose of this study is to investigate the perceived influence of academic factors, extracurricular experiences, behavioral patterns, attendance tendencies and school practices that either strengthen or inhibit the desire of potential first-generation college students to remain in high school and graduate. A secondary purpose of this study is to examine the perceived influence of participation in a special academic program, Upward Bound, on the high school graduation rate of potential first-generation college students. Lastly, critical race theory (CRT) will be examined as it relates to factors that inhibited first generation high school students from remaining in high school and to graduate.

RESEARCH QUESTIONS

1. What were academic factors, extracurricular experiences, behavioral patterns, attendance tendencies and school practices that strengthened or inhibited the desire of potential first generation college students to remain in high school and graduate?
2. What was the perceived influence of participation in Upward Bound on the high school graduation rate of potential first-generation college students?
3. What inequities can be identified from the examination of academic factors, extracurricular experiences, behavioral patterns, attendance tendencies and school practices through the lens of critical race theory?

OPERATIONAL DEFINITIONS

Potential first-generation college student is defined operationally as a student who (a) has not matriculated into an institution of higher education as a degree seeking student and for whom (b) neither parent with whom the student resides has attained a baccalaureate degree or higher. Potential first-generation college students are more likely to be low-income in comparison to their counterparts who reside with one or more parents that have earned a baccalaureate degree or higher. These students also are likely to be underserved. Upward Bound summer bridge program is defined operationally as the final level of participation in the Upward Bound Program at a university within the southwest in the United States where students who are recent high school graduates (i.e., in June 2011) enrolled in college credit prior to their matriculation to the college of their choice as a degree seeking student in the Fall 2011 semester.

LIMITATIONS

This study investigated perceptions of students who persisted and graduated from high school in order to understand characteristics of students who are potential first-generation students who did not become dropouts. Therefore, participants of this study do not include dropouts, although several participants acknowledged that they could have easily dropped out of school without support from Upward Bound and caring high school teachers and administrators. In addition, since this is a qualitative study that is based on context, the findings of this study cannot be generalized to other settings.

POPULATION

The population for this study consisted of the 22 participants who graduated in the 2011 class of their high school and enrolled in the summer bridge program of the Upward Bound Program at a university within the southwest in the United States. These students were from diverse ethnic groups such as Hispanic American, African American, Asian American, Native American, and Anglo American.

SAMPLE

A convenience sample consisted of nine Upward Bound former participants. These individuals were 18 years or older who graduated in the 2011 class from their respective high school and were a part of the summer bridge program at a university within the southwest region of the United States.

There were two strategies for undertaking this phenomenological research. The hermeneutic phenomenology that has been espoused by Van Manen and the psychological phenomenological approach that has been advocated by Moustakas (Creswell, 2018). The approach by Moustakas was used which focused on directing attention away from the researcher and highlighting the experiences of the participants. The procedures used were pinpointing a topic to investigate, bracketing out the investigator's experiences and gathering data from individuals who have had contact with the situation. Following these steps, the investigator analyzed the information that was gathered identifying important statements or quotations and placing the statements into themes.

Next, the investigator developed a textual description of the experiences of the persons (what participants experienced), a structural description of their experiences (how they experienced it in terms of the conditions, situation, or context), and a combination of the textual and structural descriptions to convey an overall essence of the experience (Creswell, 2018). Lastly, the investigator connected qualitative inquiry to CRT .

CRT research is connected to qualitative inquiry by examining the stories of people of marginalized groups through the use of interviews. The transcripts of the interviews were examined for themes that are related to

CRT. Solorzano and Yosso (2002) envisioned critical race methodology as a framework that explored the impact of race and racism in all components of the research procedure from the statement of the problem to the research question, data collection and analysis and the conclusion. As a theoretical/philosophical perspective, situating research in CRT worldview means the entire inquiry including the introduction, the statement of the problem, data collection and analysis and the conclusion are constructed from that perspective.

Using semi-structured interviews, this study investigated the perceived influence of academic factors, extracurricular experiences, behavioral patterns, attendance tendencies and school practices that strengthened or inhibited the desire of potential first-generation college students to remain in high school and graduate. In addition, the perceived influence of participation in Upward Bound on the high school graduation rate of potential first-generation college students was examined along with themes from CRT such as inequities.

After having received approval from institutional review board, participants were asked to read and sign an informed consent form. In addition, the informed consent form was explained orally, and the participants were sent a copy of this instrument by e-mail. Nine participants who submitted a signed, informed consent form were asked to participate in an interview conducted in-person and a follow-up. There was no monetary incentive provided for participating in the study.

Data gathering tools included a self-report form for demographic data such as gender, grade-point average, ACT/SAT scores, and graduation from high school., an interview protocol, in-depth interviews, transcripts of the interviews, notes from a journal that was kept by the researcher, and documents from the participants' files such as letters of commendation, honors, and awards. The transcripts of the interviews were used to identify themes from CRT such as intersection of identities and inequities experienced by the participants.

The type of interview that was appropriate to collect descriptive information from the potential first generation college students was the in-depth interview. The interview was conducted within the Upward Bound office at a university within the southwest region of the United States. The responses to the interview questions were recorded on two sets of recorders. The completed recordings were sent to a transcriber who produced the text of the interviews. The participants were given copies of the interviews and allowed to provide feedback and edit. The transcripts were analyzed for themes and patterns by the researcher and a second coder.

The results from the interviews were labeled as "Participant A through I." The decoded list of the names of the participants and the researcher's notes and journal are kept in a locked file cabinet. Reports of results of the study did not disclose the names of the participants.

The findings have been organized by holistic analysis whereby specific themes related to maintaining continuous enrollment in high school, factors that assisted with the process of continuous enrollment and themes related to inequities and other factors related to CRT were identified and described.

To achieve credibility, as recommended by Lincoln and Guba (1985), attention was given to interviewing participants and triangulating of the data by obtaining and considering multiple sources of information: (a) interviews of the participants; (b) researcher's notes during the interview; (c) researcher's journal; and (d) documents such as letters, honors, and awards, and so on. In addition, participants were given the opportunity to view and edit and transcripts for accuracy (i.e., member checking). Along with reviewing transcripts, participants were were interviewed a second time to provide feedback.

To achieve validation, the investigator identified themes that developed from the study (Eisner, 1991). In addition, to the identification of themes, the investigator searched for information that may have disconfirmed the themes. Other forms of validation employed as offered by Creswell (2018) were to spend time with the participants and earn their trust as well as checking information with the participants to ensure that it was correct.

For reliability, two different coders were used to code the data. The results from the coders were compared and discussed. The differences in the coding process were minor. In keeping with CRT, the coders examined the data for inequities and other themes related to the theory.

RESULTS

What were academic factors, extracurricular experiences, behavioral patterns, attendance tendencies, and school practices that strengthened or inhibited the desire of potential first-generation college students to remain in high school and graduate?

Academic Factors

Most students interviewed knew a potential first generation college student personally who had dropped out of high school. Several participants perceived that some students dropped out of school because they were lazy and didn't want to do the work. However, respondents cited cases whereby students dropped out because they had serious personal or family problems and felt that they had no other recourse.

Extracurricular Activities

Schools that Upward Bound students attended have a "no pass, no play" policy regarding participation in extracurricular activities. Since students themselves choose the extracurricular activities in which they participated, they have a personal interest and, thereby, are likely to be intrinsically motivated to be involved. This no pass, no play policy served as extrinsic motivation for students to maintain acceptable grades.

Behavioral Patterns

One participant in the study who had had disciplinary action administered by her high school made the observation that school officials should not leave students alone in a room with their parents unless the officials are reasonably sure that the parents know how to engage in responsible problem solving.

Attendance

Several participants in the study cited a reason that some students dropout is because they don't understand the subject matter in one or more classes, get too far behind to pass, and reason that there is no use for staying in school.

School Practices

The majority of participants in the study preferred teachers who reached out to them rather than choosing to wait for the student to ask for help whenever a problem existed. What was the perceived influence of participation in Upward Bound on the high school graduation rate of potential first-generation college students?

Academic Factors

Participants in the study recognized that the mission of Upward Bound was to prepare them to successfully complete high school and to pursue higher education until graduation. They perceived that the educational opportunities afforded by Upward Bound gave them distinct academic advantages over their peers and enabled them to improve their academic performance in high school. Participants in the study felt that Upward Bound prepared them to succeed academically in college; participants particularly felt that their science classes taught by tenured, full professors at a university within the southwest region of the United States were rigorous and prepared them for college.

One student said that prior to being enrolled in Upward Bound, she was satisfied with earning grades of C. Now that she has the aspiration of being the first in their family to earn a college degree, she stated that she has started making the honor roll and no longer is satisfied with making grades of C in her high school courses.

Prior to their enrollment in Upward Bound, some participants in the study were satisfied with earning a regular diploma to graduate. Several participants in the study cited that they made the decision after their enrollment in Upward Bound to graduate with a distinguished diploma.

Extracurricular Activities

Participants in the study perceived that Upward Bound encouraged and supported their active participation in high school extracurricular activities.

Attendance

Participants in the study said that they never considered dropping out of high school after enrolling in Upward Bound because they didn't want to be withdrawn from the program for any reason.

Behavioral Patterns

Participants in the study perceived that they felt closer to students at their high school who also were enrolled in Upward Bound than their counterparts not enrolled. Participants shared that a cluster of students enrolled in Upward Bound would sit together at their high school during lunch and regularly spend time together.

School Policies

The Upward Bound director serves as an advocate for participants at their high schools. Participants in the study perceived that they would like for their high schools to be more like Upward Bound.

What inequities can be identified from the examination of academic factors, extracurricular experiences, behavioral patterns, attendance tendencies, and school practices through the lens of critical race theory?

CRITICAL RACE THEORY

Critical race theory promoted the study of the role of race and racism in understanding the inequities between dominant and marginalized groups (Decur & Dixon, 2004; Ladson-Billings & Tate, 1995). It also explored unequal power balances and access to resources as a result of politics, economics, and gender (Taylor et al., 2009). This theory sought to uncover information that is sometimes forgotten when examining race and privilege along with examples of exclusions. Therefore, this theory can play a central role in uncovering the stories of marginalized populations that are different from the stories that are perceived by the dominant society. This is referred to as counterstorytelling (Leonardo, 2013).

The participants in the study spoke to the following factors that negatively influenced high school graduation rates among the potential first generation college: first, school administrators and teachers failed to recognize that some potential first generation college students may have to work to supplement the family income as well as cope with personal problems. These situations can be further exacerbated when school counseling services are not available to them. This is an example of marginalized populations lacking access to services that are made available to all students.

A second factor that participants perceived as negatively influenced high school graduation rates was that administrators and teachers seemed to approach their responsibilities from a culture of intimidation. The perceptions of the persons in power can impact marginalized populations.

A third factor perceived to negatively influence high school graduation rates was feelings of uncertainty and fear encountered by potential first-generation college students in response to disciplinary action. This is another example of how the perceptions of persons in power can impact marginalized groups.

A final factor judged to negatively influence high school graduation rates was the lack of a responsible, caring adult with whom potential first-generation college students felt they could communicate and from whom they might seek advice and assistance when problems arose. Viewed from CRT, persons from marginalized groups are often denied opportunities that persons from the dominant society enjoy. With the use of qualitative research and its focus on listening to voices through interviews and CRT using storytelling as one of its tools, the two can be used in combination to promote social justice for marginalized groups. Since the participants in this study had the courage to lift their voices, the researchers hoped to broadcast their concerns to stakeholders, school administrators, school counselors, teachers, the media, and others in an effort to inform them of practices that make a difference in promoting high school graduation for students from marginalized groups.

REFERENCES

Creswell, J. W. (2018). Qualitative inquiry & research design: Choosing among five approaches. (4th ed.). SAGE Publications.

Decur, J., & Dixon, A. (2004). "So when it comes out, they aren't surprised that it is there": Using critical race theory as a tool of analysis of race and racism in education. *Educational Researcher, 33*, 26–31. https://doi.org/10.3102/0013189X033005026

Eisner, E. W. (1991). *The enlightened eye: Qualitative inquiry and quantitative approaches.* SAGE Publications.

Ladson-Billings, G., & Tate, W. F. (1995). Toward a critical race theory of education. *Teachers College Record, 97*, 47–68. https://www.unco.edu/education-behavioral-sciences/pdf/TowardaCRTEduca.pdf

Leonardo, Z. (2013). The story of schooling: Critical race theory and the educational racial contract. *Discourse Studies in the Cultural Politics of Education, 34*(4), 599–610. https://doi.org/10.1080/01596306.2013.822624

Lincoln, Y. S., & Guba, E. G. (1985). *Naturalistic inquiry.* SAGE Publications.

MacIver, M. A. (2011). Gradual disengagement: A portrait of the 2008–09 dropouts in Baltimore City Schools. *Education Digest, 76*(5), 52–56. https://files.eric.ed.gov/fulltext/ED553164.pdf

Solorzano, D. G., & Yosso, T. J. (2002). Critical race methodology: Counter-story-telling as analytical framework for education research. *Qualitative Inquiry, 8*(1), 23–44. https://doi.org/10.1177/107780040200800103

Taylor, E., Gillborn, D., & Ladson-Billings, G. (Eds.). (2009). *Foundations of critical race theory in education.* Routledge.

INTRODUCTION TO CASE STUDY 12

This report of dissertation study is illustrative and important for a variety of reasons. It highlights the importance of recognizing and "managing" personal experience which will always shape the lens through which inquiry is conducted. While this is true in any inquiry, it is especially the case in qualitative inquiry where the researcher acts as the "instrument" for data collection, determining relevance, importance, and so on, impacting what is examined in the first place and how meaning is constructed in the second and finally how that meaning leads to conclusions and recommendations. This researcher started from the perspective that Black males face inequity in higher education and endeavored to recognize how that perspective might influence the work. They also began from the perspective that the purpose of qualitative research is to address and resolve social injustice. This beginning perspective provided the impetus for the application of critical race theory as a framework for the study. This declaration of framework and intent provides one basis for credibility.

This case study also demonstrates the very real situation of researchers who are honestly interested in advancing equity and social justice. They often are positioned such that they have personal purposes which influences the conduct of inquiry and the interpretation of results. In the present report, it is clear that the researcher was intent on completing the requirements for graduation—dissertation—and the report describes the frustration associated with the elaboration of methods which extended the time for completion. This honest reflection and reporting highlight the constant possibility that research however well intentioned, can be an exploitative exercise since

Qualitative Research With Diverse and Underserved Communities, pages 215–225
Copyright © 2024 by Information Age Publishing
www.infoagepub.com
All rights of reproduction in any form reserved.

regardless of other outcomes it advances the personal goals of the researcher. This "case study" also reflects the advantage of collaboration with other researchers. This is important as a bracketing mechanism in that it can facilitate the recognition of perspectives which are likely to impact the enterprise as well as provide the benefit of the experience of another in framing and executing the work. In this case the dissertation committee members provided perspectives for methodology which positively impacted the quality/authenticity of the final product. Last, this report of research amply demonstrates the emergent nature of qualitative research—a true demonstration of learning from action and acting from learning.

CASE STUDY 12

ELEVATING THE VOICES OF BLACK MALE COLLEGE STUDENTS THROUGH CRITICAL QUALITATIVE INQUIRY CASE STUDY CONTEXT

Dante Pelzer
Medical University of South Carolina

The Black men who enter colleges and universities do so having already internalized a barrage of negative messages about their perceived masculinity and chances of academic success. Over the course of their lives, collegiate Black men have had to refute deficit messaging about their academic success, confront stereotypes about their masculinity, and challenge negative perceptions about criminality. Unfortunately, college does not provide a reprieve for Black men as assumptions about their place and fit on college campuses are still questioned by peers, faculty, administrators, and campus

Qualitative Research With Diverse and Underserved Communities, pages 217–225
Copyright © 2024 by Information Age Publishing
www.infoagepub.com
217

police. This rings especially true at predominantly White institutions, where Black male enrollment is typically low and the history of marginalization and racism is deeply rooted. Given this context, more recent higher education qualitative studies have provided platforms for Black male college students to narrate their own identity development journeys, often from multiple perspectives (Cuyjet, 2006; Harper & Davis, 2012; Harper & Quaye, 2007; Harris et al., 2011).

This qualitative case study critically examines how interpretations, constructions, and demonstrations of masculinity are uniquely experienced and narrated by Black men attending a predominantly White institution (PWI). Black men attending colleges and universities do not arrive as blank slates, so central to this study was acknowledging the importance of childhood socialization processes and situating those experiences in the current collegiate context.

Given the scope of this study, the following research question was developed:

RQ: *How is masculinity constructed, demonstrated, and narrated by Black male undergraduates attending a predominantly White institution, taking into consideration pre-collegiate and collegiate contexts?*

POPULATION DESCRIPTION AND SAMPLING TECHNIQUES

Given the stated research question, the site selected for this study was a large research university located in the southeast United States. Consistent with previous research on collegiate Black men, this study provided a space for Black men to narrate and make meaning of their own masculine development journeys. Studying this population is important as these students make up less than 5% of all college students at PWIs yet have hyper-visible and invisible experiences on college campuses (National Center for Education Statistics, 2023). As underrepresented students on PWI campuses, it is paramount that university leadership recognizes how Black men show up to their campuses and how they may navigate different spaces as their unique masculine selves.

Ten undergraduate students participated in this study. The number of study participants is consistent with the goals of narrative research which aims to illuminate the fullness of the lived experiences of a few rather than extrapolate data findings across multiple settings (Merriam, 2009). Only men who completed at least one year of schooling were recruited, because it was important for them to have the ability to reflect on their interactions with peers, faculty, and staff at the university. Purposive sampling techniques were used to select participants in a way that achieved maximum variation and group heterogeneity (Creswell, 2013; Merriam, 2009). The goal was to recruit participants with different academic standing, campus involvements, family backgrounds, and sexual orientation, among other factors.

Gatekeepers were used to recruit participants which included advisors to predominantly Black student organizations and Black male employees who mentored Black male undergraduates. To recruit LBGTQ students and transfer students, I directly emailed the Transfer Student Leadership Center and the LGBTQ Student Association. Snowball sampling was used to identify student athletes willing to participate in the study.

Three Black male alumni were also recruited to talk about their experiences as undergraduates at the university. When studying a single site, it is important to fully understand how the site has conditioned the social environment of the sample population (i.e., Black male college students). Data from the alumni interviews were used to provide a contextual understanding of the research site—that is, "How have Black male students historically experienced racism, what have been the academic and social expectations of Black men on campus, and so on?" Alumni were also recruited using snowball sampling and the results yielded one alumnus from the 1960s, one from the 1980s, and one from the 1990s/2000s.

CRITICAL NARRATIVE INQUIRY: A MULTI-FRAMEWORK APPROACH

Illuminating the voices of Black male collegians is central to the exploration of the research question, as such, this study was grounded in critical narrative inquiry which merges critical race qualitative research and narrative methodologies. The goal of critical narrative inquiry is to critique and challenge dominant ideologies and empower minoritized individuals to be agents of social change (Merriam, 2009). If colleges, particularly PWIs, want to create a culture where Black men expect to demonstrate masculinity in authentic ways, university leaders must interrogate how racism and anti-Blackness in policies, practices, and social environments impact the experiences of their Black male students. Additionally, campus administrators must provide opportunities for Black men to have voice and agency in how they continue to develop a sense of self, absent the negative stereotypes that surround their existence.

Critical Race Theory

Central to critical narrative inquiry is understanding its connection to critical race theory (CRT). CRT calls for society to challenge dominant and hegemonic ideologies and create new narratives that are authentic to the cultural histories of its members (Yosso et al., 2009). CRT consists of the following five elements: (a) centrality and intersectionality of race and racism; (b) challenge to dominant ideology; (c) commitment to social justice; (d) centrality of experiential knowledge; and (e) interdisciplinary perspectives. Though all five elements of CRT are relevant to this study, the fourth element was most central to investigating the research question as it calls for the exploration of "lived experiences of subordinate groups through storytelling, family histories, parables, and narratives" (Solórzano, 1997, p. 7).

Narrative Research

Narrative research was the second framework that guided this study. Creswell (2013) described narrative research as the study of experiences expressed in lived and told stories of individuals. Narrative research has a story-telling quality that empower participants to examine themselves and identities. Moreover, narrative inquiry has the power to de-establish normative epistemologies and elevate new perspectives about social phenomena (Merriam, 2009). Narrative inquiry aligns synergistically with the CRT framework used in this study as participants had multiple opportunities to examine, reflect upon, and narrate their masculine identity journeys from childhood to college.

INQUIRY PROTOCOL

Given the case site, one large PWI in the southeast, it was imperative to use multiple research methods to achieve data saturation which allowed me to make informed analyses about the experiences of the men attending this institution. Furthermore, the use of multiple collection methods established data reliability and trustworthiness. Each method is described below.

Interviews

Each student participated in two interviews lasting between 45–80 minutes; alumni participated in one interview lasting approximately 45 minutes. Interviews followed traditional narrative research techniques which called for a loosely structured interview protocol (Creswell, 2013). Interviews started with a broad, open-ended question that allowed participants to narrate their own story about masculinity. Follow-up questions were asked to allow participants the chance to fully explore the research question. In an effort to ensure authenticity in participants' reflections and storytelling, they were given latitude to deviate from follow-up questions which is also consistent with critical narrative research. The first student interview focused on pre-college socialization as it pertains to masculinity development. The second interview centered on participants' collegiate experiences with masculinity. Conducting two rounds of interviews with distinct foci allowed for a more in-depth exploration of the students' childhood and collegiate experiences. The alumni interviews were more broadly focused on their university experiences and employed the same loosely structured interview format.

Focus Group

For this study, a focus group was conducted after both undergraduate interviews were completed. Focus group research allows participants to respond to the comments of others in the group, which creates an open atmosphere for the researcher's topic to be explored (Creswell, 2013). Themes gleaned from the literature review served as starting points for the focus group discussion. To control the flow of conversation, a semi-structured interview protocol was used. The focus group conversation added depth and breadth to the experiences explored during the interviews, and participants reported feeling a sense of validation after interacting with other men who shared similar experiences and motivations.

DATA ANALYSIS

Interviews and Focus Group Analysis

Qualitative thematic coding was used to analyze interview and focus group data. Prior to reading interview transcripts, my subjectivities were bracketed. Bracketing is the process of suspending one's assumptions, theories, and emotions related to the topic being studied, so that analysis begins with a "blank" slate (Creswell, 2013; Fischer, 2009). I kept a journal throughout data collection and analysis stages, and this is where my bracketed assumptions were kept for personal processing.

After interviews were transcribed, the analysis process began with open coding which consists of creating a preliminary list of labels that capture the essence of a phrase or sentence in the transcript (Strauss & Corbin, 1990). In this study, three transcripts were initially analyzed using open and axial coding. The result of open and axial coding was the creation of the initial coding scheme which was applied to all 20 student interview transcripts and the focus group transcript. Open and axial coding was also completed for the alumni interviews. As transcripts were coded using the initial coding scheme, new codes emerged. Staying true to the iterative process of qualitative research, the coding scheme was updated, and transcripts were re-analyzed using the most current coding scheme.

Open and axial coding occurred in Microsoft Word—using the highlight and comment tools. After the coding scheme was created, it was reproduced in NVivo®, a qualitative research data management and analysis software. Next, all transcripts were imported into NVivo for final coding. In NVivo, chunks of text were highlighted and dragged/dropped into "nodes," which is NVivo terminology for a code folder. Each node—each consisting of text from several transcripts—were analyzed for emerging themes. Themes pertaining to interview and focus group data were presented in the "findings" section of the study. Each theme was supported by quotes of varying lengths which is consistent with basic qualitative research techniques.

Participant Stories

In addition to the thematic findings, participant data was presented in narrative form. Participant stories were created for each student using their individual interview data. Interview transcripts were summarized and paired down to 3–4 pages. To keep the narratives as authentic as possible, each was written in first-person using slang and colloquialisms consistent with each student's interview transcripts. Presenting participants' experiences as narratives is consistent with the CRT principle that calls for members of minoritized groups to tell their lived experiences through storytelling, family histories, parables, and narratives, with a goal of disrupting pejorative social narratives about people of color (Ladson-Billings & Tate, 2006; Solórzano, 1997).

CHANGES IN STRATEGY AND UNANTICIPATED OUTCOMES

Despite a researcher's best efforts, every study has its challenges and unexpected situations; this study was no different. Described in the following sections are two unanticipated outcomes in the data collection and analysis phrase of this study. None of these changes derailed the study, and in hindsight, the study would lose some of its uniqueness and character if these components were not added.

The first unplanned outcome was the decision to interview alumni. Given the scope of the study, exploring Black masculinity at one institution, it was suggested by a dissertation committee member that interviewing Black male alumni could help present a fuller picture of the institution and provide additional points from which to analyze the undergraduate student data. Interviewing the alumni extended the study's length and time but provided valuable insight into how Black men experienced the university and demonstrated identity through the years.

The second shift in strategy occurred when the decision was made to present each participant's story in first-person. After listening to and reading participants' interviews multiple times during the analysis stage, I was compelled to find a unique way to present participants' stories and do so in a way consistent with the underlying research methodologies. These stories were included in the body of the chapter, before the presentation of thematic findings, and provided additional context from which to analyze the study. The participant stories added a richness and authenticity that could not be captured in block quotes or in my own interpretation of the data.

SUMMARY OF STUDY FINDINGS

Reporting of the thematic analysis followed the personal narratives. What was quite evident in the data analysis was the emergence of stories and anecdotes that did not support negative stereotypes and characterizations of Black masculinity. Moreover, participants' masculinity journeys served as counternarratives that disrupted and challenged long held perspectives on Black maleness. Each student's personal story was a unique and powerful example of resistance, and collectively, their narratives produced six themes (three pre-collegiate and three collegiate) that answered the research questions regarding their masculinity development. These themes focused on ignoring negative stereotypes associated with Black males (e.g., being more than criminals, athletes, womanizers); exploring gender roles, sexual orientation, and gender identity; and centering academic success as a positive trait of Black maleness.

From childhood to college, these men overcame personal challenges and systemic obstacles. They were vocal about what they perceived to be masculine, what was taught and learned as masculine, and what they expected of themselves. Some men were supported throughout their identity development journeys while others were ridiculed for their gender expression, academic interests, and personal relationships. But through it all, the participants' narratives and experiences challenged master narratives about Black men and disrupted troublesome generalities about Black male academic, social, and professional achievement. Ultimately, the men in this study demonstrated how complex, varied, and nuanced Black men are and how negligent it is to constrict the understanding of Black masculinity to universally accepted tropes and negative characterizations.

REFLECTIONS AND RECOMMENDATIONS

As I reflect on my approach to this study, several lessons come to mind, but here, I offer two considerations for those conducting a single-site qualitative study: (a) diversity of methods is paramount to reaching data saturation and (b) getting transcription help is not a sin.

I entered the dissertation process thinking I was going to simply mimic the pilot study I conducted in my advanced qualitative research class, but on a larger scale. I quickly learn from my own research on qualitative inquiry and from my dissertation committee that interviewing 10–15 students one time each would not allow me to fully explore my research question nor achieve data saturation. After consulting with my committee, I added a second interview and a focus group to my study. Additionally, it was recommended by a committee member that I conduct archival research on the research site and interview Black male alumni who attended the institution. These recommendations were provided during the data collection phase. I was initially frustrated by the extra work as it was pushing back my time to completion, but in the end, the incorporation of additional research methods increased the richness and complexity of my data and provided me more opportunities to draw conclusions and make analytical connections.

I was taught early in my doctoral studies that qualitative research is a labor of love that requires the researcher to be immerse in their data. I interpreted this as me transcribing all 24 of my interviews. I transcribed the first five interviews. The process was rewarding and insightful, but also laborious and was causing me to pushback my study timeline. I was relieved when I found out from my dissertation chair that there was no shame in using a transcription service. The remaining 19 interview recordings were sent to a transcription service which came at a cost, but the time I saved by not transcribing myself was valuable.

By completing this study, I discovered that qualitative research is rigorous and laborious yet necessary as scholars strive to liberate the voices of historically marginalized groups. Moreover, qualitative research requires patience as its processes are fluid, iterative, and labor intensive. But the result that labor is vibrant, rich, and contextually complex narrations of human life.

REFERENCES

Creswell, J. W. (2013). *Qualitative inquiry and research design: Choosing among five approaches.* SAGE Publications.

Cuyjet, M. J. (2006). *African American men in college.* Jossey-Bass.

Fischer, C. T. (2009). Bracketing in qualitative research: Conceptual and practical matters. *Psychotherapy Research, 19*(4–5), 583–590. https://doi.org/10.1080/10503300902798375

Harper, S. R., & Davis, C. H. F., III. (2012). They (don't) care about education: A counternarrative on Black male students' responses to inequitable schooling. *Educational Foundations, 26*(1), 103–120. https://files.eric.ed.gov/fulltext/EJ968820.pdf

Harper, S. R., & Quaye, S. J. (2007). Student organizations as venues for Black identity expression and development among African American male student leaders. *Journal of College Student Development, 48*(2), 127–144. https://doi.org/10.1353/csd.2007.0012

Harris, F., III, Palmer, R. T., & Struve, L. E. (2011). "Cool posing" on campus: A qualitative study masculinities and gender expression among Black men at a private research institution. *Journal of Negro Education, 80*(1), 47–62. https://muse.jhu.edu/pub/417/article/806869/pdf#info_wrap

Ladson-Billings, G., & Tate, W. (2006). Toward a critical race theory of education. In A. D. Dixson & C. K. Rousseau (Eds.), *Critical race theory in education: All God's children got a song* (pp. 11–30). Routledge.

Merriam, S. B. (2009). *Qualitative research: A guide to design and implementation.* John Wiley & Sons.

National Center for Education Statistics, Integrated Postsecondary Education Data System (2023). Fall enrollment component. [Interactive Data Tool.] Retrieved from https://nces.ed.gov/ipeds/SummaryTables/report/270?templateId=2701&years=2021,2020,2019,2018,2017,2016,2015,2014,2013,2012&expand_by=1&tt=aggregate&instType=1&sid=a48e9cf5-953a-4bc7-944e-70d78fedb1ea

Solórzano, D. G. (1997). Images and words that wound: Critical race theory, racial stereotyping. *Teacher Education Quarterly, 24*(3), 5–19. https://www.jstor.org/stable/23478088

Strauss, A., & Corbin, J. (1990). *Basics of qualitative research: Grounded theory procedures and techniques.* SAGE Publications.

Yosso, T. J., Smith, W. A., & Solórzano, D. G. (2009). Critical race theory, racial microaggressions, and campus racial climate for Latina/o undergraduates. *Harvard Educational Review, 79*(4), 659–690. https://doi.org/10.17763/haer.79.4.m6867014157m7071

CASE STUDIES SECTION III

INTRODUCTION TO CASE STUDY 13

This example describes teachers as researchers utilizing students in a graduate course focusing on the potential of collecting the experience of teachers working in a school which is very diverse and includes not only what are usually recognized as minoritized and disadvantaged groups but also members of developmentally delayed and disadvantaged groups. The authors discuss the usefulness and potential contributions of various "teacher as researcher" activities for aiding them in getting to know students from diverse backgrounds, supporting students' learning needs, and enhancing all students' experiences in the classroom and school and assumes that teachers are important, well positioned and as such are significantly influential in any work done with those who are not from majority or "power groups. The study considers the graduate students' completed course assignments focusing on "teachers as researchers" to explore the potential of this approach to determine value (community based), inform, and educate. The authors conclude that these exercises have potential to give teachers a richer, more complete view of their pupils' life experiences and the connections of that experience to the classroom with implications for teacher behavior and decision making since teachers have the responsibility to engage in curricular and instructional efforts which are observably beneficial for all students and that this work has potential to inform knowledge about and general perspectives of the life experience of pupils from marginalized and disadvantaged populations.

Qualitative Research With Diverse and Underserved Communities, pages 229–241
Copyright © 2024 by Information Age Publishing
www.infoagepub.com
All rights of reproduction in any form reserved.

CASE STUDY 13

TEACHER AS RESEARCHER ACTIVITIES TO BUILD RELATIONSHIPS AND SUPPORT LEARNING

Julia Ellis
University of Alberta

Charney Randhawa Docherty
Calgary Board of Education

ABSTRACT

Class members in a graduate course explored a number of "teacher as researcher" activities and exchanged ideas about the usability and potential contributions of these for helping them to get to know students, to support students' learning needs, and to add to students' positive experiences in the classroom and school. This chapter draws upon the completed course assignments of one of the teachers in the course to illustrate the activities and teachers' reflections about their value. Like others in the course, the case study teacher concluded that these activities can provide a deeper more comprehensive picture for teachers not just about students' prior knowledge, but about their lived stories

Qualitative Research With Diverse and Underserved Communities, pages 231–241
Copyright © 2024 by Information Age Publishing
www.infoagepub.com

as well. Teachers saw the activities as being valuable to use with all new topics in the curriculum. There were brief activities for beginning new topics and other activities for concluding or reviewing completed topics.

SOCIETAL CONTEXT: DIVERSITY AND THE IMPORTANCE OF RELATIONSHIPS IN TEACHING

Teachers come into teaching with positive expectations about caring for students and supporting their success in learning. Once in the classroom they can experience overwhelming diversity and find themselves lacking the tools for "managing that diversity and capitalizing on that strength in the classroom" (Immordino-Yang, 2013, p. 23).

Working well with diversity in the classroom in the context of addressing curriculum topics is challenging enough. So too is the path to building relationships with students. Experienced teachers typically state that their teaching works best once they have established relationships with students (e.g., Ford, 2017). Immordino-Yang (Sparks, 2019) has clarified that relationships are not only about friendliness and engaging socially with students. Instead, she argued that teachers' deep relationships are based on their knowledge of students' potential, their interests, their strengths and weaknesses, their curiosity, and their habits of mind. Without getting to know students in an on-going way, it is difficult for teachers to show respect for students' cultures or to learn how their cultures shape their meaning-making with curriculum topics.

FOCUS OF INQUIRY: TO EXPLORE THE VALUE OF SELECTED TEACHER AS RESEARCHER ACTIVITIES

A graduate course about teachers as researchers invited class members to explore a number of "teacher as researcher" activities and to exchange ideas about the value and usability or potential contributions of these. This chapter draws upon the work of Charney Randhawa Docherty, one of the course participants and co-author of this chapter, as a case study.

SAMPLE AND POPULATION OF INTEREST

Charney Docherty was one of 20 teachers enrolled in a Teacher as Researcher online course in Spring 2017. She is co-author of this chapter and course assignments she completed serve as the case study material. At the time of the course Charney Docherty described her teaching context in this way:

> I work at a very diverse school that includes English language learners, Aboriginal learners, a cluster of students with autism spectrum disorder (ASD)

diagnosis that are being integrated, mixed families, single parent families, Syrian refugee students and students from a variety of socioeconomic backgrounds including poverty. My official title at my school is a learning leader. My role this year has included teaching in a grade 4/5 classroom, supporting the transition of ASD students into the classroom, providing literacy support to struggling students and working as a teacher coach to mentor teachers in literacy teaching from Grades 1–5.

CONTEXT: A SPRING 2017 ONLINE COURSE ENTITLED TEACHER AS RESEARCHER

In the graduate course on teachers as researchers, course participants practiced using and designing

- activities that could help them to get to know students better, build student–teacher relationships, and build classroom community;
- activities that can help them learn students' related interests, assumptions, preconceptions, preoccupations and motivations pertaining to new curriculum topics; and
- activities that can provide opportunities for students to use interests or talents, work collaboratively, experience recognition for and validation of their ideas and talents, and draw upon and express funds of knowledge or lived experience.

Course participants were not required to do the activities with students in their own classrooms. Instead, they completed many of the activities themselves and designed ones to use with classes in the future. Conversation and writing in small discussion groups fostered reflective engagement with these activities.

CASE STUDY: QUALITATIVE CASE STUDY WITH AN EVALUATIVE EMPHASIS

In this case study we present: background information about Charney Docherty's teaching and leadership responsibilities; instructions for three teacher as researcher activities; some illustrative examples of Charney Docherty's completed assignments for these activities, and her reflections about the usability and value of these teacher as researcher activities.

THREE TEACHER AS RESEARCHER ACTIVITIES

The following teacher-as-researcher activities are presented in the case study:

- *Activity 1:* Using open-ended or self-expressive activities to learn students' preoccupations or pre-conceptions
- *Activity 2:* Using attributes trees or idea trees to learn students' prior knowledge or preconceptions
- *Activity 3:* Using open-ended creative assignments to conclude curriculum topics and incorporate students' interests and talents

Instructions for these activities are provided in Figures 13.1, 13.2 and 13.3. Additional examples of these activities were provided in supplementary course readings—Ellis (1998), Ellis (2005), and Ellis (2007).

Read the examples in the table below (Ellis, 1998a).

Context	Open-Ended or Self-Expressive Activity
Using a *story* as a starter or using a *curriculum topic* as a theme	
Grade 12 social studies class	Students are invited to make posters portraying their "actual" and "ideal" worlds.
At the conclusion of the story, *Witch of Lok Island*, in Grade 3	Students were invited to imagine that they each had their own magic staff that could help people with problems or difficulties. They were asked to make drawings to show who they would help and with what situations.
Again in a Grade 3 class the students listened to the story of *Johnny Maple Leaf*.	Before the end of the story, as the leaf was floating to the ground, the students were asked to imagine that they could float anywhere. They were asked to draw where they would go and what they would do there.
At the beginning of a unit on municipal government in Grade 5	Students are asked to each make a poster advertising all the changes they would like to make in the city in the role of mayor.
At the beginning of a futuristic science fiction unit in an advanced Grade 9 English class	Students were asked to develop their own versions of "ideal education systems."
After hearing a story about a magic mirror in Grade 2	Students were invited to draw the frame for their own magic mirror and to draw a picture inside the frame to show the kind of magic it has. (As a follow-up, students can tell or write a story about the picture.)
After hearing a story about a scarecrow entitled *Spray for a Friend*.	Students were asked to imagine that they had a can of magic spray. They were to make a drawing of the spray can with a picture on the can to show what kind of magic it had.

Write three of your own ideas for open ended activities that a teacher could use. You can use a curriculum topic as a point of departure for an activity or a story that is read to/with the class.

Figure 13.1 Activity 1: Open-ended or self-expressive activities to learn preoccupations.

Imagine that at the beginning of a new curriculum topic you will have a class work together to make an attributes tree or idea tree related to the topic. This is a useful way to learn students' related interests, beliefs, experience, and vocabulary.

So for example, to start a unit on insects, the class could make an attributes tree about all the ways that insects can be the same or different from each other.

Prompt Questions for Brainstorming for Attributes Trees

Concept or Topic of Attributes Tree	First Question to Prompt Brainstorming	Second Question to Prompt Brainstorming*
Insects	What are all the ways that insects can be the same or different from each other?	What are all the ways that insects can be the same or different from other living creatures?
Communities	What are all the ways that communities can be the same or different from each other?	What are all the ways that communities can be the same or different from other places people live?

* The purpose of this second question is to jar students into recognizing and stating attributes that are so taken for granted that they might not even think to mention them.

To help students have a sense of what you are working towards when making an attributes tree, first have them make one about something very familiar and meaningful like "What are all the ways that games can be the same or different from each other?"

To help students think about a large number of different characteristics and attributes, first have the class brainstorm many different examples of the entity of interest. For example, before making an attributes tree about all the ways that games can be the same or different from each other, you could first have the class brainstorm all the different games they know. Seeing the list of games can help them think of characteristics and attributes more quickly.

Each branch on the attributes tree would have the name of a different attribute, such as "how many players," "where it is played," "equipment needed," "how players win," and so forth. Twigs on each branch would give examples of different values each attribute can have. On the branch called "Equipment," the twigs would be words like ball, net, bat, and so on.

For some topics you might want to have the class make an *idea tree* instead of an attributes tree. An idea tree is framed as "What are all the different *ways* there are to [do something—e.g., make friends, celebrate something, cook food?]" Idea trees can also be framed as "What are all the different *kinds* of [something, e.g., games, snacks, gifts, and so forth] there are?" So for example, some of the branches on an idea tree about games might be team games, board games, computer games, and so on.

Figure 13.2 Activity 2: Making attributes trees or idea trees at the beginning of new curriculum topics.

Using open-ended creative assignments at the end of a topic can provide opportunities for students to review curriculum content while also providing contexts for students to use other knowledge, interests, or skills and talents.

Sample formats:

Create a poster/mural/dance/song/game/news hour interview/YouTube video/skit/ or funny commercial to show how you/your group/your favorite character/your favorite animal etc. could teach/use or demonstrate etc. key ideas you learned about [curriculum topic].

Examples:

Grade 5: Draw your idea for an interesting toy to sell. To make an infomercial about the toy, create a poster or song or dance or funny commercial that uses some of the advertisement techniques learned in the media literacy unit.

Grade 2: After completing a unit on small crawling and flying animals, students are asked to design their own insects and draw habitats for them. As a creative challenge each student selects (from those offered) one interesting art material element (a feather, some sequins and glue, bright colored felt, pipe cleaners in different colors, etc.) to incorporate as a key feature in the design of their insect.

Figure 13.3   Activity 3: Using open-ended creative assignments to conclude curriculum topics

COMPLETED ACTIVITIES AND REFLECTIONS
BY CHARNEY DOCHERTY

Figure 13.4 shows one of the ideas Charney Docherty presented for "Activity 1: Using open-ended or self-expressive activities to learn preoccupations." In brief—as part of creating the contents for a time capsule—the idea was to invite students to write letters to the students of the future to

Our school is celebrating its 10th anniversary this coming year. There is a big celebration planned and as a staff we have been thinking of ways to mark this occasion with our students. One idea is the creation of a time capsule that could be buried and uncovered in the future at a big school anniversary. As a part of the time capsule one possible open-ended activity could be to invite students to write a letter to the students of the future to share what their lives are like in 2017.

This letter would help a teacher understand the lived stories of their students as members of our school community and even the experiences of their lives outside of school. It may also guide a teacher to plan activities to support needs or interests that are uncovered. This would be helpful in creating authentic and engaging tasks in the classroom.

Figure 13.4   Example for Activity 1: Using open-ended or self-expressive activities to learn preoccupations.

share what their lives were like in 2017. Teachers in this course and others have noted that although they have sometimes provided students with self-expressive activities like these, they had not systematically studied the students' products with the specific intention of learning about students' preoccupations, values, beliefs, and lived experiences.

Figure 13.5 presents one of Charney Docherty's activities for "Activity 2: Using attributes trees or idea trees to learn preconceptions." In having students prepare an attributes tree about plants, a science unit in Grade 4, she anticipated learning students' prior knowledge, existing vocabulary, misconceptions, and related interests. She felt that using this strategy would be more engaging and informative than simply asking students to tell all they know about plants.

Figure 13.6 presents two of the examples Charney Docherty provided for "Activity 3: Using open-ended creative assignments to conclude topics." In the first example she reported on having students complete creative projects to show their learning about Wetland ecosystems and Waste and our

---

An attributes tree can be used prior to beginning the Grade 4 science topic, Plant Growth and Change, to learn student preconceptions. In the past I have come to understand students' prior knowledge of the topic by just asking them to share orally in a large group what they know already about plants. The responses have been quite limited and random, requiring a great deal of digging on my part. However, a stronger "pre-assessment" approach to learn their existing knowledge, vocabulary, and beliefs would be to use an attributes tree.

I would begin the attributes tree work with a question to prompt initial brainstorming: "What are all the ways that plants can be the same or different from each other?" Students would brainstorm responses to this question and then categorize these ideas onto a tree. As I take their suggestions to place similar or related ideas on a branch, we could come up with a label or category for the branch. Most of the brainstormed words or ideas would become twigs on main branches. The words—water, sun, air—would be twigs on a branch about what plants need. I would anticipate that the main branches would be categories or attributes such as "what plants need," reproduction methods, stages in their life cycle, and so forth.

As a second brainstorming prompt I could ask: "What are all the ways plants can be the same or different from other living things?" This question could prompt students to think of ideas they may have not considered before, such as that plants don't move, they make their own food, and so forth. This activity would provide excellent information to guide me to the next teaching steps and areas of focus in this topic.

As a warm-up before starting the attributes tree, I could help the class to start thinking about plants by having each student draw an interesting plant or by having the whole class brainstorm a list of interesting or favorite plants. This start-up activity could make the brainstorming for the attributes tree easier to do.

Figure 13.5 Example for Activity 2: Using attributes trees or idea trees to learn preconceptions.

Example 1:
With Grade 4/5 students I recently completed an interdisciplinary unit that integrated the Grade 4 science topic, Waste and Our World, and the Grade 5 science topic, Wetland Ecosystems. I used open-ended creative assignments at the end of our study to engage students in a project that both demonstrated their learning and that also persuaded others to make a difference to our environment—a key idea in both of these curriculum topics. They were presented with the challenge to create something that will show what they have learned but also persuade others to take actions that help our earth. We began by co-creating goals and rubrics that provided guidelines for what the project must include. The audience project was the school community. Students brainstormed possible project ideas and as a class we narrowed down the choices to the following:

1. Create a work of art that shows what you have learned and that will persuade others to take action to help our earth.
2. Write a song that shows what you have learned and that will persuade others to take action to help our earth.
3. Make a presentation that shows what you have learned and that will persuade others to take action to help our earth.
4. Make a poster to show what you have learned and that will persuade others to take action to help our earth.

There were many different projects but some of the creative assignments that emerged from this were:

- A group of three boys wrote and recorded a rap song that told students about the dangers to our wetlands. The recording was distributed to the staff who shared and discussed the lyrics with their students.
- My artistic quiet student worked independently and created a series of three water-color paintings. One showed the land of Alberta in the day of the dinosaurs, one showed the land today with construction and buildings, and the last one showed what it will look like in the future. He gave each a very thought-provoking title.
- A group of students created posters and put them up in all the classrooms that were used as lunchrooms. It showed students how to sort their recycling and garbage.
- Two students created a presentation on how to pack a waste free lunch using puppets they borrowed from the kindergarten class. They presented to each class in the school and challenged them to meet the requirements.
- Two students filmed a commercial sharing the dangers of pollution and what kids can do in their daily lives to reduce greenhouse gases. I sent the commercial to all staff and it was shared in every classroom.

Example 2:
An open-ended assignment could be used for students to demonstrate and share their knowledge about "Bullying." In our K–5 school we teach a program called Promoting Alternative Thinking Strategies (PATHS). It is a research-based program that teaches and builds upon students' problem-solving skills and strategies as part of our Health and Wellness curriculum. A key component of this program is teaching students about bullying with topics ranging from understanding what it is to how to respond. An open-ended assignment that students could use to demonstrate and share their learning would be to have them create either a skit/role play, a poster, or a work of art that shows the following things: the dynamics of bullying situations; what to do if you are bullied; what to do if you are a bystander.

Figure 13.6 Examples for Activity 3: Using open-ended creative assignments to conclude topics.

World. The class brainstormed ideas for these products. In her reflections on this activity she commented:

> Culminating this study with open-ended creative activities was very successful. As stated by Ellis (1998), I discovered that "these creative activities provide a space where children can engage both what they know and what they can think, dream, or imagine" (p. 66). Similar to the findings in this article my students cooperated, were engaged, demonstrated pride in their work and used modes of expression that appealed to them (Ellis, 1998).

> I do think involving them in brainstorming possible activities really promoted their engagement further and gave them a sense of ownership. Kids always seem to be able to "think outside the box" better than adults so I was amazed at their creativity. The kids still sing the rap song. In fact, it's still in my head too! Of course, being preteens they accessed technology and set it to a beat so it was surprisingly well done.

For Example 2, Charney Docherty anticipated having students prepare performances and presentations to show their learning from the health topic of Bullying. As noted in her reflections on this example, she expected a number of benefits from this activity:

> By having students express their learning and knowledge about the bullying topic in a project context that appeals to them, I would be able to allow them choice in representation, promote engagement, allow collaboration and still be able to collect evidence about student learning. Additionally, if students share this work with the school community through presentations or putting up their posters and art, they would have authentic audiences that make their work meaningful and offer validation or recognition. The details or stories about bullying highlighted in their presentations could also help me learn about what their lived experiences or issues with bullying are. The activity could also help me uncover concerns, as well as experiences with bullying that they may have or are undergoing. It could identify bullying issues that students may not be willing to share in other forums.

FINDINGS

Like others in the course, Charney Docherty, concluded that the teacher as researcher activities could easily be incorporated into their teaching practices and would provide ongoing opportunities to their students and provide opportunities for students to use their interests and talents in school. Also, like others in the course, she expressed surprise or frustration that although she is student centered in her teaching approaches there is so much more that she could have been doing to accomplish her goals. At the end of her last assignment, she wrote:

As I considered and worked through the activities and strategies examined and completed in this course, I was constantly reflecting on how I could easily apply them in my own practice in order to gain a deeper understanding of all students. I must admit that these reflections lead me to feel excited to incorporate the strategies and witness the benefits in the near future. However, my reflections also made me feel frustrated. The frustration I felt was with myself. As an educator, I have always tried foremost to focus on student success through establishing strong student relationships, creating a safe and caring learning environment and using a student-centered approach in my teaching practice. I believe every student can succeed. These values are at the core of my teaching philosophy so I felt uncomfortable in the recognition that there was so much I could do differently to ensure that I was focusing more intentionally and thoroughly on understanding my students. Therefore, upon reflection, there are many modifications or additions I could have used in my tasks in order to work more interpretively so that my students are even more so at the center of teaching and learning. I am excited at having the opportunity to implement these changes, to improve my pedagogy but more importantly to help me support my students to be successful, recognized and understood as individuals.

WHAT WAS LEARNED ABOUT THE TEACHER AS RESEARCHER ACTIVITIES?

The first activity, "Using open-ended or self-expressive activities to learn preoccupations," was seen by teachers in the course as providing an open space to share concerns. Charney Docherty expressed that view in this way:

> I think that this activity has the potential to enable some students to share concerns or difficulties that they may be experiencing personally or at school. It could be a respectful way to involve students in sharing personal themes or ideas and in the process also uncover areas of interest.

The second activity, "Using attributes trees or idea trees to learn preconceptions," was seen by class participants as being better than simply asking students to brainstorm or share what they already know about a topic. Making the attributes trees or idea trees gave more focus and interest. Class members noted that without an activity like this at the beginning of a topic they felt they had sometimes ended up spending too much time teaching the parts of the content that students already knew beforehand. In discussion groups Charney Docherty wrote:

> I also often ask students to just "tell me what they know" about a topic. I know this comes from our teacher training in which we were taught to assess prior knowledge. However, I hadn't considered how students may be motivated by

the desire to please in these situations and this has caused me to think differently about the questions I ask. Furthermore, after engaging in the activities this term, I can now recognize how open-ended activities can provide a deeper more comprehensive picture for teachers not just about students' prior knowledge, but about their lived stories as well. This has been a true "Aha!" for me from this course, one that will impact how I begin new topics!

The third activity, "Using open-ended creative assignments to conclude a topic," was well received by class members. The general view was that because the structure of these assignments included clear criteria (e.g., the product or performance had to show key ideas learned in the unit) the activities could be open-ended and provide space for creativity or the use of talents and interests while also supporting curriculum goals. As noted in Charney Docherty's reflections, students are cooperative and focused when working on these creative activities and their ideas are often better than what teachers can plan. Students' sense of ownership of the activities also supports their engagement. The activities provided opportunities for talents to be used and appreciated and the products and performances, as anticipated in Charney Docherty's plans for the bullying topic activities, could also provide insight into students' assumptions and related lived experiences.

REFERENCES

Ellis, J. (1998). Creative assignments that promote learning and understanding. In J. Ellis (Ed.), *Teaching from understanding: Teacher as interpretive inquirer* (pp. 57–78). Garland.

Ellis, J. (2005). Creative classroom teaching. In J. L. Kincheloe (Ed.), *Classroom teaching: An introduction* (pp. 241–260). Peter Lang.

Ellis, J. (2007). Creative problem solving. In J. Kincheloe & R. Horn (Eds.), *Educational psychology: An encyclopedia* (pp. 295–309). Greenwood.

Ford, J. E. (2017, January 31). *Student–teacher relationships are everything.* EducationWeek. https://www.edweek.org/teaching-learning/opinion-student-teacher-relationships-are-everything/2017/01

Immordino-Yang, M. H. (2013, Spring). The science of social learning. *Futures in Urban Ed* magazine (pp. 22–23), USC Rossier School of Education.

Sparks, S. D. (2019, March 12). *Why teacher–student relationships matter: New findings shed light on best approaches.* EducationWeek. https://www.edweek.org/ew/articles/2019/03/13/why-teacher-student-relationships-matter.html

INTRODUCTION TO CASE STUDY 14

The authors demonstrate multiple important considerations in using qualitative methods which are considerate of culture including feminist research methods, the importance of interrogating (researcher) bias, considering philosophical bases (both of the researcher and the community), notions and consequences of power and positionality including impact on those from marginalized groups, reflexivity and emphasizes that the recognition, discovery, "capture," and careful consideration of voice is an essential aspect of work with minoritized and disenfranchised groups and individuals. This is best illustrated in this example by the authors' application of these ideas with a frequently marginalized community/population in research and program evaluation and changes the typical research approach of inquiry of a group for knowledge to one of providing an opportunity for that group to express itself. This was possible given the illustrated focus on relationship building and genuineness as the basis for data collection procedures, acknowledging local expertise, and recognizing the consequences of belonging to a marginalized group. The authors believe that adopting a feminist research methodology allowed them to work with and for participants while better serving the study aims of knowledge generation. By incorporating feminist techniques, established institutional demands and power structures can be challenged, resulting in research processes and outcomes that are advantageous for historically marginalized and excluded communities as well as addressing researcher/evaluator interests and purposes.

Qualitative Research With Diverse and Underserved Communities, pages 243–263
Copyright © 2024 by Information Age Publishing
www.infoagepub.com
243

CASE STUDY 14

ON INTERROGATING BINARIES AND ATTENDING TO POWER THROUGH FEMINIST RESEARCH METHODOLOGIES IN ENVIRONMENTAL EDUCATION

María C. Ospina
University of California, Davis

Alycia M. Drwencke
University of California, Davis

Jenna M. Turpin
University of California, Davis

Emily L. Pascoe
University of California, Davis

Kaitlyn A. Murray
University of California, Davis

Rebecca L. Godwin
Piedmont University

Sarah T. Abusaa
University of California, Davis

Rylie Ellison
University of California, Davis

Christopher C. Jadallah
University of California, Davis

Katherine A. Dynarski
University of Montana

Qualitative Research With Diverse and Underserved Communities, pages 245–263
Copyright © 2024 by Information Age Publishing
www.infoagepub.com
245

ABSTRACT

Equity-oriented methodological approaches, such as feminist research methodologies, provide frameworks to guide diverse forms of qualitative research that honor community knowledge and engage, rather than exclude, historically marginalized groups. In this chapter we outline a case study of "Program Evaluation"—a participatory research team that employs feminist research methodologies to study the development of young people's identities at the intersection of gender, science, and leadership in a place-based, outdoor education program. We provide evidence from our collaborative research process to pictorialize the ability of qualitative research to operationalize feminist values of interrogating binaries and attending to power. In interrogating binaries, we embrace a paradigm shift towards the subjective, attend to emotion in research, recognize the multiplicity of our roles, and center relationships in the research. To attend to power, we work in a collaborative, distributed power structure, center the voices of people of marginalized genders in the research design, create opportunities for reflexion, practice allyship, and utilize feminist frameworks for assigning credit for the work. This structure opens up opportunities for doing justice-oriented research with and for marginalized communities, but also has challenges. It is slow work that works in opposition to the "publish or perish" culture of academia and there are multiple constraints that may make this work difficult to implement. Feminist research methodologies create the opportunity for change within the research enterprise while better valuing, honoring, and elevating the voices and knowledge of historically marginalized communities.

As researchers committed to advancing equity and justice with and for people of marginalized gender, racial, ethnic, class, and/or sexual identities, it is imperative that we reflexively attend to the situated nature of knowledge production not just in our methods, but our broader methodological approach. Researchers increasingly use the language of *methodology* to name a study's underlying assumptions about knowledge, reality, and the role of research in society, while using the language of *methods* to describe specific tools for data collection and analysis (Wilson, 2008). It is a study's methodology that drives and informs how different methods are used, and with and by whom (Tuck & McKenzie, 2014); thus, equity-oriented researchers must consider the methodological approach driving their investigations.

Feminist research provides an example of an equity-oriented methodological approach to guide diverse forms of qualitative research. The movement started gaining traction in the early 1970s, when feminists began denouncing traditional positivist methods that disregard the complexities of social life (Naples, 2017). Instead, feminist methodologies employ a more holistic approach which values the social context, lived experiences, and perspectives of the researcher, while also acknowledging how these may contribute to biases against minoritized groups (Harding, 1998; Naples, 2003; Smith, 1987). As a counter-system to the rigid and often extractive structures of conventional academic research (Caretta et al., 2018), feminist research methodologies (hereafter, FRMs) represent a path forward to challenge traditional research hierarchies, confront pressures imposed by the neoliberal university, and generate novel ways of working with and for diverse and historically marginalized communities (Caretta & Faria, 2020). While feminist methodologies arose largely in opposition to the dichotomy of emotion and rationality, where women—who are traditionally seen as being more emotional than rational and often incapable of both—were less capable of organizing due to their emotional ties (Mumby & Putnam, 1992), we demonstrate how emotional ties can center individuals from diverse marginalized groups. This is especially critical as researchers embedded in an educational program that seeks to affect social change rooted in the needs and desires of historically marginalized groups. In these ways, the process of the research is as important a site for catalyzing change as the products of the research and the educational program itself.

To this end, we describe the feminist methodological approaches that our research team employs in our ongoing inquiry of the development of young people's identities at the intersection of gender, science, and leadership in a place-based, outdoor education program. In this chapter, we explore the question: "What are some approaches to FRMs?" and highlight examples from our collaborative and distributed research process to illustrate how qualitative researchers can operationalize feminist values. Program Evaluation, through action research, demonstrates how feminist research methodologies support transformative change in order to better value, honor, and elevate the voices and knowledge of historically marginalized communities, while also transforming the research enterprise.

CASE CONTEXT

Girls' Outdoor Adventure in Leadership and Science (GOALS) is a free summer science and leadership program for high school girls and gender expansive youth, run by volunteers at the University of California, Davis, in partnership with Sequoia and Kings Canyon National Parks (SEKI). GOALS aims to transform science, technology, engineering, and math (STEM) fields, the outdoors, and society by investing in the professional and personal development of people who are marginalized due to varied intersections of their gender, racial, ethnic, class, and/or sexual identities. Youth scholars spend 2 weeks backpacking, contributing observations and measurements to citizen science projects, conducting original research, and taking part in a place-based, culturally sustaining curriculum. While the forward-facing parts of GOALS focus on youth, GOALS also provides a flexible framework for volunteers—almost all of whom are women and nonbinary people in STEM—to collaboratively design and administer the program through skill-sharing and hands on problem-solving in grant writing, lesson planning, designing backcountry scientific experiments, and fundraising. The program framework also provides professional development and reflection opportunities for paid trip leaders and SEKI scientists who participate in the trip. Taken together, the GOALS community consists of youth scholars who participate in these trips, SEKI scientists and trip leaders who facilitate the youth experience, and a broad base of volunteers—organized in committees—who lead and carry out program design and implementation. One of these committees is *Program Evaluation*, composed of nine volunteers—the authors of this chapter—who evaluate the GOALS program and conduct original research. In our research, we include youth scholars, trip leaders, SEKI scientists, and GOALS volunteers as participants. The overlapping relationships between the broader GOALS network and research participants is illustrated in Figure 14.1.

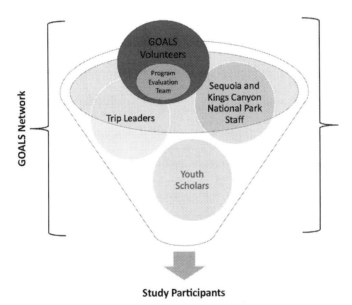

Study Participants

Figure 14.1 The overlapping relationships among the Girls' Outdoor Adventure in Leadership and Science (GOALS) network and research participants are illustrated. The GOALS community consists of youth scholars who participate in the trips, Sequoia and Kings Canyon National Park (SEKI) Staff who assist with trip logistics and engage in activities with scholars on the trip, trip leaders that facilitate the experience and volunteers who lead and carry out program design and implementation. Within the group of volunteers exists Program Evaluation, a team that evaluates the GOALS program and conducts original research. In our research, we include youth scholars, trip leaders, SEKI Staff, and GOALS volunteers as study participants.

As members of this committee and research team, we have met weekly since January 2019 to carry out two primary objectives: program evaluation (i.e., evaluating if we are meeting the needs of marginalized youth with respect to an outdoors learning experience, identifying and disseminating program-level changes) and conducting original research (i.e., exploring the role of nonformal learning and education in facilitating transformative experiences through interviews, focus groups, photovoice, and document analysis). Many of us are also embedded within other facets of the broader GOALS network, for example, in writing the curriculum or coordinating field logistics, allowing us to incorporate broader perspectives of the program into our research. Looking at the community of GOALS holistically across all stakeholder types, our membership represents the community in terms of class, gender, race, ethnicity, sexual orientation, languages spoken, level of experience, immigration status, and field of work—although we recognize the need to further diversify our team.

APPROACHES TO FEMINIST RESEARCH METHODOLOGIES WITHIN PROGRAM EVALUATION

In this chapter, we explore the connections between the approaches to FRMs and the practices of the GOALS Program Evaluation committee by focusing on two interconnected approaches: interrogating binaries and attending to power, as shown in Figure 14.2. It is important to note that this team did not set out to explicitly employ FRMs, but that our desire to work holistically and intentionally led us to co-design ways of interacting that can be understood through this lens. Our thinking and writing in this chapter are informed by feminist, queer, decolonizing, humanizing, and other critical literatures, and by drawing from our varied research and experience-based backgrounds. For example, several group members are graduate students in fields such as ecology and epidemiology. Analytic tools from such fields are useful for examining systemic trends and contextualizing experiences of marginalization in broader narratives and histories specific to time and place. The ways in which we enact and understand FRMs are inextricably tied to how we engage with the other parts of our lives that collectively create us; our other bodies of knowledge. In the following sections, we explore the connections between theory and practice through a series of vignettes drawn from researcher reflections and discuss how they embody and relate to the broader body of literature: first under the theme of "Interrogating Binaries," then under "Attending to Power."

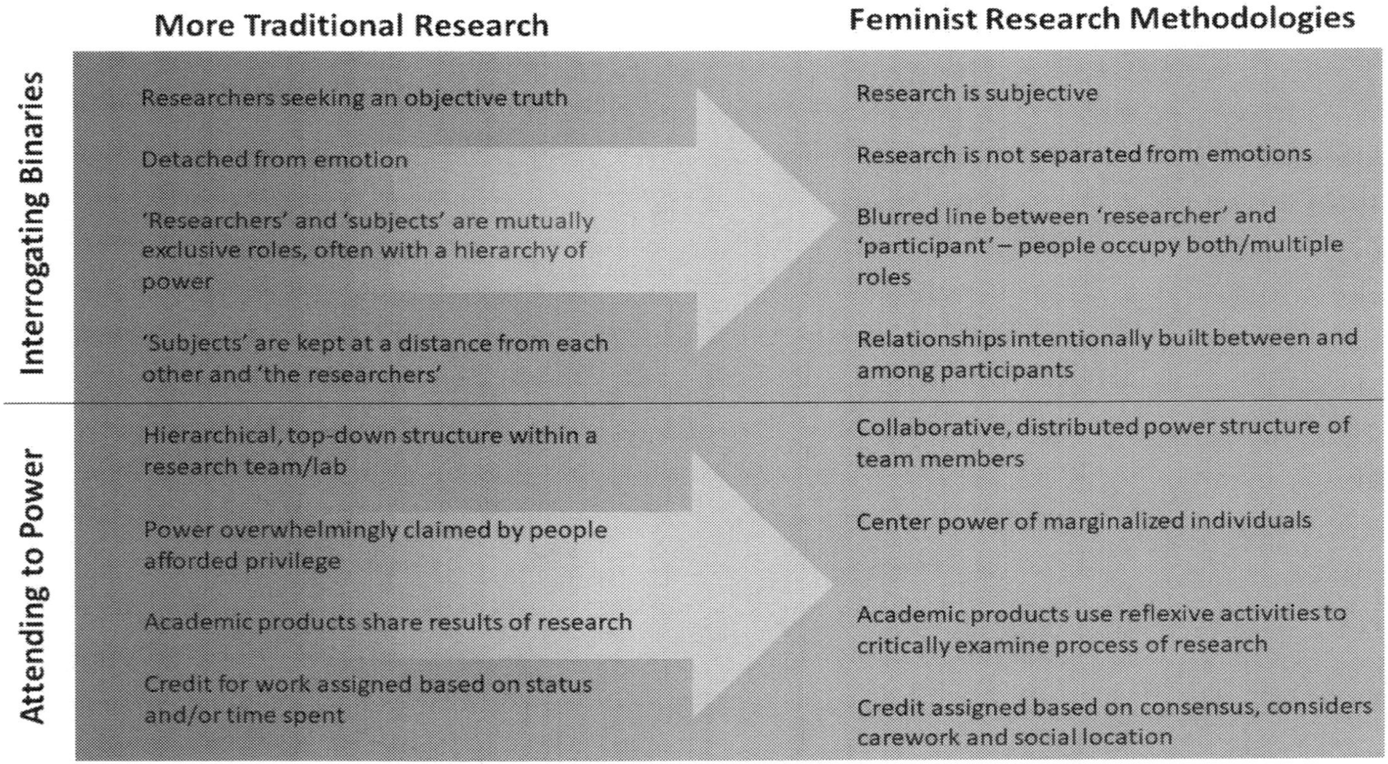

Figure 14.2 A framework for understanding the shifts Program Evaluation undertakes to enact feminist research methodologies. FRMs are not mutually exclusive from more traditional research practices but seek to interrogate binaries and attend to power more explicitly.

Interrogating Binaries

The process of interrogating binaries through our research and methods can be categorized into:

1. undertaking a paradigm shift (i.e., from attempting to be neutral observers to embracing the subjectivity of research);
2. attending to emotion in research (i.e., research is not separate from emotion);
3. recognizing the multiplicity of our roles (i.e., deconstructing the slash of the researcher/subject); and
4. centering relationships (i.e., viewing the relationships between and among participants as a part of the process).

In our research, we embraced the axiom that "the absence of self in research is an impossibility—we cannot be absent from feelings, emotions, and relationships as we are part of the environment. [...] research *is* rooted in the development of relationships; reality *is* dependent on the development of relationships" (San Pedro et al., 2017, p. 669). The power of this research is not in the absence of relationships, emotion, and care—maintained through rigid binaries—but rather through the explicit acknowledgement and centering of these inseparable components of self and community (Ahmed, 2014; Atkinson et al., 2000; Holland, 2007).

Taking up approaches to FRMs required and facilitated a critical shift in our understanding of research. Rather than serving as neutral, external observers doing value-free, positivist research on an objective reality, we recognized emotion as a part of the knowledge seeking process (Hesse-Biber, 2013), and recognized that all research is subjective, selective, and biased (Mays & Pope, 1995). In the case of GOALS, this meant honoring the emotions and complex ties each of us had to the work outside our roles as researchers.

Before we were ever researchers, we were GOALS volunteers. Each of us had invested time in curriculum, mentorship, field logistics, finance, and fundraising. We carried unique emotional ties to GOALS, and had a shared impetus in developing research that reflected our individual understandings of the GOALS mission. We shared a desire to improve the program by evaluating how effectively it serves its participants and demonstrating GOALS' value by documenting participants' stories and sharing these stories across committees and groups at the university level. Further, we shared emotional ties to conducting and analyzing research to investigate if and how participation in GOALS facilitates personal transformation. Many of us have our own experiences of marginalization in STEM and the outdoors; we specifically joined to help co-create the kind of program we wished existed for us as young people.

We interrogate binaries by recognizing the presence of self in research, as our values and emotions guided the research process (Jaggar, 1989; Wilson, 2008). In positioning ourselves as researchers, it was important to also acknowledge our own voices as knowledge: our experiences as GOALS volunteers were critical sources of wisdom as we developed our priorities and practices as a research team (Krumer-Nevo, 2009). We recognized ourselves and our relationships as inseparable from the research. Our relationships to each other, to other volunteers, to scholars, to our emotions, and to the organization at large are the lifeblood that sustains our research. In the same way, our research serves to further connections—between us, among other volunteers, among scholars—throughout the research process (Wilson, 2008).

This shift towards deconstructing the "slash"—which imposes a separation, for example between the researcher and the participant, or the professor and the student (San Pedro et al., 2017)—and interrogating hierarchical binaries of researcher/participant required a shift in how we thought of research. While typical research might be characterized as the extraction of data from a lived context, analyzed behind closed doors to create a beneficial product that can be reported out, we sought ways of thinking differently—that is, analyzing relationships, considering hierarchical power structures, and integrating diversity (Beetham & Demitriades, 2007)—about the research's form, products, and processes while still recognizing and attending to the power dynamic that exists between researchers and participants. Through attention and care at each step of the research process, we shifted from traditional research methods to employing a methodology where the *process* of research is as critical as its *products* (Israel et al., 2012; Paris & Winn, 2014; Ropers-Huilman & Winters, 2011).

At the end of an interview Sashay made parallels between the value of reflection in the GOALS curriculum and the research process: "I'm really glad this [interview process] is part of GOALS now. I just think it's really, really neat cause I think it'll also help just with everybody with reflection, which is an important part of growth." While we tracked these reflections from scholars and trip leaders, we also noticed how we—and other GOALS volunteers—were changed by the process of the research.

As our methodology required us to think differently about the process and products of the research, it became clear that the interviews were not only for data collection, but also functioned as spaces for reflection, relationship building, reconnection, and empowerment for the participants as well as us, the researchers. While the data (and subsequent analysis and reporting) are one product, these moments of healing and growth that emerge from the process are equally important. Recognizing the false binary of product and process impacted our ways of moving through interviews—allowing us to set down protocols and questions in favor of creating spaces that allowed us to hear, voice, and respond to our collective needs as they emerged.

Perhaps the most common binary reproduced in traditional social science research is that between researcher and subject (Hesse-Biber, 2013). Throughout this research, Program Evaluation has sought to include an expansive network of participants in our study, including "researchers," volunteers, students, educators, and community stakeholders, many of whom wear multiple hats within the organization. During a focus group of volunteers, we were able to make space for reflection across various roles, rather than expecting participants to adhere to a single or primary perspective.

> Over the course of data collection, we encountered a number of barriers in scheduling and recruiting volunteers to focus groups, resulting in just two volunteers ("subjects") and four facilitators ("researchers") in attendance for the final focus group. When the two volunteers asked if everyone around the table was participating in the focus group, Chris had to make an impromptu decision and responded: "Um, so, we're all [gesturing to the three other Program Evaluation members and himself] technically facilitating the focus group since we're all part of the Program Evaluation committee. [...]That being said, even though we are all helping facilitate the focus group, I think we're all also going to be participating as well. So also sharing our responses and our reflections too in that spirit of wanting to have more of a discussion."

In these moments, the boundary of who was a participant and who was a researcher was negotiated and changed as members of the research team recognized the multiplicity of their roles as volunteers alongside the other participants. In a more traditional setting, the focus group would have likely been cancelled or maintained a rigid format that could have made the participants less open to sharing their perspectives. Still, through consistent conversations amongst volunteers, we bring awareness to the power dynamic that exists between volunteers and participants (see section "Attending to Power" below). By doing so, volunteers navigate conversations with participants with care to not exploit the power dynamic and to instead offer space for others to enact power when possible. This approach blurs the traditional binary roles between researchers and participants, making room to honor the experiences and contributions of our participant-researchers. The researcher/subject binary is further complicated by the existence of complex relationships between people in the GOALS network and in the study, illustrated in the following vignette.

> Within our research team are best friends, cohort mates, collaborators, lab-mates, acquaintances, friends, and drinking buddies. When thinking about our volunteer 'subjects' in the study, there are people whose sofas we've crashed on and who we follow on social media. We have served as professional references for each other and have held others as they cried. Some people on our team meet monthly with scholars ("subjects") to help them apply for college. Others are emailing a scholar's AP Environmental Science teacher to brainstorm lessons. When thinking about the story of this research, it's the woven intimacies and connections that can't be fully spoken in the pages of a manuscript, that cannot be confined to binary roles of "researcher" and "subject."

Relationships are a critical part of the research process (Ropers-Huilman & Winters, 2011; San Pedro et al., 2017) and a critical piece of deconstructing the binary of "researcher" and "subject." Rather than viewing these relationships as potentially muddying or distancing ourselves from an "objective truth,"

> feminist researchers tend to use these relationships as the impetus for empowering and improving the lives of women, and also as a way to strengthen their understanding of the research topic. As they attend to these relationships, they acknowledge that the subjectivity and power each participant embodies is hard to understand. Throughout, the overarching purposes of understanding and change are integrally tied to the reflective relationships that are formed (Ropers-Huilman & Winters, 2011, p. 678).

In the case of GOALS, we utilize this expanded network of participants, the dual nature of our own roles, and the network of connections within, among, and beyond each "researcher" and each "subject" to acknowledge the multiple valid ways of being, experiencing, and knowing (or being known) outside of a binary system.

Attending to Power

The work of Program Evaluation also enacts FRMs by explicitly attending to power. Of course, interrogating binaries allows us to attend to power more completely and successfully, both within our research group and in how we interact with other participants, but we take additional steps to name and attend to power beyond interrogating binaries. We accomplish this in two main ways: through women's voice and reflexive processes. This section will walk through examples of how we

1. work in a collaborative, distributed power structure;
2. acknowledge the power of women's and other marginalized people's voices and knowledge—inclusive of people within and outside the Program Evaluation committee;
3. incorporate reflexive processes in traditional academic practices; and
4. utilize feminist frameworks for assigning credit to our work.

Throughout these examples, we discuss both the dynamics of attending to power within our group and in our interactions with others.

Within our research group of undergraduates, graduate students, post-docs, and faculty from disciplines such as the biological sciences and social sciences, each individual has vastly different research knowledge and experiences. In a traditional setting, the most "senior" researchers or those with a background in methods we would utilize might have grabbed the reins through the assumption that they are better equipped to lead a research group. As a result, people with access to specialized knowledge, skills, and expertise are privileged in the research process without naming how power and privilege (especially in terms of race, gender, age, and class) shape and constrain individuals' abilities to access these same things (Gutierrez y Muhs et al., 2012). Even without intentionally applying FRMs, our group understood that we did not want to operate under standard power dynamics because we recognized that our unique perspectives and experiences were critical sources of knowledge (Krumer-Nevo, 2009) that would collectively allow us to navigate our research path. This led to the decision to do research as a collective, with individual members taking on different roles at various times as it suited their needs, capacities, and interests, rather than organized into a formal lab structure led by a senior principal investigator.

The research design and study questions have also been shaped by the practice of centering women's voices, including the voices of women and girls outside of Program Evaluation.

As we brainstormed potential research questions, it became apparent that if we were to be conducting research, it ought to be guided by the needs, desires, and goals of participants across the GOALS network, especially those whose identities were multiplicatively marginalized in science, the outdoors, and schooling. The team undertook a coordinated effort to gather and analyze data to understand the most salient themes, concerns, and needs of each group (youth scholars, SEKI partners, and GOALS volunteers). We did so by analyzing previously collected surveys, filmed interviews, written materials and learning artifacts from the GOALS trip, and oral feedback sessions with stakeholders. Throughout these processes, we asked others to share what they wish the world knew about them and their experiences, and how having that information shared may affect their lives. Through these questions we drafted our research design and methods.

Voice has been a root metaphor in feminist research (Krumer-Nevo, 2009), and the process of co-developing the research questions and design centered on the voices of participants across the GOALS network. Rather than "giving voice" to the "voiceless" we engaged in dialogues that focused on ensuring "women's voices can be heard on their own terms" (Yost & Chmielewski, 2013, p. 243), flattening the traditional hierarchies and artificial binaries of researcher/participant or adult/youth. Critical in this shift is a recognition of ourselves as researchers as agentic participants in this conversation. Grande, San Pedro, and Windchief (2015) elaborated on this, writing,

> In the typical (Western) clinical and educational settings, conversations tend to be one-sided, with one person asking questions while the other is answering. In such one-sided interactions, only one demand is stated: "Tell me who you are in the absence of me." The inherent asymmetries of power raise yet another question: "What is at stake (and whose interests are served) in a power dynamic where only one person is asked to reveal him- or herself?" (p. 112)

In co-designing the research process, Program Evaluation sought to explore what is made possible when we turn towards the wisdom of our own communities, where each member holds specialized and situated knowledge. However, embedded in the practice of listening to the voices of people of marginalized genders—ourselves, other participants, and community members in the broader GOALS network—is the need to attend to the intersections of power that arise from our social locations along other axes of difference: particularly in terms of race, ethnicity, and age. We do this through action research by creating and embedding reflexive processes throughout our work, where we collectively reflect on our own position in the research as it relates to broader systems of power.

The use of reflexive processes to attend to power within our group and with other participants proved to be even more important during 2020. On May 25th 2020, three months into the COVID-19 pandemic, George Floyd was murdered by police officers, catalyzing national protests and collective uprisings as part of the Movement for Black Lives. With our third interviews with scholars and trip leaders scheduled to take place in the following weeks, our team recognized how these events would not only undoubtedly affect the participants (inclusive of the researchers) on a personal level, but also affect the data collected. After grappling with how to address these topics, it became clear that it was necessary to discuss what was going on and how to proceed. We decided that within the context of the interview we would turn off the recorders and have frank conversations about how we, the scholars and the trip leaders were understanding, coping, and thinking about the events in the world, and if there were resources, support, or other things we could help each other access.

While this move was a critical part of our methods and methodology, it intentionally did not produce data that were recorded. Drawing from (Tuck & Yang, 2014), "These stories are not simply y/ours to take" (p. 234). The refusal in research to prioritized care—in both the reluctance to have these conversations and in the act of shielding both pain and wisdom—not only inhibits community building but is also actively harmful to all research participants. As White and/or otherwise privileged researchers, our practices of allyship needed to extend within and beyond our research. Erskine and Bilimoria (2019) describe White allyship as

> a continuous, reflexive practice of proactively interrogating Whiteness from an intersectionality framework, leveraging one's position of power and privilege, and courageously interrupting the status quo of predominantly White [...] leadership by engaging in prosocial behaviors that foster growth-in-connection and have both the intention and impact of creating mutuality, solidarity, and support of Afro-Diasporic women's career development and leadership advancement. (p. 319)

GOALS had been going through an extended process of critique and reorganization as the group grappled with having unclear roles and decision-making power centralized in a group of un-elected White women who served as a defacto leadership team. In a series of meetings the members of GOALS worked to restructure our organization. This was the explicit beginning of our continual work to "courageously [interrupt] the status quo" of "white-dominated organizational leadership" by changing the structure of our organization (Erskine & Bilimoria, 2019, p. 320). Within Program

Evaluation, we intentionally disrupt the hierarchical structure and predominantly White leadership by sharing facilitation roles, valuing the voice and experience of all members, and implementing reflexive processes—through open discussions on how to proceed—to attend to power.

The use of reflexive processes within our Program Evaluation team consists of an open working style that focuses on informality rather than hierarchical structures and responsibilities. This form of distributing hierarchical relationships (Caretta & Faria, 2020) allows us to attend to power and create a more relaxed working environment where individuals are empowered to share their opinions, take on additional responsibilities regardless of their experience, and advocate for themselves. Group members share the responsibility of developing meeting agendas, taking notes, and spearheading various projects in order to allow each member to put their capacity towards areas of the research they find value and meaning in. As our group evolves, we continue to check in and redistribute tasks as needed. While much of this ebb and flow is organic, we create intentional moments of pause to critically evaluate how we work together that attends to power, as shown in the example below.

In preparing to write this manuscript, we engaged in a weeks-long process of creating a set of ten key reflexive questions, designed to help us locate ourselves in our work. We each spent a week answering these questions privately, then devoted multiple meetings to collectively reading and discussing our answers. Through this process we answered questions like: "What is your role in this group? Is this the role you want to be occupying?"; "In what ways has your voice come through or not in this work?"; "How have you designed this to reflect your story?"; "Whose story are we telling through this research and evaluation?"; (Alternatively: Who does this work serve?) "How so"?"; "Why?"; "Is this the story we should be telling?"; "What barriers exist to truth in this research/evaluation?"; "In what ways does how we operate work in alignment with our values? In opposition?" By anonymizing answers to these questions, we all felt we could more effectively discuss various perspectives and could more readily come to an informal consensus about how to proceed.

Throughout this process, we take traditional academic processes (i.e., the preparation of a manuscript, the creation of a conference talk), and create moments that allow us to critically review our work and gauge what we are doing well, areas for improvement, or determine future directions, particularly as they relate to flattening hierarchies of power. Just as we use these moments to evaluate our working relationships as a research team, we use them to evaluate how we can shift the tangible benefits of this work (i.e., authorship, advancement in the academy) in more just ways. We acknowledge that the ability to engage in this work—unpaid, volunteer work—is a privilege. Therefore, how credit is assigned to this work is similarly shaped and constrained by systems of power. Rather than following a hierarchical method of determining authorship—where higher positions are given to the most senior researchers or to the people who did the most intellectual or physical work—our team has adopted feminist methodologies in determining author order (Liboiron et al., 2017). We strive to acknowledge the value of all of our team members' contributions while also considering the power of authorship on individuals' current career and life stages, understanding authorship as a way to honor carework and other forms of under-valued labor, and as a tool for correcting injustices in how credit is typically under-assigned to people with marginalized identities (Liboiron et al., 2017). In this way, we acknowledge that *all* members of the research team have made critical intellectual and physical contributions to a given product, where no one's efforts are more or less central. Authorship then is based not on who has the most time or prior skills (manifestations of privilege and access), but on a consensus-based model of care and justice.

DISCUSSION

Utilizing approaches to FRMs has provided our team with opportunities that a traditional hierarchical structure would limit. For instance, group members share ideas as well as decision-making power, which Maria described as an "informal consensus framework." Throughout our time working together, our group has never explicitly stated we need to come to a general consensus that is reflective of everyone's voice; yet, during meetings, our team offers space for all members to share their perspective. We consciously ask for the opinions of group members without pressuring individuals to contribute beyond their capacity. This collective decision making process aspires to give each group member's voice the same amount of weight, while allowing individuals their own autonomy in the process. For example, individuals explore specific areas of interest and take on varied levels of responsibility based on what feels feasible at that time.

However, adopting FRMs comes with challenges as well—a substantial one being a slow rate of progress compared to other traditional research approaches. Despite this challenge, we advocate for "slow scholarship" to produce rigorous and ethical research (Caretta & Faria, 2020). Understandably, the voluntary nature of the project and dynamic workload favors prioritizing other responsibilities over this project, particularly academic obligations tied to funding or scholarly progress. The slower pace can also be exacerbated by the already labor-intensive nature of qualitative research which takes a high level of mental capacity and devoted time, limiting our group to individuals who are privileged enough to have said capacity. As individual volunteers progress in their lives outside of Program Evaluation, we have adapted to changes in career, members in multiple time zones, and interactions shifting to a virtual format during the COVID-19 pandemic. While this flexibility can be beneficial, these changes further complicate the ability to make progress on analyzing data, which requires multiple steps and iterations with the group decision making process. Actively incorporating feminist practices into our research process, such as creating space for reflection and sharing, has allowed us to address some of these challenges. For instance, we shifted our practice around weekly meetings to have different facilitators take turns in sharing responsibilities for planning and coordination after members of our team who had been assuming said responsibilities informally shared during a reflection meeting that doing so limited their capacity to participate in other ways.

Beyond these challenges, institutional constraints pose additional barriers to the process of feminist research. For those working at research-focused universities in particular, institutional imperatives and academia's pervasive "publish or perish" culture might be in tension with the time-and-labor intensive nature of feminist research (Caretta & Faria, 2020). For early career or non-tenured scholars and those from frequently marginalized groups in particular, whose time is often heavily academically consumed, engaging in such research can be difficult. Within our group, the accessibility of this work is further restricted by the institutional constraint of requiring Program Evaluation members to be institutional review board (IRB) certified. The need for this certification limits openness of the group and ability to frequently add more members that could share the workload. This need also creates a rigidness that requires a certain and consistent level of commitment from members in addition to their other academic responsibilities, which is unique to this committee compared to the rest of the GOALS organization. This in turn limits how credit is assigned. For example, this chapter—which discusses the dynamics of the Program Evaluation committee—has an author list that is defined and constrained by the IRB. Our research is also not traditionally structured with a principle investigator (PI), who holds greater political capital within the university, or has increased access to funding to cover research costs, including support for labor. Knowledge building as a team and leveraging resources individual members may have access to have helped to bridge these gaps, but our team is still composed of volunteers with less institutional power, and other academic obligations that may take precedence over GOALS.

While we describe our particular feminist approach to qualitative research, this is not a prescriptive document. There are multitudes of ways to approach research with feminist methodologies that can all be effective.

FRMs are meant to highlight the complexity of existing and the multiple valid ways of knowing, being, and organizing (Beetham & Demetriades, 2007). We have not provided an all-inclusive list of FRMs and their applications, but rather a case study of how we implement them. Considering the context and constraints of a group can inform which elements of feminist methods to utilize for greater success, if any. Still, we encourage other groups to interrogate binaries and attend to power as our team has grown closer and has greatly benefited from these approaches to FRMs. Some institutional constraints or hostile contexts may prohibit the successful integration of FRMs to a specific situation. Do not be discouraged if feminist methodologies cannot be implemented into every collaboration. Our methodological approach can be used as a field guide that can be adapted on a case by case basis to promote success.

CONCLUSION

Implementation of feminist research methodologies is critical to creating a more inclusive and dynamic research processes. Through the use of these methodologies, while interrogating binaries and attending to power, opportunities to honor the various forms of knowledge are created. Valuing and elevating these voices requires listening to and acknowledging the community wisdom, particularly of marginalized groups. In centering these forms of knowledge, we intentionally value the perspectives of the researcher and participant. We take into account facets such as lived experiences and social context in order to effectively attend to power in the research setting. There is no one "correct" way to employ feminist research methodologies, and doing so can be challenging; however, Program Evaluation has successfully achieved a healthier working environment and more insightful research processes by adapting FRMs. Adapting feminist research methodologies helped us to better serve research goals of knowledge production and equitable distribution of power, allowing us to work with and for participants. Incorporating feminist practices challenges traditional institutional pressures and power structures so that the research process and products are beneficial for communities historically marginalized and excluded from both the process and products of research.

AUTHOR NOTE

We have no conflicts of interest to disclose. Correspondence concerning this article should be addressed to María C. Ospina, Department of Evolution and Ecology, 1 Shields Ave., Davis, CA 95616.

REFERENCES

Ahmed, S. (2014). *Cultural politics of emotion.* Edinburgh University Press.

Atkinson, P., Coffey, A., Delamont, S., Lofland, J., & Lofland, L. (Eds.). (2000). *Handbook of ethnography.* SAGE Publications.

Beetham, G., & Demetriades, J. (2007). Feminist research methodologies and development: Overview and practical application. *Gender & Development, 15*(2), 199–216. https://doi.org/10.1080/13552070701391086

Caretta, M. A., Drozdzewski, D., Jokinen, J. C., & Falconer, E. (2018). "Who can play this game?" The lived experiences of doctoral candidates and early career women in the neoliberal university. *Journal of Geography in Higher Education, 42*(2), 261–275. https://doi.org/10.1080/03098265.2018.1434762

Caretta, M. A., & Faria, C. V. (2020). Time and care in the "lab" and the "field": Slow mentoring and feminist research in geography. *Geographical Review, 110*(1–2), 172–182. https://doi.org/10.1111/gere.12369

Erskine, S. E., & Bilimoria, D. (2019). White allyship of Afro-Diasporic women in the workplace: A transformative strategy for organizational change. *Journal of Leadership & Organizational Studies, 26*(3), 319–338. https://doi.org/10.1177/1548051819848993

Grande, S., San Pedro, T., & Windchief, S. (2015). Indigenous peoples and identity in the 21st century: Remembering, reclaiming, and regenerating. E. P. Salett & D. R. Koslow (Eds.), *Multicultural perspectives on race, ethnicity, and identity* (pp. 105–122). The National Association of Social Workers.

Gutierrez y Muhs, G., Niemann, Y., Gonzalez, C., & Harris, A. (2012). *Presumed incompetent: The intersections of race and class for women in academia.* Utah State University Press. https://digitalcommons.usu.edu/usufaculty_monographs/103

Harding, S. G. (1998). *Is science multicultural?: Postcolonialisms, feminisms, and epistemologies.* Indiana University Press.

Hesse-Biber, S. N. (2013). *Feminist research practice: A primer.* SAGE Publications.

Holland, J. (2007). Emotions and research. *International Journal of Social Research Methodology, 10*(3), 195–209. https://doi.org/10.1080/13645570701541894

Israel, B. A., Eng, E., Schulz, A. J., & Parker, E. A. (2012). *Methods for community-based participatory research for health.* John Wiley & Sons.

Jaggar, A. M. (1989). Love and knowledge: Emotion in feminist epistemology. *Inquiry, 32*(2), 151–176. https://doi.org/10.1080/00201748908602185

Krumer-Nevo, M. (2009). From voice to knowledge: Participatory action research, inclusive debate and feminism. *International Journal of Qualitative Studies in Education, 22*(3), 279–295. https://doi.org/10.1080/09518390902835462

Liboiron, M., Ammendolia, J., Winsor, K., Zahara, A., Bradshaw, H., Melvin, J., Mather, C., Dawe, N., Wells, E., Liboiron, F., Fürst, B., Coyle, C., Saturno, J., Novacefski, M., Westscott, S., & Liboiron, G. (2017). Equity in author order: A feminist laboratory's approach. *Catalyst: Feminism, Theory, Technoscience, 3*(2), 1–17. https://doi.org/10.28968/cftt.v3i2.28850

Mays, N., & Pope, C. (1995). Qualitative research: Rigour and qualitative research. *Bmj, 311*(6997), 109–112.

Mumby, D. K., & Putnam, L. L. (1992). The politics of emotion: A feminist reading of bounded rationality. *Academy of Management Review, 17*(3), 465–486. https://doi.org/10.2307/258719

Naples, N. A. (2003). *Feminism and method: Ethnography, discourse analysis, and activist research.* Psychology Press.

Naples, N. A. (2017). Feminist methodology. In *The Blackwell encyclopedia of sociology* (pp. 1–6). American Cancer Society. https://doi.org/10.1002/978140516 5518.wbeosf042.pub2

Paris, D., & Winn, M. T. (2014). Preface: To humanize research. *Humanizing research: Decolonizing qualitative inquiry with youth and communities* (pp. xiii–xx). SAGE Publications.

Ropers-Huilman, R., & Winters, K. T. (2011). Feminist research in higher education. *The Journal of Higher Education, 82*(6), 667–690. https://doi.org/10.1080/00221546.2011.11777223

San Pedro, T., Carlos, E., & Mburu, J. (2017). Critical listening and storying: Fostering respect for difference and action within and beyond a native American literature classroom. *Urban Education, 52*(5), 667–693. https://doi.org/10.1177/0042085915623346

Smith, D. E. (1987). *The everyday world as problematic: A feminist sociology* (1st ed.). Northeastern University Press.

Tuck, E., & McKenzie, M. (2014). *Place in research: Theory, methodology, and methods.* Routledge.

Tuck, E., & Yang, K. W. (2014). R-words: Refusing research. In D. Paris & M. T. Winn (Eds.), *Humanizing research: Decolonizing qualitative inquiry with youth and communities* (pp. 223–247). SAGE Publications.

Wilson, S. (2008). *Research is ceremony: Indigenous research methods.* Fernwood Publishing.

Yost, M. R., & Chmielewski, J. F. (2013). Blurring the line between researcher and researched in interview studies: A feminist practice? *Psychology of Women Quarterly, 37*(2), 242–250. https://doi.org/10.1177/0361684312464698

INTRODUCTION TO CASE STUDY 15

The writers employed an innovative mixed method approach to address some concerns raised in the literature regarding interviews as sources of information related to learning and academics as well as concerns about potential bias in self-report methods. The case study uses an effort to better understand graduate Chinese students' experiences with writing in a second language as a vehicle for this approach. Selected participants received an electronic questionnaire which was followed by an interview using ambiguous pictures to elicit affect and information and provide one basis for "triangulation" as a means of demonstrating "validity." This approach was then followed by a more traditional interview which endeavored to solicit information from respondents concerning the challenges of the requirements of their writing intensive coursework. The authors present the results of their efforts focusing on the utility of the methodology as an approach to the collection of information from individuals belonging to culturally diverse (from United States cultures) groups. The authors suggest that this approach resulted in greater confidence among the researchers in the accuracy of their data, and that the provision of a more unstructured approach than typical offered respondents a greater opportunity and offered the possibility of greater confidence in response since this approach was indirectly collecting information about respondents' experience rather than their efforts and failures with academic writing for coursework.

This case study offers some interesting perspectives for consideration—it opens the door to "storytelling" as a mechanism for "capturing" lived experience which can serve as an important means for in depth understanding

Qualitative Research With Diverse and Underserved Communities, pages 265–277
Copyright © 2024 by Information Age Publishing
www.infoagepub.com
265

of a particular phenomena without the necessity of self reference (that is indirect), stories have the potential for the expression of affect and the "projection" of self in the story experience, and finally stories may be useful for extending beyond the phenomena of interest. They can serve as a mechanism for exploring how cultural identity (including individual and community history) "influences" experience.

CASE STUDY 15

USING AMBIGUOUS PICTURE FOR DATA TRIANGULATION IN QUALITATIVE RESEARCH

The Case of Exploring Writing Anxiety Among Chinese Graduate Students

Fang Liang
Florida State University

Jeannine Turner
Florida State University

ABSTRACT

Chinese graduate students in U.S. colleges and universities can be disadvantaged within the system because English is their second language. One aspect that has received little empirical attention is Chinese graduate students' academic writing anxiety within English-speaking countries. Our mixed-method study addressed this gap in a unique way. Instead of a simple combination of survey and interviews, we used an ambiguous picture as an indirect method to get information regarding Chinese graduate students' experiences of aca-

Qualitative Research With Diverse and Underserved Communities, pages 267–277
Copyright © 2024 by Information Age Publishing
www.infoagepub.com
267

demic writing anxiety. This indirect method helps triangulate data obtained from two self-report sources, screening survey and interviews. We first discussed the limitations of self-reported data, then presented the rationale for using an ambiguous picture for data triangulation. We proceeded to use our study of Chinese graduate students' writing anxiety to illustrate that using an ambiguous picture as an indirect method can improve the validity of data obtained from self-report measures and provide important nuanced findings.

Although Chinese students are the largest international student-group in U.S. colleges/universities, they are a minority within the system. Although some researchers (e.g., Kagawa et al., 2011; Park et al., 2008) considered international students to be similar to immigrants, Zhang-Wu (2018) explained that immigrants are usually permanent residents of the host country, while international students hold short-term visas and maintain their native citizenship. However, this does not provide a clear picture of Chinese college students' experiences.

In our study, we focused on Chinese graduate students, who were pursuing majors that required a great deal of academic writing. One aspect that has received little empirical focus is Chinese graduate students' academic writing anxiety within English-speaking countries. Because English is their second language, Chinese graduate students are a disadvantaged group. Research on writing anxiety with English as a second language is relevant because academic writing is an indispensable part of graduate students' requirements. Writing anxiety may cause procrastination (Onwuegbuzie & Collins, 2001), can negatively impact students' writing performance (Daly, 1985), and may cause attrition at the dissertation stage (Marshall et al., 2017; Wynne et al., 2014). To better understand Chinese graduate students' experiences with writing in a second language, we conducted a mixed-method study. We used writing anxiety surveys to select participants with various levels of writing anxiety and invited them to participate in interviews. However, instead of simply interviewing students, we used a unique approach to begin the interview process: an ambiguous picture of a student at a computer. Our purpose for this chapter is to illustrate the usefulness of ambiguous pictures to support robust data triangulation, thus improving the validity of qualitative analysis. We first describe limitations of qualitative research, then explain why ambiguous pictures can be a useful way for overcoming some disadvantages of interviews. Lastly, we use our study as an example to show how using ambiguous pictures supports data-triangulation.

LIMITATIONS OF QUALITATIVE DATA

Although conducting qualitative research can help explore phenomena in-depth, scholars have concerns regarding the validity of qualitative data, especially when studying students' learning processes (Fryera & Dinsmore, 2020). Pekrun (2020) pointed out that interviews are a type of self-report, and therefore "subject to response sets and memory biases" (p. 189), which are also survey limitations. Simply combining questionnaires with interviews may not reduce bias. Thus, using indirect methods may be useful to improve the rigor of data analysis. We propose that one indirect method to elicit interview participants' information is through ambiguous pictures. In this case, researchers are not asking participants to describe themselves. Instead, researchers simply ask participants to tell a story about the picture. As we describe below, this process allows participants to project their thoughts/feelings regarding the intended topic. Below, we discuss the rationale of using ambiguous pictures as an indirect method for psychological assessment.

AMBIGUOUS PICTURES IN QUALITATIVE STUDIES

The method of using ambiguous pictures for psychological assessment is inspired by the Thematic Apperception Test (TAT), as picture-story exercises. Developed by Murray and Morgan (1935/1981), participants are asked to tell stories triggered by ambiguous picture-cards. By eliciting a person's imagination, the story reveals information about his/her life-views, as well as his/her perceptions and emotions. While the reliability and validity of TATs have been challenged, evidence has accumulated that support this approach. For example, in Meyer's (2003) meta-analysis, after comparing the psychometric data reported by projective TAT-assessments with those from alternate measures, the author concluded that TATs "produce reliability and validity coefficients that appear indistinguishable from those found for alternative personality tests, for tests of cognitive ability, and for many medical assessment procedures" (p. 328). In practice, TATs, and similar assessments, are still used as diagnostic tools by psychologists around the world (e.g., Piotrowski, 2015). More importantly, some researchers have made innovative adaptations to projective techniques (Piotrowski, 2015). In this light, we propose that adapting TATs, to elicit storytelling, can be extended to the realm of educational psychology. Indeed, although TATs have been an assessment for personality and emotions in clinical and social psychology, they have also been shown to have high adaptability for various research purposes (Miller, 2015). In our study, the TAT technique was modified to elicit participants' beliefs and feelings towards academic writing and their habitual writing behaviors. We used an ambiguous picture (Figure 15.1) to elicit participants' stories of academic writing, and we used the stories to triangulate data obtained from surveys and interviews. Although this research strategy is quite novel, the approach has been supported by a recent study. McCredie and Morey (2019) combined the use of TAT and self-report methods for personality assessments, asking

Figure 15.1   Ambiguous writing picture.

participants ($n = 455$) to complete a multiple-choice adaptation of TAT, along with two self-report instruments. Their results suggested that "TAT performance can correlate meaningfully with similar constructs assessed using self-report methodology when comparable structured response formats are used" (p. 1845). Next, we briefly describe our study purpose, participants, data sources, and results.

CASE STUDY

We use our qualitative study, *Exploring Writing Anxiety Among Chinese Graduate Students in An American Educational Setting* (Liang & Turner, 2021), to illustrate using an ambiguous picture to triangulate data obtained from other direct self-report sources. This study explored various levels of academic writing anxiety that Chinese graduate students experienced, their perceived causes for writing anxiety, and how they managed their writing anxiety. We recruited 11 Chinese graduate students enrolled in various graduate programs at a public university in a southern U.S. state and used three data sources.

Surveys

First, we used an online screening survey, *Survey for Second-Language Writing Anxiety Among International Graduate Students*, to select participants. We adapted the survey from the Daly-Miller (1975) *Writing Apprehension Scale.* Five items assessed participants' writing anxiety via two constructs: *avoidance behaviors* (e.g., "I avoid academic writing") and *fear of evaluation* (e.g., "I am afraid of academic writing when I know that my work will be evaluated"). Four items were used to assess writing confidence (e.g., "I feel confident in my ability to express my ideas clearly in academic writing"). All items used a 6-point Likert scale (1 = *not at all true,* 6 = *extremely true*). Each subscale demonstrated good reliability: total writing anxiety ($a = .77$), avoidance ($a = .71$), fear ($a = .65$), and writing confidence ($a = .77$). Initial data were obtained from 41 volunteers. Using these initial surveys, we identified three participants as low anxiety, four as moderate anxiety; and four as high anxiety; and invited them to participant in face-to-face interviews.

Thematic Apperception Test

As our second data source, we used an ambiguous picture to elicit interview participants' perceptions, beliefs, feelings, and behaviors regarding their English academic writing. The picture showed a person writing with a computer (Figure 15.1). In the picture, neither gender, ethnicity, nor facial expressions could be seen. A brief instruction was provided under the picture, which asked participants to look at the picture and describe the person's feelings and thoughts.

The interviewer also prompted: "Could you describe what happens in this picture? What is the individual in the picture probably feeling? What could happen next?" Participants' average time of storytelling was approximately 1 minute, 30 seconds. The timespan used for describing the picture was not associated with participants' levels of writing anxiety (determined by writing anxiety survey). For example, participants with high levels of writing anxiety did not tell the shortest (or longest) stories.

Interviews

Our third source of data were individual open-ended interviews to obtain information regarding Chinese graduate students' experiences of academic writing anxiety in their American setting (e.g., "What makes you anxious when you write? What helps you manage the writing anxiety?"). The interviews, including the picture narrative, took from 24 to 46 minutes.

Results

The analysis showed that Chinese graduate students' writing anxiety was related to English being their second language and low levels of writing confidence. For students with high writing anxiety, their anxiety could be traced back to their Chinese educational system (emphasis on high achievement through effort, Kirkpatrick & Zhang, 2011; Stankov, 2010), and the concomitant shaping of their beliefs about intelligence (whether intelligence is fixed or can grow with practice/learning). All participants described, through the pictures and/or interviews, they felt some writing anxiety. For many, their Chinese cultural/educational background—which emphasizes social comparisons and judgments of competence—played a role in their forming a belief that intelligence is fixed, which imposed a burden on their academic writing. However, many participants described ways they regulated their writing processes, as well as using emotion regulation strategies to alleviate their writing anxiety. Some of these strategies were effective in managing writing anxiety and writing progress, while others (such as procrastination) did not alleviate anxiety and interfered with writing progress. In the next section, we report the triangulation of data from surveys, picture projection, and interviews.

DATA TRIANGULATION

Table 15.1 compares results from our three sources of data. Below, we describe how the indirect data source (ambiguous picture) supported data

TABLE 15.1   Comparison of Three Types of Data

Pseudonym	Scores for Writing Anxiety/ Confidence	Picture Stories (Anxiety, Lack of Regulation/Writing Process, Regulation)	Interview Quotes
Low-Anxiety Group			
Chun	2.33/4.50	0/7 The person is typing in his ideas based on his draft under the keyboard. He is entirely focusing on the writing.	I coordinate my schedule for coursework and writing, then concentrate on writing.
Ying	2.75/4.75	0/4 I think this person feels confident . . . he knows what he's gonna write.	I have got academic writing experiences so that I know how long a writing task takes; I plan accordingly.
Hui	2.80/5.00	3/0 If this person has so much left to write, he will feel too nervous to put out anything, not knowing what to do.	I know I would be extremely anxious if I put off all tasks to the last few days, so I make sure to complete my weekly tasks, finishing everything a week before.

(continued)

	Scores for Writing Anxiety/ Confidence	Picture Stories (Anxiety, Lack of Regulation/Writing Process, Regulation)	
TABLE 15.1 Comparison of Three Types of Data (continued)			
Pseudonym			Interview Quotes
Medium-Anxiety Group			
Jinguo	2.40/3.75	1/4 I think this person had a brainstorm before writing and produced an outline.	I do not procrastinate. I would read the requirements the day when a writing task is assigned. I have a routine workflow for writing.
Hai	3.00/2.75	2/1 This student is worried about his deadline and he will push himself at this time to finish the writing task.	My first priority is to overcome that [writing anxiety]. I tried to look for some academic materials, like reference papers or something to keep myself, back to the topic.
Xiaomei	3.20/5.25	2/2 It is perhaps the night before the assignment is due, the student takes out all the references he read to write, but he is anxious because he did not organize the materials when reading them.	My way (of overcoming anxiety) is to write for one or half an hour no matter what. Even if I can't produce anything, at least I am engaged (with the task).
Lanming	4.60/5.00	1/4 I guess this person is writing something and he or she needs to use the resource, needs the tools such as calculator, the book or writing some draft, write down the to-do list.	When you make a plan, you don't make a big plan you cannot achieve. You chop it down into sub-steps, each step achievable.
High-Anxiety Group			
Fen	3.40/2.75	3/1 It is very likely that the person is catching a deadline and feeling anxious.	[After receiving feedback on writing assignment] I felt shocked, a lot of pressure, when knowing I made so many mistakes. That experience still has impact on me when I write.
Lin	4.20/2.75	6/0 The writer just has all the negative feelings. I mean maybe he or she is desperate or worried, frustrated.	Theoretically, I know how to cope with it (writing anxiety), but I'm not going to apply it. I doubt it. I just procrastinate.

(continued)

	Scores for Writing Anxiety/Confidence	Picture Stories (Anxiety, Lack of Regulation/Writing Process, Regulation)	Interview Quotes
TABLE 15.1		**Comparison of Three Types of Data (continued)**	
Pseudonym			
Yuhua	4.40/2.75	5/0 This person is trying to finish a work by the due date...obviously I think the whole process is frustrating.	My writing is a downward spiral. I don't enjoy it and I'm anxious about that. I pushed back and then I just tried to meet the requirements and tried to meet the due date. And then I got feedbacks...that make me feel like I'm not good at this.
Fangping	4.80/2.75	5/0 The person feels it hard to express what he wants to, so he procrastinates, all the way, till the day before deadline. He is really anxious.	I do not want to start [writing] because, based on previous feedback, I always had a lot of mistakes. So, I think I can't do it and don't want to do it.

from direct self-reports. The agreement of various sources of data indicated the validity of using ambiguous pictures for triangulating data in qualitative studies.

Valid data triangulation meant aligning data from the three sources (i.e., survey-scores, stories about the picture, and narratives from interviews). To be specific, participants who had low scores for writing anxiety tended to describe writing-processes and self-regulated writing-behaviors when they told the picture-story, then described similar processes/behaviors in their interviews. Similarly, participants with high writing anxiety scores described the person in the picture as worried or anxious, and in interviews, reported their own anxious feelings in writing tasks.

The table shows comparisons among data sources in the study. In the second column, are scores for participants' writing anxiety and writing confidence obtained from surveys. Participants are divided into low-, medium-, and high-anxiety groups. The third column indicates the number of times a participant mentioned writing anxiety-related feelings/issues, as well as the number of times each talked about writing processes/self-regulatory behaviors and provides quotes. The last column presents interview quotes that aligned with the ambiguous-picture narratives.

The table indicates a general pattern: high writing anxiety students tended to focus on describing the anxious feelings/behaviors regarding lack of self-regulation in their stories and interviews; whereas, low-anxiety students tended to describe writing processes and self-regulation behaviors in their stories and interviews. Worth noting, one participant seemed to be misplaced, with a low writing anxiety score, and a story that included anxiety. However, results indicated her data triangulated. Hui had a low anxiety score and high writing confidence. However, she mentioned anxious feelings three times when telling the picture story. In the interview, she described about her own experiences. When narrating the story, Hui was using the memory of experiencing anxiety during her first semester at graduate school. After years of study, Hui explained she is not generally anxious about writing now, because she puts forth effort to not procrastinate. If she procrastinates, she feels anxiety. Had we only used surveys and interviews, this nuance would have been missed. Furthermore, the comparison between her direct self-report and indirect narrative provided an important theme for the study (i.e., importance of self-regulation). Hui, along with the cases of Jingguo, Lanming, and Fen, showed that, if they use effective self-regulation strategies, they can manage their anxiety and complete the writing task. On the contrary, if they do not use self-regulation strategies, their anxiety could be triggered, with negative impacts.

CONCLUSION

We have showcased, with our study on Chinese graduate students' academic writing anxiety within an American educational setting, that using an ambiguous picture as an indirect method can improve the validity of data obtained from self-report measures and provide important nuanced findings. Fryera and Dinsmore (2020) stated that "the limitations sections of educational research articles are replete with apologies" (p. 3), and one of the reasons for the apologies is "the self-report nature of data" (p. 3). In this case, including ambiguous pictures as an indirect method of data-elicitation can be one way of making the self-report data more robust. We hope that our innovative method helps reduce some of the apologies for qualitative studies and boost educational researchers' confidence in reporting their qualitative results.

REFERENCES

Daly, J. A. (1985). Writing apprehension. In M. Rose (Eds.), *When a writer can't write* (pp. 4382). Guilford.

Daly, J. A., & Miller, M. D. (1975). The empirical development of an instrument to measure writing apprehension. *Research in the Teaching of English, 9*(3), 242–249. https://www.jstor.org/stable/40170632

Fryera, L. K., & Dinsmore, D. L. (2020). The promise and pitfalls of self-report: Development, research design and analysis issues, and multiple methods. *Frontline Learning Research, 8*(3), 1–9. https://doi.org/10.14786/flr.v8i3.623

Kagawa, M., Hune, S., & Park, J. (2011). Asian American college students over the decades: Insights from studying Asian American first-year students from 1971 to 2005 using survey research data. *AAPI Nexus: Policy, Practice and Community, 9*(1–2), 119–126. https://doi.org/10.36650/nexus9.1-2_119-126_Park

Kirkpatrick, R., & Zang, Y. (2011). The negative influences of exam-oriented education on Chinese high school students: Backwash from classroom to child. *Language testing in Asia, 1*(3), 36–45. https://doi.org/10.1186/2229-0443-1-3-36

Liang, F., & Turner, J. E. (2021). *Exploring writing anxiety among Chinese graduate students in an American educational setting* [Manuscript under review]. Department of Educational Psychology and Learning Systems, Florida State University.

Marshall, S. M., Klocko, B., & Davidson, J. (2017). Dissertation completion: No longer higher education's invisible problem. *Journal of Educational Research and Practice, 1*, 74–90. https://doi.org/10.5590/JERAP.2017.07.1.06

McCredie, M. N., & Morey, L. C. (2019). Convergence between Thematic Apperception Test (TAT) and self-report: Another look at some old questions. *Journal of Clinical Psychology, 75*, 1838–1949. https://doi.org/10.1002/jclp.22826

Meyer, G. J. (2003). The reliability and validity of the Rorschach and Thematic Apperception Test (TAT) compared to other psychological and medical procedures: An analysis of systematically gathered evidence. In M. Hilsenroth & D. Segal (Eds.), *Comprehensive handbook of psychological assessment* (pp. 315–342). John Wiley & Sons.

Miller, J. (2015). Dredging and projecting the depths of personality: The Thematic Apperception Test and the narratives of the unconscious. *Science in Context, 28*(1), 9–30. https://doi.org/10.1017/S0269889714000301

Murray, H., with Christiana D. Morgan. (1981). A method for investigating fantasies: The Thematic Apperception Test. In E. Shneidman (Ed.), *Endeavors in psychology: Selections from the personology of Henry A. Murray* (pp. 390–408). Harper & Row. (Originally published 1935)

Onwuegbuzie, A. J., & Collins, K. M. T. (2001). Writing apprehension and academic procrastination among graduate students. *Perceptual and Motor Skills, 92*, 560–562.

Park, J., Lin, M., Poon, O., & Chang, M. (2008). Asian American college student and civic engagement. In P. Ong (Ed.), *The state of Asian America: Trajectory of civic and political engagement* (pp. 75–98). LEAP Asian Pacific American Public Policy Institute.

Pekrun, R. (2020). Self-report is indispensable to assess students' learning. *Frontline Learning Research, 8*(3), 185–193. https://doi.org/10.14786/flr.v8i3.637

Piotrowski, C. (2015). Projective techniques usage worldwide: A review of applied settings. *Journal of the Indian Academy of Applied Psychology, 41*, 9–19. https://www.researchgate.net/publication/273004208

Stankov, L. (2010). Unforgiving Confucian culture: A breeding ground for high academic achievement, test anxiety and self-doubt? *Learning and Individual Differences, 20*(6), 555≠563. https://doi.org/10.1016/j.lindif.2010.05.003

Wynne, C., Guo, Y., & Wang, S. (2014). Writing anxiety groups: A creative approach for graduate students. *Journal of Creativity in Mental Health, 9*(3), 366–379. https://doi.org/10.1080/15401383.2014.902343

Zhang-Wu, Q. (2018). Chinese international students' experiences in American higher education institutes: A critical review of the literature. *Journal of International Students,* 8, 1173–1197. https://doi.org/10.5281/zenodo.1250419

INTRODUCTION TO CASE STUDY 16

The author employed snowball data collection methods via social media to identify the 30 study participants and is notable for its inclusion of critical race theory (CRT) as a framework for data collection and analysis. While CRT has been vilified as a radical ideological notion rather than a conceptual orientation to the experience of Black (and other minoritized) groups based on historical events and interpretations of race relationships over time since the founding of the United States this example describes CRT in terms of a logical explanation of the context of experience and uses CRT ideas as a lens through which collected experience is considered and meaning making proceeds. Also notable in this example is the identification of participants from 19 different institutions from across the United States. Their demographics were unique in their representation of an intersection representing ages from 22–48, social economic class, sexual orientation, and religious and marital status. The process started with the collection of quantitative data to include background information such as previous educational backgrounds, age, and degree completion dates. The authors use the term *racial battle fatigue* which is notably defined as the outcome of continuous physiological, psychological, cultural, and emotional managing with race-related microaggressions in less-than-ideal and racially hostile or unsupportive environments in the situation of a campus environment. This is an example of how a multi-stage, iterative approach framed from a CRT perspective was used for coding and analysis of the data.

Qualitative Research With Diverse and Underserved Communities, pages 279–291
Copyright © 2024 by Information Age Publishing
www.infoagepub.com

CASE STUDY 16

IN THE TRENCHES

Building a Composite Character to Understand the Experience of Black Men in Graduate Education

Jesse Ford
University of North Carolina at Greensboro

ABSTRACT

Existing narratives in circulation highlight the multiple challenges facing by Black doctoral students in higher education. These challenges often stem from isolation (Ingram, 2013), racial microaggressions (Griffith & Ford, 2023; Shavers & Moore, 2014), and the multitude of challenges associated with socialization into the academy. This chapter highlights the methodological approach used in my dissertation, "In the Trenches: Black Men in the Academy Navigating Racial Primed Environments." A composite character using 30 Black men was created to frame 30 Black men's experiences and their journey through graduate education.

In recent years, researchers have taken an interest in the retention, matriculation, and graduate experiences of students of color (Perez-Felkner

---

Qualitative Research With Diverse and Underserved Communities, pages 281–291
Copyright © 2024 by Information Age Publishing
www.infoagepub.com
281

et al., 2020; Bertrand Jones et al., 2015). More specifically, scholars have called for more concrete approaches to understanding the experiences of Black people in academic settings (Bertrand Jones et al., 2020; Jackson et al., 2020). While not absent from past and contemporary scholarship, Black experiences provide a shifting narrative of the continued significance of race and racism in America and, subsequently, higher education. Perhaps, the most visible gap in understanding these race-related experiences is at the graduate student level (Ingram, 2013). Since the 1970s, Black student attrition has been staggering between 40–70% in graduate degree completion (Sedlacek, 1987). Moreover, in 2019, less than 8% of students who received research doctorates identified as Black/African American (National Center for Science and Engineering Statistics, 2019). This statistic is more concerning given that Black men account for 34.1% of all doctoral degrees earned by Black graduate students. Without reflecting on the direct obstacles faced by Black men in graduate education, the experience goes unacknowledged, unexplored, and greatly undervalued. Thus, this chapter aims to add to the increasing body of research that informs institutional practices on Black men in graduate education.

A BRIEF REVIEW OF THE LITERATURE

Contemporary research demonstrates an empirical link between racism and education (e.g., Constantine et al., 2008; Smith, 2004). In addition to experiences of racism (Ingram, 2013; Scott & Johnson, 2021), Black men in graduate programs are highlighted as having a lack of role models (Platt, 2015), challenges navigating the hidden curriculum (Platt, 2015), and feelings of doubt and incompetence (Ingram, 2013). These experiences, for Black graduate students, which are often not contended in isolation (Ford, 2020), are complicated by racial microaggressions (Ford, 2020; Ingram, 2013; Johnson-Bailey et al., 2009). Pierce and team (1978) highlight racial microaggressions as "subtle, stunning, often automatic, and nonverbal exchanges which are 'put downs' of blacks by offenders" (p. 66). Mirco is a phrase that emphasizes the word small and draws attention to minor and infrequent events that affect people of color. As such, Smith (2004) defines racial battle fatigue as a side effect of continuously enduring race-related microaggressions.

Racial battle fatigue is the psychological, physiological, and emotional stress reaction Black Americans undergo as a result of being subject to racism on a daily basis (Smith, 2004). This model has three elements, each of which has a distinct race-related stress response: psychological (e.g., frustration, anxiety), emotional/behavioral (e.g., inadequate school/work performance, procrastination), and physiological stress (e.g., insomnia, headache). Race-related stress is caused not only by having to deal with a racial interaction or experience, but also by anticipating having to deal with one. Moreover, race-related stressors are attributed to many mental health problems Black people are diagnosed with each year (Smith et al., 2011). Aside from racialized experiences (Ford, 2020; Ingram, 2013), inadequate socialization is cited as an obstacle to Black men's academic performance in graduate programs (Ford, 2020, Platt, 2015).

Socialization, or "the process by which persons acquire the knowledge, skills, and dispositions that make them more or less effective members of their society" (Weidman et al., 2001, p. 4). More specifically, for students of color, McCoy and Winkle-Wagner (2015) state,

> Socialization is a one-way socialization process, by which students are required to leave behind their communities, pasts or identities, may have particularly negative consequences for racially underrepresented students as they are expected to adapt to the norms of campus that are often predominantly white. (p. 426)

This socialization process, which is different from White students, fails to account for the identities, cultural backgrounds, and familial upbringing students of color have before entering the graduate programs (McCoy & Winkle-Wagner, 2015). Moreover, traditional graduate student socialization approaches often fail to account for the impact of racial microaggressions and racial battle fatigue in education, which is a significant challenge for Black men (Ford, 2020). To understand their experiences, a qualitative inquiry was guided by the following research question: "How do race-related microaggressions influence Black men socialization experiences graduate education?"

METHODOLOGY

Study Research Design

Qualitative research, according to Merriam (1998), is "an umbrella concept covering several forms of inquiry that help us understand and explain the meaning of social phenomena with as little disruption of the natural setting as possible" (p. 5). Moreover, Pasque and team (2012) state critical qualitative inquiry calls for scholars and practitioners to understand the "inequitable world-as-it-is and helpful in imagining a more equitable world-as-it-could-be" (Pasque et al., 2012, p. 3). To make the world appear as it could be, researchers must acknowledge the world as it is, which calls for society to acknowledge American society's historical racially constructed realities. We must move beyond colorblind identities in research and abolish our historical inequity and patriarchal culture in order to render the world visible (DeCuir & Dixson, 2004). With these aspects in mind, narrative inquiry as a method anchored this work. Narrative inquiry investigated the racialized context, since it is difficult to research Black men without knowing their racialized identities.

Recruitment and Participants

Criterion and snowball sampling were used to recruit participants for this research. Recruitment for this study was conducted through social media platforms. The 3-day recruitment process culminated in the selection of 30 participants based on the following criteria:

- must self-identify as a Black man[1] (i.e., African, Black American, African Caribbean, African Latina, Black, or Multiracial);
- must be enrolled or recently graduated from an in-person doctoral program at a HWI within five years or less; and
- must be pursuing or have pursued a social science doctoral degree.

Collectively, the researcher desired to understand the lived experiences of 30 Black men from 19 different institutions from across the United States. Participants ages ranged from 22–48 and held a host of other identities which influenced their experiences by social economic class, sexual orientation, and religious and marital status.

Data Collection and Analysis

The data collection and analysis process began by asking prospective participants to fill out a demographic questionnaire, which collected background information such as previous educational backgrounds, age, and degree completion dates. To explore the research question deeper, each participant took part in two one-on-one semi-structured interviews. Interviews lasted for 60–90 minutes with the average time of all interviews being 71 minutes. Both interviews were used to explore different components of the socialization process (academic preparation, mentoring, and professional development, as outlined by Bertrand Jones & Osborne Lampkin, 2013). The first interview centered on racial battle fatigue in the day-to-day experiences of the participants. Racial Battle Fatigue is the outcome of continuous physiological, psychological, cultural, and emotional managing with race-related microaggressions in less-than-ideal and racially hostile or unsupportive environments (campus or otherwise; Ford, 2020). The second interview explored the socialization experiences, as outlined by Bertrand Jones and Osborne-Lampkin (2013), as necessary components of academic socialization.

Following the interviews, the data was transcribed and analyzed for authenticity, and a discussion with the participants was held to clarify interpretations and assumptions in order to confirm the data's accuracy and credibility. A multi-stage, iterative approach was used for coding and analysis of the data. The coding process was divided into two rounds, with NVivo 12 and a conventional paper and pencil analysis approach used in each. To gain a better understanding of the data, holistic coding at the paragraph level was used first. Holistic coding is often employed when the researcher understands what was found within the data (Miles et al., 2014). Provisional coding, the second round of coding, was used by the researcher to pull emerging codes from literature and guiding frameworks. Within this study, provisional codes include racism, mentoring, professional development, and academic preparation. Sub coding was also used to generate additional codes from the provisional and holistic process, which was based on data collected from the first interview for the second one. While participant recruitment was not an issue in this process, the number of participants was an unanticipated consequence which led to the method approach.

The data gathered and analyzed from these two interviews, as well as the application of the guiding frameworks were used to triangulate the data. The term triangulation was described by Bogdan and Biklen (2007) as "the use of multiple data sources or theoretical perspectives" (p. 275), and it was used to obtain a better understanding of the racialized and gendered experiences of the participants. Member checking was employed with all participants and a peer debriefer to triangulate the reliability and validity. The data collected served as the basis for the methodological approach used in this chapter.

Methodological Approach

In addition to the data collection and analysis process, critical race theory (CRT) anchored the methodological approach. Parker (2015) proposed, "CRT can be used as methodology and as a theory in and of itself that can analytically and conceptually frame a study" (p. 202). By using CRT as a methodology, Kim (2015) outlines it should be used

> to understand how white supremacy and its subordination of people of color have been created and maintained in the United States and to be committed to social justice by working toward eliminating racial oppression as part of the largest goal eradicating all forms of oppression. (p. 43)

The views of Kim (2015) and Parker (2015) highlight the significance of CRT in higher education research and center the racialized experiences of Black men in this scholarship.

In the context of CRT, Kim (2015) outlines eight tenets of CRT, however this scholarship focuses on the sixth tenet as a method and uses a counterstories approach to provide a vehicle to share narratives that are not often told. Critical race theorists utilize stories, dialogues, and testimonies to counter the existing dominant narratives on race and discrimination (Parker, 2015). Bell (1995) positions these methods, as highlighted by Parker (2015), as vital to challenging historical racial power dynamics. Furthermore, counterstories equip scholars to use the art of storytelling as a method to break complacency, contest the status quo, and center Black voices (DeCuir & Dixson, 2004; Delgado, 1989).

Solórzano and Yosso (2002) positioned composite stories or characters as a prominent type of counternarratives and

> draw on various forms of "data" to recount the racialized, sexualized, and classed experiences of people of color. Such counterstories may offer both biographical and autobiographical analyses because the authors create composite characters and place them in social, historical, and political situations to discuss racism, sexism, classism, and other forms of subordination. (p. 33)

While the argument can be made that counterstories are creative writing, Solórzano and Yosso (2002) contend composite counterstories are "grounded in real life, not fiction" (p. 36). Furthermore, Griffin and colleagues (2014) state composite stories are

> perspectives from the margins; reveal struggles for equitable treatment and opportunity; validate and build community among those who suffer similarly; expose barriers that inhibit success and derail social consciousness; creatively position quotidian experiences as critical cultural commentary; teach those unfamiliar about marginalization; and challenge and transform the imposition of domination. (p. 1355)

THE CREATION OF EDDIE, A COMPOSITE CHARACTER

Eddie, a composite character, was developed to accurately tell the lived experience of the 30 participants. Composite character scholarship is critical to Black men's experiences in the academy as their voices are rarely amplified in higher education research (Griffin et al., 2014), which reflects their absence from the professoriate and decimal numbers in the education system (Ford, 2020). The composite story approach was utilized for two distinct reasons: (a) to disrupt the dominant master narrative with a large qualitative sample size and (b) to show the challenges Black men face in the academy across 19 institutions in the United States. Common themes from their experiences were extracted and were used to build on existing literature on Black men in the academy.

FINDINGS

The findings resulted in the identity responsive early career socialization model[2] (Figure 16.1; Ford, 2020), which places identity at the core of Black men's graduate education experiences. The paradigm places the Eddie's prominent personalities at the forefront of their interactions (i.e., race, gender, sexual orientation, religion, etc.). Eddie's identities are present during his socialization experiences (mentoring, academic preparation, and professional development), but he is often subjected to racialized microaggressions, which lead him to receive various forms of stress (anticipatory stress, behavioral stress, physiological stress, physiological stress).

Four major themes emerged from this scholarship during the socialization of Black men in graduate education: anticipatory stress, behavioral stress, physiological stress, physiological stress. Collectively these stressors impact Eddie simultaneously during mentoring, professional development

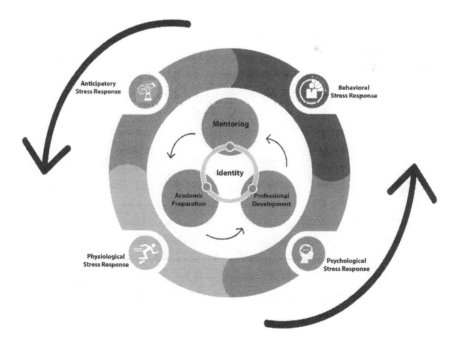

Figure 16.1 Identity responsive early career socialization model.

and academic preparation experiences. When asked about his classroom experiences, Eddie asserted:

> It never fails. In class, someone always says something that I perceive as a microaggression. Even when I address it with the professor, a white woman, they often tell me I am overreacting, but how does she understand my experiences in the stress it causes.

These findings are consistent with Ingram (2013) and Ford (2020) on Black men experiences in the classroom. Eddie also highlighted the absences of same-race, same-gender mentors in his experience. To demonstrate this point, Eddie explained,

> I am supported here, but the mentorship is missing. My faculty here think they cover all of the bases because I am financially covered, but there are parts of this process my white professors just don't understand. Furthermore, all of our faculty are White women. They are great, sometimes a few insensitive microaggresive comments, but it is just not the same as building relationships with someone who looks like me.

Eddie's narrative tells the story of racialized experiences in graduate education for Black men. His story provides a snapshot of the major themes across the data and highlights the significance of racially responsive early career socialization model.

MAJOR TAKEAWAYS AND RECOMMENDATIONS FOR PRACTICE

The creation of Eddie as a composite character was employed to find common themes amongst 30 participants. While not commonly used in qualitative research, this method allows for incorporating large numbers of participants to tell a story. Eddie's creation is the first large scale composite story of a Black man navigating the doctoral study in the academy. Additional studies should be explored to learn more about the collective experience of other disenfranchised populations in education.

This work calls for educators to rethink the role of race and the impact of racism on Black men's socialization, like Eddie, who are learning to navigate racially primed environments. While Eddie's story is a composite narrative of 30 Black men, the experiences highlighted are not new. Scholarship, which highlights the battles with race and racism for Black men in the academy at HWIs, dates back to the 1970s, however racial climate issues date back to the origins of Black people in the United States. In conclusion, as scholars, educators, and practitioners cultivate Black men scholars, it will be imperative to provide a new method for socialization into the academy of Black men, like Eddie, in graduate programs.

NOTES

1. Must be a person of African descent and biologically born a man.
2. Formerly known as the Racially Responsive Early Career Socialization Model

REFERENCES

Bell, L. A. (2007). Theoretical foundations for social justice education. In M. Adams, L. A. Bell, & P. Griffin (Eds.), *Teaching for diversity and social justice* (pp. 1–14). Routledge.

Bertrand Jones, T., Ford, J. R., Pierre, D. F., & Davis-Maye, D. (2020). Thriving in the academy: Culturally responsive mentoring for Black women's early career success. In *Strategies for supporting inclusion and diversity in the academy* (pp. 123–140). Palgrave Macmillan.

Bertrand Jones, T., & Osborne-Lampkin, L. (2013). Black female faculty success and early career professional development. *Negro Educational Review, 64*(1–4), 59–75. https://eric.ed.gov/?id=EJ1014334

Bertrand Jones, T., Osborne-Lampkin, L., Patterson, S., & Davis, D. J. (2015). Creating a "safe and supportive environment:" Mentoring and professional development for recent Black women doctoral graduates. *International Journal of Doctoral Studies, 10*, 483–499. http://ijds.org/Volume10/IJDSv10p483-499Jones1748.pdf

Bogdan, R. C., & Biklen, S. K. (2007). *Qualitative research for education: An introduction to theory and methods* (5th ed.). Allyn & Bacon.

Constantine, M. G., Smith, L., Redington, R. M., & Owens, D. (2008). Racial microaggressions against Black counseling and counseling psychology faculty: A central challenge in the multicultural counseling movement. *Journal of Counseling & Development, 86*(3), 348–355. https://doi.org/10.1002/j.1556-6678.2008.tb00519.x

DeCuir, J. T., & Dixson, A. D. (2004). "So when it comes out, they aren't that surprised that it is there": Using critical race theory as a tool of analysis of race and racism in education. *Educational Researcher, 33*(5), 26–31. https://doi.org/10.3102/0013189X033005026

Delgado, R. (1989). Storytelling for oppositionists and others: A plea for narrative. *Michigan Law Review, 87*(8), 2411–2441.

Ford, J. (2020). *In the trenches: Black men in the academy navigating racialized encounters* [Doctoral dissertation, The Florida State University].

Griffin, R. A., Ward, L., & Phillips, A. R. (2014). Still flies in buttermilk: Black male faculty, critical race theory, and composite counterstorytelling. *International Journal of Qualitative Studies in Education, 27*(10), 1354–1375.

Griffith, T. O., & Ford, J. R. (2023). Say her name: The socialization of Black women in graduate school. *Journal of Student Affairs Research and Practice, 60*(3), 279–292.

Ingram, T. N. (2013). Fighting FAIR (feelings of alienation, isolation, and racism): Using critical race theory to deconstruct the experiences of African American male doctoral students. *Journal of Progressive Policy & Practice, 1*(1), 1–18.

Jackson, L., Ford, J. R., Randolph, C., Schleiden, C., Harris-McKoy, D., & McWey, L. (2020). School climate as a link between high school Black males' math identity and outcomes. *Education and Urban Society,* 53(4). https://doi.org/10 .1177/0013124520931453

Johnson-Bailey, J., Valentine, T., Cervero, R. M., & Bowles, T. A. (2009). Rooted in the soil: The social experiences of Black graduate students at a southern research university. *The Journal of Higher Education, 80*(2), 178–203.

Kim, J. H. (2015). *Understanding narrative inquiry: The crafting and analysis of stories as research.* Sage.

McCoy, D. L., & Winkle-Wagner, R. (2015). Bridging the divide: Developing a scholarly habitus for aspiring graduate students through summer bridge programs participation. *Journal of College Student Development, 56*(5), 423–439. https:// eric.ed.gov/?id=EJ1070613

Merriman, S. B. (1998). *Qualitative research and case study applications in higher education: Revised and expanded from case study research in education.* Jossey-Bass.

Miles, M. B., Huberman, A. M., & Saldaña, J. (2014). *Qualitative data analysis: A methods sourcebook* (3rd ed.) SAGE Publications.

National Center for Science and Engineering Statistics. (2019). *Doctorate recipients from U. S. Universities: 2019* (NSF 21-308). National Science Foundation.

Parker, L. (2015). Critical race theory in education and qualitative inquiry: What each has to offer each other now? *Qualitative Inquiry, 21*(3), 199–205.

Pasque, P., Carducci, R., Kuntz, A., & Gildersleeve, R. (2012). *Qualitative inquiry for equity in higher education: Methodological innovations, implications, and interventions.* John Wiley & Sons.

Perez-Felkner, L., Ford, J. R., Zhao, T., Anthony Jr, M., Harrison, J. A., & Rahming, S. G. (2020). Basic needs insecurity among doctoral students: What it looks like and how to address it. *About Campus, 24*(6), 18–24.

Pierce, C., Carew, J., Pierce-Gonzalez, D., & Wills, D. (1978). An experiment in racism: TV commercials. In C. Pierce (Ed.), *Television and education* (pp. 62–88). Sage.

Platt, C. S. (2015). Everyday struggle: Critical race theory and Black male doctoral student experience. In C. S. Platt, D. B. Holloman, & L. W. Watson (Eds.), *Boyhood to man-hood: Deconstructing Black masculinity through a life span continuum* (pp. 107–130). Peter Lang.

Scott, S., & Johnson, J. M. (2021). Racial realities: Exploring the experiences of Black male doctoral candidates in "All But Dissertation" status. *International Journal of Doctoral Studies, 16,* 171–187. https://doi.org/10.28945/4701

Sedlacek, W. E. (1987). Black students on White campuses: 20 years of research. *Journal of College Student Personnel, 28*(6), 484–495. https://eric.ed.gov/?id =EJ367021

Shavers, M. C., & Moore III, J. L. (2014). Black female voices: Self-presentation strategies in doctoral programs at predominately White institutions. *Journal of College Student Development, 55*(4), 391–407.

Smith, W. A. (2004). Black faculty coping with racial battle fatigue: The campus racial climate in a post-civil rights era. In D. Cleveland (Ed.) *A long way to go: Conversations about race by African American faculty and graduate students* (pp. 171–190). Peter Lang.

Smith, W. A., Hung, M., & Franklin, J. D. (2011). Racial battle fatigue and the miseducation of Black men: Racial microaggressions, societal problems, and environmental stress. *Journal of Negro Education, 80*(1), 63–82.

Solórzano, D. G., & Yosso, T. J. (2002). Critical race methodology: Counter-storytelling as an analytical framework for education research. *Qualitative Inquiry, 8*(1), 23–44. https://doi.org/10.1177/107780040200800103

Weidman, J. C., Twale, D. J., & Stein, E. L. (2001). *Socialization of graduate and professional students in higher education: A perilous passage?* John Wiley and Sons.

INTRODUCTION TO CASE STUDY 17

This study examined benefits and challenges of the Haiti Compact, a post 2010 earthquake in the Ayiti alliance of U.S. higher education institutions in partnership with Haitian NGOs. Study research questions were (a) "What are the perceived benefits and challenges of partnerships between I/NGOs working in Ayiti and American member schools of the Haiti Compact?"; (b) "To what extent do I/NGOs working in Ayiti, and American member schools of the Haiti Compact perceive their partnerships to be reciprocal, mutually beneficial, and social justice-oriented?"; and (c) "How is the perception of partnership influenced by historical and political relationships between Ayiti, the United States of America, and the West?" Study participants included an ethnically and nationally diverse individual including Haitian Compact member schools, NGOs, and U.S. university partners.

The researchers used an extreme case study design employed to explore the unique and differing socially constructed real-life context of the Ayisyen and American perspectives, experiences, and sources. The case study approach is appropriate for studying small groups, partnerships, examining relationships, illustrating unusual cases, and providing detailed descriptions of study phenomena.

Qualitative Research With Diverse and Underserved Communities, pages 293–303
Copyright © 2024 by Information Age Publishing
www.infoagepub.com

CASE STUDY 17

THE HERMENEUTIC CIRCLE IN AYITI

A Method of Analysis to Amplify Individual and Collective Ayisyen Voices

Jessica Darnell Brazell-Brayboy
Westminister University

CONTEXT

Following the catastrophic 2010 earthquake in Ayiti (Haiti), five American universities associated with Break Away organization for alternative breaks formed the The Haiti Compact: Higher Education With Haiti. The unique consociation of U.S. universities was formed to engage "U.S. campuses in effective, responsible, and sustainable service work in and for post-earthquake Haiti...ensuring consistent and mutually beneficial support" (Murphy, 2016, p. 176). The purpose of the study was to thoroughly investigate HC as a theoretical and functional experiential education partnership model developed with Ayisyen partners within the context of collective response to the 2010 earthquake in Ayiti. Conducted over a 2-year period, the instrumental case study investigated international partnerships

Qualitative Research With Diverse and Underserved Communities, pages 295–303
Copyright © 2024 by Information Age Publishing
www.infoagepub.com

between select American universities and I/NGOs affiliated with the HC to determine the extent of "effective, reciprocal, and equitable international partnership" (Longo & Saltmarsh, 2011, p. 82). The preeminent context of Ayiti's postcolonial and neocolonial state, the role of the West in Ayiti's past and present, particularly the United States, and tenets of ISL pedagogy necessitated an extensive literature review to clarify the parameters of the case and the context in which the case is situated.

INQUIRY FOCUS

The study sought to answer three specific questions through cogent avenues of inquiry: (a) "What are the perceived benefits and challenges of partnerships between I/NGOs working in Ayiti and American member schools of the Haiti Compact?"; (b) "To what extent do I/NGOs working in Ayiti and American member schools of the Haiti Compact perceive their partnerships to be reciprocal, mutually beneficial, and social justice-oriented?"; and (c) "How is the perception of partnership influenced by historical and political relationships between Ayiti, the United States of America, and the West?" The research questions were designed to better understand the qualities of benefits and challenges of the HC partnerships because they had become long-term, and reportedly reciprocal and mutually beneficial despite historic context and structural inequalities between Ayiti and the United States of America.

CASE/SAMPLE/POPULATION OF INTEREST

The HC is a case within a bound system of the 2010 earthquake in Ayiti, the American universities affiliated with BreakAway that eventually identified as the HC, the BreakAway organization, and the I/NGOs with whom the American universities partnered with for alternative break trips. Because partnership was the focus of investigation, only participants representing partnerships in which both the HC member school and the I/NGO were examined. Selected partnerships were: American University and the Asosyasyon Peyizan Fondwa, American University and Fonkoze, American University and University of Fondwa, College of William and Mary and Sonje Ayiti, College of William and Mary and Grace Children's Hospital, and University of Maryland and Mennonite Central Committee. The individuals representing these organizations represent a wide range of ethnically and nationally diverse professionals working and living both in Ayiti and the United States of America. At the time of study, the selected parties had produced fruitful lasting partnerships with measurable outcomes.

POSTCOLONIAL AND NEOCOLONIAL CONDITIONS
OF THE INQUIRY

"The Haiti of today cannot be understood without knowledge of its complex and often tragic history" (Dubois, 2012, p. 13). Its past and present are characterized by long-term political and economic entanglements with Western powers as well as authoritarian political practices (Farmer, 2011). Ayiti's capital, Port-au-Prince, was occupied by the United States for 20 years (1914–1934) during which the United States imposed significant educational reforms (Santo Domingo Military Government, 1920) which "convinced many Haitians that a sinister motivation was at work" (Dubois, 2012, p. 282). During the occupation, "the attitude of Americans was a constant source of bitterness that profoundly shaped the Haitian social experience" (Dubois, 2012, p. 285). The U.S. occupation of Ayiti began a difficult and tense relationship between the United States and its southern neighbor that is felt today in international policies, the current occupation of Ayiti by the United Nations, and the large sums of Western aid flowing into the country.

Ayiti was born out of the earliest phases of globalization and though it has been a sovereign country for over two hundred years, the country's long history of non-Ayisyen control has made disengaging from the colonial experience nearly impossible due to the significant remains of indirect colonial control (neocolonialism). Ayiti's neocolonial state is the defining condition in which this qualitative study was conducted. Furthermore, it is the defining condition of the individual Ayisyens served by the Ayisyen I/ NGOs partnering with the HC.

METHODOLOGY FOR INQUIRY

In this investigation, the broad phenomenological assumption of individual and combined experiences informed the selection of a constructivist paradigm and qualitative case study design. Ontologically, the constructivist paradigm of qualitative research assumes no absolute reality exists but that multiple context and time dependent realities create a socially constructed reality. Case study methodology for the study was selected because it utilizes multiple methods of empirical investigation to analyze a singular case within a real-life context (Creswell, 2013). A particularly fitting methodology for the investigation of the HC, it is appropriate to studying a small group or partnership, for investigating relationships (Yin, 2009), suitable for illustrating "a unique case, a case that has unusual interest in and of itself and needs to be described and detailed" (Creswell, 2013, p. 98), and particularly fitting to understanding and describing "an event from the point of view of the participant" (Mertens, 2010, p. 235).

The imminent post/neocolonial context of the partnerships and all aspects of Ayisyen culture demanded the selection of a methodology with a design capacity for the non-negotiable and ethical inclusion of Ayisyen and American perspectives, experiences, and sources. The case at hand was, and still is, a unique case, also known as an extreme case, because it has emerged in atypical and unreplicatable circumstances (Yin, 2009).

PROCESS AND PROTOCOL FOR INQUIRY

The hermeneutic circle was the primary method used to attach meaning to collected and analyzed data from observations, interviews, documents, audiovisual materials and online data. A hermeneutic approach to data interpretation is compelled by questions of cause and meaning (von Wright, 1971) and assumes a lack of transparency in meaning due to the profound subjectivity of personal experience and perception; it recognizes the lack of objectivity the researcher brings to the study. The primary mechanism employed for making meaning in the hermeneutic approach is the hermeneutic circle—an ideal interpretive tool for crossing historical, cultural, and social gulfs. The hermeneutic circle is a structured way of moving between part and whole, in a circular pattern, between the historic context and present, along with the individual and collective narratives of participants. Moving back and forth between part and whole, individual and collective narrative, past and present creates a circuitry for meaning-making.

During the course of simultaneous data collection and analysis, particularly during interviews, I, the researcher, entered interviews of study participants with inescapable preliminary conceptions that informed an imagined sense of the whole. As simultaneous data collection and analysis was conducted, I amended and re-imagined the whole through what I encountered in part (i.e., interview, document, observation). For example, when a participant would reference an Ayisyen proverb, I would ask for the proverb to be explained. This deepened my understanding of why the proverb had been shared and what cultural values were held by the speaker. This enabled me to better investigate identified cultural values present in other data sources and thus move back and forth between part and whole, the individual and collective narratives of participants. This allowed me to find deeper meaning in the data.

INFORMATION PROCESSING/ANALYSIS

The analysis of data collected was a recursive and dynamic process. As the study progressed and themes emerged, the ongoing process of analysis became more directional and intense. The process was characterized by examination of pieces of the phenomenon to make sense of the whole. Though intuition is an essential element of qualitative analysis, it was necessary to select analytic techniques to guide analysis. A holistic analysis was conducted through categorical aggregation of collected data and direct interpretation of individual instances until a full picture of the case's history fully emerged. Presenting a descriptive account of the HC established an evidentiary base, which was essential so that the case and analysis of the case are distinguishable. Data was compressed and linked together; once the collective narrative emerged, a more directional and intensive phase of analysis began. It is essential to note that data collection and analysis is a recursive process enacted in the initial stages of data collection.

Two primary analytic strategies were used to analyze the case: simultaneous data collection and analysis, and thematic analysis. Ongoing analysis guided the researcher to maintain focus, identify the saturation point, and manage the high volume of data. Data was made sense of through organizing it in different arrays including capturing data in visual displays, noting the frequency of references and events, and examining chronological and/or temporal schemes. Thematic analysis was used to identify emergent themes significant to understanding the phenomenon. The process of coding disaggregated the data into manageable bits or units. As data was coded, it was constantly compared and contrasted to successive segments of data, a process that paralleled the use of a hermeneutic circle during data interpretation. Collected data was coded in a priori content and non-content specific schemes. Content specific codes were derived from the original research problem and questions born out of existing literature. Data triangulation was implemented by using different sources to determine consistency of data. Methodological triangulation is the use of multiple methods of inquiry to substantiate the authenticity of data collected. A variety of methods were used to collect data from multiple sources as a way of understanding the nature of partnerships between HC member schools and I/NGOs working in Ayiti. Triangulation was used to analyze within and then across subunits to confirm themes.

UNANTICIPATED INFLUENCE

Political instability and inclement weather were identified as potential events that could threaten travel to Ayiti to conduct in-person interviews and site visits but neither created significant interference. While interviews could have been conducted remotely, it would have significantly interfered with the researcher's ability to develop rapport and trust with participants and would have eliminated naturalistic observation altogether. Fortuitously, there were no events or outcomes that challenged recruiting or retention efforts. The individual accounts of partnership experiences had strong evident themes even across subunits of analysis. Saturation was easily reached, and a clear collective narrative emerged while the researcher was still in Ayti.

While I, the researcher, had extensive experience living and working in low income postcolonial countries with complex iterations of neocolonialism, I was unable to anticipate prolific impact of significant Western presence in Ayiti through I/NGOs, international policies of other countries regarding Ayiti, and the contentious presence of the United Nations would have on this body of research. One I/NGO representative explained that the length of time Ayiti has interacted with Westerners in exploitive and dependent dynamics has created "fatigue." Another American representative described encountering "wariness of do-gooders" during initial meetings with I/NGOs.

Interview participants' responses to questions overtly addressed the context of colonialism in all its stages, American interventions in Ayisyen government, a culture of international aid and development, the ongoing United Nations MINUSTAH operation (which was curtailed in October 2017), and the wave of relief operations following the 2010 earthquake. Participants boldly and directly exerted the postcolonial historical and neocolonial political context of Ayiti to be unequivocally inseparable from the partnerships I was researching. One participant keenly spoke to the intertwined nature of post-colonialism and its direct influence of partnerships bound in the contemporary case by referencing the context of international relations between Ayiti, the West, and the United Nations as non-reciprocal. The unanticipated direct impact of colonialism on this body of research was profound and ultimately became the scaffolding in which all data collection, analysis, and interpretation was conducted.

EMERGENCE AND EVOLUTION OF INQUIRY

The initial stage of research design was formatted to accommodate Ayisyen non-conversational in English through Kreyól translations of consent forms and interview protocols. Once simultaneous data collection and analysis began, it became evident that all staff members at I/NGOs were multilingual professionals with extensive experience conversing with American English speakers, thus negating the need for Kreyól translators and documents.

SUMMARY OF FINDINGS

Evident commonalities emerged from the diverse stories and responses of participants spoken in individual vernaculars characteristic of their lived experiences. The emergent themes were grouped by the topic participants were speaking to as the collective narrative of participants came forward. *Resipwosite* (reciprocity), *benefis mityèl* (mutual benefit), and *solidarite* (solidarity) are the themes of the collective told through a hued rondure of subthemes. The subthemes associated with resipwosite, benefis mityèl, and solidarite emerged unevenly and intertwined, indicating the complexity and sophistication of symbiotic quality among the distinct themes. Additionally, the data indicated the three themes were nested—resipwosite was necessary to establishing benefis mityèl, and solidarite could only be reached with resipwosite and benefis mityèl present, though simultaneous development of themes did occur.

Participants most often described and discussed resipwosite in terms of relationships, persistence, selection and choice, dignity, unforeseen challenges, and the negotiation of partnership standards. Participants were generally more hesitant when discussing partnerships and the degree to which they are ge benefis (mutually beneficial) though the authority with which they answered questions of this topic increased as they themselves introduced terms of financial and non-financial cost and motivation(s). Finally, emergent themes of solidarite were largely situational, recognizing and addressing context of the partnerships and a variety of types of solidarite. The particular knowledge of this bound case is generalizable, to an extent; it can be used by practitioners and educators to understand the nuances of partnerships and what generalizable factors might influence other similar partnerships.

RECOMMENDATIONS FOR QUALITATIVE RESEARCH

A hermeneutic approach was unequivocally valuable in crossing relational and cultural borders present in neocolonial Ayiti; the method deeply enriched my ability, as a qualitative researcher, to understand the quality and nature of partnerships within the case. I recommend the hermeneutic method of analysis to any researcher seeking to develop a rapport of trust with study participants and to elicit deep meaning from data. I relied heavily on the hermeneutical circle to make sense of the complex and interconnected responses of participants as well as simple questions regarding the benefits and challenges of participating in partnerships associated with the HC. For example, among the first questions posed to interview participants was: Is there a benefit to the I/NGO or university you represent when working with X university or X I/NGO? This question was followed by a contrasting question: Are there challenges as well? I/NGO participants frequently responded to these questions by citing examples from prior work with other groups as if it were easier to speak about HC partnerships by illustrating their answers through other like experiences. Using examples of previous partnerships as a starting point, participants began to speak to the nature of their work and eventually seemed comfortable speaking directly about their partnerships with schools from the HC. The developing comfort level of participants parallels findings that trust is built overtime as a relationship that yields dignity for those involved.

The equal inclusion of community voice in this body of research was intended to interrupt neocolonial cultural hegemony in academic literature. In this vein, my second recommendation for engaging with diverse and underserved communities through qualitative research is to readily incorporate indigenous language and terms into your research and thus introduce non-hegemonic knowledge into the knowledge economy. In doing so, we as researchers interrupt cultural hegemony by giving currency to the community of people who helped make knowledge known by their participation in research projects. For example, in this case study, Kreyól vernacular and proverbs were intentionally centralized in this body of work. Central findings and themes of the research are presented in Kreyól rather than English so as to centralize the imbued Ayisyen flavor and meaning. Introducing vernacular diversity to the body of research was an ethical decision to interrupt the historic exploitation of Ayiti by means of cultural imperialism. One way this was done in the case study dissertation was to include Kreyól proverbs in chapter headings. For instance, the findings chapter included the proverb, "Fòk de klòch sonnen pou konn verite-a," which translates as, "You must hear two bells ring to learn the truth." The meaning of the proverb is clear, fitting to the purpose of the chapter, and communicates a cultural truth that has been often oppressed by colonizer and unwanted intruders.

A third and final recommendation to researchers engaging with groups of people from diverse and underserved communities is to approach your work with cultural humility that elevates the dignity of the community or population with whom, or about whom, you are generating knowledge.

REFERENCES

Creswell, J. W. (2013). *Qualitative inquiry and research design: Choosing among five approaches* (3rd ed.). SAGE Publishing.

Dubois, L. (2012). *Haiti: The aftershocks of history.* Picador.

Farmer, P. (2011). *Haiti after the earthquake.* Public Affairs.

Longo, N. V., & Saltmarsh, J. (2011). New lines of inquiry in reframing international service learning to global service learning. In R. G. Bringle, J. A. Hatcher, & S. G. Jones (Eds.), *International service learning: Conceptual frameworks and research* (pp. 69–85). Stylus.

Mertens, D. M. (2010). *Research and evaluation in education and psychology: Integrating diversity with quantitative, qualitative, and mixed methods* (3rd ed.). SAGE Publications.

Murphy, J. D. (2016). Resipwosite as a guiding framework for rethinking mutual exchange in global service learning parterships: Findings from a case study of the Haiti Compact. In M. A. Larsen (Ed.), *International service learning: Engaging host communities* (pp. 175–188). Routledge.

Santo Domingo Military Government. (1920). *Santo Domingo: Its past and its present condition*. Santo Domingo City: Dominican Republic.

von Wright, G. (1971). *Explanation and understanding, contemporary philosophy*. Cornell University Press.

Yin, R. K. (2009). *Case study research: Design and methods*. SAGE Publishing.

INTRODUCTION TO CASE STUDY 18

This case study employed a narrative methodology informed by the arts and delivered as a way of inquiry with people and communities who endure multiple forms of oppression. It is an example of how female Black literacy learners can benefit from a narrative methodology informed by the arts and rooted in African and Black storytelling traditions. This work illustrates the "power" or stories as a vehicle for understanding experience, culture and the individual and collective efforts to survive and thrive. They regarded storytelling and telling stories were used to heal, celebrate, and liberate. Although stories are the foundation of qualitative research, researchers' development of qualitative methodologies grounded in Black storytelling traditions remains largely unexplored. Black scholars continue to challenge researchers studying Black experiences to reflect on qualitative inquiry's methodological imperatives and commitments.

In addition, the work demonstrates the potential of creative expression as a means of organizing experience, evoking affect, and providing a means of communication which is not delimited by vocabulary or facility with language. Also illustrated are justification, analysis, and synthesis procedures and the difficulties and opportunities of a narrative method informed by creative expression ("the arts"). The authors utilized the arts to plot, map, and gather archives of the daily lives of these women and demonstrate how narrative researchers who are arts-informed have the opportunity to center the experiences and worldviews of Black immigrant mothers with little literacy in their work.

Qualitative Research With Diverse and Underserved Communities, pages 305–317
Copyright © 2024 by Information Age Publishing
www.infoagepub.com
305

This chapter presents a call to action and presents a guide to rooting arts-informed narrative methodologies in work with marginalized and disenfranchised communities. This case study uses the maternal practices of Black immigrant mothers with limited literacy skills to illustrate the reimagining of an arts-informed narrative methodology. The process reveals considerations and possibilities for analyzing and synthesizing research findings into creative nonfiction graphic short stories (e.g., zines).

CASE STUDY 18

AN ARTS-INFORMED NARRATIVE METHODOLOGY ROOTED IN BLACK FEMINIST PERSPECTIVES AND BLACK STORYTELLING TRADITIONS

Stephanie Fearon
York University

African communities worldwide embody a cultural legacy of storytelling and telling stories. We draw on our indigenous storytelling traditions to articulate our healing, dreams, joys, and fears. We wield our stories to enact resistance, reimagine futures, and nurture "psychic self-preservation" (Rodriguez, 2006, p. 1070). Diasporic African communities continue to use stories to ask and answer epistemological and ontological questions in our voices and across generations (Onuora, 2012, 2015). Our stories affirm us as legitimate narrators of our own lives—past, present, and future.

Although stories are the foundation of qualitative research, the development of qualitative methodologies grounded in African storytelling

Qualitative Research With Diverse and Underserved Communities, pages 307–317
Copyright © 2024 by Information Age Publishing
www.infoagepub.com

traditions remains largely unexplored in scholarship (Banks-Wallace, 2002). Black thinkers have long urged researchers, especially those engaging Black women, to uphold the validity of African epistemologies as analytical, conceptual, and representational tools of inquiry (Dei et al., 2000; Wane, 2005). Black feminist scholars, like Dillard (2000, 2018) and Banks-Wallace (1998, 2002), have responded to this call to action by introducing frameworks that center Black women's stories, knowledge, and power as intellectual and cultural production (Banks-Wallace, 1998; Dillard, 2018). These Black feminist scholars inspired me to root arts-informed narrative methodologies in Black feminist perspectives and African storytelling traditions. This re-envisioning resulted in the development of a comprehensive analytic process where Black women participants' oral accounts are compiled into creative nonfiction graphic short stories.

CHAPTER OVERVIEW

This chapter presents arts-informed narrative methodology as a valid approach to inquiry with individuals and groups who experience multilayered oppressions. The chapter is organized in a case study format to illustrate the ways in which an arts-informed narrative methodology grounded in Black feminist and African storytelling traditions can be used to serve Black women literacy learners. The chapter details the rationale, analysis, and synthesis processes, along with the challenges and possibilities of an arts-informed narrative methodology.

CASE STUDY CONTEXT

In 2018, I began a qualitative research study investigating the relationships between Black immigrant mothers and their children's schools. I conducted in-depth, individual interviews with Black immigrant mothers living in Canada. Throughout the research process, participants divulged their struggles with literacy and its impact on how they navigated educational institutions, like their children's schools. Participants recounted their experiences with anti-Black racism and detailed its intersections with other forms of oppression, like sexism, xenophobia, and ableism. Their narratives of being Black immigrant mothers and adult literacy learners accentuated the profound and creative strategies that Black women draw on to resist anti-Blackness within their communities and public institutions. This early work incited my recent research study on community activism amongst Black mother literacy learners.

FOCUS OF INQUIRY

As an arts-informed researcher investigating the activism of Black mother literacy learners, I reflected on the following methodological questions:

- What insights does current scholarship on arts-informed narrative methodologies offer around the use of storytelling to reveal the resistance work of Black mother literacy learners?
- How might an arts-informed narrative methodology promote the agency of Black immigrant mother learners within the research process?
- How might Black storytelling traditions guide arts-informed narrative researchers' decisions around methods for data analysis and synthesis?

RESEARCH SAMPLE DESCRIPTION

The purpose of this arts-informed narrative study was to explore with six African Caribbean women living in Toronto their maternal experiences as adult literacy learners. Specifically, I sought to understand how these particular Black immigrant mothers engaged in activism within their communities. A purposeful sampling procedure was used as it enabled me to yield the most information about the phenomenon under study. Since I sought to locate African Caribbean women literacy learners in Toronto, a snowball sampling strategy, sometimes referred to as network or chain sampling (Miles & Huberman, 1994; Patton, 2002), was employed. Participants were asked to refer other African Caribbean mothers whom they knew to be literacy learners.

The inclusion criteria were as follows:

- women that self-identify as Black immigrants from the English-speaking Caribbean;
- live in the Greater Toronto Area;
- women who have engaged in motherwork;
- women at least 21 years of age and competent to formally give consent for the interview;
- identify as an adult with limited literacy; and
- completed at at least two years in a community-based adult learning program.

RESEARCH SAMPLE RATIONALE

Black immigrant communities in Canada are diverse and longstanding, re-flecting 150 different countries of origin (Statistics Canada, 2019). Long-established Black immigrants in Canada are mostly from the Caribbean accounting for roughly half of the Black immigrant population in the country (Statistics Canada, 2019). The deep-rooted presence of Caribbean immigrant communities is further revealed in that most first, second, and third generation Black Canadians identify their ethnic origins as Caribbean (Statistics Canada, 2019). Many of the early African Caribbean migrants to Canada were working-class women who arrived through the country's 1955 West Indian Domestic Scheme. The Scheme reflected pervasive racist and sexist ideas that deemed African Caribbean women as best suited for do-mestic work regardless of their skills, qualifications, and interests in other areas (Crawford, 2003). Anti-Black racism and their employment responsi-bilities prevented many of these early African Caribbean immigrants from pursuing formal education in Canada and improving their literacy skills.

Data on adult literacy continues to highlight the dire literacy concerns amongst immigrant populations (Elfert & Walker, 2020). However, limited literature is dedicated to the adult literacy experiences of Canada's largest Black immigrant population—the African Carribean community. Canada's striking historical relationship with African Caribbean mothers further stresses the importance of excavating and amplifying the stories of these particular mothers who have limited literacy skills.

METHODOLOGY FOR THE INQUIRY AND RATIONALE

For the study, I used the arts to help plot, map, and collect the archives of the everyday experience of Black women literacy learners in Canada (Sharpe, 2016). An arts-informed narrative methodology relies on empiri-cal data informed by the literary genre and comprises personal narration and cultural stories (Onuora, 2012, 2015). This methodology allows the researcher to participate in meaning-making by storying memories relayed from conversations with participants.

By using an arts-informed narrative methodology, my study on Black immigrant mother learners' maternal practices and activism, as Cole and Knowles (2008) explain, intertwined "the systematic and rigorous quali-ties of conventional qualitative methodologies with the artistic, disciplined, and imaginative qualities of the arts" (p. 59). For the study, I used informa-tion, descriptions, and direct quotations from participants' transcripts and reconstruct them in order to take readers on a narrative journey through lived experiences recalled from memories (Onuora, 2012, 2015).

To ensure participants' access and engagement in the research process, participants, a community visual artist and I compiled findings into a series of graphic short stories. Graphic short stories honored the experiences of the participants with limited literacy skills by using images, text, and creative imagination "to order, make sense of, and give significance to often fragmented recollections of the past" (Onuora, 2015, p. 15). In so doing, the study was able to communicate, in a structured, creative, and accessible form, the insights gleaned from the information shared by participants. This arts-informed narrative methodology asserted the places of the Black immigrant mothers who participated in the study as trusted narrators of their own stories.

METHODS OF ANALYSIS AND SYNTHESIS

The study's methods of analysis and synthesis built upon a process I developed for my doctoral dissertation (Fearon, 2020). I also relied on Banks-Wallace's (1998, 2002) texts as a foundation to reimagine a comprehensive framework whereby research findings are restructured into creative nonfiction graphic short stories. This analytic process revealed the depth of participants' maternal experiences and the ways in which those experiences inform their activism. The study's method for data analysis included the following:

1. locating the interviews within the historical context and cultural norms,
2. demarcation of boundaries for individual stories,
3. thematic and functional analysis of stories,
4. grouping stories according to themes and functions,
5. comparison of story themes and functions across participant interviews, and
6. restructuring participants' memories into written and graphic storied accounts.

Locating the Interviews Within the Historical Context and Cultural Norms

Hartman (2020) affirms the necessity for those engaged in the study of Black women and girls to listen to and read intently their stories. Hartman (2020) describes the analytic process she undertook when investigating the histories of Black women and girls. She writes, "It required me to speculate, listen intently and read between the lines" (p. 56). I heeded Hartman's suggestions and, as part of the analysis process, I listened intently to audio recordings of each participants' individual, in-depth interview. Through intent listening, I made provision of the historical context and cultural norms underlying the study. The social-cultural-political context in which a study is conducted influences story creation, telling, and interpretation (Etter-Lewis, 1993; Goss & Barnes, 1989; Hurston, 1990; Livo & Rietz, 1986; Mishler, 1986). I transcribed each interview and assigned pseudonyms to participants. The process of transcribing and reading the transcripts solidified, challenged, and expanded my initial grasp of the historical context and cultural norms that shaped the interviews. As suggested by Banks-Wallace (2002), I documented directly onto the transcripts references made by participants to specific historical events and cultural conditions.

Demarcation of Boundaries for Individual Stories

Banks-Wallace (2002) reminds researchers that a crucial component of the analysis process is to define a story in a manner consistent with the population under investigation. Stories consist of narrative and dialogue. A narrative is a running account of the sequence of events or plot, while the dialogue captures discussion (Livo & Rietz, 1986). Analytic methods used by many qualitative researchers place more significance on the plot (Mueller, 1999; Polanyi, 1985). In fact, Mishler (1986) argues that researchers frequently suppress or selectively delete dialogue deemed to be unrelated to a particular storyline of interest to the research. Conversely, dialogue is a defining feature of African oral storytelling traditions. It is not just what is said but how it is said that determines the meaning of a story (Collins, 2000; Goss & Goss, 1995; Stewart, 1997). In order to analyze the data, I had to establish story boundaries that were consistent with participants' Caribbean experiences. For this study, temporal and spatial boundaries were used as the guides to distinguish one story from another in each interview. These boundaries indicated when the participant talked about an event outside the present context (Livo & Rietz, 1986). I identified keywords used by participants, noting how the words were said, to denote story boundaries.

Thematic and Functional Analysis of Stories

Thematic and functional analysis focused on the text of the story as told by the participant-storyteller (Banks-Wallace, 2002). Banks-Wallace (2002, p. 416) presents researchers with questions to guide the analysis of stories told by participants during in-depth interviews: (a) "What is the point of the story?"; (b) "What function does this story serve in this context?"; and (d) "What key words and/or phrases are used to tell the story?" For this study, I used the aforementioned questions to inform the thematic and functional analysis of the stories shared by participants during the interviews.

Thematic categories were determined inductively and in concert with the conceptual framework. Hartman (2020) recounts the ways in which researchers often pathologize the stories shared by Black women. She writes, "[Researchers] fail to discern the beauty and they see only the disorder, missing all the ways Black [women] create life and make bare need into an arena of elaboration" (p. 23). When determining the thematic categories, I continued to honor participants as thinkers and prioritized key words and phrases they used to tell their stories.

Identifying these key words and phrases provided me with insights into the embodied context of the storyteller's world (Sewall, 1998). Understanding why specific words and phrases were chosen to describe an event or convey an idea, as well as how the words were said, was critical in ensuring the correct interpretation of participants' stories (Cannon, 1995; Etter-Lewis, 1993; Hine, 1989; Hurston, 1990).

Like Hartman (2020), I "broke open" the stories by listening to and reading intently memoried accounts shared by participants. I paid attention to participants' reactions when they told particular stories. To further help me "read between the lines" and discern the stories' meaning, I noted in the transcript margins personal feelings elicited when listening to and reading the storied accounts. In so doing, I created an audit trail documenting how I centered participants' experiences and put them in conversation with the literature when deciding thematic categories.

Grouping Stories According to Themes and Functions

Banks-Wallace's process for analyzing stories rooted in African oral traditions calls for the grouping of participants' stories into themes. I analyzed each identified story shared by participants in the interviews separately. For each participant, I created a Venn diagram labeled with the thematic categories. I reviewed each interview transcript, focusing on the stories shared. For each participant, I titled their stories and grouped them into thematic categories on a Venn diagram. The Venn diagram allowed me to highlight the ways a participant's story addressed multiple themes. The Venn diagrams were housed in a virtual folder that I created for each participant.

Comparison of Story Themes and Functions
Across Participant Interviews

I created a master Venn diagram for the study. Similar to that of the participants', the master Venn diagram was labelled with the thematic categories. I referenced participants' diagrams and plotted the titles of each story collected across interviews onto the master chart. I highlighted stories that were emotive and addressed the questions guiding the study. I created a chart outlining how each highlighted story connected to the study themes and answered the research questions.

Restructuring Participants' Memories
Into Storied Accounts

Banks-Wallace (2002), Collins (2000), Goss and Goss (1995), and Stewart (1997) write of the prominent role dialogue figures in African storytelling traditions. With the aim to prioritize participants' voice and their relationships with one another, study findings were reconfigured as a series of graphic short stories. Each graphic short story began as dialogue. I took direct quotes from the interviews and used creative imagination to order participants' recalled memories as dialogue. I then included description as a way to reinforce the meaning captured in the dialogue. Description also enabled me to set participants' stories within a social, political, and historical context. On two occasions, a community visual artist and I connected with study participants for feedback on the stories. Participants suggested images to accompany the written storied accounts. Participant insights were documented on a storyboard and shared with participants for additional feedback. This process of centering dialogue and participant insights underscored the importance of who was saying what to whom, and how they were saying it. The creative and imaginative qualities of literary and graphic arts ensured that study findings reflected the emotive and accessible qualities of African storytelling traditions.

FINDINGS

The study presented participants' conceptualization of their motherwork as a form of activism. Black immigrant mothers who were literacy learners understood their motherwork as integral to the health and well-being of Black immigrant women and children within their network. In the graphic short stories, participants organized and carried out resistance aimed at particular social contexts and institutions. Each graphic short story captured Black mother literacy learners' activism as comprising (a) formal and nonformal arrangements to care for children; (b) transmission of intergenerational knowledge, values, and worldviews; (c) working with members of their networks to create spaces where Black immigrant mother learners and their children are able to heal from injustices; and (d) collaborating with members of their support network to establish a space, spanning time and geography, where Black immigrant mother learners come together and organize acts of resistance.

CHALLENGES AND POSSIBILITIES FOR QUALITATIVE INQUIRY

Storytelling provides arts-informed narrative scholars with opportunities to center the worldviews and experiences of Black immigrant mothers with limited literacy. This chapter provided researchers with a field guide to facilitate and expand upon methodologies in ways that uphold Black mother learners as active agents in the research process. Arts-informed narrative methodologies are not above criticism and do reify power differentials between the researcher and participants. For example, who holds the power to determine the stories selected and the format in which they are shared? How are participants engaged in data analysis and synthesis?

In this light, I put forward the following critical self-reflection and discussion questions:

- What worldviews, values and goals inform your methodological decisions? How do they align with those of the participants?
- How will you engage in research methodologies that honor and amplify the voices of Black communities who experience intersecting oppressions?
- How will participants practice decision-making agency within the research process?

Arts-informed narrative researchers are encouraged to devise strategies to ensure that participants play more active roles in the study's design and implementation. I welcome fellow arts-informed researchers to approach research with Black communities in ways that honor our stories as a method of study to enact resistance and secure our liberation.

REFERENCES

Banks-Wallace, J. (1998). Emancipatory potential of storytelling in a group. *Journal of Nursing Scholarship, 30*(1), 17–21. https://doi.org/10.1111/j.1547-5069.1998.tb01230.x.

Banks-Wallace, J. (2002). Talk that talk: Storytelling and analysis rooted in African American oral tradition. *Qualitative Health Research, 12*(3), 410–426. https://doi.org/10.1177/104973202129119892

Cannon, K. (1995). Surviving the blight. In G. Wade-Gayles (Ed.), *My soul is a witness: African American women's spirituality* (p. 1926). Beacon.

Cole, A. L., & Knowles, J. G. (Eds.). (2008). *Handbook of the arts in qualitative research: Perspectives, methodologies, examples and issues.* SAGE Publications.

Collins, P. H. (2000). *Black feminist thought: Knowledge, consciousness, and the politics of empowerment.* Routledge.

Crawford, C. (2003). Sending love in a barrel: The making of transnational Caribbean families in Canada. *Canadian Woman Studies, 22*(3–4), 104–109. https://link-gale-com.ezproxy.library.yorku.ca/apps/doc/A111401773/AONE?u=yorku_main&sid=bookmark-AONE&xid=7a04e4d2

Dei, G. J. S., Hall, B. L., & Rosenberg, D. G. (2000). *Indigenous knowledges in global contexts: Multiple readings of our world.* University of Toronto Press.

Dillard, C. B. (2000). The substance of things hoped for, the evidence of things not seen: Examining an endarkened feminist epistemology in educational research and leadership. *International Journal of Qualitative Studies in Education,* 13, 661–681. https://doi.org/10.1080/09518390050211565

Dillard, C. B. (2018). Let steadfastness have its full effect: (Re)Membering (re)search and endarkened feminisms from ananse to asantewaa. *Qualitative Inquiry, 24*(9), 617–623. https://doi.org/10.1177/1077800417745103

Elfert, M., & Walker, J. (2020). The rise and fall of adult literacy: Policy lessons from Canada. *European Journal for Research on the Education and Learning of Adults, 11*(1), 109–125. https://doi.org/10.3384/rela.2000-7426.rela9203

Etter-Lewis, G. (1993). *My soul is my own: Oral narratives of African American women in the professions.* Routledge.

Fearon, S. (2020). *For our children: Black motherwork and schooling* [Unpublished doctoral dissertation]. University of Toronto. https://tspace.library.utoronto.ca/bitstream/1807/103353/4/Fearon_Stephanie_202011_PhD_thesis.pdf.

Goss, L., & Barnes, M. (1989). *Talk that talk: An anthology of African-American storytelling.* Simon & Schuster.

Goss, L., & Goss, C. (1995). *Jump up and say!: A collection of Black storytelling.* Simon & Schuster.

Hartman, S. (2020). *Wayward lives, beautiful experiments: Intimate histories of riotous Black girls, troublesome women and queer radicals.* Norton, W. W., & Company.

Hine, D. C. (1989). Rape and the inner lives of Black women in the Middle West: Preliminary thoughts on the culture of dissemblance. *Journal of Women in Culture and Society,* 14, 912–920. https://www.jstor.org/stable/3174692

Hurston, Z. N. (1990). *Mules and men.* Perennial Libraries.

Livo, N., & Rietz, S. (1986). *Storytelling: Process and practice.* Libraries Unlimited.

Miles, M. B., & Huberman, A. M. (1994). *Qualitative data analysis* (2nd ed.). SAGE Publishing.

Mishler, E. (1986). *Research interviewing: Context and analysis.* Harvard Press.

Mueller, J. (1999). Narrative approaches to qualitative research in primary care. In B. Crabtree & W. Miller (Eds.), *Doing qualitative research* (2nd ed., pp. 221–238). SAGE Publishing.

Onuora, N. A. (2012). *Anansesem (storytelling nights) African maternal pedagogies.* [Unpublished doctoral dissertation]. University of Toronto. https://tspace.library .utoronto.ca/bitstream/1807/67307/6/Onuora_Adwoa_201211_PhD_ thesis.pdf

Onuora, N. A. (2015). *Anansesem: Telling stories and storytelling African maternal pedagogies.* Demeter Press.

Patton, M. Q. (2002). *Qualitative research and evaluation methods* (3rd ed.). SAGE Publishing.

Polanyi, L. (1985). *Telling the American story: A structural and cultural analysis of conversational storytelling.* Ablex.

Rodriguez, D. (2006). Un/masking identity: Healing our wounded souls. *Qualitative Inquiry, 12*(6), 1067–1090. https://doi.org/10.1177/1077800406293238

Sewall, I. (1998). *The folkloral voice.* Qualitative Institute Press.

Sharpe, C. E. (2016). *In the wake: On Blackness and being.* Duke University Press.

Stewart, C. (1997). *Soul survivors: An African American spirituality.* Westminster John Knox Press.

Statistics Canada. (2019). *Diversity of the Black population in Canada: An overview.* Minister of Industry.

Wane, N. N. (2005). African Indigenous Knowledge: Claiming, writing, storing, and sharing the discourse. *Journal of Thought, 40*(2), 27–46. https://www.jstor .org/stable/42589823

INTRODUCTION TO CASE STUDY 19

A case study approach was used to explore a partnership between a K–12 charter school and a university. Researchers examined the influence of participation in diversity equality and inclusion professional development on interactions with diverse and underserved ethnic groups, the application of diversity and equity inclusion training into classroom practices, and influence on diversity and equity inclusion diversity training on institutional perceptions of marginalized staff members. An improvement inquiry methodological approach was utilized. This approach focuses on tasks, processes, and tools used and effects on organizational policies, structures, and norms. This approach is unique as it hones in on specific work-related problems, assesses variation in performance, provides a vehicle for measuring organizational change and improvement, provides a disciplined process to guide change, and facilitates improvement within and across an organization. The process is based upon democratic engagement of different sectors in a network within the organization.

Qualitative Research With Diverse and Underserved Communities, pages 319–333
Copyright © 2024 by Information Age Publishing
www.infoagepub.com

CASE STUDY 19

DIGGING DEEPER AND REACHING OUT

Using Qualitative Research to Include Voice in Diverse and Underserved Communities

Margery Covello
Lindley Academy Charter School

Kwanza A. Cogdell
Lindley Academy Charter School

Caroline Lembo
Lindley Academy Charter School

Ronald W. Whitaker, II
Cabrini University

ABSTRACT

This chapter focuses on a case study of a partnership between a K–12 Charter School organization and university in the northeast region of the United

Qualitative Research With Diverse and Underserved Communities, pages 321–333

States; that is focused on co-constructing an inclusive infrastructure that is affirming and supportive of all stakeholders. Improvement Inquiry (Bryk et al., 2015) is utilized as a methodological approach towards accessing change. Additionally, this chapter concludes with recommendations for K–12 and university partnerships to consider.

QUALITATIVE RESEARCH FOR DIVERSE AND UNDERSERVED COMMUNITIES

The year 2020 brought the worst and the best of humanity: acts of hatred and of love, words of division and unification, feelings of hope and helplessness. This tumultuous back drop thrusted committed individuals at Lindley Academy Charter School, an American Paradigm School, to focus on conversation and action around bias, prejudice, racism, and equity to deconstruct and reconstruct mindsets, and to sustain open and honest conversations that include the voices of the voiceless, marginalized, underrepresented, and devalued.

This is Lindley Academy Charter School's journey to involve the voices of community members. We engaged Cabrini University, our professional development school (PDS) partner to join us. The purpose of Lindley Academy and Cabrini University's long-standing partnership is to mutually support and collaborate, creating positive educational outcomes for our staff and students. Previous partnership work together focused on how teacher development is not "an individual process, but rather, communities in common alignment play a major role in nurturing aspiring teachers" (Whitaker et al., 2020, p. 26). Our commitment to learning in public, identifying and addressing emerging trends, acknowledging long standing issues, and supporting each other as we individually and collectively find our voice, is what makes our journey unique, yet scalable and replicable. Access to Lindley Academy was possible because of the researchers' affiliation and experience. Three of the researchers are educators at Lindley Academy and one is an educator at Cabrini University. It is extremely valuable to be a researcher in your own community. As such, Lindley Academy Charter School was chosen for this case study.

Including all voices requires we have all found our own voice—that we are all race fluent. Our working definition of race fluency is the ability to talk about bias, prejudice, racism, and equity in support of community success. The problem that precipitated the inquiry was that we realized that our staff and faculty were not race fluent. Our premise is that in order to create an anti-racist school environment we had to first be able to talk about race not only from an academic, intellectualized, removed, broadstrokes perspective, but also from a personal, soul searching, and up-close perspective.

The following facts will provide the reader with a sense of our community and the backdrop in which we exist. Lindley Academy is a renaissance public charter school in North Philadelphia, specifically the Logan section of the city. Lindley is composed of 750 intelligent, athletic, creative, and innovative learners in kindergarten to eighth grade and 85 faculty and staff members. All students are eligible for free or reduced lunch, have a variety of social and emotional issues, and have the expectation that school is a nurturing environment in which they will become college or career ready. 92% of students identify as Black and 25% of the faculty identify as Black.

Statistically, compared to the state averages as reported by City Data.com (n.d.) and the Census Reporter (n.d.), the residents of the Logan section of the city are more likely to be young, poor, Black, unemployed, have a longer commute to work, and are less likely to hold a college degree or be a homeowner. From a lived experience perspective, the Lindley community feels deeply the burden of multiple recent crises—health, social, economic, equity, and political.

Families are believers in the value of a high-quality education as evidenced by their own words shared in written comments regarding their feelings and observations about a Lindley education. Parents share, for example, "I believe in the mission and appreciate the education my child is receiving"; "Greatness and achievement is possible with a Lindley education"; and "We here at Lindley academy are a family. The school is a great support system in the Logan area." Families are engaged partners in their child(rens) education as evidenced by high participation at academic progress conferences, school wide events, and responsiveness to outreach from school personnel. Lindley staff, families and students aspire to live by the Lindley Lion ROAR ideals: respect myself and others, outstanding attitude, achieve excellence, and responsible for my choices and actions. The ROAR is recited every morning as a school community.

STRATEGIC DIVERSITY LEADERSHIP

In adherence with Williams (2013), the aim of our inclusivity efforts is to move beyond the diversity crisis model. Specifically, as Williams (2008) argues that the diversity crisis model starts with educational leaders putting the majority of efforts into getting rid of an "embarrassing incident (e.g., someone being called a racial slur), but ultimately these planning efforts lack implementation. To that end, he argues for the need for educational leaders to become strategic in our diversity planning, in a manner that includes clearly defined goals, tactics, phases, progress indicators, and outcome indicators (Williams, 2013).

Thus, in collaboration with Cabrini University we identified four action items to develop an equity plan in the Spring of 2020:

1. Form a committee to establish our assessment purpose and questions.
2. Determine our methodology for the equity audit.
3. Develop a plan with actions items and desired outcomes etc.
4. Engage in a cycle of continuous improvement.

We leaned in and asked ourselves the following questions. The impact of teachers' attitudes on marginalized students' academic achievement is well researched. Douglas et al. (2008), Hinojosa and Moras (2009), and Coleman (2007) among many others conclude that teachers' views of marginalized students from a deficit perspective rather than a potential perspective contribute to negative academic achievement outcomes for marginalized students. Our initial professional practice musings, based on this research included the following guiding questions:

- How do we come together as a community of learners to be more worthy education partners to our predominantly Black student population and their families?
- Can we come together to recognize that racism is and has been a global pandemic, in and of itself?
- Are we willing to accept that especially when it comes to race that we have a lot of work to do and that the work may be difficult, messy, and unwelcomed by some?
- What steps can a predominantly white staff take to involve all voices in an effort to support the success stories of a predominantly Black student body?
- How do we facilitate the sustained inclusion of the voices of all community members urgently, methodically, and joyfully?
- Are we willing to be vulnerable and to be transparent in our learning?

Educators must be "responsive to the emerging needs of the community and the larger society, not only as regards the changing context of the world of work and employment but also to the political, cultural and social changes taking place" (Starratt, 1993, p. 13). When considering the current educational environment for marginalized students we are once again reminded that "it is totally unrealistic to expect students to take full advantage of the intellectual and personal development opportunities without some assistance from the institution (Ender et al., 1984, p. 12). Alkire (2019) adds about the current state of schools in marginalized communities that "these systems cannot be broken down by simply going along with the flow of things and moving in tandem as usual. The only way to combat racist regimes is by inciting knowledge and passion into our students and future teachers by showing the honesty of these racist practices" (para. 2). This case study explored the following research questions:

1. What influence can diversity equity and inclusion (DEI) professional development that encourages vulnerability and discomfort have on staff and faculty members' perceptions of their own race fluency to include marginalized voices?
2. What impact can diversity equity and inclusion (DEI) professional development that encourages vulnerability and discomfort have on staff and faculty members ability to identify needed changes in their classroom practices to include marginalized voices?
3. What effect does consistent diversity equity and inclusion (DEI) professional development that encourages vulnerability and discomfort have on how marginalized staff members feel about school?

In February of 2020, two staff members facilitated a professional development: *How to Educate African American Students Regardless of Trauma.* As a result of this training, the faculty and staff requested the creation of a Cultural Competency Book Club, and then the Commonwealth mandated COVID-19 school building closure happened. The whole world and especially the world of education changed. We quickly regrouped to provide training on virtual teaching for faculty and staff, to provide continuity of education for our students, to deploy 750 devices, to launch a neighborhood wide food service program, as well as to continue to provide all of the supports that our families have come to expect; however, we could not let the Book Club idea go. It was an idea that would not be pushed to the back burner and thus two staff members took on the responsibility for facilitating what came to be known as the Lindley Academy Cultural Competency Book Club from March until June. It was a voluntary book club that was made up of what we liked to refer to as a cohort of the willing. At the end of each book club meeting we identified action items. The book club identified five critical areas: on-going professional development for staff and faculty, family engagement, student involvement, curriculum implementation, and community involvement. These five action items became the foundation for Lindley Academy Charter School's 4 Steps Toward Equity. The four components are: staff and faculty, community, students, and systems and stuff (curriculum). To guide our work, we created a mission statement: "Lindley Academy Charter School at Birney will faithfully through conversation and action shape a caring school community that supports Black Lives Matter and shines a light on all injustices in pursuit of systemic equity." The 4 Steps Toward Equity were rolled out to all staff and faculty members at a professional development in August using the graphic found in Figure 19.1.

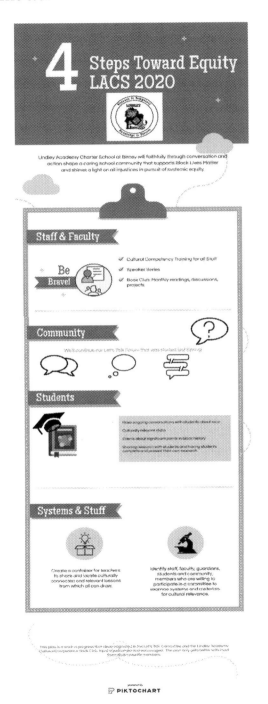

Figure 19.1 4 Steps toward equity.

We prioritized this work by making it mandatory for faculty and staff to "get uncomfortable about race" (Mayo, 2019, 00:01:10). In doing this, we included equity work in the regular professional development schedule. We moved, rescheduled, and made room for these meetings.

Our objective for the staff and faculty step is based on a simple premise, as stated earlier, that race fluent faculty and staff members will be a better education partner to students and their families than a faculty and staff who is race inarticulate. This step has two parts: the first is a speaker series in which we partnered with four groups of professionals who are well respected, based on a career commitment to equity work. The second part is the Cultural Competency Book Club. The book club is facilitated by staff members who volunteer and are supported by the original book club facilitators. Without doing the work required to become race-fluent while simultaneously expecting the traditionally voiceless to speak up keeps us squarely on the ill begotten path of relying on Black community members to bear the sole burden of effecting change (Trepczynski, 2020). As educator Dwayne Reed (2020) stated, "White supremacy won't die until White people see it as a White issue they need to solve rather than a Black issue they need to empathize with."

The objective for the community step, was born out of the murder of George Floyd and the subsequent need for the community to share deep emotions. Lindley staff members channeled the rage and harsh realities of the racial unrest into what was aptly named the "Let's Talk Forum" as a way to process the acute pain students and other community members felt at the time and continue to feel. To introduce the forum, the following statement was shared with the community.

> Our school was founded on the simple principles that a first-rate education is the birthright of every individual, all children can learn, and every child will be challenged to reach his or her full potential. We work tirelessly to help children reach that potential. They deserve a world that does the same. Let's Talk Forum was created as a Zoom conversation to discuss inequality and justice issues that are affecting the health and wellbeing of communities of color.

At the time of this writing, three Let's Talk Forums have taken place.

The work that we intend to do in the Student Step on research and culturally relevant clubs has proven to be more difficult than we have expected in a virtual environment. Even though Lindley is 100% virtual right now, "school" is a rigorous all day academic experience. We overestimated our students' appetites for additional online interactions. We look at this overestimation as our miss, not a deficit of our students. Until the time when we can safely return to the school building, we are committed to placing student voices at the center of the Let's Talk Forums.

Objectives for the systems and stuff (curriculum) step include creating a task force of stakeholders to examine the current ELA, social studies and science curriculum to determine cultural appropriateness and reviewing the caring school community, our SEL curriculum, and our math curriculum for culturally relevant revisions. In addition, everyone has access to Google Classroom to submit culturally relevant lessons that they have developed and would like to share with their colleagues.

The pandemic and subsequent closing of the school building created some anticipated and unanticipated consequences. For example, we were unable to anticipate students' appetite for online programming after school hours. We learned that there is very little appetite for this. This affected our ability to include student voices as meaningfully as we would have liked. In addition, we were able to anticipate and subsequently capitalize on the advent of robust online training which gave us access to national DEI experts. In a pre-COVID-19 environment, we would have likely constrained ourselves to inhouse or regional experts. Lastly, this work affected staff members in various ways. Discussions of the realities through which our Black staff members live daily triggered mental and emotional shutdowns and renewed trauma. Black staff members felt pressured to host their white counterparts' discomfort and defensiveness toward cultural competency professional development.

IMPROVEMENT INQUIRY AS A METHODOLOGICAL APPROACH

Bryk et al. (2015) suggests that improvement science (or inquiry) "addresses the reality by focusing on the specific tasks people do, the processes and tools they use and how prevailing policies, organizational structures, and norms affect this" (p. 27). The principles of improvement inquiry include: (a) making the work problem specific and user centered, (b) focusing on variation in performance, (c) seeing the system that produces the outcomes, (d) measurements for improvement, (e) disciplined inquiry to drive improvement, (f) the importance of network improvement communities, and (g) living improvement within and across our organization.

Further, in order to construct an inclusivity environment, which values the perspectives, voices, and expertise of all stakeholders, when addressing problems of practice, improvement inquiry is a methodological lens that aids in the process of building organizational and inclusivity capacity within our context. Specifically, improvement inquiry gives us shared language, values, and accountability mechanisms that provides our context with inclusivity foundational building blocks.

We identified Improvement Inquiry (Bryk et al., 2015; Duquesne Collective Action Network, 2020) to guide our process for information gathering, information analysis, and action step identification, because true educators view themselves through the lens of a learner.

Improvement inquiry has an intense, cutting-edge, and reflective nature; therefore, the researchers believe that the principles of improvement inquiry are a good match for the subject matter of this research. With most professional developments, the process is to plan it, facilitate it, ask participants to complete a feedback form, and then never give the feedback more than a passing glance. Frequently, feedback results look at "How did we do as presenters?" as opposed to "What should we do next as a community?" We followed this flawed process many times. We were humbled by how insightful, thoughtful, and sometimes anguished, the feedback was after the first 4 Steps Toward Equity sessions. It demanded a response. Responding to feedback from each session was identified early on as a critical step to continuous improvement. Summarizing the feedback and resharing it was critical to learning transparently as a community.

Using design thinking—especially the principles of design-based implementation research (Anderson & Shattuck, 2012; Dolle et al., 2013, LeMahieu et al., 2017)—and cross-sector collaboration based on democratic engagement (Saltmarsh, 2017), the network seeks to develop a process of improvement inquiry that will help schools and communities get better at getting better and to sustain that improvement mindset for the long-term (Bryk et al., 2015; Peurach, 2016).

INFORMATION ANALYSIS

Our approach for analyzing our ongoing work aligns with using design thinking. Explicitly, we utilize the tenets of design-based implementation research (Anderson & Shattuck, 2012; Dolle et al., 2013; LeMahieu et al., 2017). It is our aspiration to engage in a process of improvement inquiry that will help our partnership with enhanced effectiveness, sustainability, and continuous improvement (Bryk et al., 2015; Peurach, 2016). Our inquiry focus remained relatively consistent throughout this study. Based on the feedback we collected from the staff and faculty, we share the emerging findings.

The first research question explored the influence diversity equity and inclusion (DEI) professional development that encourages vulnerability and discomfort may have on staff and faculty members' perceptions of their own race fluency to include marginalized voices. Based on feedback response analysis, the researchers note the following emerging findings. Most of the staff and faculty who participated in the feedback process when asked, "As a result of your participation in the 4 Steps to Equity class so far, do you think you are more race-fluent (able to discuss race-related topics) than when the class started?" responded positively which we categorized into the following thematic responses: "Yes, very much so"; "Somewhat, I am a work in progress"; and "I am already race-fluent but have learned some new things." Based on these results we conclude that our staff and faculty have positive perceptions of their ability to become increasingly race-fluent to include the voices of marginalized students and families in their educational practice.

The second research question examined whether DEI professional development that encourages vulnerability and discomfort can have an impact on staff and faculty members ability to identify needed changes in their classroom practices to include marginalized voices. Based on an analysis of the responses to feedback, the researchers conclude that staff and faculty can identify needed changes in their classroom practices, Staff and faculty identified over 150 actions that they would incorporate into their practice. Some examples include, "I need to be careful never to seem surprised when my students master a skill"; "I'll use positive narration vs. simple praise"; "If I am praising scholars for simpler tasks, I need to motivate them to complete more difficult tasks"; "I'll re-focus on empowerment and meeting with parents to include them as a partner"; and "Since these sessions I feel that I speak up much more than before about racism." These actions were grouped thematically around expectations, word choice, mindset, relationships, caring school community, academics, and families.

The last research question considered whether consistent DEI professional development that encourages vulnerability and discomfort has an effect on how marginalized staff members feel about school. A review of the responses to feedback results in the conclusion that consistent DEI professional development can have a positive effect on how marginalized staff members feel about school. For example, "Keep on with these PDs. They are great!"; "Thank you for inviting me to this valuable PD experience"; and "Keep up the sessions. I truly believe we are doing something amazing here." As researchers we were encouraged by these positive results in such a short period of time.

What we are learning about getting a staff ready to include voice:

- Prioritize the work. This is not about "finding" or "making" time. It is not about time at all. It is about priorities. We can't change the amount of time we have to accomplish our goals. Time is finite. Move something off of your professional development calendar to make space for equity work.
- Including voice builds hope. This hope is evidenced in community members' feedback which include statements like, "I am so happy

that these sessions are happening and scheduled to continue happening"; "This is very important work and I am proud of the team for engaging with it"; and "I am very happy that this is actually happening and we are having these conversations!!"

- Like all schools, color blindness, White silence and microaggressions exist in our community; however, when called out in our community there is an active willingness to do the work required to be better partners to our Black students and their families.

- Improving race fluency is possible in a short amount of time. When we asked staff if they are more race fluent as a result of participation in the Book Club and Speaker Series most faculty and staff members self-reported, "Yes, very much so" and "Somewhat, I am a work in progress."

- Improving practice is possible in a short amount of time. Staff members self-report very concrete examples of culturally relevant improvements to their practice. These responses are grouped thematically, by caring school community, academics, family, and overall and reshared with the faculty and staff as a growing resource.

What we learned about qualitative research:

- Just start. Do not let perfection be the enemy of good. We recognize and acknowledge that we are not putting on a magic show. It is OK if the work is not flawless. Keep going anyway.

- Evolution is not a sign of failure. Let the process evolve as new and better information becomes available. When reasons for change emerge whether by logic or instinct, act upon them. It is OK to receive feedback that we'd rather not have heard. Hear it anyway and use it to collectively and individually dig deeper.

- Respond to feedback along the way. Do not wait until the end of the feedback collection to make changes that can and should be made in real-time. Truly valuing the voices demands that we act immediately on what we are hearing.

- Create an iterative process. View the work as a looping process in which there is always space for improvement, adaptation, and more voice.

We are proud of the work that has happened so far and continues today. If we have not made it clear yet in this summary, let us emphasize now that this has been a whole community effort and responsibility for keeping the work alive does not rest with just one individual, one group or one institution. Special thanks goes to Cabrini University's Center for Urban education, Equity and Improvement, the Let's Talk Committee; the Leadership

Team at Lindley Academy; Lindley's amazing faculty and staff; our colleagues at American Paradigm Schools; and most importantly our students and families. When we reflect on the progress, we have made in such a short time, we are more convinced than ever that good things happen in Philadelphia. Good things.

REFERENCES

Alkire, S. (2019, January 20). *The school system is failing Black students.* Black Feminist Collective. https://blackfeministcollective.com

Anderson, T., & Shattuck, J. (2012). Design-based research: A decade of progress in education research? *Educational Researcher, 41*(1), 16–25. https://doi.org/10.3102/0013189X11428813

Bryk, A. S., Gomez, L. M., Grunow, A., & LeMahieu, P. G. (2015). *Learning to improve: How America's schools can get better at getting better.* Harvard Education Press.

Census Reporter. 19141. (n.d.). *19141.* Accessed November 22, 2020. http://censusreporter.org/profiles/86000US19141-19141/

City Data.com. (n.d.). *19141 zip code (Philadelphia, Pennsylvania) detailed profile.* Accessed November 22, 2020. http://www.city-data.com/zips/19141.html

Coleman, B. (2007). *Successful White teachers of Black students: Teaching across racial lines in urban middle school science classrooms* (AAI3289276) [Unpublished doctoral dissertation]. University of Massachusetts–Amherst.

Dolle, J. R., Gomez, L. M., Russell, J. L., & Bryk, A. S. (2013). More than a network: Building professional communities for educational improvement. *Teachers College Record, 115*(14), 443–463. https://doi.org/10.1177/016146811311501413

Douglas, B., Lewis, C. W., Douglas, A., Scott, M. E., & Garrison-Wade, D. (2008). The impact of White teachers on the academic achievement of Black students: An exploratory qualitative analysis. *Educational Foundations*, Winter–Spring, 47–62. https://files.eric.ed.gov/fulltext/EJ839497.pdf

Duquesne Collective Action Network. (2020). Lessons learned in the pursuit of social justice in education: Finding a path and making the road. In R. Papa (Eds.), *Handbook on promoting social justice in education* (pp. 71–104). Springer. https://doi.org/10.1007/978-3-030-14625-2_98

Ender, S. C., Winston, R. B., Jr., & Miller, T. K. (1984). Academic advising reconsidered. In R. B. Winston, Jr., T. K. Miller, S. C. Ender, & T. J. Grites (Eds.), *Developmental academic advising* (pp. 3–34). Jossey-Bass.

Hinojosa, M. S., & Moras, A. (2009). Challenging colorblind education: A descriptive analysis of teacher racial attitudes. *Research and Practice in Social Sciences, 4*(2), 27–45. https://digitalcommons.sacredheart.edu/sociol_fac/6

LeMahieu, P. G., Grunow, A., Baker, L., Nordstrum, L. E., & Gomez, L. M. (2017), Networked improvement communities: The discipline of improvement science meets the power of networks. *Quality Assurance in Education, 25*(1), 5–25. https://doi.org/10.1108/QAE-12-2016-0084

Mayo, L., (2019). *Let's get uncomfortable: It's time to talk about race* [Video]. TED Talks. https://www.ted.com/talks/lori_mayo_let_s_get_uncomfortable_it_s_time _to_talk_about_race

Peurach, D. J. (2016). Innovating at the nexus of impact and improvement: Leading educational improvement networks. *Educational Researcher, 45*(7), 421–429.

Reed, D., [@TeachMrReed]. (2020. June 4). *White supremacy won't die until White people see it as a White issue they need to solve rather than a Black* [Tweet]. Twitter. https://twitter.com/TeachMrReed/status/1268559506809786368

Saltmarsh, J. (2017). A collaborative turn: Trends and directions in community engagement. In J. Sachs & L. Clark (Eds.), *Learning through community engagement: Vision and practice in higher education* (pp. 3–16). Springer.

Starratt, R. J. (1993). *Transforming life in schools: Conversations about leadership and school renewal.* Australia Council for Education Administration.

Trepczynski, S. (2020, June 1). Black and brown people have been protesting for centuries. It's White people who are responsible for what happens next. *Time.* https:// time.com/5846072/black-people-protesting-white-people-responsible-what -happens-next/

Whitaker, R., Conway, T., Bryde, B., Ritter, M., & Covello, M. (2020). Green light, yellow light, red light: A case study that explores should the PDS partnership proceed, slow down, or stop? In E. Garin & R. West Burns (Eds.), *Clinically based teacher education in action: Cases from professional development schools* (pp. 22–26). Information Age Publishing.

Williams, D. A. (2008). Beyond the diversity crisis model: Decentralized diversity planning and implementation. *Planning for Higher Education, 36*(2), 27.

Williams, D. A. (2013). *Strategic diversity leadership: Activating change and transformation in higher education.* Stylus Publishing.

INTRODUCTION TO CASE STUDY 20

This study examined undocumented immigrants focusing on (a) the impact of socio-political discourse on identity, (b) their social interactions, and (c) influence on academics. Study research questions were (a) "In what ways, if any, does the larger socio-political discourse on undocumented immigrants and immigration have on the social identity (re)formation of undocumented Latinx students? In what ways does this larger discourse magnify one's undocumented status?"; (b) "How does an undocumented status impact social interaction with peers, teachers, staff, and strangers encountered in everyday life?"; and (c) "How do social relations with the aforementioned individuals influence academic experiences and outcomes?" The initial research methodology was participant observation. The selected research is the story of the lived experiences of an undocumented immigrant.

The researcher documented experiences developing the research design. Initially, the researcher made weekly visits to a high school of a friend for 6 months. During class lectures, the researcher would take detailed field notes and document interactions with friends. Also, the researcher interacted daily with the study population and conducted workshops about access to college, financial aid, and college culture. However, testimonials was the final selected study methodology. The study sample consisted of 12 gender-balanced students that identified as Latinx and undocumented, four were in high school, four in community college, and four in a 4-year university. Testimonials allow underserved and underrepresented communities of color to describe lived experiences through personal lens and place the experiences within the context of individual stories and. life histories.

Qualitative Research With Diverse and Underserved Communities, pages 335–344
Copyright © 2024 by Information Age Publishing
www.infoagepub.com

The study was also selected because the introduction provided an example of crafting a profile of experiences which can be an effective way of sharing interview data and providing the foundation for analyzing and interpreting data. Profiles are generally written in the words of the participant. It allows the participant to be presented in context, to clarify the intentions of participants, and to convey the sense of process and time. In other words, the researcher comes to know and understand the lived experiences of the participants through their stories and provide a reflection of the consciousness of the person. Profiles allow the researcher to share what has been learned from interviews through storytelling. The study presented is a variation of a crafted profile in that the researcher is the participant telling the story. Nevertheless, the crafted profile allows the reader to see the meaning making of self and the social world.

The profile was created from detailed field notes documenting weekly observations and experiences during family, school, and university interactions. These experiences formed the foundation for dissertation research and recommendations for conducting qualitative research. The particular piece was selected because the introductory section provided an example of crafting a profile as an analytical tool.

CASE STUDY 20

QUALITATIVE RESEARCH WITH UNDOCUMENTED IMMIGRANTS

Ana K. Soltero López
California State University, Fresno

In February of 1985, I crossed the U.S.–Mexico border illegally and settled in Los Angeles, California. I entered the United States at the age of one and a half using the birth certificate of my U.S.-born cousin. My prescribed identity as an "illegal alien" was unknown to me until the year 1994 when California's Proposition 187 was introduced, which sought to preclude "illegal aliens" from social services such as healthcare and public education. I remember my mother trying her best to explain to an 11-year-old the process of migration she had chosen in order to have a better life. Already confused by what she told me, my mother proceeded to explain to me the importance of censorship given my vulnerable immigration status. She explained that if my status were to be disclosed, I would be deported to Mexico, a country I did not know.

The fear that was instilled in me negatively impacted my childhood. I was no longer the carefree, talkative, friendly child I had been. I became very

Qualitative Research With Diverse and Underserved Communities, pages 337–344
Copyright © 2024 by Information Age Publishing
www.infoagepub.com

reserved and often times had to think twice before answering questions by friends or teachers; fearing I would reveal something that would cause them to report me to immigration services. To reduce my fear and anxiety, I simply decided to cease the close relationships I had with most of my peers and teachers. At school, I spoke only when spoken to and if applicable would stick to a simple "yes" or "no" responses. The restricted social life I had created for my safety remained the same for several years. I started my senior year and became depressed about the realization that my undocumented status would prevent me from going to college. Discouraged but hopeful, I applied to several schools anyway. In my mind, I had agreed that simply being admitted to colleges and universities would be an achievement. Luckily, my prayers were answered and my petition for permanent residency was accepted. I became a United States legal permanent resident in March of 2002 and was able to pursue my dreams of a college education.

I start this chapter with my testimonio because my lived experiences were a large part of what inspired me to become an educational qualitative researcher. As a first-generation college student, I sought opportunities to serve underserved youth and families. I committed to ensuring that youth with similar backgrounds to mine would not have to endure the unnecessary challenges of the TK–12 pipeline. I wanted, in particular, to inform immigrant youth and their parents about college, financial aid, and career pathways. In seeking opportunities to do this work, I landed a position with a longitudinal mentorship program where I mentored a seventh-grade undocumented student and her family. I also served as the liaison between the local schools and the university. Unbeknownst to me, I had started my career as a qualitative researcher as I collected detailed field notes documenting my weekly observations and conversations between the family, schools, and university. My personal experiences influenced the professional experiences I sought, and thus, propelled me to pursue a career as a qualitative researcher and educator.

In this chapter, I highlight my qualitative dissertation project focused on Latinx undocumented students. The chapter is organized with four pieces of advice about qualitative research. I also describe my process of answering the what, who, why, how, where, and when. I close the chapter with additional considerations.

ADVICE #1: READ THE LITERATURE

If you are new to qualitative research, it is important that you take coursework and/or read extensively about this methodological approach. There is an abundance of books, journals, and other resources that discuss at length the how-tos of interviewing, focus groups, participant observation, action research, just to name a few. The more well-read you are, the better informed you will be about the numerous methods of qualitative research. Relatedly, awareness of theoretical frameworks is equally important. Take inventory of the frameworks you know and like and ask yourself why you gravitate towards them. Understanding your interest in certain methods and theoretical frameworks will come in handy as you begin designing your qualitative study. Aside from knowledge on methods and theories, you should read as much as you can on the research topic(s) that interest you. After all, besides writing a methods and frameworks chapter/section, you will also be writing a literature review that will show your mastery of the topic and assert yourself as an emerging scholar who is filling the voids in the literature.

I begun learning about qualitative methods as an undergraduate via required coursework for my majors, some which required pilot studies. Moreover, my position in the aforementioned mentorship program evolved my application of methods such as participant observation, interviews, focus groups, and analyses of fieldnotes, and interview transcripts. I learned a tremendous amount from working closely with the doctoral students who I shadowed and provided additional reading material. By the time I was in my doctoral studies and ready to write my dissertation proposal, I felt confident in my ability to successfully carry out my own qualitative research. My undergraduate preparation as a Chicana/o/x studies and psychology double major had also exposed me to many theoretical frameworks that further guided the research projects I completed. As a graduate student, I knew that I was drawn to critical frameworks, such as critical race theory. My dissertation work was informed by Latina/o critical theory, which uses narratives, counterstories, and testimonios as methodological tools to address genuine problems within the education of Latinx students. My project addressed the five tenets: (a) intersectionality of race and other factors, (b) challenging dominant ideology, (c) centrality of experiential knowledge, (d) commitment to social justice, and (e) using a transdisciplinary approach (Delgado & Stefancic, 2001; Solórzano & Yosso, 2001). In the sections that follow, I will describe my process by trial and error, techniques, and lessons learned.

ADVICE #2: UNDERSTAND THE IMPORTANCE OF YOUR RESEARCH QUESTION(S)

Aside from knowing the methods and frameworks that interest you, it is important to keep in mind that your research question(s) help dictate suitable methods and frameworks. Your research questions help you answer "what." For example, my final dissertation research questions inquired: (a)

"In what ways, if any, does the larger socio-political discourse on undocumented immigrants and immigration have on the social identity (re)formation of undocumented Latinx students? In what ways does this larger discourse magnify one's undocumented status?"; (b) "How does an undocumented status impact social interaction with peers, teachers, staff, and strangers encountered in everyday life?"; and (c) "How do social relations with the aforementioned individuals influence academic experiences and outcomes?" A few things can be gathered from my questions, it tells us that my focus population is undocumented students, and it also tells us I had three foci on this population: (a) the impact of socio-political discourse on identity, (b) their social interactions, and (c) influence on academics. These details help answer the "who," to a degree, but the big question any qualitative researcher always needs to be able to answer is the "So what?" or "Why?" As a doctoral student, my professors and peers asked me this repeatedly. This exercise helped me verbalize out loud my argument to the importance of researching these specific factors about undocumented students. It helped me determine that my methodology would include qualitative methods. Moreover, I was forced to ponder the impact I wanted my study to have. After all, this project was personal and I was not just doing this project to get a PhD, I was driven by a need for positive change. I was highly committed to making changes that would benefit the academic and social journeys of undocumented students. Regularly answering "So what?" from the inception to completion of my study also strengthened my identity and confidence as a qualitative researcher.

ADVICE #3: BE FLEXIBLE

Once I was able to convincingly articulate my study and its importance, I was given the greenlight from my advisors to write my proposal. My methods chapter answered the "How?"; "Where?"; and "When?" of my study. I originally set out to study undocumented Latinx K–12 students labeled as English language learners (ELL). As I read the literature, I recognized the dearth of research on ELL undocumented students. At the time of my dissertation studies, the dominant literature on undocumented students focused on high achieving, college-track students, with minimal research on students that did not fit this profile. I had this very specific population in mind and set off to identify schools and teachers that had such population. Fortunately, a friend from college became a high school teacher and was teaching ELL students many of whom were undocumented and gave me access to her classroom. I intentionally sought this out as an opportunity to pilot my work before doing a larger-scale study. Prior to visiting my friend's classroom, I reached out to her principal and set up a meeting to discuss my project at length. The principal was intrigued with my work and welcomed any feedback that would help her and other staff to better serve this population and thus official access was granted to this site.

For this pilot study, the "Where?" became my friend's high school and the "When?" resulted in 1 or 2 weekly visits for two periods. My chosen method: participant observation. During lectures, I would sit in the back of the class and take detailed field notes. At other times, I supported my friend in walking around the class and helping students with classwork and practicing their English-speaking skills. My friend cultivated a strong sense of community among her students. There was an evident sense of respect for one-self and others, and a college culture. My friend and I would do workshops about access to college, financial aid, college life, and other topics that interested them. We invited their inquiries about college and careers. Due to limited resources and the perceived low expectations of these students, they had not met with the college counselor and knew little to nothing about getting to college. In the half year that I spent with these students, my friend and I noticed the impact that our workshops and candid conversations about our experiences as children of immigrants, native Spanish speakers and first-generation college students had on the students. They spoke more highly of themselves and recognized that their funds of knowledge, though unacknowledged in their schooling, were characteristics that motivated them towards their future. In turn, my time with them inspired me and confirmed my desire to conduct a larger-scale study with this same demographic.

My original research questions focused on undocumented Latinx high school ELL students and I sought a sample size of at least 50 students. I began emailing teachers, principals, and counselors across the Los Angeles area. The majority never responded, and thus, a lesson on flexibility was learned. During check-ins with my advisors, they would ask me how much more time I wanted to spend on recruitment and cautioned me that reaching the specific population and sample size could take me years. Thus, after much thinking, I decided to alter my research questions so they were not as narrow, broaden the eligibility of my sample, and change my method. My final project was a sample of 12 gender-balanced students that identified as Latinx and undocumented, four were in high school, four in community college, and four in a 4-year university. They were recruited from three high schools, one community college, and two four-year universities in Southern California. I had also switched my method to testimonio complementary to my use of Latina/o critical theory as my framework.

I chose testimonios because communities of color are recognized as natural storytellers (Banks-Wallace, 2002). Passed from generation to generation, oral histories sustain culture, values, and language, but also valiant stories of struggle, resistance, trauma, and displacement that are common among marginalized communities (Angueira, 1988; Benmayor, 1988; Brabeck, 2003). For example, the historical denial of testimony by slaves and free Blacks against Whites in court, rejected the voices, experiences, and histories causing the further subordination of Blacks (Howard, 1973). However, these exact same testimonies are inserted in academic discourse and are used to disprove and challenge knowledge that is accepted as fact (Bailey,1980; Blassingame, 1975).

The incorporation of testimonios as a methodological tool for academic research, challenges traditional westernized methodological practices because it moves towards a social justice-based research that is guided by the participant and not the researcher. This method is unlike traditional in-depth interviews because it privileges the storytelling ability of participants and maintains its integrity by limiting interpretation (Haig-Brown, 2003). Suited to my dissertation research, testimonios are recognized as "a verbal journey of a witness who speaks to reveal the racial, classed, gendered, and nativist injustices they have suffered as a means of healing, empowerment, and advocacy for a more humane present and future" (Perez Huber, 2009, p. 644). Given the consistent social and political attacks on immigrant communities, there was no better time to voice their experiences.

ADVICE #4: BE CONSCIOUS OF YOUR PRIVILEGE(S)

The last recommendation I want to offer is of utmost importance when conducting research on diverse and underserved communities. I am a firm believer that to do qualitative research that is guided by social justice principles, researchers must acknowledge their privileges, such as race/ethnicity, gender, class, sexuality, immigration status, language, phenotype, and so on. For example, I was conscious about my privilege as a graduate student with a bachelor's and master's degree, who spoke English fluently, and had become a naturalized U.S. citizen. I struggled with the complexities and nuances of being both an insider and outsider and documented these feelings and emotions in researcher memos.

The shared characteristics between my informants and I outweighed the differences. My former undocumented status afforded me a direct connection and insights that harnessed a deeper criticality and understanding on the topic of undocumented students. For example, my recruitment approach consisted of emails and class presentations in which I forged an intimate connection to students by sharing my own testimonio of my experiences as an undocumented student throughout my K–12 education. There is something powerful about having the lived experience of the population you are studying. This shared common experience transforms the researcher–researched dynamic. This shared experience also helped with data collection and analysis. After each testimonio was recorded, it was transcribed and reviewed for emerging themes alongside the informants. The process of sharing an authentic narrative of a life-long journey helped both the informants and I theorize and co-construct stories of struggle, survival, and resistance (Perez Huber, 2009). My goal in the analysis phase was to capture the individual experiences of each informant yet highlighting the commonalities in all their experiences.

Though these commonalities were a plus, there were power dynamics at play I could not ignore. I struggled with recognizing that these youth were sharing their stories with me and I would be awarded a PhD. This huge benefit to my education and career surpassed what I could offer them. While their stories would advance my career, I struggled with feeling like I could not change the systemic barriers they spoke about that made their lives and academic goals that much harder to achieve. Similarly, though I mentored and shared resources with them, it was limited, as overtime my contact with these students was lost, whereas my advancement was life-long. After almost two decades of maintaining an active research agenda focused on undocumented students, I continue to have a healthy struggle negotiation my privileges. More importantly, I celebrate the small victories that have contributed to changes in practices and policies that benefit undocumented students. These small but accumulated triumphs are chipping away as the systemic barriers that seek to maintain the marginalization of undocumented students. This is what keeps me inspired and continuing to do research with and for undocumented immigrants.

CONCLUSION

The core foundation of my work with and for undocumented students is social justice. To properly enact social justice research, it is vital that qualitative researchers approach prospective informants with humility and transparency. At the time of my data collection, undocumented students were the hot topic in research. My informants shared with me that they constantly got requests for participation in research studies. As they explained, they responded to my call because I was transparent in my approach and vulnerable in sharing my story. This comfort made them share their testimonio unapologetically or "sin pelos en la lengua." They appreciated that they could also speak in English and Spanish. The intentional incorporation of their interpretation in the analysis process made them feel truly part of the study and not just study subjects. These practices led to them never feeling pressured or forced to maintain their participation. These lessons learned from my informants are things I have continued to present day.

I encourage all qualitative researchers to ask themselves "So what?" about their topic and disentangle the meaning and contribution of your project to your respective field and to yourself. Sit in discomfort for as long as it takes, and become comfortable in knowing that your project will likely hit bumps along the way, such as informant and site rejections, revision to research questions, adaptation of methodology, and so on. This is all part of the research process and developing a researcher identity. Above all, stay true to your commitment to impose positive change that centralizes and legitimizes the existence, humanity, and identity of populations that structural and systemic racism continue to marginalize. Your research will make a difference.

REFERENCES

Angueira, K. (1988). To make the personal political: The use of testimony as a consciousness raising tool against sexual aggression in Puerto Rico. *Oral History Review, 16*(2), 65–93. https://www.jstor.org/stable/3675072

Bailey, D. T. (1980). A divided prism: Two sources of Black testimony on slavery. *The Journal of Southern History, 46*(3), 381–404. https://doi.org/10.2307/2207251

Banks-Wallace, J. (2002). Talk that talk: Storytelling and analysis rooted in African American oral tradition. *Qualitative Health Research, 12*(3), 410–426. https://doi.org/10.1177/104973202129119892

Benmayor, R. (1988). For every story there is another story which stands before it. *The Oral History Review, 16*(2), 1–13. https://www.jstor.org/stable/3675066

Blassingame, J. W. (1975). Using the testimony of ex-slaves: Approaches and problems. *The Journal of Southern History, 41*(4), 473–492. https://doi.org/10.2307/2205559

Brabeck, K. (2003). Testimonio: A strategy for collective resistance, cultural survival and building solidarity. *Feminism and Psychology, 13*(2), 252–258. https://doi.org/10.1177/0959353503013002009

Delgado, R., & Stefanic, J. (2001). *Critical race theory: An introduction.* NYU Press.

Haig-Brown, C. (2003). Creating spaces: Testimonio, impossible knowledge, and academe. *Qualitative Studies in Education, 16*(3), 415–433. https://doi.org/10.1080/0951839032000086763

Howard, V. B. (1973). The Black testimony controversy in Kentucky, 1866–1872. *The Journal of Negro History, 58*(2), 140–165. https://doi.org/10.2307/2716826

Perez Huber, L. (2009). Disrupting apartheid of knowledge: *Testimonio* as methodology in Latina/o critical race research in education. *International Journal of Qualitative Studies in Education, 22*(6), 639–654. https://doi.org/10.1080/09518390903333863

Solórzano, D. G., & Yosso, T. J. (2001). Critical race and latcrit theory and method: Counter-storytelling. *International Journal of Qualitative Studies in Education, 14*(4), 471–495. https://doi.org/10.1080/09518390110063365

INTRODUCTION TO CASE STUDY 21

This report details the phenomenological examination of the provision of leadership opportunities to students with disabilities by their teachers and vice principal. There are a number of important illustrations of qualitative methods with minoritized or disadvantaged participants. One important idea to note is the emergent nature of the inquiry design—while many qualitative researchers allow the prompts and data collection guides (e.g., interviewer guides, focus group moderator's guide) to evolve, this study demonstrates the openness of the researcher to consider alternative designs even as they began the study with one approach in mind. Another illustration provided by this study is the importance of proper informed consent. While this is always a feature of research conducted in university settings in particular, often the consent document is presented in a manner that is inaccessible to the participant and serves more to "protect" the researcher and their institution than the participants to the research. The assurance of confidentiality and data security were instrumental to accessing authentic data and thus were key elements of what was included in the consent.

Decision making regarding inclusion of participants is also key. While there were several teachers in the study who would have and wanted to provide information and perspective, the researcher determined that these possible informants were "different" from those targeted and could have been possibly too inexperienced to offer a perspective that was likely to be useful to the inquiry. While this decision may have been in error (it is a "testable question"), the researcher chose to suffer the possibility of a "false

Qualitative Research With Diverse and Underserved Communities, pages 345–355
Copyright © 2024 by Information Age Publishing
www.infoagepub.com
All rights of reproduction in any form reserved.

negative" rather than risk a "false positive." This is often a critical decision for researchers and one all too often, neglected or ignored. The notion of false positive or negative reflects the reality of the near impossibility of completely and accurately demarcating a demographic or experiential category. This is based on the notion that real human experience is continuous rather than a collection of discrete episodes.

Finally, this research demonstration is illustrative of the important idea of organizational review. It is essential that researchers do not take upon themselves solely the responsibility for oversight for research projects. The possibility of conflict of interest always looms large and the limited perspective may constrain the researcher from identifying risk to participants that others may more easily discern. This is a crucial point given the nature of the work or social scientists who may believe that their exploration of human experience is at worst intrusive but certainly, never poses a risk. Even in instances where research is deemed to be "nonregulated," it is good practice for researchers to request a review from a "disinterested" colleague to ensure the rights and welfare of participants are respected and protected.

CASE STUDY 21

A PHENOMENOLOGICAL CASE STUDY ON LEADERSHIP OPPORTUNITIES FOR STUDENTS WITH DISABILITIES

Tan King Lok
University of Malaya, Malaysia

Donnie Adams
University of Malaya, Malaysia

Student leadership has been studied globally especially in the area extracurricular activities (Hancock & Jones, 2012). These activities are pivotal for students' holistic growth and development where vital skills such as teamwork (Kaselman et al., 2015; Simonsen et al., 2014), socializing (Van De Valk, 2008), critical thinking as well as time and conflict management (Amirianzadeh, 2012) are cultivated. Thus, Chapman et al. (2011) postulated that student leadership in extracurricular activities should involve a whole-school approach. Adams, Harris, and Jones (2017) adds to this by

Qualitative Research With Diverse and Underserved Communities, pages 347–355
Copyright © 2024 by Information Age Publishing
www.infoagepub.com
All rights of reproduction in any form reserved.

suggesting the inclusion of students with disabilities as a collective school approach towards social inclusion.

Consequently, leadership opportunities for students with disabilities have gained increased recognition in the 21st century (Carter et al., 2011; Coffey & Lavery, 2017; Klisz, 2014). Scholars observed that apart from developing friendships and relationships with their non-diagnosed peers, students with disabilities who participate in co-curriculum activities were able to develop their physical health, most importantly their leadership skills (Adams, Harris, & Jones, 2017; King et al., 2003).

MALAYSIAN CONTEXT

In Malaysia, students with disabilities are commonly segregated from their non-diagnosed peers in classrooms (Solish, Perry, & Minnes, 2010; Adams, 2017). This stagnates the country's National Education Philosophy's vision that "every student will have knowledge, thinking skills, leadership skills, bilingual proficiency, ethics and spirituality and national identity" (Ministry of Education, 2013, p. 67).

Unfortunately, the lack of opportunities for students with disabilities to lead in co-curriculum activities has become a common occurrence in schools. Teachers' resistance towards social inclusion (Bennett, Wells & Rank, 2009), their scepticism on the benefits of leadership experiences for students with disabilities (Black et al., 2014), the limited opportunities in leadership programmes (Hauerwas & Mahon, 2017), and the perceptions of the society (Hauerwas & Mahon, 2017) are among the many challenges faced by students with disabilities to nurture their leadership potential.

The Malaysia Education Blueprint (2013) outlines that schools encourage the inclusion and participation of students with disabilities in co-curriculum activities, and yet there are often barriers or factors that restrict participation and accessibility to these activities. Therefore, the belief of equality for students with disabilities remains questionable in Malaysian schools even as it aims towards a more inclusive society (Adams, 2017; Chapman et al., 2011).

Klisz (2014) posits that a supportive school environment helps in nurturing the leadership potential for students with disabilities. Above all, the support and encouragement of the school leader and teachers are the most vital factors (Coffey & Lavery, 2017; Duong, Wu, & Hoang, 2019; Hancock et al., 2012). Therefore, school leaders and teachers are encouraged to plan for providing opportunities for students with disabilities to participate and lead in co-curricular activities (Adams, 2017; Lieberman, Arndt, & Daggett, 2007).

As a contribution to building a more substantial knowledge base on underrepresented, marginalized and/or disadvantaged community in

Malaysia, this chapter reports the application of a phenomenological case study approach to explore the lived experiences of the vice principal in special education and teachers in providing leadership opportunities for students with disabilities. The study intends to answer the following research question: What are the leadership experiences and opportunities in co-curriculum activities for students with disabilities in a selected school in Malaysia?

POPULATION AND LOCATION

The school selected for this study is a high school that offers the Special Education Integration Program (SEIP) for students with different types of disabilities. The school has a population of 83 students with disabilities and 12 teachers with special education qualification and training. Located in Kuala Lumpur, several students in this school compete in international sports games representing Malaysia. They are renowned athletes with recent achievements in winning gold medals at the recent 2019 Special Olympics World Games in Abu Dhabi, United Arab Emirates.

In addition, the coaches for these athletes were also the vice principal and teachers. Therefore, they were targeted as the population of interest in order to explore their lived experiences in coaching and providing leadership opportunities for students with disabilities in this school. Table 21.1 demonstrates the summary of the interviewees' demographic background.

METHODOLOGY

Phenomenological Case Study

A myriad of heterogeneous frameworks and approaches can be chosen when designing a qualitative study. Creswell and Poth (2017) observed that over the years, qualitative frameworks or approaches are found across

TABLE 21.1 Profile of the Interviewees

Interviewees	Years of teaching experience in current school	Highest academic qualification	Gender
VP	8	Master's Degree	Male
T1	9	Bachelor's Degree	Female
T2	3	Bachelor's Degree	Female
T3	3	Bachelor's Degree	Female
T4	3	Master's Degree	Male

social, behavioural and health science literature and the approaches that commonly surface are Narrative Research, Phenomenology, Grounded Theory, Ethnography and Case Study. However, the approaches may not be holistically, theoretically, or methodologically describe a given study as certain studies evolve in parallel and partly in sequence (Flick, 2018). Denzin and Lincoln (2018) claimed that qualitative research is a field of inquiry that can crosscut different disciplines, fields, geographical location, subject matter, and the variation of the research context affects each study differently. The definition of qualitative research is relative depending on the approaches decided by the qualitative researchers (Creswell & Poth, 2017; Flick, 2018; Ritchie et al., 2013; Yin, 2017).

The research design of a qualitative study is to "understand, explore and detail the complex understanding of a contemporary issue" (Creswell & Poth, 2017, p. 45). This study begins as a specific case, a specific case that will be described and analyzed as it focused on the perception of school vice principal in special education and special education teachers. While this study intends to determine the phenomenon in depth, and within its real-world context itt has yet to be clearly evident as a 'case study' (Yin, 2017), in this case, 'phenomenology' is combined with the 'case study' approach to explore undisclosed knowledge of reflection, perception, consciousness and expression (Merleau-Ponty, 1962; 2012). Therefore, phenomenological case study was selected to "uncover" the lived experiences of the vice principal in special education and teachers in providing leadership opportunities for students with disabilities.

According to Crawford (2016), phenomenological case study is an advantageous approach to understand human experience (i.e., teachers providing leadership opportunities and coaching students with disabilities) based on the perspective of the participants (school vice principal in special education and special education teachers). The data collected will offer rich, descriptive knowledge to the field of study, and this will disclose new knowledge and practical understanding of the phenomenon realistically (Adams & van Manen, 2017). Phenomenological case study was utilized to explore the lived experiences (Ferm Almqvist & Christophersen, 2017; Mourlam, De Jong, Shudak, & Baron, 2019) of the vice principal in special education and teachers in providing leadership opportunities for students with disabilities.

Research Procedure

The execution of this study began with the insights presented in Klisz's study (2014), conducted in the Midwest US. In this study, the scholar proffers that little research exists on inclusion for students with disabilities, especially the participation of these students in extracurricular activities, not to mention leadership opportunities. , his study intended to explore the topic in the Malaysian context. Considering the cultural and demographical differences, this topic is hardly discussed in the literature. Therefore, a literature review was conducted in reputable databases such as Scopus and Web of Sciences to identify relevant studies on student leadership development, student leadership challenges, student leadership opportunities, challenges of students with disabilities in school, extracurricular activities, and challenges of students in extracurricular activities.

Discovering relevant literature helped to formulate the research questions and research objectives of this study. Next, a semi-structured interview protocol was formulated. The protocol is important to allow participants provide a fresh commentary (Creswell & Poth, 2017) on the problem investigated. A set of open-ended questions was crafted in the interview protocol to explore the experiences of the vice principal in special education and teachers on providing leadership opportunities for students with disabilities in co-curriculum activities.

The interview protocol consists of a total number of 29 questions and the questions were divided into 4 major sections: (a) Section A: Demographic Background; (b) Section B: Leadership opportunities for students with disabilities in co-curriculum activities; (c) Section C: The challenges faced by students with disabilities in leading co-curriculum activities; (d) Section D: Suggestions to improve the leadership development of students with disabilities in leading co-curriculum activities. Under the four major sections, substantive questions were formulated, followed by a set of research sub-questions in each of the sections were phrased to be answered by the interviewees.

Prior to the data collection, a pilot test of the interview protocol was conducted with an experienced vice principal in special education and a special education teacher to refine the interview protocol and to prepare for the actual data collection process (Creswell & Poth, 2017; Yin, 2017). To ensure the highest standard of research ethics (Yin, 2017), permission was obtained from the university to conduct the pilot study. A pilot study is conducted to ensure the interview protocol is easily understood and the questions are answerable. We further refined the interview protocol after piloting the interview protocol. After which, permission was obtained from the Malaysian Ministry of Education (MoE) to conduct the actual research.

the procedures suggested by Creswell and Poth (2017) were followed to ensure credibility. . Consent from participants for recording the interviews were obtained before recording.. They were also informed and acknowledged that the interview was voluntary. Therefore, they were free to share any information, and it would not be shared with any unauthorized third party. All interviewees signed the interview consent form as evidence of their acknowledgement and consent.

Guaranteeing the confidentiality and anonymity of their identity and that information shared would be secured was intended to keep them comfortable when answering the questions during the interview sessions. Each of the interview sessions was conducted in a distraction-free but visible location within the school areato prevent any possibility of misconduct during the interview sessions. Before the interview began, the interviewees were provided a choice of being interviewed in *Bahasa Malaysia* or English as this step allowed the interviewers to express their thoughts and perception precisely (Yin, 2017). The interviewees agreed to the roughly 50 minute interviewsthrough the medium of Malay language. Most interviewees find that language more helpful for expressing their views and experiences.

Data Analysis

The process of data analysis involves equating and organising data, conducting preliminary read-through of the database, coding and organising themes and forming the representation of the data interpretation (Creswell & Poth, 2017). First, a group of native Malay language speakers with good competency in English translated and transcribed the audio collected, which was in Malay language into English. To ensure the transcripts were accurately translated and transcribed, the transcripts were verified bythe participants through the pre-agreed communication channel, *WhatsApp Messenger.*

Information that might harm the interviewees are not disclosed to conform to ethical issues. Hence, this study developed a set of labels to represent each interviewee (Creswell & Poth, 2017; Wolcott, 1990). Table 21.2 indicates the representation of each interviewee.

A thematic analysis approach was selected to analyse the data in this study. A constant comparative analysis (Glaser & Strauss, 1965) was utilised to generate codes and form key themes. Next, all code labels were reviewed again and reduced by merging similar or overlapping codes.

Finally, a qualitative data analysis software ATLAS.ti™ was utilized to code and and generate emergent themes. To achieve trustworthiness of the findings, accepted standards for this research design were applied to the

TABLE 21.2 Interviewees Labels	
Interviewees	**Labels**
Vice principal in Special Education	VP
Special Education Teacher 1	T1
Special Education Teacher 2	T2
Special Education Teacher 3	T3
Special Education Teacher 4	T4

analysis process followed by inquiry audit, which was conducted to establish dependability (Lincoln & Guba, 2000).

CHALLENGES

The data collection stage presented few challenges. Several passionate special education teachers who were interested to provide their views were not selected for this study as they did not have enough teaching experiences in the school. They confessed that they are new to the school, have less than 3 years of teaching experiences and it was decided they could not contribute rich information due to limited participation in the school activities.

SUMMARY OF RESEARCH FINDINGS

This section summarizes the findings of this study. Two emerging themes emerged from the study. The vice principal and teachers shared students with disabilities were provided with leadership opportunities such as leading a group during the extracurricular activities. These students were also provided many opportunities to perform tasks and responsibilities. However, the opportunities are available for them was based on the classes and activities in which they participated. These findings suggest that students with disabilities are highly encouraged and supported to lead in co-curriculum activities as a group leader, especially the uniform body scouts in this context. A leadership position in clubs, societies and uniform bodies could aid develop their leadership potential. Students were also assigned tasks and responsibilities. In this way, they could be trained to be responsible which is an important component in their leadership practices.

RECOMMENDATIONS

This study contributes to the knowledge base on underrepresented, marginalized and/or disadvantaged community in Malaysia. It reports the application of a phenomenological case study approach to explore the lived experiences of the vice principal in special education and teachers in providing leadership opportunities for students with disabilities. Findings of this study provides valuable insights to several parties, namely: policy makers, special education teachers, schools, parents, and the community. The findings of this study are presented as a preliminary finding to develop a more inclusive society.

Future studies may consider articulating the leadership development of students with disabilities in extracurricular activities or other leadership development activities, in the context of primary schools and universities; and how leadership opportunities impact their future career or the relevance between leadership opportunities and the career transition. As the nature of this study is limited, it is also highly encouraged to explore views of student leaders with disabilities on the opportunities to access and experience leadership in extracurricular or other development activities.

REFERENCES

Adams, C., & van Manen, M. A. (2017). Teaching phenomenological research and writing. *Qualitative Health Research, 27*(6), 780–791.

Adams, D. (2017). *The effectiveness of the buddy support system in special education in Malaysia.* Paper presented at SEAMEO SEN ICSE 2017 (2nd International Conference on Special Education), Sarawak, Malaysia. Retrieved from https://publication.seameosen.org/pdf/icse/2017/A15.03.pdf

Adams, D., Harris, A., & Jones, M. S. (2017). Exploring teachers' and parents' perceptions on social inclusion practices in Malaysia. *Pertanika Journal of Social Science and Humanities, 25*(4), 1721–1737.

Adams, D., Semaadderi, P., & Tan, K. L. (2019). Student leadership and development: A panoramic view of trends and possibilities. *International Online Journal of Educational Leadership, 2*(2), 1–3.

Carter, E. W., Swedeen, B., Walter, M. J., Moss, C. K., & Hsin, C. T. (2011). Perspectives of young adults with disabilities on leadership. *Career Development for Exceptional Individuals, 34*(1), 57–67.

Chapman, C., Ainscow, M., Miles, S., & West, M. (2011). *Leadership that promotes the achievement of students with special educational needs and disabilities: A review of literature.* National College for School Leadership.

Coffey, A., & Lavery, S. (2017). Student leadership in the middle years: A matter of concern. *Improving Schools, 21*(2), 187–200.

Glesne, C. (2016). *Becoming qualitative researchers: An introduction.* Pearson.

Hancock, D., Dyk, P. H., & Jones, K. (2012). Adolescent involvement in extracurricular activities: Influences on leadership skills. *Journal of Leadership Education, 11*(1), 84–101.

Imada, D., Doyle, B. A., Brock, B., & Goddard, A. (2002). Developing leadership skills in students with mild disabilities. *Teaching Exceptional Children, 35*(1), 48–54.

Jelas, Z. M., & Mohd Ali, M. (2014). Inclusive education in Malaysia: Policy and practice. *International Journal of Inclusive Education, 18*(10), 991–1003.

Klisz, T. A. (2014). *Disability and access: Leadership opportunities for students with disabilities in high school* (Seniors Honours Theses). Eastern Michigan University.

Meijer, C. J., & Watkins, A. (2019). Financing special needs and inclusive education from Salamanca to the present. *International Journal of Inclusive Education,* 1–17.

Lee, L. W., & Low, H. M. (2013). 'Unconscious' inclusion of students with learning disabilities in a Malaysian mainstream primary school: Teachers' perspectives. *Journal of Research in Special Educational Needs, 13*(3), 218–228.

Plano Clark, V. L., & Creswell, J. W. (2015). *Understanding research: A consumer's guide,* (2nd ed.). Pearson Education.

Yeo, L. S., Chong, W. H., Neihart, M. F., & Huan, V. S. (2016). Teachers' experience with inclusive education in Singapore. *Asia Pacific Journal of Education, 36*(1), 69–83.

INTRODUCTION TO CASE STUDY 22

The author explored the intersections of two high school math teachers' identities as math teachers and as gay and lesbian individuals using a case study approach and material from his dissertation. The author's main goal was to demonstrate how the participants' leadership characteristics affected inclusivity and their role modeling in the classroom.

This original method of incorporating the case study technique is one tactic that offers a thorough, all-encompassing understanding of an often complex subject in its actual context. In this instance, the author believed that underrepresented students might envision themselves working in mathematics-related fields when they observed underrepresented adults in teaching jobs. In this case study, the demographic of interest was math teachers, who seemed to include queer theory to show an understanding of the binary concepts that aren't frequently connected to arithmetic. By emphasizing their identities and classrooms, this case study further adds to the experience of gay and lesbian math instructors in high school. Furthermore, it should be mentioned that even if the participants identify as gay and lesbian, they serve as role models.

Qualitative Research With Diverse and Underserved Communities, pages 357–367
Copyright © 2024 by Information Age Publishing
www.infoagepub.com

CASE STUDY 22

A GAY MATHEMATICS TEACHER AND A LESBIAN MATHEMATICS TEACHER EACH WALK INTO THEIR CLASSROOM

An Exploration of a Case Study

Kyle S. Whipple
University of Wisconsin, Eau Clair

ABSTRACT

The following is comprised of excerpts of a dissertation in which the research-er utilized the methodology of case study while investigating the intersection-ality of mathematics teacher identity with gay and lesbian identity in two high school mathematics teachers. The purpose of this condensed version is to provide insights into the inner workings of the case study methodology.

Qualitative Research With Diverse and Underserved Communities, pages 359–367
Copyright © 2024 by Information Age Publishing
www.infoagepub.com
359

CONTEXT FOR THE INQUIRY

Mathematics fields are traditionally dominated by white, heterosexual, cis-gendered males (Hill, 2009), and education is a field dominated by white, heterosexual, cisgendered females (Gray et al., 2013). Because of this combination, few racially and sexuality marginalized youths see themselves represented in mathematics classrooms (Sapon-Shevin, 2004). The struggle for LGBTQ+ students in public schools can be eased with teachers, counselors, and staff who create a sense of community through Gender and Sexualities Alliance (GSA) clubs and other organizations that celebrate LGBTQ+ students' identities (Wimberly et al., 2015). LGBTQ+ mathematics educators who are out with their identities in their school districts can help create a bridge for LGBTQ+ students to a mathematics related degree and employment. In order for LGBTQ+ mathematics educators to support LGBTQ+ learners, LGBTQ+ mathematics educators need to find ways to share and discuss their own LGBTQ+ identities, and the sharing of LGBTQ+ identities in a heteronormalized institution such as a school is fraught with challenges and the possibility of being labeled as a social outcast.

FOCUS FOR THE INQUIRY

This study aims to address the following questions: (a) how does the intersection of LGBTQ+ identity and mathematics identity impact secondary mathematics teachers' abilities to create inclusive spaces in their schools? and (b) how do out LGBTQ+ secondary mathematics teachers accept their duty to serve as role models for all students?

CASES

The participants are two high school mathematics teachers who are out with their gay and lesbian identities in their schools. Using my personal knowledge of secondary LGBTQ+ mathematics educators and my resources through online groups such as the Trans Teacher Network, the American Educational Research Association (AERA) Queer Studies Special Interest Group, and the LGBTQ+ Research and Researchers Facebook group, I issued a call for participants who live in the Midwest. There were five initial responses and out of those responses, I purposefully selected two teachers for the case study, Brayden and Wendy (pseudonyms). These participants were chosen by their willingness to participate in the data collection and their proximity to my location.

CONDITIONS

In the review of the literature, there is a gap in studies concerning secondary LGBTQ+ mathematics teachers. Queer pedagogy has only weakly been implemented in mathematics courses and creating inclusive curricula that covers higher order mathematical thinking is an important part of giving LGBTQ+ students access to career success. Racially marginalized teachers have been considered in the context of their mathematics identity and their ability to serve as role models; yet, the same has not been done for LGBTQ+ mathematics teachers. This study aims to investigate secondary LGBTQ+ mathematics teachers in the areas of identity, inclusion, and serving as role models.

METHODOLOGY

This case study followed the methodology proposed by Yin (2014) with the teacher as the unit of analysis. To create triangulation, I collected data from multiple sources: audio recorded interviews, observations, field notes, and digital photos of artifacts from the classrooms of the participants. Yin is particularly useful for my work as he argues against the dichotomization of quantitative and qualitative research methods (Yazan, 2015), which is a strong connection to the queer theory framework. I chose the method of case study as it allowed me to conduct in-depth research into two LGBTQ+ mathematics teachers and to describe their identities, and in particular their leading identities in their mathematics classrooms, and how those identities impact inclusion and serving as classroom role models (Black et al., 2010). Spending significant time in the teachers' classrooms allowed me to witness the two mathematics teachers in their school context.

PROCESS

The case study consisted of data collection from two high school mathematics educators who are out with their gay and lesbian identities in their schools. The data collection took place over two 8-week periods of the fall semester; the first portion of the semester I worked with Brayden and the second portion of the semester I worked with Wendy. The two participants gave an audio-recorded pre-observation interview and a post-observation interview, each with open-ended questions. The interviews were semi-structured to allow for a free exchange of ideas and a conversational style discourse. The pre-interviews helped establish the mathematics identities of the teachers and their perceived levels of inclusion; while the post-interviews allowed me to gain explicit details into noticings I made during the observations. Along with the interviews, there were classroom observations and detailed field notes for each session. There were also reflections by the researcher following each observation and digital photos of artifacts from the classrooms. All of the evidence was collected with the goal of understanding the gay and lesbian identities and the mathematics identities of each of the teachers, as well as how each teacher incorporated inclusion into the classroom and the positionality of the teacher as a role model for LGBTQ+ students.

At the time of this study, Brayden identified himself as a gay, cisgendered white man. He had been teaching secondary mathematics in public schools for 4 years, 3 of those in his current school. He had a bachelor's degree in mathematics and a master's degree in education. The high school in which Brayden taught at the time of the study could be described as third-ring suburban, approximately 30 miles from a large urban area, and had approximately 900 students.

At the time of the study, Wendy identified herself as a lesbian, cisgendered white woman. She had been teaching secondary mathematics in private schools for 14 years, 10 in her current secular school. She had a bachelor's degree in mathematics and a master's degree in mathematics education. The school where Wendy taught was located in a large urban center in the Midwest and served approximately 500 students.

ANALYSIS

The analysis of the data consisted of transcribing the interview responses, which were used in conjunction with the classroom observations, field notes including photos of the physical space, and reflections. I conducted iterative open coding (Patton, 2015). The process was inductive with the intention of finding patterns and solidifying or adjusting the importance of patterns with each iteration. Overall, I was interested in obtaining concrete examples of the intersectionality of LGBTQ+ identity and secondary mathematics teacher identity. I also highlighted each teacher's ability to serve as a role model and implement inclusive curriculum and pedagogy.

During the observations, I used field notes to detail the school environment, including the actions of the teachers, the people involved in the school, and the physical space. I paid special attention and noted the material presented and the interactions of the teacher with students. In particular, I focused on the type of identity the teacher was performing through their actions and decisions in their respective high school mathematics classrooms. The narrative of teacher determined the leading identity for a particular time in the classroom; for example, if the teacher was presenting an example, then the problem, along with the discussion with the students, were used to conclude the leading identity. In case of contradictions, such as the physical placement of Safe Zone stickers, I highlighted that as a key finding with an opportunity for further analysis.

While transcribing the interviews, I kept track of responses relevant to the research questions through highlights with comments. Using these highlighted notations, I created a list of 49 original codes. As I created each code, I noted the timestamp of the transcription from which the code originated. I then used a slideshow program to create a platform in which it would be easy to move the codes. I began with ten slides—nine slides each contained five codes, and one slide contained four—which were placed in chronological order of appearance in the transcripts. I then grouped the codes together into like bundles based on the topics of the codes. Using this method, I was able to create five different bundles. Next, I looked through each bundle and was able to create three final themes from the original 49 codes: mathematics teacher identity, LGBTQ+ identity, and school environment as it pertains to both the building and mathematics classrooms. Once I had the three themes, I organized the codes into groups within each theme based on commonalities. In the mathematics teacher identity theme, there were nine codes related to teacher identity and four codes related to mathematics identity. In the LGBTQ+ teacher identity theme, there were eight codes related to LGBTQ+ identity as it pertains to the self and six codes related to LGBTQ+ identity as it pertains to others. Finally, in the school environment theme, there were 14 codes related to the environment of the building and eight codes related to the environment of the classroom.

CHALLENGES

Finding participants was challenging. The intersection of the identities of mathematics teacher and out LGBTQ+ do not have a large population, so finding willing participants who also would be close enough in proximity to observe took time. There were five potential participants and of those, Braydon and Wendy were willing. Brayden taught in a school district approximately 7 hours from my location, so I had to arrange for housing accommodations during the data collection period. Wendy was located in the same urban area as me. Both teachers agree to allow me to enter their classrooms and observe at will, so reaching saturation for data collection within their classrooms was possible. However, finding mathematics teachers all along the LGBTQ+ spectrum was not.

FINDINGS

This research revealed striking similarities between the teaching styles of Brayden and Wendy, including their curriculum development and pedagogical approaches to inclusion. From the findings in this research, I define pedagogical inclusion in classrooms to be demonstrated when teachers use discourses and interactions to create an atmosphere where students are seen as an integral part of the learning process and are free to make mistakes as they work through mathematics problems. Both teachers believed their gay or lesbian identity was a part of who they were as individuals, but their mathematics teacher identity really drove the curricular decisions they made. During curriculum writing, both teachers had mathematics teacher as their leading identity. However, when it came to pedagogy and social interactions, both teachers had their gay or lesbian identity as their leading identity and created inclusive and welcoming mathematics classrooms. As mathematics teachers, Brayden and Wendy both acted as role models for all students.

Despite the strong gay and lesbian identities of the two teachers, the mathematics teacher identities emerged from the data to be the focal point of Brayden's and Wendy's identities. They showed this strong identity through their eagerness to emphasize how much time and effort they put into creating inclusive mathematics curricula in mathematics content areas that more organically had opportunities for inclusive pedagogies. Brayden and Wendy felt their curricula on statistics concepts were better suited for inclusion through problem contexts and questions. While teaching statistics concepts, both teachers used data sets that conveyed inclusion and diversity issues central to answering the problems. Furthermore, these problems in statistics furthered students' understanding of how data and statistical analysis aided in critical discourses belonging to inclusion and diversity. Brayden showed in statistics students could be encouraged to choose project topics based on their lived experiences. For example, he had a student complete a linear regression project using the number of followers on Instagram and the winner of *Ru Paul's Drag Race*. He also included a problem where students completed a statistical analysis on the number of people of color pulled over for traffic violations near the school. One statistics problem I observed Wendy use in her class was based on the number of Confederate Statues erected in a given year and how those years related to the time of the Civil War. The students quickly noticed that the highest number of statues were erected during the Jim Crow era.

However, both teachers admitted that they struggled to connect mathematics teaching and learning to LGBTQ+ people in Algebra II. Brayden wrote his curriculum for Dual Credit College Algebra without extensive inclusion and for Wendy, the same was true for AP Calculus BC. Neither teacher was able to find the balance between covering the appropriate mathematics material and creating relevant problems that incorporated inclusion of LGBTQ+ experiences in their courses outside of statistics. Therefore, in the broader curricular contexts, both Brayden and Wendy were intentionally challenging the official curriculum (Apple, 1993) by brining gay and lesbian contexts into statistics. Apple (1979, 1993) argues that curricula are documents generated by people in power and those curricula perpetuate dominant cultural views. The marginalization of LGBTQ+ issues in mathematics curricula is not just a matter of not finding an organic connection to mathematics problems, but is part of a larger discriminatory culture of the dominant group. I argue that without deliberate attempts by Brayden and Wendy to challenge the dominant narrative of mathematics culture, gay and lesbian issues would not have become parts of their mathematics pedagogy, curricula, and learning environment. These findings suggest that more mathematics teachers, especially LGBTQ+ identified, deliberately need to include marginalized experiences of LGBTQ+ people in the written mathematics curricula, and in the implemented curricula to recognize the LGBTQ+ culture.

Brayden and Wendy considered themselves role models for all of their students, including both cisgendered heterosexuals and those on the LGBTQ+ spectrum. The teachers believed by being open with their gay and lesbian identities and through their sponsorship of extracurricular activities, students would see them as role models. Given the findings in research on the importance of both race and gender of teachers and the influence on students pursuing careers in mathematics (Bottia et al., 2015; McCray et al., 2002), Brayden and Wendy serving as role models for LGBTQ+ mathematics students could potentially lead to more LGBTQ+ students interested in mathematics or mathematics-related degrees in college. However, some studies have shown the limitations of role model theory for underrepresented groups, including women and people of color. For example, in a study of influence of male and female role models Cheryan and colleagues (2011) found that the female role models did not have significant influence on female students' aspirations and beliefs in success in STEM fields. Similarly, another study (Carrington et al., 2008) found a teacher's gender had hardly any impact on mathematics performance or attitude towards mathematics. Therefore, there is a cautionary note as to the extent of the positive influence of role models on LGBTQ+ students' mathematics achievement or aspirations.

GROWTH AS A QUALITATIVE RESEARCHER

My ability to understand the qualitative research method developed through this study. While I spent 20 years as a mathematics teacher, I did not have significant time to watch others teach, and I had never seen another LGBTQ+ identified mathematics teacher in action. I established a deep appreciation for both Brayden and Wendy as I watched them engage their students in mathematics content. Taking time to construct a thorough analysis of their identities, use of inclusion, and willingness to serve as role models for LGBTQ+ identified students gave me a deeper understanding of their experiences as gay or lesbian mathematics teachers. Although I already knew from my years as a teacher that one observation does not paint a complete picture of a classroom, I learned that observing, collecting, and analyzing data over many weeks can.

REFERENCES

Apple, M. W. (1979). *Ideology and curriculum.* Routledge.

Apple, M. W. (1993). The politics of official knowledge: Does a national curriculum make sense? *Teachers College Record, 95,* 222–241.

Black, L., Williams, J., Hernandez-Martinez, P., Davis, P., Pampaka, M., & Wake, G. (2010). Developing a 'leading identity': The relationship between students' mathematical identities and their career and higher education aspirations. *Educational Studies in Mathematics, 73*(1), 55–72.

Bottia, M. C., Stearns, E., Mickelson, R. A., Moller, S., & Valentino, L. (2015). Growing the roots of STEM majors: Female math and science high school faculty and the participation of students in STEM. *Economics of Education Review, 45,* 14–27.

Carrington, B., Tymms, P., & Merrell, C. (2008). Role models, school improvement and the "gender gap": Do men bring out the best in boys and women the best in girls? *British Educational Research Journal, 34,* 315–327.

Cheryan, S., Siy, J. O., Vichayapai, M., Drury, B. J., & Kim, S. (2011). Do female and male role models who embody STEM stereotypes hinder women's anticipated success in STEM? *Social Psychological and Personality Science, 2,* 656–664.

Gray, L., Bitterman, A., & Goldring, R. (2013). Characteristics of public school districts in the United States: Results from the 2011–12 Schools and Staffing Survey (NCES 2013–311). U.S. Department of Education. Retrieved April 7, 2016 from http://nces.ed.gov/pubsearch

Hill, R. J. (2009). Incorporating queers: Blowback, backlash, and other responses to workplace diversity initiatives that support sexual minorities. *Advances in Developing Human Resources, 11*(1), 37–53.

McCray, A. D., Sindelar, P. T., Kilgore, K. K., & Neal, L. I. (2002). African-American women's decisions to become teachers: Sociocultural perspectives, *International Journal of Qualitative Studies in Education, 15*(3), 269–290.

Patton, M. Q. (2015). *Qualitative research & evaluation methods.* Sage Publications, Inc.

Sapon-Shevin, M. (2004). Being out, being silent, being strategic: Troubling the difference, *Journal of Gay & Lesbian Issues in Education, 2*(2), 73–77.

Wimberly, G. L., Wilkinson, L., & Pearson, J. (2015). LGBTQ student achievement and educational attainment. In G. L. Wimberly (Ed.), *LGBTQ issues in education: Advancing a research agenda* (pp. 121–139). American Educational Research Association.

Yazan, B. (2015). Three approaches to case study methods in education: Yin, Merriam, and Stake. *The Qualitative Report, 20*(2), 134–152.

Yin, R. K. (2014). *Case study research: Design and methods, 5th edition.* Sage Publications.

ABOUT THE EDITORS

Jeton McClinton holds a PhD in community college leadership and has served as an educational leadership faculty member for 15 plus years at Jackson State University. She teaches courses in research design and qualitative research methods. Dr. McClinton has published numerous journal articles on the recruitment and preparation of teachers. She has a strong higher-education leadership background, having worked with traditional and nontraditional students. She also holds significant academic scholarship credentials with research experience in educational technology, leadership development, and distance education. The synergy between these areas helps profile Dr. McClinton as an innovator—highly driven and committed to quality and growth in her workplace. She has served as editor, coeditor, and/or author of three books *Infusing Undergraduate Research Into Historically Black Colleges and Universities Curricula* (Emerald Publishing, 2015), *Dyslexia Is Not a Disease—It's a Learning Difference: Theoretical and Practical Approaches to Teaching Struggling Readers With Learning Differences* (CreateSpace Independent Publishing, 2015), and *Mentoring at Minority Serving Institutions: Theory, Design, Practice, and Impact* (Information Age Publishing, 2018).

Arthur E. Hernandez, a professor at the University of the Incarnate Word, has completed advanced study in educational psychology, clinical psychology, and curriculum and instruction. He is a nationally certified school psychologist, nationally certified counselor, and a diplomate of the American Board of Psychological Specialties. He served as a member and chair of the Texas Board of Examiners of Psychologists and has held both academic and

Qualitative Research With Diverse and Underserved Communities , pages 369–370
Copyright © 2024 by Information Age Publishing
www.infoagepub.com

research appointments. In addition to serving as director of the American Evaluation Association's Minority Serving Institutions program, he serves as mentor and on the advisory board for the Leaders in the Equitable Evaluation and Development (LEEAD) initiative and has recently completed his term on the RISE Advisory Board—a field advancement effort that aims to better understand and strategically improve the lives and outcomes of boys and men of color in the United States. He is also currently appointed to the Joint Committee on Standards for Educational Evaluation—an international coalition of professional organizations concerned with the quality of evaluation inquiry.

Alma L. Thornton is a professor in the dxecutive PhD program at Jackson State University where she serves as the qualitative methodologist. Her career spans more than 30 years of experience, developing and implementing applied qualitative research. She has served as chairperson of the Department of Sociology and director of the Center for Social Research at Southern University and A&M College, and guest editor of the *Journal of Race, Gender, and Class*. In 2012, Dr. Thornton was named the Louisiana Legislative Researcher of the Year as a result of her cumulative research in the areas of nutrition and food insecurity, workforce development, housing, alcohol and other drug abuse, and HIV/AIDS. More recent qualitative studies include the investigation of community engagement and perceptions of policing.

ABOUT THE CONTRIBUTORS

Sarah Abusaa is a PhD student in epidemiology at the University of California, Davis. She studies how the ecology of recently introduced mosquito populations in the California Central Valley influences human-vector interactions and the implications for potential disease transmission. Her interests include population ecology, data visualization, critically examining scientific histories, infectious disease epidemiology, and public health. Sarah works on curriculum development and program evaluation for Girls Outdoor Adventures in Leadership and Science (GOALS). She is devoted to constructing accessible and uplifting spaces for scientific study that confront and break down institutional legacies of racism and colonialism in STEM fields, influenced in part by her experiences as a queer BIPOC scientist. She joined GOALS as someone working for such spaces to exist for future generations of scientists and outdoor enthusiasts.

Donnie Adams is a senior lecturer at Department of Educational Management, Planning and Policy, Faculty of Education, University of Malaya. He obtained his PhD in educational leadership from the University of Malaya. He is a recipient of the University of Malaya's Bright Sparks scholarship and a recipient of University of Malaya's Excellence Award 2016: PhD Completion in Less than 3 Years. He is actively involved in research and development work towards the area of leadership in special educational needs and school-wide reformation of inclusive education agenda in Malaysia.

Qualitative Research With Diverse and Underserved Communities, pages 371–385
Copyright © 2024 by Information Age Publishing
www.infoagepub.com
371

Afshan Amjad has teaching experience both in Canada and internationally at various levels. Currently, she is working as an instructor at Norquest College, Edmonton. She previously worked as an assistant professor at Aga Khan University, Karachi, Pakistan where she was involved in development and research projects. She completed her PhD in early childhood education at the University of Alberta, investigating Muslim school students' classroom experiences in a large urban area in Western Canada. Her doctoral research was funded by the Social Sciences and Humanities Research Council (SSHRC) of Canada. Her current research interests include school experiences of immigrant children, multiculturalism, diversity, race, and racism. She has published articles on immigrant children's school experiences with special focus on their over-referral for special needs classes due to cultural, religious, and linguistic differences. The unique school experiences of Muslim immigrant children in Canada is another area of interest.

Jessica Darnell Brazell-Brayboy, PhD, began her career in higher education after a transformative period of work in conflict zones in Africa. Her work has focused on developing equitable international partnerships for development and education, the values and benefits of civic and community engagement, and building equitable student affairs processes and policy to cultivate vibrant and inclusive campus culture. Jessica is a proud 9th generation mulatto American and the namesake of Darnell Rosa Leroy Brayboy Brazell Hornsby. She completed her doctoral studies at Loyola University Chicago in Higher Education in 2015.

Loyce Caruthers, PhD, is professor of educational leadership, policy, and foundations at the University of Missouri–Kansas City. She teaches courses related to educational administration and qualitative research. She also serves as coordinator of the educational doctorate program in PK–12 educational administration. Her previous professional experience includes middle school teacher, staff developer, special projects coordinator, and assistant superintendent of curriculum and instruction. Loyce also served as a director of educational equity, which involved the development and implementation of program initiatives to support school desegregation. Loyce's research involves the use of voice through narrative and critical race theory for exploring phenomena related to race, class, language or national origin, gender and other differences that may influence educators' beliefs and perceptions, and ultimately their work in schools. Recent publications include an edited book, *Womanish Black Girls/Women Resisting the Contradictions of Silence and Voice*, which received the 2019 Critics Choice from the American Education Studies Association and 2020 Society of Professors of Education Outstanding Book Award, as well as the co-authored book, *Great Expectations: What Kids Want From Our Urban Public Schools* (Information Age Publishing, 2016) with a forward by Gloria Ladson-Billings.

Her recent publications have appeared in the *Journal of Urban Learning, Teaching, and Research; Journal of Black Studies; Urban Education; The Journal of Negro Education;* and *Educational Studies.*

Kwanza A. Cogdell MAT, EdD, holds a bachelor's degree in finance, a master's degree in the art of teaching and a doctorate in educational leadership. In addition, she holds a K–6 Level II teaching certification and pre-K–12 Principal Certification. Dr. Waters has owned and operated an early childhood center and preschool as well as taught in kindergarten, 2nd grade, 3rd grade, and 4th grade. Ms. Waters has also taught GED and SAT prep courses, was a K–8 instructional coach and a K–8 assistant principal at Lindley Academy Charter School, a place she refers to as "home." She currently serves as the high school principal at Tacony Academy. However, her most important accomplishment of all is being a mom to her four awesome children: Jada, Jordyn, Nasir, and Jaden.

Margery Covello, MBA, EdD, is the CEO of Lindley Academy Charter School, an American Paradigm School. She is a "Triple Ram" earning a BS in finance, an MBA in management, and an EdD in administration and supervision from Fordham University in New York City. Dr. Covello previously was the chief of staff at American Paradigm Schools and the director of operations at Philadelphia Performing Arts Charter School. In addition, she held a variety of positions at Fordham University including director of residential life, assistant dean in the College of Business Administration, and the director of G.L.O.B.E., Fordham University's international business program. Dr. Covello lives in Philadelphia with her husband Paul Marone and their twin daughters Lucy and Rose.

Ryan Culbertson (MA, Texas Tech University) is a research fellow at Claremont Graduate University and managing director of Metaflective Strategies, a research and evaluation firm. He has worked in PK–20 education for over 15 years as an instructor, coordinator, and director at the local, state, and national levels, with focus on underserved and low-socioeconomic status student populations. His research focuses on STEM education and opportunities in PK–12 pipeline, as well as effective program assessment and evaluation.

Jacqueline Dansby, PhD, is a retired college administrator where she served as the project director for Upward Bound at St. Mary's University. She has worked extensively with potential first-generation college students with Upward Bound. In addition, she has taught first-generation college students at the community college and university levels. Jacqueline has grant writing and grant reviewer experience and has research interests with first-generation college students, grants management, and qualitative research.

Gloria Dansby-Giles, EdD, is a professor of counselor education at Jackson State University where she is actively involved in research and serves on dissertation committees. Gloria serves on several editorial boards and serves as editor of the *Journal of Counseling and Practice*. She has research interests and published articles related to social justice and equity issues such as PTSD and women, ethical issues of counselors during the coronavirus pandemic, telemental health, trauma, and first-generation college students.

Y. Falami Devoe, PhD, is affiliate faculty in the undergraduate and individualized master's programs at Antioch University. She is a womanist scholar, arts-based educator with interdisciplinary interests at the intersections of race, class, gender, sexuality, ethnography, and pedagogy. She is passionate about Black women's voices and how critical these voices are in creating new narratives and sustainable practices of healing, liberation, and well-being. As a scholar, practitioner, she integrates mindfulness, art, poetry, storytelling, and photography in her courses and presentations.

Charney Randhawa Docherty is an assistant principal with the Calgary Board of Education in Calgary, Alberta. During her 24 years as an educator, she has taught students in diverse communities and has been an instructional coach, both at the school level, and as part of the inclusive learning team at the system level. She is passionate about working with students, educators, and families to develop inclusive learning environments in which each student is able to access quality teaching to experience success as a learner. Her goal as an educator and leader is for each student to feel that their diversity is understood and valued as a strength that they bring to their education and school community. She has worked alongside educators and has led professional development sessions to build the capacity of teachers, leaders and school support staff in meeting the diverse needs in today's classrooms. Charney has a bachelor's degree in psychology from the University of Alberta, a bachelor's degree in education from the University of Calgary, and has received her master's degree in education from the University of Alberta.

Carmen Dones, EdD, is a Latino first-generation college student who earned her terminal degree in education from California State University, Northridge. She currently serves as a community college dean of instruction, as well as a faculty member in the dental hygiene baccalaureate degree program and the bachelor's degree completion program. She is also a licensed dental hygienist in California. Dr. Dones was instrumental in transforming the dental hygiene associate degree program into a baccalaureate level program. She is student centered and dedicated to student equity and success. She serves as a mentor for Latino students striving to enter the community college bachelor's program, as well as for students in the doctorate program at her alma mater.

Alycia Drwencke is a regional dairy management specialist for Cornell Cooperative Extension. In her current role, Alycia works with dairy producers on education, research, and outreach to continually improve management within the industry. Alycia received her MS in animal biology from the University of California, Davis. Throughout her MS, Alycia studied innovative detection and abatement of heat load in dairy cows. Her professional and research goals are to promote a holistic culture of care on dairy farms for the cows, employees, and producers. Alycia has been a part of the curriculum development and program evaluation committees with Girls Outdoor Adventures in Leadership and Science (GOALS). She strives to utilize her White privilege to promote the success of underserved and underrepresented groups in STEM and the outdoors. Alycia is committed to creating systemic change that will end the perpetuation of racism and toxic narratives within society.

Katherine A. Dynarski is a postdoctoral research associate at the University of Montana. Her research focuses on interactions between plants, soils, and microbes that shape global biogeochemical cycles. Katy first became interested in equity in the outdoors and scientific spaces after working on an all-women field ecology crew as a college student made her believe that she could be a scientist. She helped launch Girls Outdoor Adventures in Leadership and Science (GOALS) while working towards her PhD in soils and biogeochemistry at UC Davis, in hopes of expanding youth access to such identity-affirming outdoor and scientific experiences. Katy is passionate about the power of spaces outside of traditional academic hegemony to support communication, collaboration, and a re-envisioning of what it means to do science (and be a scientist).

Julia Ellis, EdD, is an emerita professor in the Faculty of Education at the University of Alberta. She has contributed articles and book chapters on the topics of interpretive inquiry, interviewing, teacher as researcher, narrative inquiry with children and youth, perspectives of "difficult" students, mentorship programs for children and youth, peer support and school leadership programs, children and place, creative classroom teaching, gender issues in the classroom, and multiculturalism in the classroom. Two of her books are: *Teaching From Understanding: Teacher as Interpretive Inquirer* (Routledge, 1998) and *Caring for Kids in Communities: Using Mentorship, Peer Support, and Student Leadership Programs in Schools* (Peter Lang, 2001). She served as producer, writer, and researcher for the television broadcast video, "Listen up! Kids Talk About Good Teaching."

Rylie Ellison grew up in the woods, hiking and camping around her hometown in Washington state. She joined Girls Outdoor Adventures in Leadership and Science (GOALS) to help marginalized communities access these spaces and share in the joy of spending time in nature. She is a recent graduate of UC Davis, where she got her PhD in agricultural and environmental chemistry developing treatment methods to reduce the environmental impacts of dairy manure and make it a better fertilizer. After grad school, she wanted to take the analytical and communication skills from research and apply it in the policy sphere. She is currently starting a new job as a science and technology policy fellow at the California Council on Science and Technology where she hopes to continue using the lessons learned from GOALS in listening to and supporting marginalized communities and working towards a more equitable society.

Philomena Essed is professor of critical race, gender, and leadership studies at Antioch University's Graduate School of Leadership and Change and affiliated researcher at the University of Utrecht's, Gender Graduate Program. She holds a PhD from the University of Amsterdam and honorary doctorate degrees from the University of Pretoria (2011) and Umeå University (2015). In 2011 The Queen of the Netherlands honored her with a Knighthood. Well known for introducing the concepts of everyday racism, gendered racism, and entitlement racism she also pioneered in developing theory on social and cultural cloning. The now classical 1984 (in Dutch) *Alledaags Racisme* (English version, *Everyday Racism*, 1990 has been republished in 2018 with additional chapters. Other books include *Understanding Everyday Racism: An Interdisciplinary Theory* (SAGE Publications, 1991) and *Diversity: Gender, Color and Culture* (University of Massachusetts Press, 1996). Her most recent book (in Dutch, 2020) called *Racismekennis* (Racism Knowledge) introduces this new concept. This publication is based on an extended republication of her earlier work on *Understanding Everyday Racism.* Essed has co-edited various volumes including: Race Critical Theories (Wiley-Blackwell, 2001); *Refugees and the Transformation of Societies* (Berghahn Books, 2004); *A Companion to Gender Studies* (Wiley-Blackwell, 2009, 'outstanding' 2005 CHOICE award); *Clones, Fakes and Posthumans: Cultures of Replication* (Brill, 2012), *Dutch Racism* (Brill, 2014), and *Relating Worlds of Racism: Dehumanisation, Belonging and the Normativity of European Whiteness* (Palgrave Macmillan, 2019). Her current focus is on humiliation, dignity, and ethics of care as experience and practice in leading change.

Stephanie Fearon, PhD, is the inaugural assistant professor (tenure-track) of Black Thriving and Education at York University. Dr. Fearon's research draws on Black storytelling traditions to explore the ways that Black families and educational institutions partner to support student wellbeing. She uses literary and visual arts to communicate, in a structured, creative, and accessible form, insights gleaned from stories shared by Black mothers and their families. Dr. Fearon's extensive academic and professional experiences has led her to work with system leaders, classroom educators, and community organizations across Canada and internationally.

Jesse R. Ford, PhD, is an assistant professor of higher education in the Department of Teacher Education and Higher Education at the University of North Carolina at Greensboro. His research interests include the sociocultural influences that affect the undergraduate, graduate, and professional experiences of underrepresented populations in academia.

Jennifer Friend, PhD, is the dean of the College of Arts and Sciences, associate provost for Academic Affairs, and professor of education at Rockhurst University in Kansas City. Her 28 years of experience in education include faculty and administrative roles in educational leadership, graduate education, and assessment. She began her career in K–12 schools as a middle grades principal and language arts teacher. Dr. Friend's research focuses on educational leadership and issues of social justice in U.S. public education. She is currently collaborating on an oral history and educational website project titled, *Kansas City Speaks: Stories of School Desegregation* (see http://kcdeseg.com/). She is the co-author of the book, *Great Expectations: What Kids Want from Our Urban Public Schools* (Information Age Publishing, 2016) and co-editor of the book, *Principal 2.0: Technology and Educational Leadership* (Information Age Publishing, 2013). Recent publications also have appeared in *Urban Education*; *National Forum of Education Administration and Supervision Journal*; *Journal of Urban Learning, Teaching, and Research*; and *Educational Studies.*

Adriana D. Glenn, PhD, is an assistant professor, RN-BSN program director, and academic coach in the School of Nursing at The George Washington University in Ashburn Virginia. She has almost 30 years of experience as a family nurse practitioner and almost 15 years of experience in higher education teaching nursing students at undergraduate and graduate levels. She has extensive experience working with undergraduate students in community settings both in the United States and in Central America. The "Heart Healthy Photovoice Exhibit" was showcased at the Smithsonian's National Museum of African American History and Culture in 2018. Dr. Glenn is often sought for her expertise in qualitative methods. She maintains an active clinical practice as a nurse practitioner for the Virginia Department of Health, City of Alexandria and GWU's Student Health Center. Dr. Glenn received her PhD in nursing from George Mason University and holds a Master of Arts in education administration (focus on education leadership) from California State University, Los Angeles, a Master of Nursing in primary ambulatory care/family nurse practitioner from the University of California, Los Angeles, and a Bachelor of Science in basic nursing from Boston University.

Rebecca Godwin is an assistant professor of biology at Piedmont University. She received her PhD in entomology from the University of California, Davis. Her research centers around the taxonomy and phylogenetics of trapdoor spiders. She teaches a number of courses ranging from introductory biology to invertebrate biodiversity. Her interests include evidence-based teaching and facilitating inclusion and accessibility through universal classroom design. Rebecca joined Girls Outdoor Adventures in Leadership and Science (GOALS), working with the program evaluation committee. She is committed to increasing societal scientific literacy and creating healthy and inclusive spaces for undergraduates of underrepresented groups to experience and participate in scientific research.

Kahlí Hedrick-Romano (PhD, The University of Texas at San Antonio) is a postdoctoral researcher at Claremont Graduate University and founder of Growth Insight, an education software and data coaching firm. She has worked in public education for over 10 years, as a secondary science educator and college instructor, and as a researcher and evaluator within the context of the education non-profit and youth development sector. Her research and evaluation expertise includes both quantitative, qualitative, and mixed methods.

Elizabeth L. Holloway is a professor of psychology in the Graduate School of Leadership and Change at Antioch University. She is a fellow of the American Psychological Association and diplomate of the American Board of Professional Psychology. She has over 35 years of experience as educator, researcher, and consultant in clinical supervision, relational practice, and respectful cultures in higher education and healthcare organizations. She has conducted teaching workshops on her model of supervisory practice and building respectful workplaces throughout the world. Her teaching, writing, and research focus on qualitative methodologies for inclusion and diversity research, relational practice in teaching and learning, and leadership for respectful engagement.

Chris Jadallah is a PhD student in science and agricultural education and a National Science Foundation graduate research fellow at the University of California, Davis. In his research, Chris examines how participatory and community-based approaches to conservation science provide a forum for collective and collaborative learning between scientists, science-related professionals, and communities. While previous work investigates biodiversity conservation in diversified farming systems, his current research with young people is focused on dam removal and watershed restoration at multiple sites throughout the Western United States. Additionally, Chris works with the Girls' Outdoor Adventure in Leadership and Science (GOALS) program at UC Davis to investigate how learning spaces can best support young people from nondominant communities in leading social change through engaging in sensemaking at the intersection of gender, leadership, the outdoors, and science. His scholarship is informed by ethnographic and participatory methodologies in addition to critical and sociocultural perspectives on learning, with implications for designing learning environments that value multiple knowledge systems to advance healthy and just social-ecological systems.

Tan King Lok is currently a research assistant for a joint international research project between the University of Malaya and UNICEF. As a passionate educator and a recent master graduate, he is very active in research work. A Social Sciences Citation Index (SSCI) journal article he recently co-authored was accepted for publication.

Anna Kirova is professor of education at the University of Alberta. Her research explored the experience of childhood that has been interrupted by immigration as well as the lived experiences of immigrant children in their daily shifting between languages and cultures as they encounter the school culture in their host country. Her international work in this area has resulted in a book: Global migration and education: Schools, children, and families. Her recent research has focused on the psychosocial adaptation of Syrian refugee families with young children. She has written extensively in peer-reviewed journals on issues regarding newcomer children's peer interactions and acceptance of immigrant children, identity formation and second language learning in ESL students, and the role of teachers in helping linguistically and culturally diverse students to adjust to the school culture. She has served as education domain leader and children, family, and youth research domain leader with the Prairie Metropolis Centre of Excellence in Research on Immigration, Integration, and Diversity. In this role, she encouraged policy-relevant research that engaged issues of importance identified by immigrant settlement agencies, schools, the health care system, and the like.

Caroline Lembo, MEd, is triple-certified in English education, library science, and reading. Currently, a "Double Hawk," this Philadelphia transplant is ecstatic to begin her interdisciplinary doctoral of education leadership studies at Saint Joseph's University in Fall 2021. After being named The New Teacher Project's "Most Effective Teacher" at West Catholic Preparatory High School, she set her sights on Lindley Academy Charter School and nosedived into thousands of packaged books with many empty bookshelves. Four months later, the first-ever Lindley Library, affectionately named "Starbooks," was born. A firm believer that every student deserves a quality education, she strives to continuously inquire deeply about educational equity, cultural competency, and what truly drives student success.

Fang Liang is a doctoral candidate in the program of Learning and Cognition at the College of Education at Florida State University. Her research interests focus on second language writing anxiety and self-regulation in second language learning.

Ana K. Soltero López, PhD, is an associate professor and the coordinator of the Bilingual Authorization program (BAP) in the Kremen School of Education and Human Development at the California State University, Fresno. She teaches courses in the multiple subject credential program and BAP that centralize culturally and linguistically sustaining pedagogies, Spanish language and literacy, critical teacher inquiry and reflexivity, and service-learning. Her primary research focus is K–20 Latinx educational access, retention, and persistence and is informed by her teaching and work with youth, educators, and communities of color.

Vicki Lynton (PhD, The University of Texas at San Antonio) is an associate professor and the developmental education coordinator for the Integrated Reading and Writing Department at Northwest Vista College. She is active in collaborative professional development focused on enhancing instruction for multilingual learners. Her research focuses on underserved populations, teaching and learning, language and literacy, and the development of academic literacy practices for multilingual learners.

Pesha Mabrie (MA, The University of Texas at San Antonio) is a doctoral candidate in the Educational Leadership and Policy Studies Department at the University of Texas at San Antonio. Mabrie's research interest includes college access and retention, student affairs employee retention, Black feminisms, and equity practices in higher education.

Kaitlyn Murray is a PhD student in science and agricultural education at the University of California, Davis. As an educator and researcher of community leadership, Kaitlyn explores how people with marginalized sexualities and genders—particularly members of the LGBTQIA community—navigate and change educational systems. Her current research examines how queer and trans youth create spaces of resistance, community, safety, and joy simultaneously within and in opposition to nonformal agricultural educational systems. She studies the gendered and racialized experiences of science, the outdoors, and leadership through her ongoing work with Girls' Outdoor Adventure in Leadership and Science (GOALS). As a GOALS volunteer, Kaitlyn has written curriculum, contributed to field logistics, organized program evaluations, and conducted research with a participatory team. Kaitlyn's research is broadly informed by her experiences as a white, rural, queer woman from the northeastern Appalachian Mountains, and draws upon critical, humanizing, and participatory methodologies to affect change through the process and products of research. Her studies of educational equity and community leadership can be found in the *Journal of Agricultural Education, Equity and Excellence in Education*, and the *NACTA Journal*.

Nesma Osman is a third-year PhD candidate at Virginia Tech. She received a Fulbright scholarship in 2016 for doing her master's degree in agricultural and extension education at Mississippi State University. She has been working as a teaching assistant since 2013 after she graduated in 2012 from Cairo University. At Virginia Tech, where she started her PhD degree in 2018, she worked as an instructor of records for an online course (LDRS 1015, Exploring Citizen Leadership) for undergraduate students. Her research area focuses on extension program planning and evaluation. Her research experiences started when she began her master's degree, and her research was on "Work motivation before and after using assistive technology by disabled agricultural workers" in May 2018. She approached a qualitative method (interview) in her thesis. When she started her PhD degree at Virginia Tech, she had two professional collaboration as a research assistant. First, she did collaborate in a departmental grant project about "graduate student experience in agriculture and life sciences" last May 2019; she approached a quantitative method (survey). The second opportunity was working on a summer project, "Cucurbit IPM for reducing pollinator exposure to key pesticides." She was responsible for data management and evaluation feedback.

Maria Camila Ospina is a third year PhD candidate and National Science Foundation graduate research fellow at the University of California, Davis. Drawing from her experience in avian behavior, communication, and conservation, Maria joined the graduate group in ecology seeking to understand how survival mechanisms (e.g., foraging, anti-predator behavior, interspecific, and intraspecific communication) in birds are impacted by anthropogenic disturbance. Maria's interest in community ecology has connections to her experience as an immigrant from Colombia: community support here in the United States helped ease her integration process. Having also worked as a community organizer and digital influencer for the immigrant community in Florida, one of Maria's central goals is to be a catalyst for marginalized people underrepresented in science to learn about the scientific process and potentially pursue a career in STEM.

Emily Pascoe is a postdoctoral researcher for the Pacific Southwest Center of Excellence in Vector-Borne Diseases (PacVec) at the University of California, Davis, where her research focuses on the ecology of ticks and tick-borne pathogens. Emily's interests lie in host-pathogen-environment interactions, pathogen diversity and ecology, microbiota-host interactions, and invasive species. In addition, Emily is passionate about making science education and communication accessible; she has written and contributed to a number of science curricula grounded in culturally relevant pedagogy and currently serves as the social media editor for the journal *Parasitology*. When she isn't conducting research, you will find her out in nature either backpacking, trail running, or attempting photography. Emily recognizes that her privileges, including as a White woman, have greatly facilitated her ability to pursue her career and hobbies. Through Girls Outdoor Adventures in Leadership and Science (GOALS), where she has participated with the curriculum, mentorship, and program evaluation aspects of the program, she hopes to find ways to positively learn from and leverage this privilege.

Dante Pelzer currently works at the Medical University of South Carolina (MUSC) where he serves as an assistant professor and the assistant director for student diversity. At MUSC, Dr. Pelzer oversees diversity and inclusion programming, advises multicultural student organizations, serves on various diversity and university-wide committees, and teaches courses within the interprofessional (IP) curriculum. Dr. Pelzer completed his PhD in higher education administration at Florida State University while working as a residence coordinator. Before arriving at Florida State University, Dr. Pelzer served as the program director for Multicultural Student Life and Off-Campus Student Affairs at Winthrop University. In this role he was responsible for planning campus-wide diversity programming, facilitating diversity and inclusion training and educational workshops, and advising the Commuter Student Association. Dr. Pelzer earned both his bachelor's degree in mass communication and master's degree in higher education from the University of South Carolina. His research focuses on Black male college achievement, Black masculinity, and the experiences of underrepresented college students.

Donna J. Peterson is an associate extension professor in the School of Human Sciences at Mississippi State University. She is a program planning and evaluation specialist with MSU Extension. In this role, her work focuses on designing and carrying out evaluations, analyzing evaluation data, reporting findings, and making recommendations for future program implementation. She also provides training and professional development for MSU Extension specialists and agents on program planning and evaluation. Dr. Peterson teaches a graduate-level course in program evaluation in the School of Human Sciences and advises graduate students on thesis and dissertation projects. Dr. Peterson earned her master's and PhD from the University of Arizona in family and consumer sciences with an emphasis in family studies and human development.

Cindy N. Phu, EdD, is a tenured assistant professor in the Department of Speech Communication at Pasadena City College (PCC). She has served as PCC's director of forensics, PCC's speech center coordinator, and was on the leadership board of the Pacific Southwest Collegiate Forensics Association (PSCFA). With over 16 years of teaching experience, she has taught numerous courses from gender communication to interpersonal communication. Her current research examines the experiences of mothering students of color. At PCC, she has helped create a family resource center for parenting students. She also served on the Women of Color Leadership task force of the International Association of Maternal Action and Scholarship (IAMAS) and is now on the organization's steering committee.

Guan K. Saw (PhD, Michigan State University) is an associate professor in the School of Educational Studies at Claremont Graduate University. His research focuses on educational inequality, underserved populations, STEM education and workforce, college access and success, and research and evaluation methodology. He is lead author for several studies appearing in *Educational Researcher, American Journal of Education, Journal of Higher Education, International Journal of Science and Mathematics Education, Hispanic Journal of Behavioral Sciences,* and *Policy Insights From Behavioral and Brain Sciences.* Saw's work has been funded by the National Science Foundation, Institute of Education Sciences, National Institute of Justice, and American Educational Research Association.

Candace Schlein is professor of curriculum studies at the University of Missouri–Kansas City. She further serves as the Director of the preparing future faculty program. Her research focuses on experiential curriculum, diversity, and narrative inquiry. Recent publications include articles in *Theory Into Practice, Frontiers in Education: Teacher Education;* and *Curriculum and Teaching Dialogue.* She is a co-author of a chapter in the upcoming *Oxford Encyclopedia of Curriculum Studies* (Oxford University Press, 2022). She is the author of *(Un)Learning to Teach Through Intercultural Professional Development* (Information Age Publishing, 2017) and co-editor of *A Reader of Narrative and Critical Lenses on Intercultural Teaching and Learning* (Information Age Publishing, 2016).

Nicola Smith-Kea is a Black, Jamaican American cisgender woman who is a policing specialist working in a philanthropic organization exploring strategies that drive transformative solutions and policy change. She has multiple years of experience in policy, research, and analysis at the international, national, and local levels. As a scholar-practitioner, her areas of expertise include the intersection of law enforcement, mental health, substance use disorders, and homelessness; community-police relationships. Her deep passion for gender equity and inclusion, has led her to also focus on recruitment, retention, and inclusion of women in law enforcement to executive leadership positions. She helps communities find solutions through intentional coordination and collaboration through the promotion of data-driven, innovative cross-system responses. She is committed to the mission of advancing police effectiveness and increasing positive encounters between police and the community.

Jeannine E. Turner is a professor in the Department of Educational Psychology and Learning Systems at Florida State University in the United States. Her research focuses on motivation, emotions, and self-regulation for learning difficult topics.

Jenna Turpin is a third-year undergraduate studying wildlife, fish, and conservation biology at the University of California, Davis. She currently studies greater sage-grouse lekking behavior as an undergraduate intern in the Gail L. Patricelli lab. Jenna works with Girls Outdoor Adventure in Leadership and Science (GOALS) on the program evaluation committee. Upon graduation, Jenna plans to become a wildlife biologist and pursue a PhD in the field of ornithology. She believes that who is doing science matters and is committed to working towards ensuring everyone—particularly those who have been underrepresented or excluded—has access to becoming a scientist.

Ping-Hsuan Wang is an English researcher at the Language Training and Testing Center, Taipei, Taiwan. He obtained his BA degree in English at National Central University and an MA in linguistics at Georgetown University. His research interests and publications include chronotopes in conversations with Taiwanese Americans (*Language in Society*), stance-taking in online comments (*Discourse & Society*), gay immigrants' coming-out narratives (*Narrative Inquiry*), and framing in family mealtime discourse. His works also appear in edited volumes, including *Gender, Sexuality and Race in the Digital Age* (Farris, Compton, & Herrera; Springer, 2020), *Taiwan: Environmental, Political, and Social Issues* (Clark; Nova Science Publishers, 2021), and *Identity Perspective From Peripheries* (Matsumoto & Östman; John Benjamins, forthcoming). He tweets @hoganindc2015.

Kyle S. Whipple, PhD, I am an assistant professor in the Education Studies Department at the University of Wisconsin Eau Claire. I graduated from the University of Minnesota with a PhD in STEM education in June 2018. My research interests are centered around LGBTQ+ teachers and their implementation of inclusive pedagogy and curriculum in mathematics and science lessons. I started the LGBTQ+ Teacher Mentors organization in 2019 to create a social network connecting college students who identify as LGBTQ+ and are pursuing degrees in education to teachers who identify as LGBTQ+. I was a public-school teacher in mathematics for 20 years, and I identify as a transman.

Ronald W. Whitaker, II is the culturally responsive pedagogy assistant professor of Education at Cabrini University. In this role, he is intentional about incorporating culturally responsive tenets into Cabrini's undergraduate and graduate education programs. At Cabrini, he also serves as the assistant dean in the School of Education, director of district and school relations, and director for the Center for Urban Education, Equity, and Improvement (CUEEI). Further, Dr. Whitaker also holds the distinction of being a Schouver Fellow at Duquesne University. The Duquesne Collective Action Network is a cross-sector, research and development collective focused on building system capacity in local schools and their communities.

Dr. Whitaker completed his doctoral degree in educational leadership at Duquesne University. He also earned a master's degree in education at the University of Pennsylvania, a master's degree in business administration at Eastern University, and two undergraduate degrees from Geneva College where he graduated magna cum laude. Additionally, Dr. Whitaker earned a certificate in culturally sustaining pedagogy from the University of North Carolina at Charlotte, and a certificate in diversity and inclusion from Cornell University. As a researcher, Dr. Whitaker has published articles on the psychology of race and racism, issues related to diversity, equity, inclusion, culturally responsive pedagogy, practices, and programming, and the societal and educational disenfranchisement of African American males. Dr. Whitaker presents his research at both national and international scholarly conferences, and within K–12 educational milieus. He is revered amongst colleagues for engaging in "tough conversations" in a respectful manner. For 15 years, he has led various programming for Black boys and men. Lastly, Dr. Whitaker was a 2016 AERA Asa Hilliard/Barbara Sizemore fellow, and a 2017 Black theology fellow at Princeton Theological Seminary/Princeton University.

Printed in the United States
by Baker & Taylor Publisher Services